Handloader's
Guide

Handloader's
Guide

Stanley W. Trzoniec

Stoeger Publishing Company

Published by Stoeger Publishing Company
55 Ruta Court
South Hackensack, New Jersey 07606

ISBN 0-88317-121-X

Library of Congress Catalog Card No.: 84-052540

Manufactured in the United States of America

Distributed to the book trade and to the sporting goods trade by Stoeger Industries, 55 Ruta Court, South Hackensack, New Jersey 07606

In Canada, distributed to the book trade and to the sporting goods trade by Stoeger Canada Ltd., 169 Idema Road, Markham, Ontario L3R 1A9

CONTENTS

HANDLOADING TODAY | Page
Chapter 1   Getting Started...11
Chapter 2   Basic Equipment 21
Chapter 3   Metallic Cartridge Components...33
Chapter 4   Putting It All Together—Handgun Ammunition 45
Chapter 5   Reloading Rifle Ammunition 59
Chapter 6   An Update on Propellants 75
Chapter 7   At the Range 91

HANDGUN SECTION
Chapter 8   American Centerfire Handgun Cartridges 101
Chapter 9   The Great .38/.357 Combination by Al Pickles 115
Chapter 10—Care and Feeding of the Modern Automatic Pistol 121
Chapter 11   Some Thoughts on Ballistics by Mason Williams 127
Chapter 12   The Power of the Max 133

RIFLE SECTION
Chapter 13   The ABC's of Bullet Casting by C. Kenneth Ramage.....................139
Chapter 14   Rifle Accuracy—Consistency is the Word by Mike Venturino 145
Chapter 15   The Twenty-two Centerfires by Dick Eades 149
Chapter 16   Just Starting Out? Try the .30/06 Springfield 155
Chapter 17   A Rebounding Cartridge—the 7mm Mauser 165

GENERAL TOPICS
Chapter 18   Additional Handloading Equipment 175
Chapter 19   Favorite Loads from American Gun Writers 183
Chapter 20   Questions and Answers 191
Reference Section...199
Index 253

Dedication

To my daughters, Carolyn and Randee . . .
my whole reason for being here

Introduction and Acknowledgments

Welcome to the pages of Stoeger's new *Handloader's Guide*. Born out of a sincere desire to supply the handloader of today with an up-to-date source book, this new volume is a culmination of ideas and discussions between myself and some of the top men in the field.

Ken Ramage, an authority on cast bullets, has penned a section relevant to the cast-bullet maker of today. As an executive with Lyman Products Corporation, Ken has the opportunity every day to test, evaluate and shoot lead bullets in a variety of shapes, sizes and calibers.

Mason Williams, one of this country's most knowledgeable ballistics experts, has written a piece on basic ballistics. For both the novice and expert, there is an education here for everyone.

Al Pickles, involved in law enforcement circles for many, many years, covers the famed .38 Special/.357 Magnum combination. Information about loads, plus honest, time-honed opinions are expressed in this fine piece.

Mike Venturino covers rifle accuracy—a goal we all strive for. Mike lives in the West, and as a dedicated shooter and handloader walks you through the steps necessary to produce good rifle handloads.

Finally, Dick Eades, a Texan with a wealth of technical knowledge of all firearms, lends his expertise on the .22 centerfires, one of my favorite subjects for sure. Dick lets you in on the secrets of small-bore shooting and blending handloading recipes.

The rest of the book is sprinkled with subjects aimed at the modern shooter in general. From basic pistol and rifle reloading to propellants and specific caliber selections, we've included meaningful facts in a no-nonsense manner. Hopefully, the book will provide an enjoyable evening's reading and after that serve as a reference work that will be used time and time again.

As no book of this type is the complete work of one man, many thanks must go to the people involved in the firearms and ammunition industry for all their help in supplying products and information. Their products are written about as a testimonial to their thoughtfulness. Special thanks go to Jerry Rakusan at *Guns* magazine for his honest advice, to Dick Deitz, Bill Siems and Johnny Falk for just being there when I needed them, and to my wife, Inge, for her constant support and confidence in me throughout the past year.

About the Author

Intrigued by firearms since childhood and early experiences with a .22 Long Rifle, Stan Trzoniec finds that today this avocation occupies a good part of his life.

Aside from writing for just about every major firearms periodical on the newsstands today, the author is a Contributing Weaponry Editor for *Survive* magazine and Special Products Editor for *Guns* magazine. *Guns* was the first to publish his full color photographs on its pages and he has been thankful ever since. Trzoniec is very lucky in that he can combine his profession as a commercial/industrial photographer with his writing and turn out some beautifully illustrated work.

In talking to many editors, he found that there are plenty of good writers around but in many instances quality photography was lacking, especially for magazines that use full color layouts exclusively each month. "There was simply a void to be filled and I filled it," he states. In addition to meeting his monthly editorial requirements, he also finds time to accept photography assign-

ments for *Outdoor Life* magazine, Remington Arms and Charter Arms.

Not claiming to be an expert, but a person knowledgeable in many fields of firearms endeavor, Trzoniec leans towards the modern semi-automatic high-volume pistol if pushed for a speciality. He thinks the potential for autoloaders is there not only for self defensive use, but for law enforcement use as well. The revolver is not forgotten though, and his opinion of it is high. While the automatic pistol is fine in many respects, the revolver can digest many loads that are out of the question for use in self-loaders. The single-shot pistol is another avenue of relaxation and excitement as witnessed by the introduction of the .357 Maximum by Remington. Trzoniec feels that in the long run the Max will find a permanent home with the single-shot pistol because the problems of flame cutting and barrel erosion are eliminated in a closed breech gun.

On the subject of rifles, Trzoniec tries them all.

Each has its own particular niche to fill. From the California-styled Weatherbys, to the modern classics, automatics and pumps, they are all finely crafted products. In the field, Stan uses his trusted Remington Classic chambered in the time-honored .270 Winchester. As the summer approaches, his fancy turns to varmint shooting with some of his sporter-weight rifles. With a shotgun, he likes to shoot trap and dabbles a little in the reloading of shotgun shells but only for competition use. When time permits he likes to go big game hunting either in the West or in Canada. Close to his home in Massachusetts he can drive a short distance and forget his troubles when roaming the New England countryside in the fall.

Handloading holds a particular fascination for Trzoniec because of its diverse nature. What other activity combines math, trajectory problems, ballistics, muzzle energy and velocity statistics? All to get a rifle to keep its shots inside one minute of angle.

As for equipment, Trzoniec is well prepared with a complete reloading area, chronographs, motorized Nikon cameras and a ballistics program for his Apple IIe computer to sort out all the data. When he writes on handloading, he keeps stressing the need for safety on all fronts and tries to present the material in an easy manner so that even the novice can follow along. Complicated data only serve to turn people off. Trzoniec's philosphy of writing about firearms is brief—keep it simple, yet informative.

This is his second book; the first title, *Modern American Centerfire Handguns*, was published a few years ago and an update is planned. With the growing interest in handguns in general, keeping up with the influx of new designs, models and calibers is a constant learning process.

For a complete diversion, Trzoniec turns to his power boat for fun on the waterways of the Northeast, and to his automobiles. He likes to keep them in tiptop shape and running perfectly.

In addition to his commercial photography activities, Trzoniec shares his business with his wife, Inge. Together, they operate a custom frame shop, a retail photography store and a picture gallery.

Chapter 1
Getting Started

The reloading of sporting ammunition is so closely allied with all facets of the shooting sports that they are virtually inseparable.

For instance, the competitive sharpshooters depend on their handloads to print groups as small as a 25-cent piece at distances ranging from 50 to 100 yards. In a hunting situation, a trophy bull at 300 yards is going to be a lot easier to take by a hunter who knows his rifle and ammunition. He is confident that his rifle will place the bullet precisely, if he does his part. All that time at the reloading bench and out at the range are about to pay off.

Going back in time, we find the development of handloading actually started with the introduction of the metallic cartridge. This was in 1866 and the company was called Winchester. Then, about 1867, a group of entrepreneurs formed the Union Metallic Cartridge Company; later to become Remington Arms Company.

Before the self-contained metallic cartridge, a cap and ball combined with a little black powder was all the frontiersman had to take care of his shooting

needs. When smokeless powder and repeating rifles entered the scene a major demand for loading components was created, and continues today.

Some unenlightened shooters still ask, "Why should I handload when I can buy all the ammunition I want over the counter from such companies as Federal, Frontier, Remington or Winchester?" In response to this important question I offer three equally important answers: economy, versatility and accuracy.

In these days of inflation and uncertain prices, any way we can save money and still enjoy our sport is a move in the right direction. Every shooter would like to become a better shot, and this takes practice—lots of practice. But this means expending ammunition, and ammo costs money. Plain and simple. However, reloading can cut your ammo costs dramatically.

Let's work out an example using one of our most popular handgun cartridges, the .357 Magnum. As of this particular date and time, good quality, factory-fresh, high-performance, jacketed ammunition runs, on the average, about 32.5 cents a round. Now, if we take the same components, which includes new brass, a hundred jacketed 158-grain bullets, an equal number of primers, and enough powder to complete the job and reload, our basic cost tumbles to about 24 cents a round. This is for the first firing.

Since the brass cases are good for about 15 to 20 loadings, we can now prorate this cost thus lowering the price of reloads to about a dime per round. Getting interested?

And, if you don't like the muzzle blast of the thunderous magnums, lead bullets are available for plinking, target or small game hunting. By buying lead bullets, and ignoring the initial cost of the brass, .357 reloads cost under six cents a round for 100 units complete and ready for firing. Shooters who cast their own bullets enjoy an additional saving. After their investment in equipment is paid off,

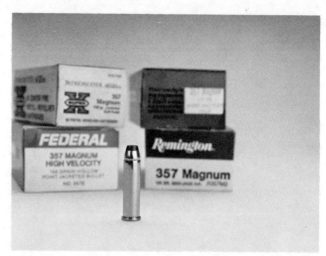

For discussion purposes, let's say .357 Magnum factory ammo costs 32.7¢ per round (box of 50).

For the handloading of accurate ammunition, a place of your own is needed. This photo shows the author's setup with everything arranged in order to avoid confusion.

For discussion purposes, let's say reloaded .357 Magnum ammo, using new brass, costs 23.35¢ per round (12.5¢/case; 7.87¢/jacketed bullet; 1.85¢/powder and 1.13¢/primer), per 100 rounds. Additional reloadings eliminate the one-time cost of the brass, bringing the cost per round down to 10.85¢.

For discussion purposes, let's say reloaded .38 Special ammo, using new brass, costs 17.39¢ per round (11.4¢/case; 4.45¢/wadcutter lead bullet; .41¢/powder and 1.13¢/primer), per 100 rounds. Additional reloadings, without the brass cost, bring the cost per round down to 5.99¢.

they can scrounge lead wheel weights or linotype metal for lead and costs can be brought down to an unbelievable one and a half cents per round. Incredible, isn't it?

The example cited was for handgun ammunition, but rifle costs are proportionable. Since the average rifleman in all probability shoots fewer rounds per year than a handgunner, the savings will be more noticeable.

After economics, the second reason to handload is versatility. Here, the combinations of powders, bullets and even primers all add up to an impressive variety. Take one caliber, the famed .30/06 Springfield. The '06 has been around since the turn of the century and in that time has garnered a good following. It's not hard to see why.

First, it was this country's standard military cartridge for a long time and a huge quantity of brass was made for the armed forces. A lot of this brass trickled down to the civilian shooting populace in the form of once-fired brass. Firearms manufacturers were quick to turn out many fine sporting rifles for this cartridge, and have continued to do so for over 80 years. Few calibers can touch the '06 for longevity and popularity.

Along with good rifles and plentiful brass, consider the half-dozen bullet makers offering .30-cal-

iber bullet weights in 100, 110, 130, 150, 165, 168, 180, 190, 200 and 220 grains and you begin to see what I mean by versatility. For instance, one bullet maker, Hornady Bullets of Grand Island, Nebraska, has a lineup of 18 bullets in .308 caliber. And, depending on the application, you have your choice of hollow points, spire points, full metal jackets or round nose designs.

If this isn't enough for you, powders and primers enter the picture. By varying the powder charge weight by as little as $1/2$ grain, or by switching from regular to magnum or bench rest primers, the reloader can change the grouping of his shots appreciably. The time spent in experimenting is certainly worthwhile with the .30/06.

The last, but certainly not the least consideration, is accuracy, which is the watchword of the handloader. With all the forces opposing the bullet as it cuts through the air, including yaw, rotational spin, gravity and pressure, it's a small wonder the modern projectile strikes the target anywhere near the point of aim. But this is the challenge of accurate shooting and the natural habitat of the handloader. Depending on his own parameters, he will, in due course, determine his own level of accuracy.

Varmint hunters, for example, have only one criterion of accuracy—extreme. For this type of hunt-

DO-IT-YOURSELF RELOADING CENTER

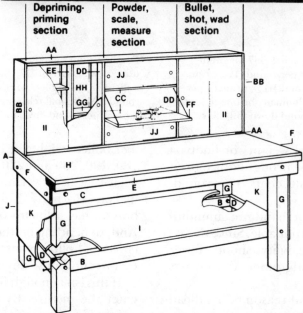

Depriming-priming section

Powder, scale, measure section

Bullet, shot, wad section

You can build this sturdy reloading bench and, at last, have a place for all your reloading tools, components and accessories. Plans are complete down to the last nut and bolt. Send $2.50 check or money order to NRMA Bench Plans, 1221 S.W. Yamhill, Portland, OR 97205. National Reloading Manufacturers Association.

The author uses a Lyman turret press (on the left) for quantity reloads such as needed for pistol competition. On the right is the Pacific press for heavier use (i.e., rifles).

Don't be afraid to use extra bracing at the corners of your reloading bench.

Keep powder up high and out of reach of curious toddlers, or keep it in a locked cabinet.

ing, where the target may be only four inches wide and shooting distances of 300 to 400 yards are commonplace, handloading is a virtual necessity. In my own case, I'm not happy unless my varmint guns will shoot half-inch groups at 100 yards from a bench rest. Big game hunters are not that particular. They handload too, but not to the point of dribbling half-grain differences in powder drops. The vital target area of a deer averages about 18 to 20 inches from brisket to backbone, so 1½- to 2-inch groups at the range are quite acceptable.

After considering the three basic factors of economy, versatility and accuracy as they apply to reloading ammunition, the logical conclusion is that one's own "custom-tailored" ammo is more satisfying than any over-the-counter commercial ammunition. Handloading can become a hobby of intense interest once you have mastered the basics, and will include such topics as ballistic coefficient, propellant, rate of twist, feet per second, foot pounds of

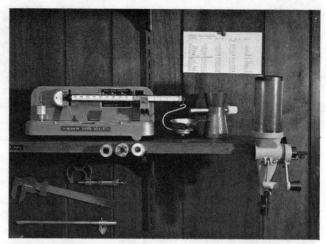

For the best possible readings, the powder scale should be placed on a shelf about eye level. Note handiness of the dribbler and powder measure.

energy and more. As a pastime, you just can't beat it. As a hobby, it's one that you will never tire of, and will grow with over the years.

The Working Area

With all this information behind you, and before we get into the equipment needed for proper reloading procedures, the first order of business is how to go about setting up a reloading work area.

While no great amount of space is needed to perform all the operations, consideration should be given to its location. A corner in the basement is good; a walled-in room is better. Not everyone lives in a private home, of course, and a basement may be out of the question. Apartment dwellers have to use their ingenuity to come up with portable or closet-

Everything should be lined up and stocked according to bullet weight and caliber. This is necessary to avoid costly mistakes later on.

As with all major components, primers should be kept separate from powder. Never take primers out of the factory boxes and store them in glass or other containers.

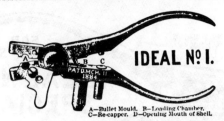

A—Bullet Mould. B—Loading Chamber.
C—Re-capper. D—Opening Mouth of Shell.

Ideal No. 1 Reloading Tool

The Ideal No. 1 tool, patented March 11, 1884 was a light, compact and complete little tool designed for loading the smaller pistol cartridges of the day. It was capable of performing all the operations required in reloading. It molded the bullet (A), deprimed the shell, seated a new primer, forced the bullet in place and crimped the shell. It did not have a bullet sizer, however. Illustration above, from the No. 4 Ideal Handbook, lists the tool's features. It weighed 20 ounces and cost $2.25 at that time. It was then available for these cartridges: ".22-10-45, .22-15-45 W.C.F., .32 Short, .32 Long, .32 S&W, .32 Ex. Long, .32 H&R, .32 M&H, .38 Short, .38 Long, .38 Ex. Long, .38 S&W, .38 M&H, .41 Short—Colt's D.A., .41 Long—Colt's D.A."

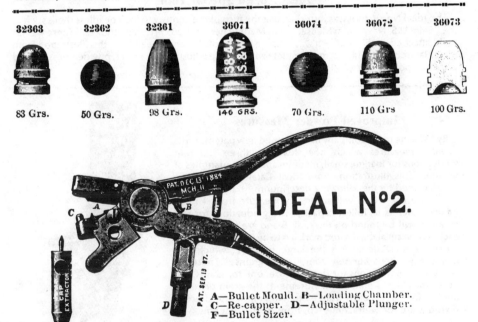

32363	32362	32361	36071	36074	36072	36073
83 Grs.	50 Grs.	98 Grs.	146 GRS.	70 Grs.	110 Grs	100 Grs.

A—Bullet Mould. B—Loading Chamber.
C—Re-capper. D—Adjustable Plunger.
F—Bullet Sizer.

Ideal No. 2 Reloading Tool

The No. 2 tool was a target pistol cartridge tool intended to load cartridges exactly like factory ammunition for the S&W and Colt target pistols on the market. An excerpt from the No. 4 Ideal Handbook says: "With it shells can be loaded with either round or conical bullet; the cuts of bullets show the different ones that can be loaded with this tool. The 100 Grs. .38 Cal. is a special of our own that has met with much favor. . . . When the mould is for round ball the tool is called Gallery, when for the conical bullet it is called Target. The purchaser can have which he desires, and with the extra moulds he can have the variety, as the tool will seat all that are of the same calibre, with the exception of the 98 Grs. (32 S. & W. Rifle), the Rifle tool will seat the other 32 Cals. with the addition of an extra adjusting screw and vice versa. The adjustable plunger will seat the ball on any charge of powder."

The No. 2 tool was then made for the .32-44 S&W Target, grooved ball; .32-44 S&W Gallery, round ball; .38-44 S&W Target, grooved ball; .38-44 S&W Gallery, round ball; .32 S&W Pocket Pistol; .32 S&W Rifle; and .38 S&W Pocket Pistol. In its nickel-plated version it cost $3.50. Separate molds were $1.50, the hollow base 100 grain mold cost $2.00 and the extra seating screw was $.50.

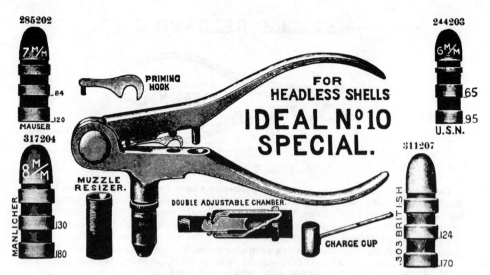

Ideal No. 10 Special Tool

The Ideal No. 10 tool was introduced at the turn of the century to load headless shells such as the "6mm U.S. Navy, 7mm Mauser, 8mm Mannlicher, and .303 British cartridges." There was no mold attached to this unit — it was simply a tong tool. As can be seen from this illustration from Ideal Handbook No. 14, it came complete with double adjustable chamber, powder measure and priming hook. It cost $2.50 complete.

Improved Powder Measures

By 1899, the Ideal Company had obtained new patents on its powder measures which now featured three different graduations for loading small, medium and large quantities of powder. This illustration, from Ideal Catalog No. 14 was accompanied by the following description: "B indicates the small measure which will accurately measure from 1 to 35 grains, which is its fullest capacity. The graduations for this measure will be found on the slide B and are for one grain each. When set at the desired mark it is to be fastened with the set-screw A, D designates the large measure, which will measure powder accurately from 30 to 140 grains...There are two sets of graduations for this measure, one for grains, the other for the old drachm measurement; the grain divisions are for five grains each from 30 to 140 grains. The drachm divisions are for ¼ drachm each, from ½ to 5 drachms."

Ideal Broken Shell Extractor

The advent of smokeless powders, with their increased pressures, also led to an increase in the number of broken cases shooters were to experience. The Ideal Company had a solution to the problem of how to remove a broken case easily — their Ideal Broken Shell Extractor, illustrated here from the Ideal Handbook No. 14. Part of the description follows: "It is made of soft steel and case-hardened. The ball run is on an incline, and the ball is made of the best steel hardened and ground to the proper size — they will last a lifetime." The unit cost only $.75.

type bench setups. In this case, flipping through the many monthly gun magazines can yield names and addresses of companies specializing in plans, one-leg loading stands and other numerous accessories geared to people faced with space problems.

On the other hand, it's obvious that the fellow with his own house has the luxury of space—ideally, a permanent, lockable area. With room to expand, it's not going to be long before he goes from pistol to rifle or even shotshell reloading. Consider your needs carefully and keep in mind that the kitchen table is out unless you can work late at night when the kids are in bed or out of the way. The last thing you need is distractions. Handloading is not a dangerous hobby, but it does require concentration on your part. With the ground rules laid down, let's see what our options are in setting up an operation, covering bench construction, design ideas and storage facilities.

First, as mentioned, a separate room is the best facility. When I moved into my house the basement was empty, so when laying out the playroom, laundry room and work areas, space was allocated for my gun room. My area measured 8 by 12 feet. After the studding of the room was completed, all lighting, electrical and security features were added. Safety items like double locks and an alarm system were installed before any paneling went up.

A built-in gun cabinet was made from rough-cut pine to fit around a chimney flue. The walls were sheetrocked, joined and filled, then wallpapered with a nice hunting scene motif. The bench was next.

Because of the inherent pressure forces associated with handloading—case resizing, priming or bullet swaging—you must build your bench so that it's very strong and perfectly stable. This is no place for 2 × 3s. Use 2 × 4s or even 2 × 6s for sturdiness all around. Don't be afraid to use extra braces in the corners. You'll find out later on that you did the right thing. Plan to bolt the assembly legs to the floor and walls. A compound press develops a lot of force in various operations and the last thing you need is a bench that moves.

With all this in mind, head for the lumber yard. The first thing to look for is material for the bench top. Formica, pressed wood or plywood all make sturdy tops. You can always nail and glue a couple dozen 2 × 4s together for a butcher block appearance. My bench was made from a damaged door returned to the yard because of a slight defect, hardly

Labels are very important in handloading. Keep everything within easy reach and read what you grab.

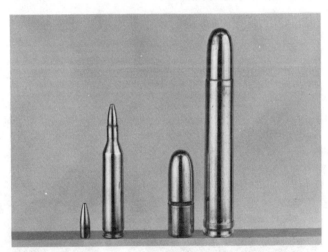
From mice to mastadons. This photo shows the tiny .17 Remington compared to the monster .458 Winchester. Note the size of the bullet alone!

For target shooting, .38 wadcutter bullets are the way to go.

noticeable and only on one side. This door measures 2 feet by 6½ feet and cost me a mere $6.

Shelving was custom made to my requirements out of 1 × 6 and 1 × 8 common pine, which was easy to work with. I found that building them in units was the best method here. Don't go to ½-inch pine; it will just bow under the weight of a lot of bullets. Square up all the edges for a nice neat job, securing the wood all around with carpenter's glue and finishing nails. When all is set and dry, a coat of stain will enhance the overall appearance.

Primers and powders should be stored separately, not only because they can interact, but also to keep them out of reach of prying young hands. Refrain from smoking in your reloading room. Guests also must leave the smoking lamp unlit until they reach safer quarters.

Other accessories to be considered in the general layout are dies, shell holders, loaded cartridges and case trimmers. Whether you are right- or left-handed will determine the proper work flow across the bench. Before anchoring any tool, run through a mock loading session just to see if the setup is exactly right for you. Obviously it should feel comfortable with everything within easy reach.

Reviewing the photos in this chapter and talking to other shooters and getting their views will help you in planning your new work area. Remember, the key to successful handloading is being organized. Not only does this keep the components flowing in an orderly fashion, but in a safe fashion as well.

Pitting one handload against the other will show just which load is best. The small group in front is what the whole game is about.

Chapter 2

Basic Equipment

When purchasing reloading equipment for the first time, equal consideration must be given to price, brand name, design, the amount of time you anticipate spending at the bench, the volume of ammo you anticipate loading and the cartridges you are going to load now and in the future.

While the price of any equipment is always important, brand names rely on their reputation, and overall quality is usually reflected in the cost of the unit. That will never change; you still get exactly what you pay for. Design features usually run parallel to the convenience aspect, with extras incorporated to entice the buyer in favoring one brand over another. On some presses, for example, heavy rams, primer catchers and snap-in shell holders are built into the unit resulting in greater efficiency and more handloads completed in a given time period.

With that in mind, those of you bent on serious competitive shooting should definitely lean toward equipment geared to turning out hundreds of rounds per hour. With long practice sessions necessary to achieve a high level of skill in the target games, this type of press is a definite asset.

On the other end of the scale are the Lee hand tools or Lyman 310 loading handles. Where loading speed is not of the essence, these products are quite adequate when only a very limited amount of loading is done for one caliber; or where possibly you may enjoy loading a few rounds around a campfire in the wilds. For a compromise, most people choose the C or O type presses readily available on today's market in many forms including the so-called reloading kits. Priced very reasonably, they are aimed at the masses, hence their unquestioned popularity.

In order for you to see exactly what you will need to reload high-quality ammunition, a list of basic equipment would be appropriate at this time. Therefore, for loading centerfire metallic ammunition in either pistol or rifle cartridges, I offer the following suggestions for the first-time buyer:

1. A good high-quality bench press in either C, O or turret model with provisions for a primer feed and a spent primer catcher.
2. One set of appropriate dies.
3. Shell holder to match the caliber.
4. Powder scale.

5. Powder measure.
6. Case trimmer with the appropriate pilot.
7. Deburring tool.
8. Case lube kit.
9. Powder funnel.
10. Primer flipper.
11. Loading block.
12. Case neck brushes.
13. Primer pocket cleaners (large and small).
14. Handloading manual.

Optional accessories—These can be acquired now or at a later date:

A. Powder trickler.

B. Tungsten carbide dies in lieu of the standard pistol die set.

C. A good set of dial calipers.

D. Two to three plastic cartridge boxes for travel use.

E. Bullet puller.

Pacific's big and brawny Double 0-7 reloading press features a new angled frame for ease of entry, "0" type construction and rugged linkage to satisfy the most discriminating reloader.

Closeup of a Bonanza press shows the snap-in, snap-out feature when using regular die sets, primer catcher and shell holder.

F. Handloader's log or notebook for range work.

G. Case tumbler.

While this list may seem awesome to the aspiring handloader, each has a purpose which we'll go over in detail. The final decision of what or what not to buy is, of course, up to the individual, but I for one would not deviate too much from this list in order to keep handloading safe, efficient and, most important of all, organized.

The initial purchase of equipment can be done item by item, or you can buy a preassembled kit. You can buy all of the items mentioned one at a time but there is no reason to. With the exception of the case trimmer, primer flipper and the loading block, all of the basic components can be purchased in reloading kit form.

Lyman Products provides an example. In their Lyman Expert Kit you get a press, dies, shell holder, powder measure and powder scale, plus

Lyman's Orange Crusher gives the big-bore handloader the edge by engineering a large opening to handle the largest of rifle cases.

presses come in C, O or turret-type designs. There is another form commonly referred to as the H, but for all practical uses, stick to the above-mentioned trio.

At one time the C press was the most popular, but nowadays has been largely replaced by other types. Turret presses, which could be called a modified C, are being manufactured by a handful of companies to supply the needs of quantity loaders. Turret presses were first marketed in the 1920s by

about a dozen extra items such as a primer catcher, powder funnel, loading manual, etc., for a modest $299.95. If you bought all of these items on a one-to-one basis the cost would then jump to $354.95, plus your time, aggravation and gas. Needless to say, reloading kits have a lot to offer the first-time operator.

That straightened away, let's begin discussing the components. Starting at the top, the first priority is a sturdy, heavy-duty bench press. After you read what I have to say, talk to other handloaders and get their opinions both pro and con. Value their words and experience. Finally, go to your local dealer and try out a few—most big shops have a bench set up with reloading components—then decide which press is best for you.

Bench presses come in all sizes, shapes and designs. Names such as Bonanza, Lyman, Pacific, RCBS, Lee, Hollywood or Bear will soon become household words to you. For general purposes,

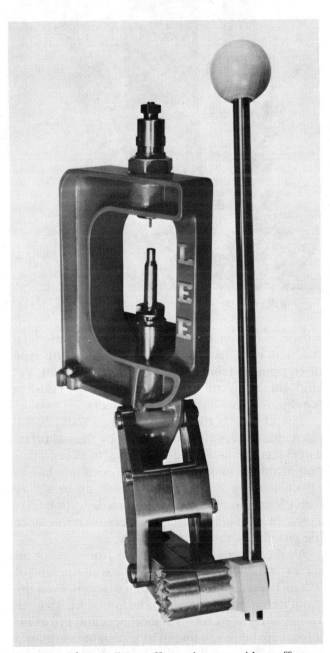

For around $30 retail, Lee offers a nice press with an offset angle and which takes all 7/8 × 14 dies.

Closeup detail of the RCBS press and its priming arm.

For loading quantity pistol loads, the Lyman turret press is the answer. Depending upon the caliber (3- or 4-die sets) you can set up and leave one cartridge when working on another.

Pacific, but their lack of rigidity in sizing modern magnum cases has, in all probability, kept this type of equipment from reaching its peak. Lyman, Pacific and Dillon still sell them; the majority going to handgunners who shoot heavy calibers.

The O type is the preferred press today. Constant attention and improvement by the manufacturers has resulted in a design equal to all the stress and strain put on it. Closing in the open side has, in effect, made a press that can stand up to a very heavy load and still keep everything distortion free. For seating match bullets with very high tolerance die sets, this press is the logical choice.

All the better presses have their features. For instance, Lyman's Orange Crusher has an opening of 4½ inches which is large enough to accept even the 8mm Remington Magnum. The famed RCBS Rock Chucker is noted for its smoothness and effortless sizing capabilities thanks to its system of compound leverage. Pacific sells a press called the 0-7, and the newer model dubbed the Double-07. Both are an-

gled at 30 degrees for improved visibility and accessibility. Bonanza's old-line Model 68 runs its O pattern parallel to the edge of the bench instead of at a right angle. The list goes on and on. In fact, at the big SHOT (Shooting, Hunting, Outdoor Trade) Show—an annual trade show devoted to the shooting sports—I literally find it hard to keep up with the constant flux of new presses and equipment introduced each year.

Other convenience factors to look for when buying an O press could include: a positive priming system; maximum strength built in so it won't bend under regular case forming or bullet swaging operations; overall smoothness of operation in general; offset handles that are adaptable for

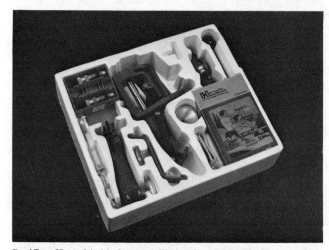

Pacific offers this kit for metallic loading. Included is a press, powder scale, dies, powder measure and complete instructions.

Over 80 years old now, Lyman's 310 tool is just the ticket for the man who likes to load his ammo in the field or in small batches.

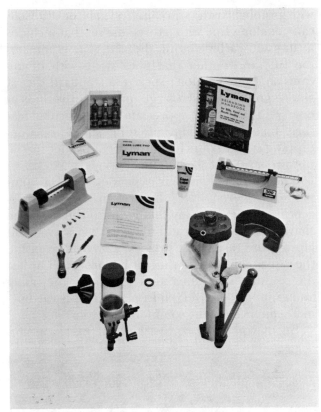

The Lyman Expert Kit has all the necessary tools to start turning out accurate reloads from the moment you get home.

southpaws if necessary; and a compound leverage system designed to give maximum force with a minimum amount of power applied to the handle.

Last on our list would be the turret press. Available from Lyman, Lee, Hollywood and most recently Forster Products, this type has a lot going for it. First off, once set up, especially for the beginner, it has the capability for consistent results without the hassle of resetting the dies every time he wants to reload. Secondly, most turrets have six mounting holes, which accommodate two complete caliber setups assuming you are using the standard three-die sets, or three-die pistol and two-die rifle plus a powder measure. Finally, there's speed! While I don't advocate running by the stopwatch every time

you hit the loading bench, by loading a certain caliber—say, the .45 ACP—by the batch you are going to surprise yourself with the amount of work you will turn out.

Turret, C or O design, the choice is yours. Consider all the options, then take your pick. Since a whole book could be written on the subject, this space, with the help of photographs, allows me only to touch on the basics. Choose wisely, but as you do, scan the three points I brought up earlier: time, volume and the cartridge being loaded.

Reloading Dies

Next to a bench press, reloading dies perhaps represent your next most significant investment. Depending on the caliber or cartridge, you are going to run into terms like tungsten carbide, small base, bench rest, trim dies, crimp dies and multi-die sets. For the present, concern yourself only with standard or tungsten carbide (T/C), in two-, three-, or four-die sets. Originally introduced by Pacific in 1930, today's modern dies still carry the $7/8 \times 14$ thread design.

Straight-walled cases, such as those associated

Like the Lyman 310 tool, this Lee entry is made for the man on the run.

with pistol cartridges in .357, .41, .44 or .45 Colt, can get along fine with a three-die set that includes a tungsten carbide sizing die. This die eliminates the fuss and bother that goes along with lubing cases so that they don't stick in a standard die. If you're going to load a large quantity of rounds at one sitting, you will appreciate this particular feature. Incorporated in the first die should be a decapping stem to punch out the spent primer on the upward stroke of the handle.

The second die is your expander, which in simple terms merely flares the neck of the case to accept the bullet in a way that helps to eliminate the shaving of lead (in lead bullets) or worse yet, collapsing the case. Most presses allow you to prime the case at this stage of the loading process. The last die completes the operation by seating the bullet and crimping (holding) it in place. This is the normal sequence for the common three-die set.

But if you are a real stickler for precision am-

For bench-resters, Lyman offers die sets that include this micrometer seating die for ultra-precise depth control.

munition, a four-die set allows you to size on the first, expand on the second, seat the bullet on the third and for extra care after you make sure the bullet is perfect, crimp it in place on the fourth.

For reloading rifle cartridges, two dies are used: the sizer/decapper and the bullet seater/crimper. The procedure for loading rifle ammo is similar to loading pistol ammo, except for sizing. Here, the shooter has a choice of just neck sizing (for special target applications) or full length resizing for general purpose or hunting requirements.

There is one point that I'd like to interject here. Consider a neck expanding die for your rifle reloading. Made by Lyman—they call it an M die—this component serves the same purpose as the number 2 die in the pistol set. A modest investment

Die makers offer several finishes. Lyman sets are chrome, RCBS dies are brightly polished and Pacific offers industrial hard chrome for long life.

To accommodate a multitude of bullet shapes with one die set, Lyman offers this Multi-Deluxe set with seating screws to match round nose, wadcutter and semi-wadcutter-type bullets.

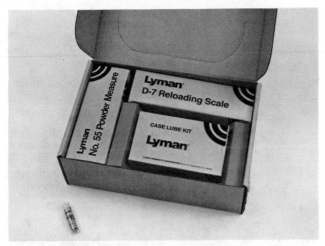

Here in one kit is all you need for measuring powder, lubing your cases and weighing all charges.

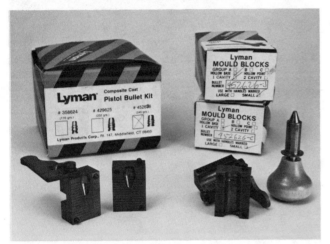

Lyman pistol bullet moulds are known for their close tolerances, durability and wide selection in pistol, rifle and shotgun slug designs.

With the powder metered in the handle, this Bonanza measure drops accurate charge weights while minimizing powder shearing.

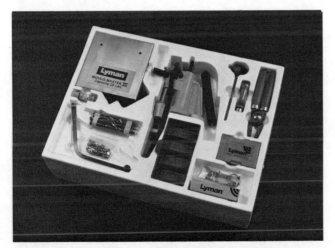

Lyman's Master Casting Kit contains everything from a furnace with a 20-pound capacity, mould guides, lube, sizer/lubricator and dippers for turning out fine lead bullets.

Drop tubes are an asset for those using large charges of slow burning powders such as 4350 or 4831. They allow the propellant to fill the case more easily.

Basic Equipment

The secret of accurate handloads is an accurate powder measure. Lyman's #55 has three micrometer-adjustable blades to regulate charges down to very fine amounts.

Quinetics makes this hand-held measure that throws charges with a very high degree of accuracy.

Closeup of the adjustment on Pacific's Multi-Deluxe measure.

Depending on its use, one measure can be better than the other. On the left is Pacific's Multi-Deluxe; on the right is the Pistol Powder Measure with a sliding bar that uses interchangeable bushings.

A powder scale is a must for measuring charges as dispensed from a powder measure.

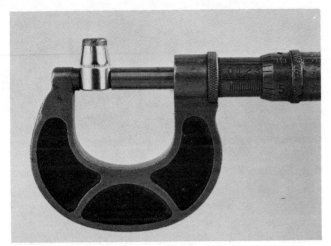

A machinist's micrometer can be used for the measurement of bullets.

Many favor a dial micrometer for its instant readings. This .38-caliber bullet measures .357 inches.

of $11 will save you a lot of frustration at the bench, especially when using cast bullets, and at the range produce increased accuracy potential.

A shell holder is just what its name implies. A very important component in any setup, the shell holder is a means for retrieving the case from any particular die, and aids in the proper alignment of the case throughout the entire operation.

For complete accuracy and, above all, absolute consistency, a powder scale running in concert with a powder measure is a must. However, if push comes to shove, and the kids need braces or shoes before you need loading gear, spring for a powder scale first. You can always weigh charges by the trickle method, or by the use of Lee's famous graduated and inexpensive charge cups. Like every other component on our list, powder scales and measures each have their own individual attractions. On powder scales look for magnetic dampening, easy-to-read numerals and a leveling screw. The powder measure should be able to dispense all kinds of propellants, whether ball, flake or the larger-grained extruded forms, with no problem.

Case trimmers act much like miniature lathes in that they trim cases on a horizontal plane. Made to close standards, sharp cutters combined with the ability to operate within thousandths of an inch will keep all your brass trimmed to industry specs so trouble in chambering won't develop later on.

Handloading manuals published by the various bullet and powder companies are essential references to be studied before you drop a single grain of propellant. For handloading involves no guesswork; everything must be done by the book. Man-

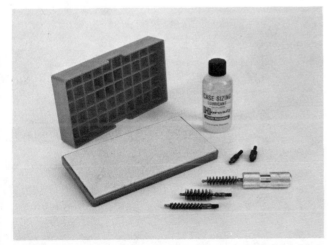

Pacific's lube kit includes everything in one package for lubing cases before they enter the sizing die.

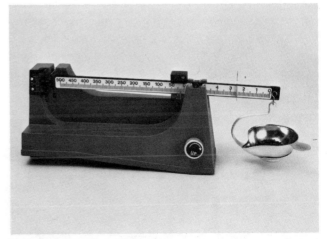

A powder scale from Lyman.

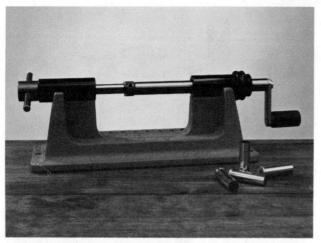

A rotary case trimmer from RCBS.

For loading cases, a cartridge tray is needed to keep all the cases upright, especially when they are filled with powder.

For reloaders on a budget, this pocket trimmer from Lee could fill the bill.

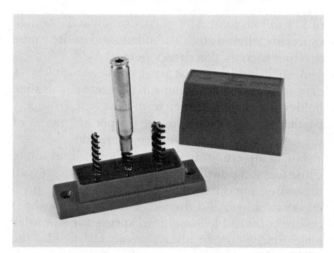

Some people prefer to use graphite as a lubricant and Bonanza makes this stand that includes brushes for .22-, .270- and .35-caliber cases.

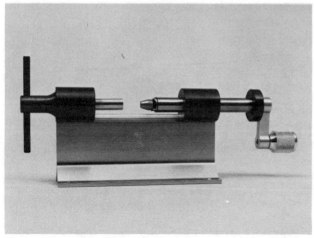

A rotary case trimmer from Forster.

For keeping your fingers off sensitive primers, this inexpensive plastic primer flipper from RCBS is just the ticket.

The amount of residue that comes from a fired case is shown in this photograph. Lee pocket cleaner is next to the .45 case.

Bullet pullers allow you to take any loads apart without destroying them. This one is from Quinetics.

uals give recommendations for the proper use of powder, primers and bullets, and include range and drop tables along with velocity figures to help you determine the correct holdover when hunting game in the field and the shot is longer than the familiar sighting-in distance at the range. But figures are just numbers on paper, and nothing beats actual practice. Sections on ballistics coefficients, pistol and rifle tables and general trouble shooting information usually complete the average bullet maker's reloading manual. Some of the manuals are free, others carry modest price tags.

The preceding few paragraphs briefly listed major investments on the part of any new or aspiring handloader. Incidentals that help to make reload-

ing life easier include such items as a deburring tool, primer pocket cleaners, powder funnel, loading blocks and a primer flipper (which turns all the primers the right way up for insertion into the loading tube). Needless to say, while I can't possibly describe each of these products in detail, you will see, as we progress in Chapters 4 and 5, exactly where they fit in.

My final comment in this chapter concerns our list of optional equipment. A few inexpensive items such as a powder trickler, cartridge boxes (for transporting ammo to the range) and a bullet puller (for mistakes) should be acquired as soon as possible. Dial calipers are available in plastic and, although they won't last as long as stainless steel, they

Depending on the caliber, some cases can be saved even though they have neck splits. The one on the left can be cut down from .357 to .38 Special; same on the second one, but not the last one (R).

Primer pockets should be kept clean to ensure 100% ignition, and these from Lee (L) and RCBS (R) are a good way of performing the task.

will serve the purpose until you decide to upgrade your equipment. Tungsten carbide dies should, if at all possible, be purchased over standard dies without reservations of any kind. A notebook is an asset as you should record all loads and data for future reference. A case tumbler is just a means of getting cases clean without the hassle of wiping each case after firing, or being out in bad weather.

If this is going to be your first step in the hobby of handloading ammunition, consider it an adventure, so to speak. The items of equipment mentioned here can be thought of as building blocks for things to come. Combining the information in this chapter with the components in the next will give you a solid foundation on which to build your knowledge of reloading. I have a feeling that in no time at all you will be solidly entrenched in this pastime. It can be a fascinating experience.

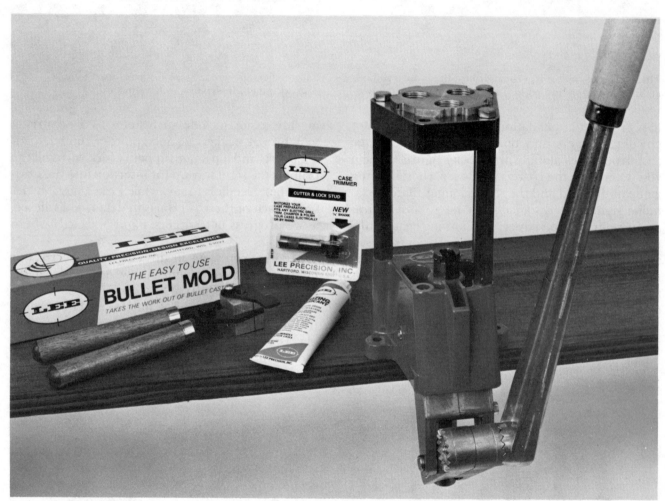

Lee Precision offers a complete line of sturdy and economical tools for both beginner and advanced handloader.

Chapter 3

Metallic Cartridge Components

Now that we have covered the list of basic equipment needed to turn out good reloaded ammunition in an organized sequence, our attention should swing toward the components, or "ingredients," if you will. This will include the cartridge case or brass, the projectile or bullet, the primer for ignition and the propellant, more commonly known as powder. The powder, by the way, is our energy source, which, when ignited by the primer, turns into a gaseous state, builds up pressure and, since pressure will always find the weakest point, liberates the bullet sending it on its way.

Starting with the major component, the cartridge case, as we know it today, has changed less over the decades than bullets, powders or even primers. Cartridge cases are classified by their case head. Pistol cases have either a rimmed or rimless case head depending on the caliber. Generally, revolvers use rimmed cartridges, and automatics fire rimless cartridges. The photos show the distinction.

Rifle cartridge cases, on the other hand, are available in rimmed, rimless, semi-rimmed, rebated rimless and belted magnum designs. The most common type is the rimless. Termed the most versatile by handloaders and manufacturers, this case is found in such favorite calibers as the .243, .270 and .30/06. Headspace is controlled by paying attention to the area between the shoulder and head; not much of an effort today if you fully resize all your brass.

The rimmed design dates back to the turn of the century and would include such examples as the .38 Special, .357 or .41 Magnums in handguns, or the .30-30, .30-40 or the .45-70 in rifles. Here, headspace is measured by the thickness of the rim itself. Semi-rimmed cartridges such as the .220 Swift and .225 WCF have a rim that juts out from the body ever so slightly and, like the popular rimless, also headspaces on the shoulder.

Next is the belted case. Found on magnum cases,

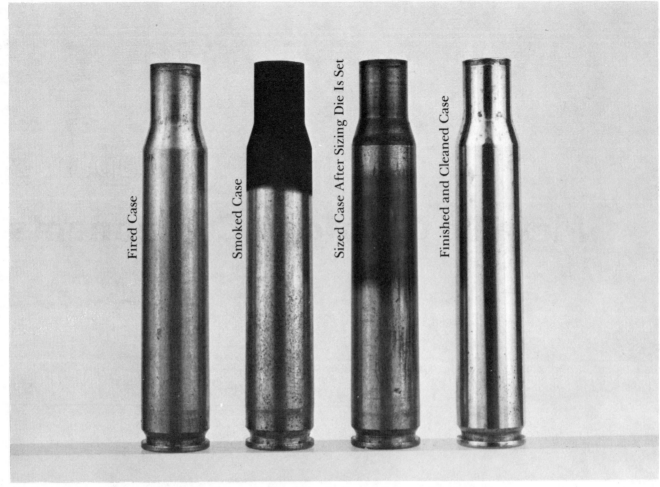

Fired Case

Smoked Case

Sized Case After Sizing Die Is Set

Finished and Cleaned Case

Four steps for proper headspace in rifles.

it is nothing more than a case with a belt around the base which is used to headspace the cartridge in the rifle chamber. This type is found on such notables as the 7mm Remington, .375 Holland & Holland and the Weatherby family of calibers. The least common, in fact it's found on only one cartridge, is the .284 Winchester. Again, this one headspaces on the shoulder area and is called the rebated rimless. In this example the case rim is actually smaller than the case head itself.

Headspace

Since we keep running into the term "headspace," perhaps a few words are in order to explain the meaning more fully. Basically, headspace is termed as that area in which a cartridge can move in a very limited front to back movement when confined in a rifle chamber. Handguns can be counted in also, but in a limited way. Here, we are talking about the Contenders chambered for rifle car-

tridges so prevalent in today's silhouette matches. As this is such a limited application, we shall confine our discussion to rifles and their cartridges.

Industry standards call for a headspace tolerance of .004" on the maximum side. While this figure does not relate to a large dimension inside a chamber, anything more could lead to dangerous situations. Excess headspace in any weapon can and will lead to case separation or gas blowback. With 40,000 to 50,000 c.u.p. (copper units of pressure) confined to a very small area, proper attention to all details when setting up your dies is an absolute must.

When you are handloading ammo for a specific rifle, tuning your brass to that particular firearm is an easy task. First, purchase brand new, factory fresh brass. Then, following the recommendations for an average load from a trusted manual, assemble the loads, using proper bullets, primers and

Without a doubt, loading manuals are the "Bibles" of handloading. Refer to them even when changing one component for another, trying a new load or checking the trajectory of one bullet against another.

Cartridges like the .44 Magnum develop high pressures and new cases used in guns like this Ruger Redhawk will help assure adequate safety margins. Note the thickness and bulk of the cylinder on this handgun.

powder, of course. Fire all these rounds in *that rifle*. Now you have what the experts call fireformed brass. This simply means the brass has taken on the exact measurements of the chamber in which it was fired. Nearly. As brass expands and contracts on firing, it's as close as possible to the chamber volume as it will ever be.

Now, to help control the headspace a few things must be done to keep all the variables constant. First, take the fired and formed case and lube it as you would any round before sizing. Then smoke the shoulder area with a candle flame. This will be your guide to exact sizing for *that particular rifle*.

Place the proper sizing die into the press, being

careful not to screw it down so far that it touches the shell holder. Next, run the case up into the die. If the shoulder doesn't make contact, turn the die down about half a turn at a time or until it just starts to "kiss" the shoulder. A ring around the brass will indicate contact. You have now sized the brass case to your rifle for a minimum headspace dimension. Naturally, this is not for the man who shoots the same caliber in three or four different rifles. He may run into trouble in chambering rounds from one rifle to another. This can be especially embarrassing on a hunt, for sure. But, if want the most accuracy from any given gun with the least amount of tolerable headspace, this is the method to use.

Every major maker of commercial factory ammunition sells top-quality components for handloaders.

Only the freshest brass and bullets should be used when reloading cases. Never buy surplus or brand names of doubtful origin.

Always consult a manual for powder recommendations.

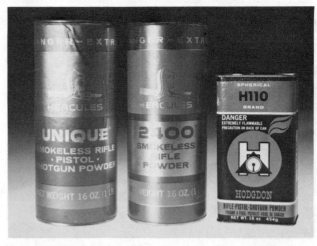

For pistol shooting, these three powders will cover most applications.

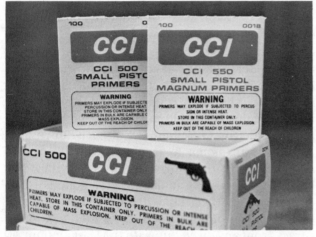

Warning labels are put on primers for good reason. Please read them.

For pistol or rifle reloads, primers such as these from Federal assure complete combustion in the cartridge case.

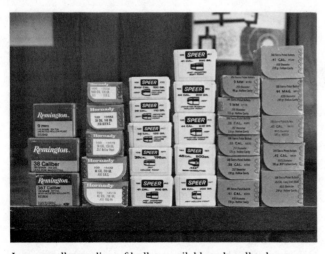

Just a small sampling of bullets available to handloaders. These are pistol bullets from 9mm to .44 caliber.

Remington offers their bullets in both factory loads and as component parts. The handloader has the advantage when he rolls his own.

By the way, this method can and should be used on belted magnum cases also. Even with a belt, this doesn't mean everything is still O.K. in the shoulder area. The belt is no panacea for solving all headspace problems, although many say it is. I've witnessed excessive headspace on a belted magnum more than once. With the higher temperatures and pressures they develop, I'd be doubly sure on the interior specs when shooting these high-velocity rounds.

Other factors associated with loading rifle brass are case trimming, and separating all cases by manufacturer's headstamp.

After you fire a case a number of times it's a good idea to check the overall case length. For this you can either purchase one of the inexpensive plastic gauges put out by such firms as Lyman or RCBS, or invest in good, stainless steel, dial calipers made by companies catering to the machine tool industry.

After verifying the overall case length, some trimming may be necessary and this is where the case trimmer comes in, as mentioned in the previous chapter. Checking the specs in the loading manual, we find the permissible overall length of the .270 is given as 2.540". The trim-to-length would be .010" below this figure of 2.530". It does little harm to trim to this length as it saves continued trimming after each firing, and also helps to keep cases in a state of uniformity throughout each loading session. With this method, you should be able to go through four or five firings without having to case trim this particular lot of brass.

Because the interior volume of cases will differ from brand to brand, it's best to segregate them by headstamp. While one load in one cartridge case may be O.K., the same load in another case may lead to pressure problems. If you have to change brands, start loading at least 10% below established charges and work up again ever so slowly.

The brass cartridge case is considered the container in which the bullet, primer and powder are united into one round. It is also the starting point on which all other operations depend. By purchasing only the best in brass, resizing intelligently and loading to conservative levels within that caliber's parameters, you can be assured of gaining all the fruits of velocity, accuracy and safety.

Bullets

Now we can move on to one of shooting's most talked about subjects—bullets. It doesn't take much

Weight
238.0 grs.

Weight
241.1

Capacity
Grains Water
79.8

Capacity
Grains Water
79.6

Remington   Winchester

Differences in cases can make a difference in capacity.

Expansion is a major consideration in any bullet construction for it often spells success or failure on a hunt. From left to right, bullets from Sierra, Hornady, Remington and Speer.

The Sierra Power Jacket bullet. Note the serrations in the bullet jacket for better expansion.

looking to discover the huge assortment of projectiles available to the aspiring handloader. With big companies such as Sierra, Speer and Hornady turning out literally millions of bullets annually, the choice can be confusing at first to beginners, and even stagger the imagination of the advanced reloader. For handgunners, the choice, while still large, is pretty well cut-and-dried depending on the application: target, hunting or defense use. Rifle bullets, because of numerous variables, demand closer attention and investigation. We'll get into rifle bullet specifics later on.

Shall we begin? Target loads for handguns require low velocity for a mild recoil sensation, plus the use of blunt or wadcutter bullets that cut per-

fectly round holes in the paper targets. This obviously makes scoring easier and has settled many an argument on the line. In the popular .38 Special this would include bullet weights of around 148 grains. Since distances are short with accuracy paramount, nothing equals this type of bullet for competition. Velocity here would be about 700 to 800 feet per second (fps), depending on the gun or the way the shooter loaded for this particular match. Hunting or defense loads call for something else again. The purpose of the load determines its beginning. I know it sounds as if you have to work backwards, and in reality you do. Let me explain.

Hornady's full metal-jacketed 9mm bullet is available to handloaders, and the parent company also loads them into its own Frontier brand ammo.

Expansion tests can be carried out by the novice to see just how a bullet reacts under stress. The two bullets on the left were fired into sand; the two on the right into pine boards.

.38 caliber handgun bullet choices. (1) 110 gr. Sierra JHC. (2) 125 gr. Sierra JHC. (3) 146 gr. Speer HP. (4) 148 gr. bevel base wadcutter. (5) 150 gr. Sierra JHC. (6) 158 gr. Hornady lead. (7) 160 gr. Speer soft point. (8) 160 gr. Hornady Silhouette. (9) 170 gr. Sierra Silhouette. (10) 180 gr. Hornady Silhouette. (11) 200 gr. Winchester lead round nose.

In all pistol calibers there are different bullet weights. In the .38 and .357 you have 110-, 125-, 140-, 158-, 160-, and 180-grain bullets. The .41 Magnum bullet comes in 170, 200 or 220 grains; and the .44 Mag in 180, 200, 225, or 240 grains. Each was designed for a special purpose.

The lighter weight selections are made for high velocity and rapid expansion where a minimum amount of penetration is needed; for example, hunting small game or varmints. The heavier slugs—either hollow- or soft-pointed versions— were engineered to produce deeper penetration, if only by sheer mass alone. Velocity is important also,

but, remember, for a jacketed bullet to do its job thoroughly it must be driven to speeds in excess of l,000 fps. As the bore size gets larger, bullets tend to get a little tougher (there are exceptions of course) so the handloader must compensate for this by driving the bullets at a higher velocity to achieve a similar degree of bullet expansion. This has been proved. One glance at any factory ammunition catalog will bear this out. For if anyone has the time, money and facilities to run all sorts of tests on bullets, it's the people at Federal, Remington, Winchester and the other bullet companies.

Remember, some loads for big cartridges like the

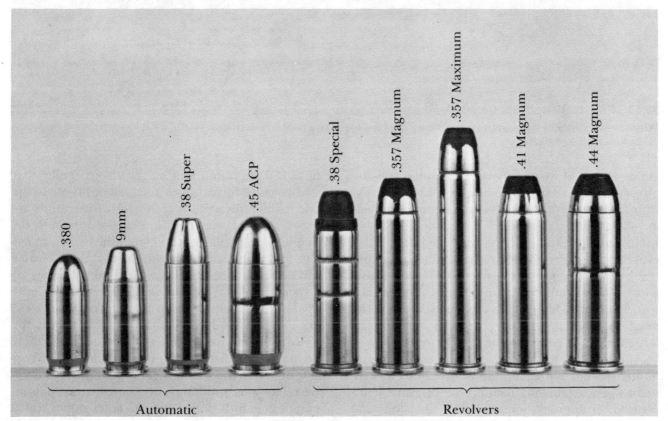

Pistol cartridges.

When working with the big magnums everything from cases to primers must be picked with careful consideration during all stages of the handloading operation.

.357, .41 or .44 Magnums were intended for one purpose—to take big game quickly and humanely. Consequently, everything from the gun to the bullets was designed to produce killing shots on bears, wild boar, deer and other big game animals. However, since these rounds do exert so much wear and tear on the gun, most of the magnum handgun cartridges were developed for revolvers. Physically, wheelguns can handle the big mags without the need for special internal parts like accelerators, large frames or cumbersome magazines.

Automatic pistols also play an important role in handgunning. With more and more law enforcement agencies turning to this type of gun for increased firepower—something I am for 100 percent—the auto is receiving increased and well-deserved attention. Full metal-jacketed bullets will ensure good feeding and reliability of these weapons. Unlike the revolver, in which the rounds are indexed by a revolving cylinder, the automatic depends on the bullet getting from the loaded magazine and up a feed ramp into the chamber before it can be fired. Since cartridges such as the 9mm, .38 Super and .45 Automatic headspace on the mouth of the case, a taper crimp is preferred to the roll crimp for dependable feeding under all conditions.

Rifle bullets are another ball game. They tend to be more specialized, and probably have to be, considering the forces of higher pressure readings, barrel lengths and longer rotational stress, plus accuracy demands put on them to reach out to 200 or even 300 yards and stay within a 3- to 4-inch circle.

Again, as with handgun bullets, rifle projectiles can be broken down into various "job descriptions" with appropriate bullet weights to suit all. Target shooting, hunting and, to a lesser extent, plinking, encompass most rifle bullet uses. To bring everything into a sharper focus, let's settle on one caliber: .308″ in diameter, .30/06 in designation.

For target shooting where a high ballistic coefficient is needed, bullets tend to be extremely streamlined; many even incorporate a boat tail design for greater stability in flight. Here, accuracy is the name of the game—placing ten shots into the smallest group possible. Depending on the maker, bullets in the .30-caliber example that we are using range from 150 to 220 grains under such names as Boat Tails, Matchkings, or Match, and carry ballistic coefficients of 450 to over 600 plus!

Before we go any further, let's explore that sexy phrase, "ballistic coefficient," or BC for short. Simply put, the BC of any bullet relates to its ability to resist air drag, keep a decent velocity and maintain a good trajectory. This is a very important factor in serious target shooting. Hunters, too, will appreciate BC on an expensive safari.

While on the subject of hunting, and still in our .30/06 class of bullets, we note that designs come in soft points, hollow points, spire points, MagTips, Partitions and with full metal jackets (FMJ). In fact, the list seems endless. In any event, to make things easier we can subdivide the list so that the hunter can see what's available and which bullets suit his intended purpose.

For the small game or varmint hunter out after meat or pelts, rather than merely pest control, full metal-jacketed bullets traveling at moderate velocities are his best bet. Predator control would call for expandable projectiles (hollow or soft points) moving at high velocities to ensure one-shot kills. These

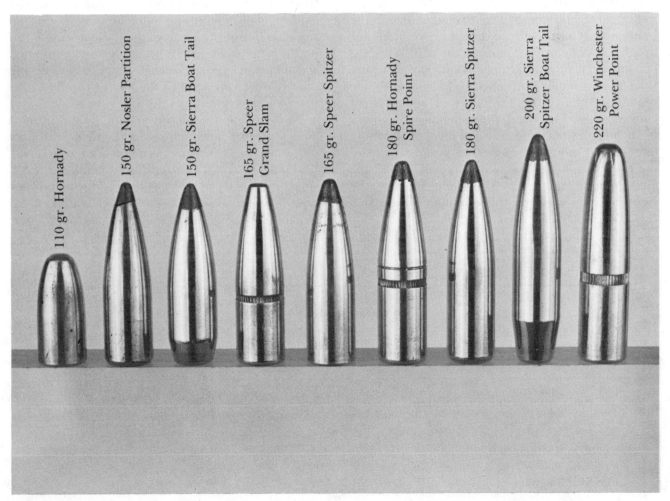

.30/06 hunting bullets.

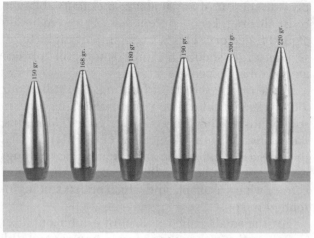

.30/06 match bullets—Sierra Matchking hollow point boat tail.

With short-barreled guns, the handloader can tailor his loads to get the most in velocity from a 2-inch barrel.

bullets produce tremendous shock when they hit, anchoring animals on the spot. Period.

Big game hunters should, if possible, match the bullet weight and caliber to the species hunted. For instance, in one of my favorites, the .270 Winchester, for antelope or mule deer at long ranges where velocity and bullet drop must be held to the bare minimum, the 130-grain bullet is an excellent choice. I also like the 150-grain bullet for black bears and deer at moderate ranges. For anything larger—elk, moose or the big bears—I'd start leaning toward a more powerful round in .30/06, the 7mm Mag or even the .300 Magnum. In short, the right bullet in the right caliber equals hunter success. Take both seriously.

To the beginner, this may seem complicated at first. However, time spent reading this book, the loading manuals and the outdoor journals and periodicals dotting the newsstands will soon put you on the right track. Then, range sessions combined with hunting experiences will enable you to decide exactly what you need in the way of proper bullet design and weight to get the job done.

Next on our list of components is the primer. This part, like powders, should be dealt with very cautiously in all respects. When working up a particular load pay strict attention to loading manual specifications when they list a cartridge or powder type. These loads have been arrived at after extensive testing, so follow the specifications to the letter.

PRIMER CHART

Primer	Federal	CCI	Remington	Winchester
Small Pistol	100	500	1½	1½-108
Small Pistol Magnum	—	550	5½	1½M-108
Large Pistol	150	300	2½	7-111
Large Pistol Magnum	155	350	—	—
Small Rifle	200	400	6½	6½-116
Small Rifle Magnum	205	450	7½	—
Large Rifle	210	200	9½	8½-120
Large Rifle Magnum	215	250	9½M	—

Before the novice loads a single cartridge, powder knowledge is a must.

Primers come in two sizes and types. Size number one measures .175″ in diameter, and is termed small pistol or small rifle. The next size is .210″ in diameter, and is called large pistol/large rifle. Magnum primers are available in both sizes. These produce a much hotter flame than regular primers and have a longer burning time to ignite large charges of slower burning powders used in loading big cases such as the 7mm and 8mm Remington Magnums.

Certain precautions are necessary when dealing with primers. Remember, primers do explode. That's their purpose—to ignite the powder. Care must be exercised in handling or loading primers into metallic cartridges. Use the right primer—small, large, standard or magnum—and leave them in their original containers. These plastic trays were designed to keep the primers apart. Do not, and I repeat *do not*, pile primers in boxes or glass jars. To do so only invites trouble. Also, it should go without

saying but I'll mention it anyhow, when loading or handling primers—*no smoking!*

In concert with primers is powder. Smokeless powder is available in three forms: flakes, extruded or spherical. An example of the flake type would be Hercules Unique; in extruded form, Accurate Arms MR-3100; and spherical, Hodgdon's BLC-2. In general terms, powders are judged on a scale relative to their burning rate. While it's very hard to pinpoint this because of other factors involved—case volume, pressure ratios or even bullet weight—nevertheless, a standard had to be established to set up guidelines for both handloaders and manufacturers alike.

In examining this rate-of-burning characteristic, we find that powders suitable for small cases, as with handgun cartridges, are termed fast. Bullseye, Winchester 231 or Unique are typical.

On the other end of the scale are the slow burners for large cases, bringing to mind Hodgdon's H-4831 or Norma's MRP (Magnum Rifle Powder). We'll go into greater detail in Chapter 6, but for the moment this will give you a head start pointing you in the right direction.

When you pull the trigger on a loaded round the following takes place: After the gun's firing pin has contacted the primer, setting it off, the powder ignites, forming a gas. As pressure builds, it forces the cartridge case backward against the bolt face and outward against the chamber. Pressure is exerted in all directions. Because the bullet is the only moveable part of the whole cartridge unit, pressure from the expanding gas acts upon it and starts it moving. Roughly four inches down the bore, pressure peaks because of the increasing amount of volume left behind. As the bullet moves farther down the barrel, its velocity increases, pressure drops and the bullet goes on its way out the barrel. All this, from trigger pull to terminal contact at, say, 100 yards distance, happens in a little over a third of a second.

Choosing the right components is a difficult aspect of handloading, but, I may add, the most pleasurable. For only after you assemble the right case, bullet, primer and powder, then watch your groups shrink at 100 yards will you experience the complete satisfaction that is so much a part of this pastime. With all this behind us, let's start putting it all together.

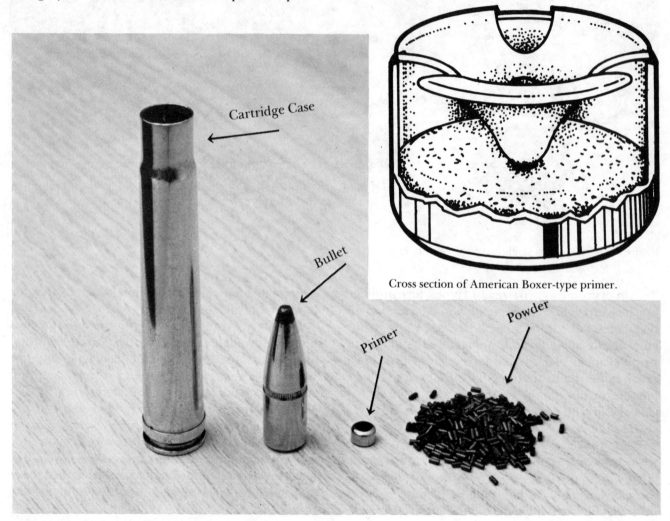

Cross section of American Boxer-type primer.

Cartridge Case

Bullet

Primer

Powder

Metallic components.

Chapter 4

Putting It All Together—Handgun Ammunition

The reloading of handgun ammunition amounts to nothing more than taking a cartridge case and running it through a number of predetermined steps. As simple as it may sound, there are a few items to be considered as you progress through any loading session.

The first is loading data. Research all your work from chapters in this book, spec sheets or from laboratory-type loading manuals such as those published by Speer, Hornady or Sierra, or from powder makers such as Hodgdon, Du Pont or Hercules. Never guess at any load, powder charge or primer size, and always consult a reputable and up-to-date handbook. To do otherwise would be foolhardy at best.

General safety precautions are a must. Never smoke or indulge in alcoholic beverages in your work area. Keep the bench clean. Only the components relative to the cartridge you are working with should be on the deck. Nothing else. Get in the habit of wearing eye protection, especially when at the priming station. Accumulated "dust" in the filler tubes can—and has—lead to detonation of primers after months of heavy loading sessions. Again, keep everything in tiptop shape.

If any problems crop up, *stop!* Don't force any equipment, as serious complications could develop. Instead, investigate the situation clearly even if you have to leave the area for a few minutes to clear your head or think over the problem. Go through the routine mentally, figure it all out, then apply corrective action.

Record all data. Labels are supplied with each box of bullets. Use them to label your loaded cartridge boxes. Use printed forms to record all loading data for future use. Use both as a cross reference. Take nothing for granted.

The loading of handgun cartridges is a shortcut to more shooting because it saves money. The photo sequence that follows shows one cartridge moving through the various loading stages. Fifty or even a hundred cases at a time can be done at one station. When these are complete, the operator can move on to the next station. But remember, *quality* before *quantity!*

All steps are not shown in complete detail as this would take almost double the number of photos and space involved. A quick check of any loading manual, die set instructions or loading press literature will fill in the blanks. Common sense and experience will do the rest.

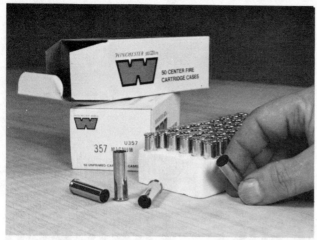

Using new brass, visually check all the cases for grit, packaging or brass chips before lubing or sending them up into your expensive carbide sizing die. Remove any foreign particles. When purchasing brass, as mentioned before, always try to get one lot number. This is the number stamped on the inside flap of the box. Serious handloaders who are interested in consistent velocities do this as a matter of course.

Lubricate all the cases if you are using standard dies. Eliminate this step if carbide dies are employed. These dies are getting more popular every year because carbide sets are cleaner, and eliminate the need for cleaning of the cases after lubing.

Insert the sizing die into the press. Check the manufacturer's recommendations with reference to clearance at the shell holder. Most die sets are adjustable and allow the handloader to set the base of the die so it just touches the shell holder on the upswing, or downswing, of the handle depending on the way your press is set up. This results in full resizing of the case in a uniform manner with no chance of partial sizing which would lead to chambering problems later on.

Insert the cartridge case into the shell holder. Here, it's a good idea to stay with one brand of both die set and shell holder.

Run all the cases all the way up into the sizing die. If a fired case is used, the primer will be expelled at this time also. Out of all the dies in the sequence, this one is probably the most important. For as the case is fired in the gun it expands, filling the chamber and acting as a gas seal. After firing, the case relaxes, but does not go back to the original factory size. This is where this die comes in. In short, we are compressing the brass back to a standard diameter so it will chamber easily.

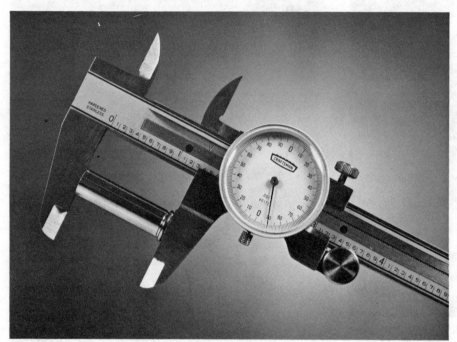

After cleaning (if lube was used) and before progressing, check each case for overall length. This is easily done on a dial micrometer, or the inexpensive plastic gauges sold by many of the loading manufacturers. This is another important step in the loading process, for if the case is overlength, it will not only lead to chambering difficulties, but possible pressure problems as well.

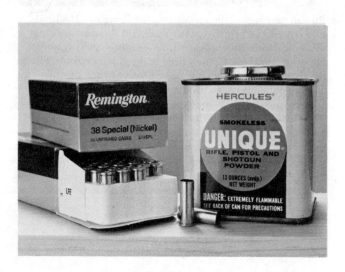

Nickel cases and Unique powder; they make a good pair in loading the .38 Special.

If any cases are overlength, check the specs, then trim those cases now to ensure proper chambering in the weapon, and an equal crimp later on in the reloading process. This can be done in a number of ways, including using a case trimmer or a trim die. Many reloaders favor the case trimmer. Once set, you can do a number of cases in a relatively short time. The other alternative, the trim die, requires that you file away the excess length. Either way, afterwards, you must again check the length.

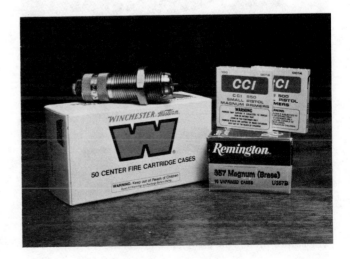

Fresh brass, tungsten carbide dies and both standard and magnum primers are your best bet for top-quality reloads.

Putting It All Together—Handgun Ammunition

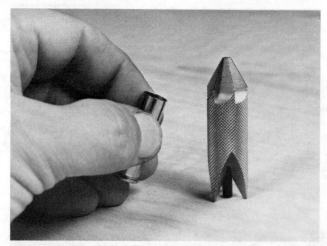

Using the deburring tool, create a slight inside chamfer using the pointed end of the tool. The opposite end will remove any burrs left over from trimming on the outside of the case. As these deburring tools are extremely sharp, care must be taken so you don't take off too much brass resulting in weak necks. One quick twist is all that is needed.

The author prefers the 230-grain bullet in the .45 ACP.

Replace the sizer die with the neck expander, setting the case flare to match the bullet base. Very close attention should be exercised here. Do not *overflare* the case. To do so will only lead to split necks and reduced case life. On automatic rounds (e.g., 9mm, .38 Super or .45 ACP) only a minute flare is needed to hold the bullet securely during the violent action of the automatic pistol.

Pick the appropriate primer from past experience, as recommended in a popular loading manual or from the chart in this book. Primers are available from most companies specializing in loading or general ammunition (e.g., Remington, Speer or Winchester) and numbers will differ. Please, before any priming is considered, make absolutely sure you have picked the right primer for the particular cartridge you are now loading.

The inside view of an RCBS tungsten carbide die. Note the very smooth surfaces for effortless sizing.

Putting It All Together—Handgun Ammunition

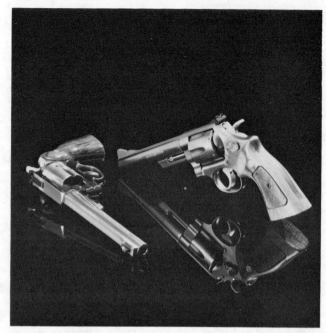

The .44 Magnum has enough powder to satisfy the hardened shooter.

Seat all primers carefully. This may be done in a number of different ways. One way is on the press as shown. Another possibility is by using a separate Lee priming tool. The third way would be to use a special tool, like the RCBS automatic priming tool. Whatever the choice, make sure the primer is fully seated in the case, flush with the bottom.

The .44 Special has always been one of America's favorite handgun calibers.

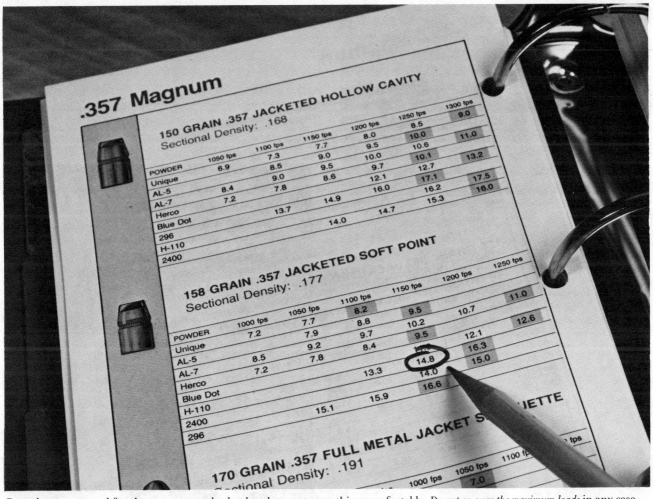

.357 Magnum

150 GRAIN .357 JACKETED HOLLOW CAVITY
Sectional Density: .168

POWDER	1050 fps	1100 fps	1150 fps	1200 fps	1250 fps	1300 fps
Unique	6.9	7.3	7.7	8.0	8.5	9.0
AL-5		8.5	9.0	9.5	10.0	11.0
AL-7	8.4	7.8	8.6	10.0	10.6	13.2
Herco	7.2			9.7	10.1	
Blue Dot				12.1	12.7	
296				16.0	17.1	17.5
H-110		13.7			16.2	16.0
2400			14.9	14.0	15.3	

158 GRAIN .357 JACKETED SOFT POINT
Sectional Density: .177

POWDER	1000 fps	1050 fps	1100 fps	1150 fps	1200 fps	1250 fps
Unique	7.2	7.7	8.2	9.5	10.7	11.0
AL-5		7.9	8.8	10.2	12.1	12.6
AL-7	8.5	7.8	9.2	9.5		
Herco	7.2		8.4	14.8	16.3	
Blue Dot					15.0	
H-110			13.3		14.0	
2400		15.1	15.9		16.6	
296						

170 GRAIN .357 FULL METAL JACKET SILHOUETTE
Sectional Density: .191

	1000 fps	1050 fps	1100 fps
		7.0	

Consult your manual for the proper powder load and start at something comfortable. *Do not go over the maximum loads* in any case. Start about mid-range, and work upwards as you gain both experience and a working knowledge of the cartridge on hand.

Even on a modest budget, loading areas can be set up in small corners to produce fine reloads.

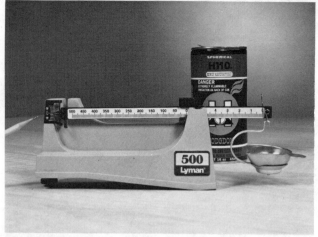

Set up the scale—zero the unit. This is important, especially with fast burning powders like Bullseye. Attention to detail here is mandatory. Overcharging could result in damage to the firearm and yourself.

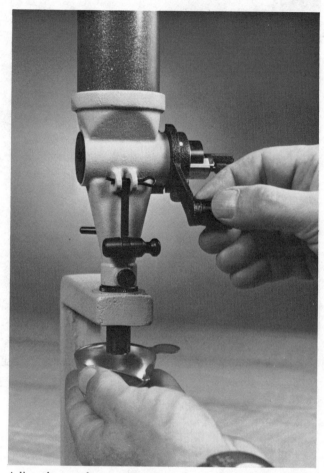

Adjust the powder measure to match your load choice. Weigh this load to confirm your setting. To see just what your average powder drop will be, throw ten charges into the pan, weigh them as a single batch, then divide by ten. If all is satisfactory, then and only then proceed with the next step.

The .25 ACP is available in very small autos.

Load all the cases in an orderly fashion following a fixed sequence, left to right, or top to bottom depending on your preference.

Then, check all cases for *double charges*. Use a penlite if necessary, but double-check *all cases*.

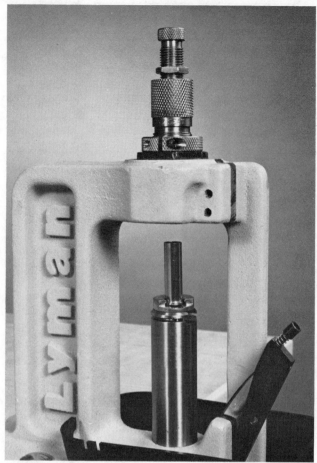

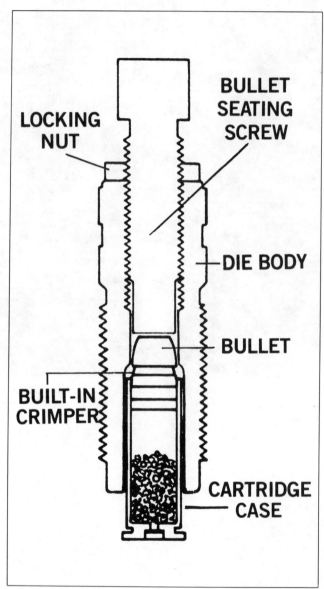

Remove the neck expander and replace it with the bullet seating die. Follow all instructions with this setup. I find it easy to insert the die base first, setting it up with the case. After this is accomplished, insert the bullet seater, adjusting it for overall length as the bullet is driven down into the case.

LOCKING NUT

BULLET SEATING SCREW

DIE BODY

BULLET

BUILT-IN CRIMPER

CARTRIDGE CASE

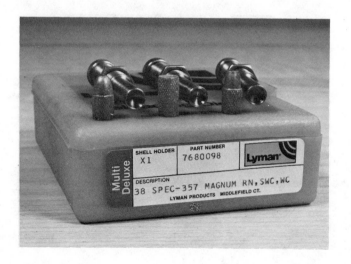

Pick the seating punch most suitable for the bullet ogive you are now loading. (Left to right: round nose, wadcutter, semi-wadcutter.)

Place the bullet into the primed, charged and flared case making sure it is straight and true with the sides of the case.

Seat the bullet for proper depth and crimping. This is done in the following general manner, but check your literature for specific instructions. Raise the ram with the bullet and case to the highest point and leave it there. Screw the seating body down until it just touches the mouth of the case. Unscrew the body about a half-turn back and leave it. This is the uncrimped position. Now lower the ram and insert the seating stem. Raise the ram again, and slowly turn the stem downward until it just contacts the bullet. By alternately raising and lowering the cartridge case, you will start to push the bullet home. When you have arrived at the pre-selected depth, stop. This is the non crimp position, perfect for autopistol rounds using the taper crimp. To crimp the bullet at the cannelure, back off the seating screw about a quarter-turn and tighten it down finger tight. Next, turn the die body down three quarters of a turn and tighten it down. This is the crimp position, just the ticket for all high-performance loads.

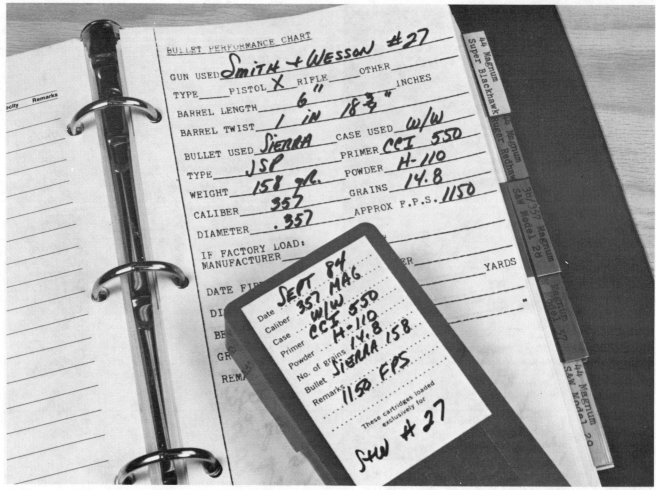

BULLET PERFORMANCE CHART

GUN USED *Smith + Wesson #27*

TYPE ___ PISTOL *X* RIFLE ___ OTHER ___

BARREL LENGTH ___ *6"*

BARREL TWIST ___ *1 in 18¾"*

BULLET USED *Sierra*   CASE USED *W/W*

TYPE ___ *JSP*   PRIMER *CCI 550*

WEIGHT ___ *158 gr.*   POWDER *H-110*

CALIBER ___ *357*   GRAINS *14.8*

DIAMETER ___ *.357*   APPROX F.P.S. *1150*

IF FACTORY LOAD:
MANUFACTURER ___

DATE FIR ___ YARDS

DI ___

BE ___

GR ___

REM ___

Date   *Sept 84*
Caliber   *357 Mag*
Case   *W/W*
Primer   *CCI 550*
Powder   *H-110*
No. of grains   *14.8*
Bullet   *Sierra 158*
Remarks   *1150 FPS*

These cartridges loaded exclusively for

S+W #27

Finally, record all data for future use. You can either make up your own record sheet as I did, or purchase any of the ones available at your local dealer. Just make sure you keep very accurate records to go over as you test each load. Weather, temperature and even different guns play an important role in all load performance. Keeping records enables you to see all these factors at a glance.

Stay away from surplus brass, both foreign and domestic, for trouble-free loads in any automatic caliber. Always use factory fresh.

Chapter 5

Reloading Rifle Ammunition

Good quality rifle ammunition is loaded in virtually the same manner as handgun ammunition. And, unless there is a dramatic change in metallic components in the near future, the process will stay essentially the same.

There are differences, however, even though the general technique is the same. Minor, but different. Basically, the loading of present-day bottleneck cartridges revolves around four operations: sizing/decapping; priming; powder charging; bullet seating. The photographs illustrate the various stages. But, there are other parts of the operation to contend with. Some steps are similar to those followed in loading handgun ammo; others are unique to rifle cartridges and require complete understanding before proceeding.

One obvious difference is that powder charges tend to be larger in rifle cases. Consequently, the powder measure must be able to dispense bulky, coarse-grained propellant. A metering chamber set up to drop, say, 10.5 grains of 2400 powder into small caliber pistol cases is inadequate for rifle cases. The better powder measures are adjustable, or have replaceable chambers that can handle all kinds of powders. Keep this in mind when shopping for a powder measure, especially if you reload a variety of cartridges, or plan to. The extra initial investment is worthwhile.

With coarse-grained propellants you will find yourself weighing each individual charge a few grains under your chosen load, then trickling the charge up to balance the beam on the scale. It slows things down but in the long run doesn't matter as rifle shooters don't expend as much ammo as do pistoleros, except riflemen involved in serious competition, and they don't mind the slower pace if it results in consistent, accurate loads.

Neck tension is very important in rifle cases. It not only holds the bullet in place when loaded, but also assures more consistent powder combustion which leads to better accuracy in all cases fired in the same gun. Therefore, proper attention has to be paid to the expander plug in the sizing die. If, when seating bullets, there is little or no resistance when seating the projectile, the plug should be checked for proper diameter. No industry is immune to the devil's misdeeds and it is possible, though highly improbable, to get a .311″ plug instead of the correct .308″.

Other problems could crop up that the handloader should look out for. Incipient head separation caused by a bad headspace situation is reason to check your sizing die for proper adjustment. Overall improper bullet/cartridge length can not only lead to difficult chambering but can also raise pressure levels. Too much lube is often the culprit causing those small dents in the shoulder area of your rifle cases.

Because these and numerous other situations can come up from time to time, I cannot overstress the importance of having a minimum of two or even three loading manuals as reference material. Compiled under laboratory conditions, these books represent hundreds of man-hours of testing, shooting and pressure readings of just about any cartridge on the market today—or yesterday. Rely on them for correct and intelligent data.

Finally, as in pistol reloading, check and double check everything. At the bench, monitor your procedures; at the range, check for signs of abnormal pressure. Flattened primers, hard extraction or ejector markings are cause for concern. If evident, use your bullet puller and recheck your loads. Don't ever fire them off just to get rid of them.

Remember, accidents never take a holiday. Conscientious practices combined with attention to all phases of the reloading operation will assure a safe, satisfying hobby.

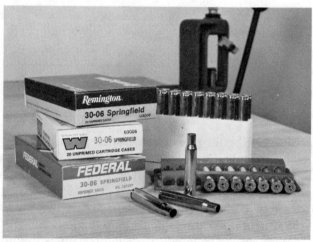

Using new brass, inspect them for grit, packaging fluff or brass chips. Whenever possible, always buy the same lot number as printed on the box. This will assure you of the same interior dimension, which is very important to velocities and good accuracy.

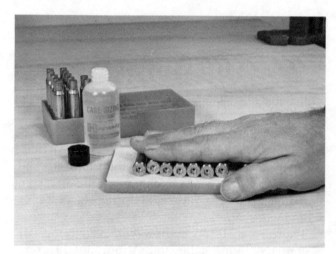

Lube all cases on the lube pad. Make sure that you use only minimum lubrication on the rifle cases. Too much lube will cause the case shoulder to collapse when the round is fired; too little could result in having a case get stuck in the die.

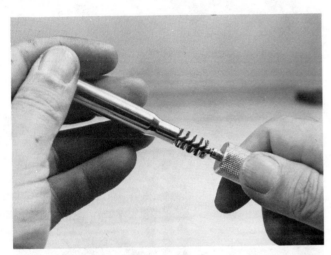

Lubricate the inside of the case necks for an easy return over the expander plug. Another possibility would be to use the new carbide expander plugs now on the market, thus eliminating this step.

Insert the sizer/decapper into the press and adjust it according to the die maker's instructions. The usual procedure advised by nearly all die makers is to screw this die into the press until it touches the shell holder when the ram (with shellholder) is in the up position. This assures full length case resizing.

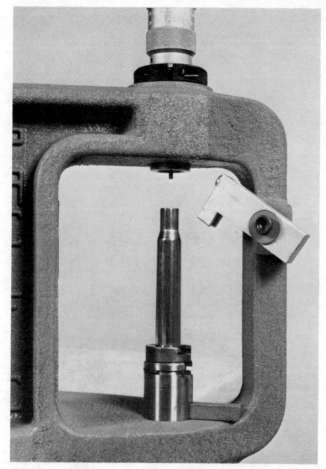

Slide a cartridge case into the shell holder, making sure it is touching the rear of the holder and is straight and ready for entry into the sizing die.

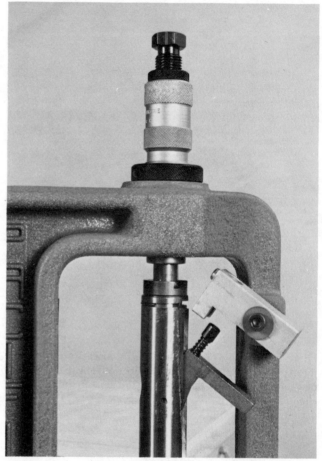

Press the cartridge case into the die by running it up completely for full length resizing. If it's a fired case, the primer will be expelled at this time. The primer pocket can be cleaned at this time with a few twirls of the cleaning tool.

Clean the case with a solvent or by tumbling before going on. Removing the lube is a definite must, as leaving any lube on the inside or outside of the brass cartridge case will contaminate the powder and primer in short order, rendering the ammunition useless.

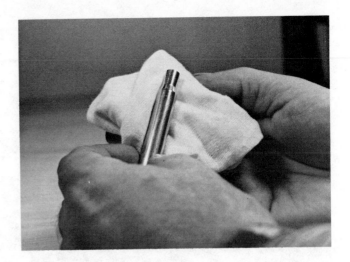

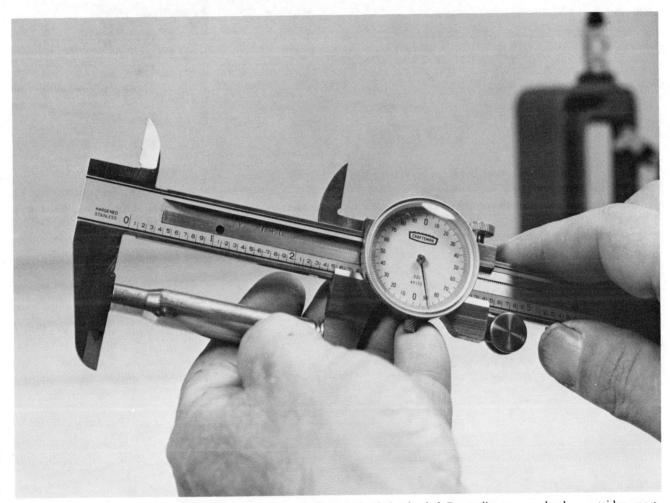

Check for case overall length by comparing factory specs to the cartridge being loaded. Depending on your load or cartridge, most cases demand trimming every fifth or sixth reload. Accepted practice allows you to trim back about .010″. Example: A .30/06 case can be allowed to grow to no more than 2.494 inches. Trimming back to 2.484 would give you enough allowance for many reloads before you have to trim again.

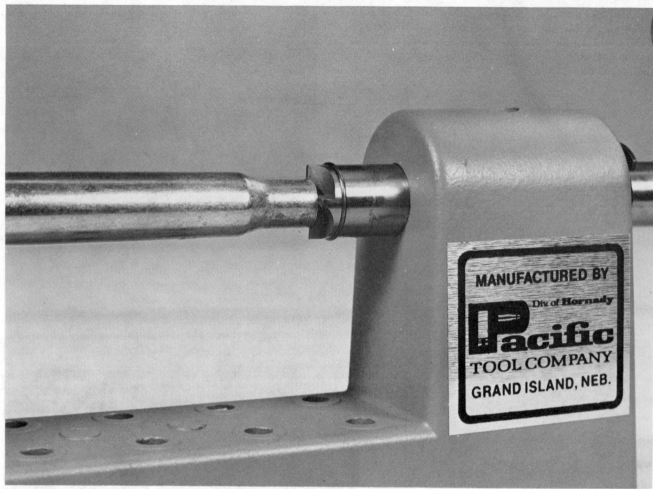

If overlength, trim the cases to the proper specifications for this caliber. You can use either a trim die or a case trimmer. With the former, you must purchase separate dies to perform the trimming operation. A case trimmer utilizes a pilot that fits into the case neck, holding it steady during the process. These pilots come in different sizes.

A prime example of a modern, top-quality rifle is this Sako from Finland. Shown is the Standard Grade, but you can move upward in both models and features, depending on your budget and preferences.

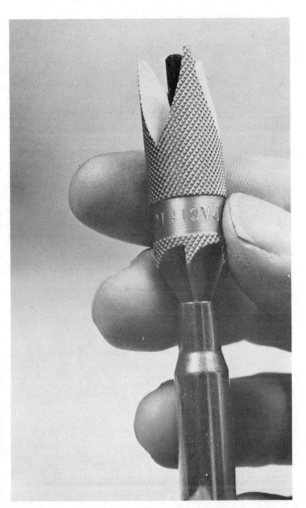 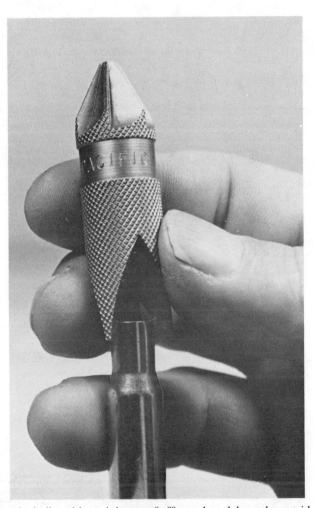

After trimming, chamfer the inside of the case mouth (left) to receive the bullet with a minimum of effort—then deburr the outside to remove all burrs (right). Please remember to use a light touch as the deburring tool is hardened steel and is very sharp.

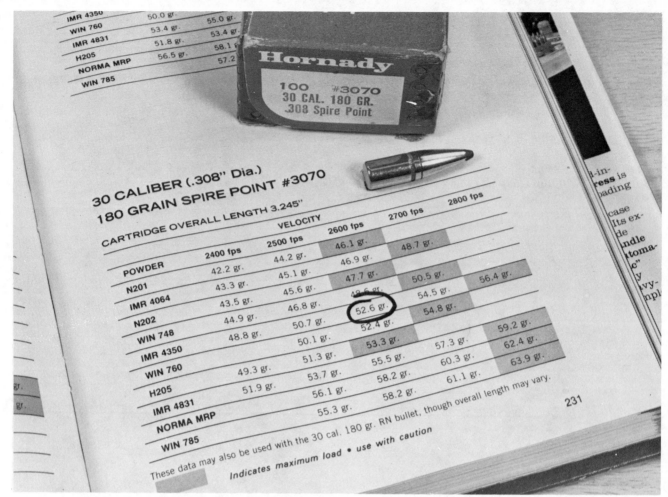

POWDER	VELOCITY				
	2400 fps	2500 fps	2600 fps	2700 fps	2800 fps
N201	42.2 gr.	44.2 gr.	46.1 gr.	48.7 gr.	
IMR 4064	43.3 gr.	45.1 gr.	46.9 gr.		
N202	43.5 gr.	45.6 gr.	47.7 gr.	50.5 gr.	56.4 gr.
WIN 748		46.8 gr.	48.6 gr.	54.5 gr.	
IMR 4350	44.9 gr.	50.7 gr.	52.6 gr.	54.8 gr.	
WIN 760	48.8 gr.	50.1 gr.	52.4 gr.		59.2 gr.
H205		51.3 gr.	53.3 gr.	57.3 gr.	62.4 gr.
IMR 4831	49.3 gr.	53.7 gr.	55.5 gr.	60.3 gr.	63.9 gr.
NORMA MRP	51.9 gr.	56.1 gr.	58.2 gr.	61.1 gr.	
WIN 785		55.3 gr.	58.2 gr.		

30 CALIBER (.308" Dia.)
180 GRAIN SPIRE POINT #3070
CARTRIDGE OVERALL LENGTH 3.245"

These data may also be used with the 30 cal. 180 gr. RN bullet, though overall length may vary.

Indicates maximum load • use with caution

231

Pick your load and primer as determined by the loading manuals.

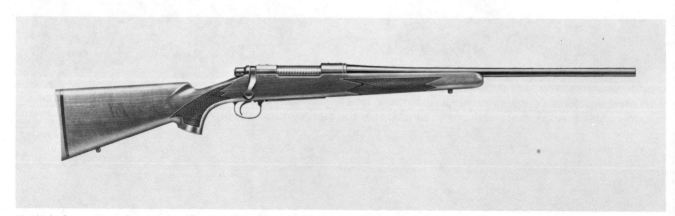

Typical of great American-made rifles chambered in .30/06 is the Remington Model 700 Classic.

Prime the case using the press primer feed incorporated in the press. This is the most popular way to prime the cases. It's fast and all the parts needed to complete this operation come with the press. Other alternatives would be hand priming tools or specialized equipment suited just for priming.

Set up the powder measure to throw a charge a couple of grains below your chosen load. Consult the chart supplied by a manufacturer or your own notes based on experience.

Zero the powder scale, then use the powder trickler to bring the charge up to the correct weight. When you are satisfied, you can then move on to the next step.

Load the case with the propellant, moving on down the line until all the cases are charged. After all cases are loaded, check to verify the charge weight.

After placing a primed and charged case into the press, raise the case and install the seater die until the crimping notch touches the neck of the case. Unscrew the die about a quarter turn, then tighten the lock ring by hand.

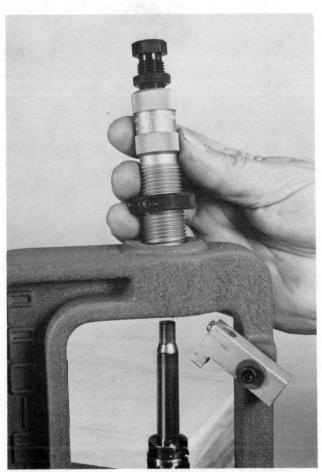

When all cases are charged and not before, move on to the next step, which is seating. Insert the seating/crimping die.

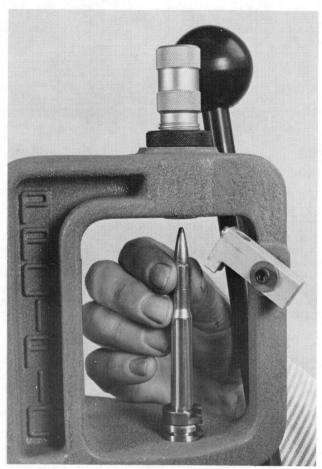

Bring the case back down and install the bullet, making sure it is straight on top of the host case.

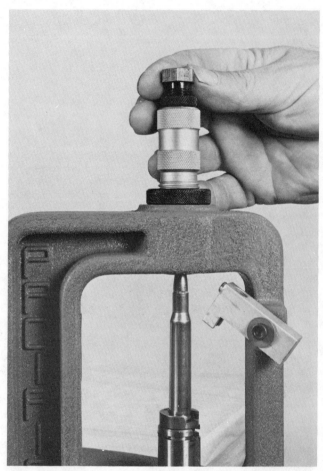

Raise the case again and adjust the bullet seater die until the correct bullet depth is attained by following the "overall length with bullet" chart pertaining to the caliber you are now loading. Verify this with your dial calipers. Here, it's a good idea to make a dummy round (one with *no powder or primer*) and check it for functioning in your particular rifle. If it's a hunting round, make three or four, load the magazine, and run each through the action. This will guarantee faultless performance in the field.

When the correct bullet depth has been attained, the crimp can now be applied at this time if desired.

This is the latest example of Remington's faith in the older cartridges. Pictured here is the Classic model in .250/3000 Savage short action rifle with the B&L 4X scope in Redfield rings and bases.

Last, record all data using a record sheet. Information that could be included would list the rifle, bullet and make, powder in grains, primer, case, overall length, velocity, date fired, temperature and group size. Another label should be made and affixed to the plastic cartridge box. In this way, mixups between loads (or the wrong cartridges) will never happen.

Chapter 6

An Update on Propellants

Powder selection for any given caliber has to be one of the more interesting facets of the entire handloading spectrum. For powder, like gasoline in a car, determines optimum performance. Fill your tank with the wrong octane, and you'll hear it all the way down the road. Fill your case with the wrong powder, and you'll see it in enlarged groups, erratic velocities and missed game.

So in essence, then, the powder is the fueling substance in any cartridge case. Used in properly measured quantities and burned in a confined space, then ignited by the primer, it forms a gas which then expands causing pressure against the bullet, propelling it down the bore.

While there are two types of powder available to shooters today—black powder and smokeless—we are concerned here with only the latter. The former is used in the shooting of muzzleloading firearms, a subject covered in other books. While early metallic cartridges were loaded with black powder, our coverage deals exclusively with modern smokeless powder in today's cartridges.

When reading about or handling modern smokeless powders you will be confronted with such terms as "progressive burning, characteristics, brand names, case volume, identification and burning rates."

When a powder is called "progressive" it refers to its ability to burn at a relatively slow rate, with a slow pressure curve. Thus, combining the right powder with the right cartridge is of paramount importance in handloading. Needless to say, I cannot overemphasize the need to constantly refer to the excellent loading manuals published by Hodgdon, Hornady, Nosler and Sierra, and the powder makers themselves: Du Pont, Hercules and Winchester/Olin.

A "characteristic" in a powder relates to its energy source, deterrents and coatings—one at a time. The energy in propellants comes from nitrocellulose and nitroglycerine. Single-based powders would include only the first ingredient; double-based, both. Deterrents slow the rate of burning by chemically treating the grains for additional control. This has many advantages for the shooter, one being a lower flame temperature, which leads to a reduction of bore erosion, especially in rifles. For flash inhibiting, a coating of potassium sulfate is added. For ease in metering through powder measures, graphite or a glazing compound could be introduced. Finally, a preservative will be added for longevity.

Brand names are very significant and tremendously important. Handloaders must recognize this when handling propellants. Although product numbers may be the same—as in H-4350 (for Hodgdon) and IMR-4350 (for Du Pont)—burning rates in some instances will be slightly different. As when making any change in a component (primer, bullet or case), handloaders will do well to start 6 to 8% (in rifles) below established charges when introducing a new powder or even a new lot number.

Case volume, although not a tangible component, will also alter performance and should be evaluated when switching brass of the same caliber. For instance, in the case of the .270 Winchester, the net capacity in grains water runs 61.5 for Remington brass; 62.1 for the Winchester brand. Such differences could cause a marked variation in both pressure and velocity readouts, so remember to start low when making a change no matter how minor it might seem in comparison to the norm.

As to powder identification, the accompanying descriptions and photographs are meant for practical reference and guidance only. Never try to match a powder (ball, flake or extruded) from an unmarked container to any of the photographs, then use it in a firearm. Since there is no absolute way of differentiating between powders, aside from analysis in a lab at the factory, what you may think is 4831 could in reality be 3031. Using the same charge weight with the faster powder will produce disastrous results.

While the brand of powder and its volume do have a definite influence on accuracy—along with bullets, primers and full length resizing—the burning rate of that propellant is another important factor. While some people see little value in listing powders according to their burning rate, I find this information helpful for both the beginner and advanced reloader. They get a perspective of where any particular propellant fits in, especially since there is such a large selection to choose from. However, in no way should a brief, general description of a powder be considered as a recommendation.

Always consult your loading manuals for specifics. Combined with intelligent cross references, burning rates do have their place in handloading. Please remember, the accounting of current propellants given here is not to be used as a guide for the selection of powder charges. Its only purpose is to show where certain powders fall within the total lineup as produced by scientific "closed bomb" tests. This, in turn, will assist you in seeing the complete picture of canister powders as they stand today.

Such an examination of powders does bring up a couple of points. The first is that the faster-burning powders are for smaller cases—generally. Of course, there are exceptions, but for the most part this is true. By this we mean pistol calibers or small rifle cases like the .30 Carbine, which need their energy fast to compensate for short barrel time and small case volume; or perhaps to work the action of a pistol, as in the case of an automatic weapon.

On the other end of the spectrum, the slower powders are reserved for bigger cases or longer barrels where energy is expended over a longer period of time. These powders are used mostly in magnum or belted cases, but over the years constant experimentation by knowledgeable handloaders and technicians using pressure barrels and chronographs has made it possible for some non-magnums to utilize slower powders like IMR-4350 or H-4831 with equal success—up to a point!

Let's cite an example. Taking our time-proven .30/06 and the 150-grain bullet, we find—in a recent manual—powders ranging from fast to slow: IMR-3031, H-4895, IMR-4064, IMR-4320, IMR-4350, IMR-4831 and Norma-MRP. On the fast end, velocities average around 2900 fps. Going to the medium to slow powders, which, incidentally, seem to be the best for this cartridge, again the average goes up to 3000 to 3100 fps. Falling behind, however, is the still slower propellant in the IMR-4831/MRP class. Here we start to lose the battle as our velocities again start to slow down to 2900 fps.

Next, information about burning rates of powders, together with a loading manual, will show that you have a choice. Right off the bat you note that the .38 Special thrives on helpings of Bullseye, W/W 231 or Unique. But for some added fun and experiments, the innovative handloader can stock up on HP38, Red Dot or Herco. Depending on his handgun, he may get better accuracy and higher velocities with the last three, but again—and I stress this heavily—a lot depends on his gun. Because no two guns are ever the same, before shooting a successful load in a different gun of the same caliber, the wise man will throttle down those loads by 5 to 6% (in handguns) until he is sure his new gun can handle and shoot the same loads with equal success.

Last, versatility will enter into the picture. Let's say you just went out and purchased a brand new shiny .300 Weatherby Magnum. Not a bad choice; a bit stiff on the recoil, but capable of taking game just about anywhere on this planet. Then, to make this a real soap opera, the store had a stock of 130-, 150-, 165-, 180- and 220-grain bullets, but regrettably had only one powder: H-4831.

No problem. For here we can use that powder with the 130-grainer to get 3600 fps; the 150-grain for 3400 fps; the 165-grain for 3300 fps; the 180-grain bullet for 3200 fps; or the 220-grain round nose for 2800 fps. So you see you don't have to run out and buy everything on the list. Pick a reputable loading manual, choose a bullet and the velocity you need for your hunting requirements in the field by consulting the drop and range tables, then pick your propellant according to loading manual recommendations.

But, before you go out and purchase a single grain of propellant, remember that there are definite rules and guidelines to follow when using canister-grade powders.

- Use only reputable brands, so marked, and purchased *brand new*.

- Keep all powders in a cool, dry location separate from all primers.

- Never smoke or consume alcoholic beverages while loading. A clear head is a must.

- Demand absolute peace and quiet while in a loading session.

- Set up a routine for work at the loading bench.

- Never switch propellants from factory tins to plastic see-thru containers for ease of identification. Light will speed the process of decomposition, making smokeless powders more susceptible to spontaneous combustion.

- Make sure all components (bullets, powders, primers) are matched to the cartridge you are loading. By substituting a .303-caliber bullet (.311″ diameter) for a .30/06 bullet (.308″ diameter), pressures will rise dramatically, causing undue stress and destruction of the weapon, and maybe you as well.

- Do not guess at the proper charge weight. Follow the loading manuals religiously, for they are the "Bibles" of the shooting sports.

- Never mix powders, or make "duplex" loads in a vain attempt to force higher velocity readings.

- Use a good scale to confirm all powder readings off a trusted powder measure.

- Never, and I mean NEVER, go above the maximum loads in any loading manual.

- Always double-check all operations for safety and uniformity in loads.

CURRENTLY AVAILABLE CANISTER-GRADE POWDERS ARRANGED IN THE ORDER OF THEIR BURNING RATES

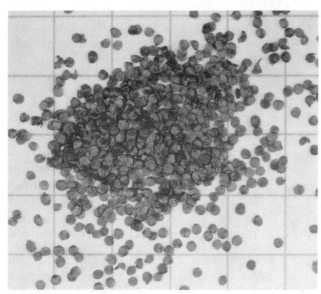

Bullseye—Around since the turn of the century, this double-based powder is the fastest available for practical use. Used widely in .38 Special target loads.

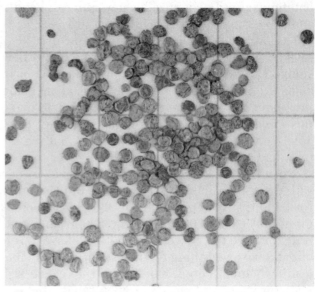

W/W 231—A high-energy ball powder finding great favor in cartridges such as the .38 Special or the .45 ACP.

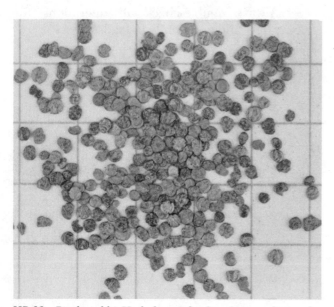

HP-38—Produced by Hodgdon. A fast burning powder used in small pistol cases.

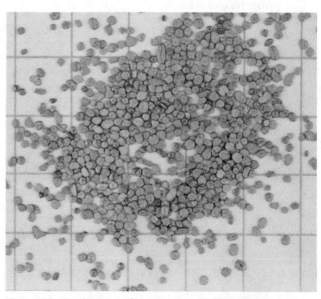

Trap 100—Made primarily as a trap and field shotgun powder. Handgunners now load it for mid-range target use.

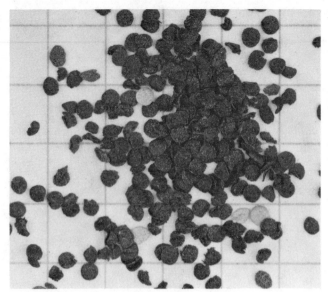

Red Dot—For economizing on one powder, both handgunners and shotgun shooters can use this powder for both applications. Especially good for light loads in the .357 Magnum or .44 Special.

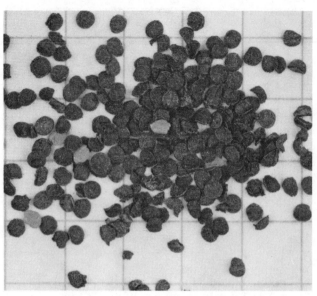

Green Dot—Slightly slower than its cousin Red Dot. Applications include medium handgun loads.

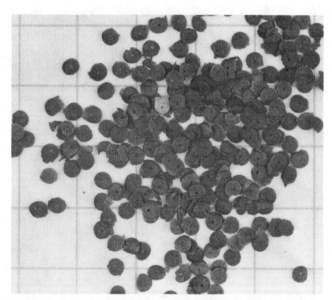

700X—Currently the only double-based powder made by Du Pont. Shotgunners involved in competition are the principal users. Can be used in handguns from .38 Special to .44 Magnum.

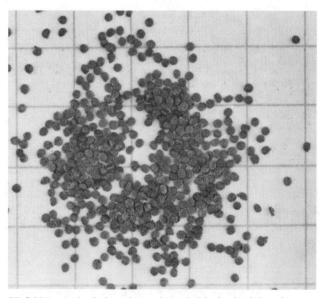

SR-7625—A single-based powder suitable for both handgun and shotgun loads. Similar to Unique.

An Update on Propellants

Hercules Unique—Very popular for all handgun loads. Can be used for light rifle loads and cast bullets. Wide availability. Very economical to use.

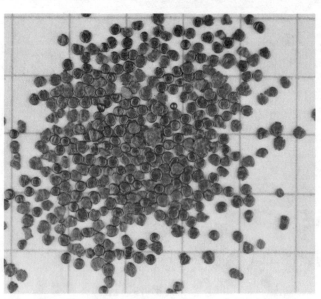

HS-6—A spherical powder by Hodgdon finding favor with those shooting magnum calibers.

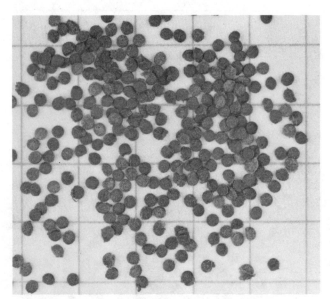

SR-4756—Very clean burning in handguns. Works very well in rifles utilizing cast lead bullets.

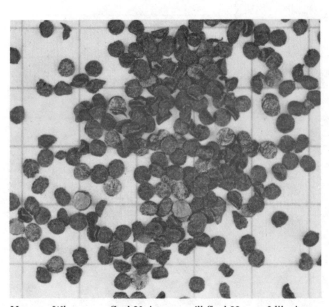

Herco—Where you find Unique, you'll find Herco. I like it, especially in large cases like the .45 Colt.

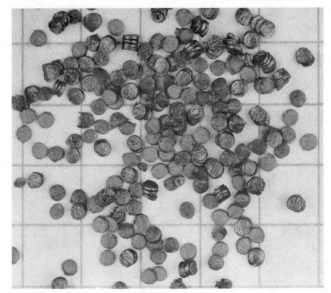

Blue Dot—Very popular in heavy, large caliber handgun applications.

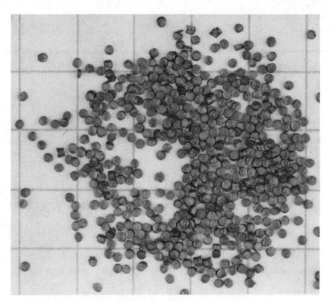

2400—A double-based, medium burning handgun powder. Popular with .41 and .44 Magnum users. For rifle use; handloaders shooting small cases like the .22 Hornet find it especially suitable to their needs.

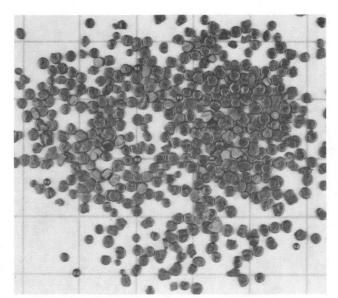

HS-7—Kissing cousin to HS-6; a wee bit slower and thus better suited for larger handgun cases.

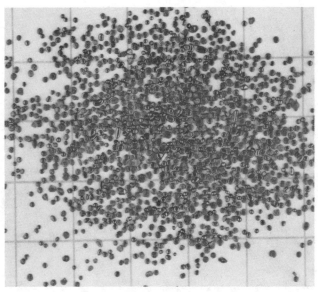

H-110—What started out as a powder for the .30 Carbine has blossomed out into a fine propellant for heavy magnum loads. Magnum primers are recommended for consistent ignition.

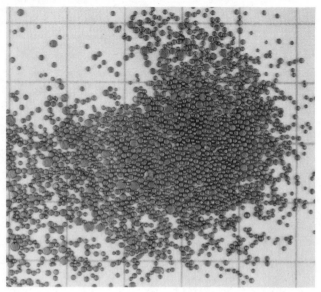

Accurate Arms 9—A ball-type powder for use in the .357, .41 and .44 Magnums.

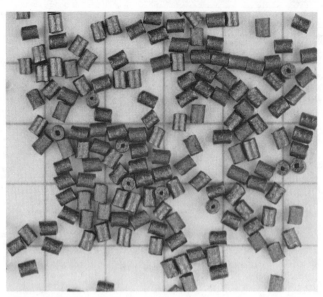

SR-4759—Reintroduced in 1973, this powder is useful in the .221 Remington Fireball. Also excellent for reduced loads in all calibers.

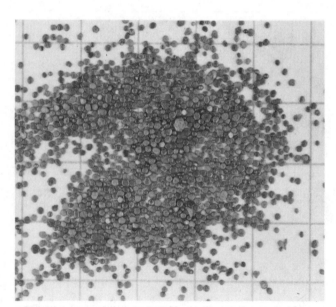

W/W 296—A top choice for all magnum handgun loads, 296 must be used as listed in the manuals for best results. Most factories use it for commercial loadings in the .30 Carbine and .357 and .44 Magnums.

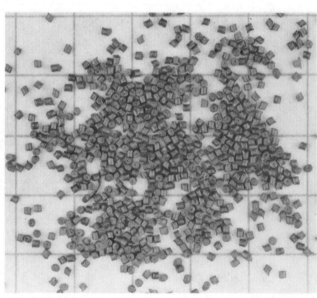

IMR-4227—The fastest burning propellant in the IMR series, it is ideally suited for handguns, rifles and .410 shotshell loading.

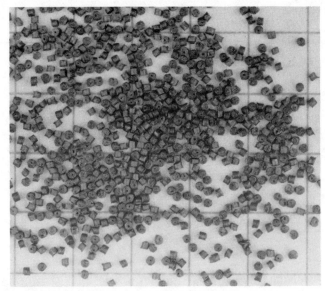

H-4227—Made by Hodgdon. By all standards a duplicate to the Du Pont brand.

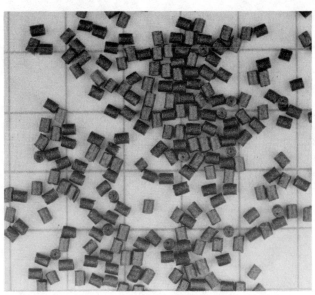

Accurate Arms MP5744—An extruded powder for use in high-velocity silhouette cartridges such as the .30 and .357 Herretts, 7mm TCU and 7mm IHMSA.

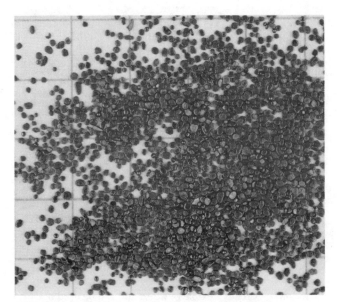

W/W 680—Suitable for small rifle cases in the .22 Hornet class.

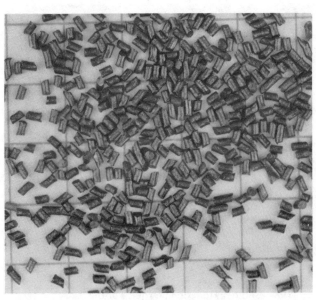

Norma 200—A good choice for the .222 Remington.

An Update on Propellants

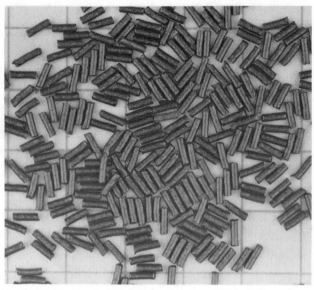

IMR-4198—An excellent choice in the .222 Remington for bench rest shooters or varminters. Wide availability makes this a good powder for competition shooters on the move.

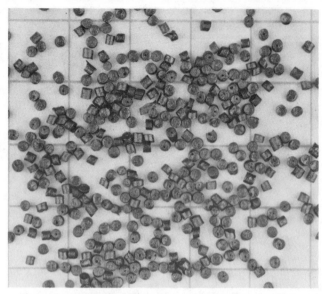

Reloader 7—Years ago there was a Reloader 7, 11 and 21. Now this one remains and, like the 4198 series, is good for smaller cases up to .30-30.

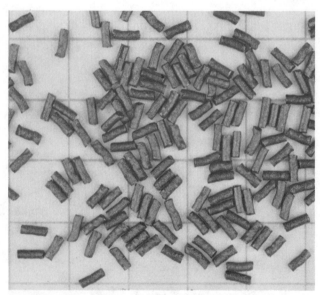

H-4198—Another Hodgdon powder. For the .222 Remington, plus straight-walled cases in the .444 Marlin or .45-70 class.

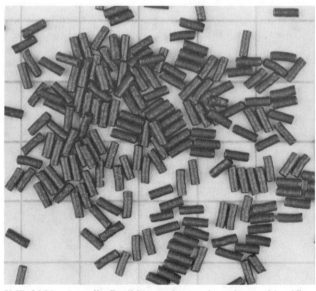

IMR-3031—A really flexible powder; and can be used in rifle cases from the 7 × 57mm to the thunderous .458 Winchester Magnum.

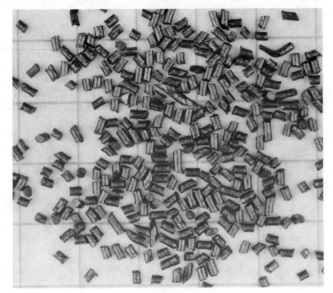

Norma 201—For use in .30-30 size cases.

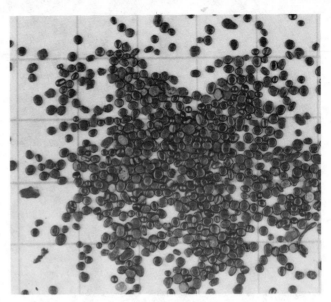

W/W 748—For use in cartridges smaller than .30/06. Especially good in .22-caliber centerfire rifles.

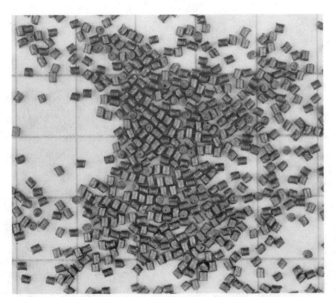

H-322—A new powder used in cases with a .22 centerfire to .308 capacity. A favorite of bench rest shooters.

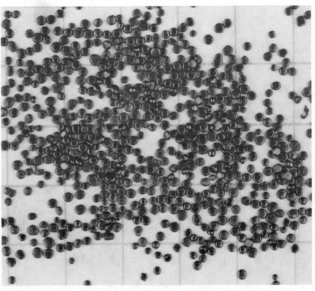

BLC-2—Again, like the preceding two, a good choice for the same cartridges.

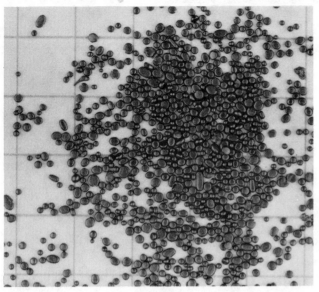

Accurate Arms MR2460—A brand new entry for loads in the .218 Bee, .222 and .223 Remington. Also for lighter weight bullets in the .22 PPC, .225 Winchester or .22-250.

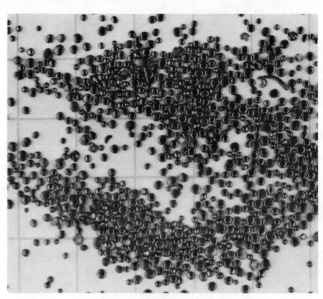

Accurate Arms MR223—A good powder for the .223 Remington or .220 Swift.

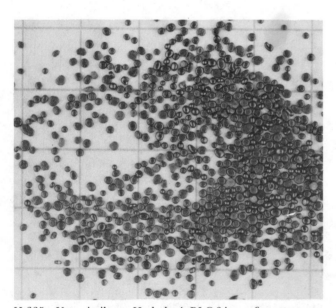

H-335—Very similar to Hodgdon's BLC-2 in performance. Economical to use.

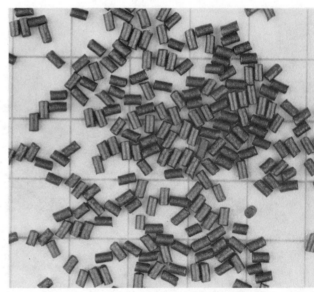

IMR-4895—Versatility is the byword here. IMR-4895 can be used in cases from the .22 centerfire to .45-caliber rifles. Very popular. Burns very efficiently in reduced loads.

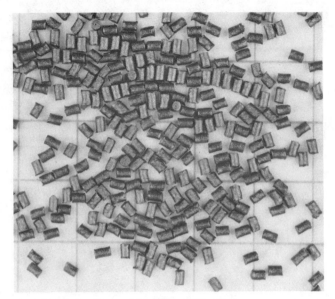

H-4895—A duplicate of the IMR-4895 offering.

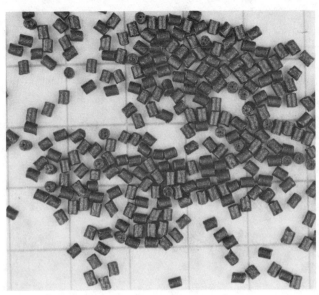

IMR-4320—A fine-grained powder for easy metering, this propellant does well in 6mm or .25-caliber applications.

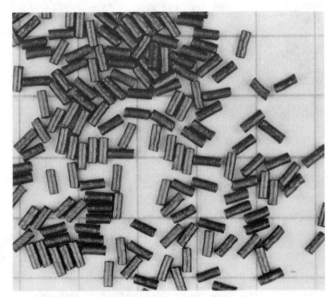

IMR-4064—Just a tad slower than the 4895 series; nevertheless, works well in straight-walled cases. Appearance is similar to 3031, but *please don't go by appearances*!

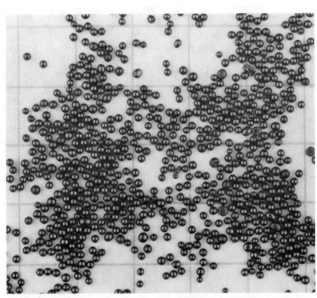

H-380—In between the 4320 and 4350, this spherical powder finds a good home with the .22-250, .220 Swift or .30/06.

An Update on Propellants

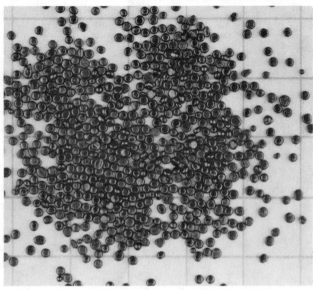

W/W760—Is a good powder for case sizes up to the .375 H&H.

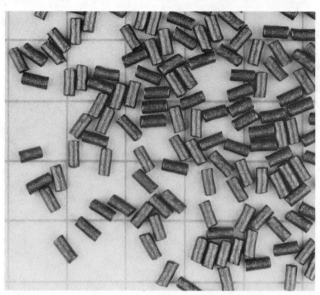

IMR-4350—One of this country's most widely used rifle powders, it is good for both standard and magnum size cases. Hodgdon markets the same powder under the H-4350 product name.

H-414—Very good in medium to large cases, including the .270 Winchester and .30/06 Springfield.

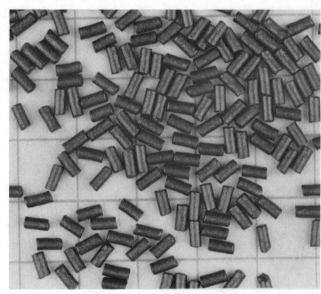

IMR-4831—The slowest burning of the Du Pont IMR series, it was introduced in 1973. Good for larger capacity cases such as the 7mm Remington or Weatherby's lineup of magnum entries, this must never be confused with H-4831, which is slightly slower.

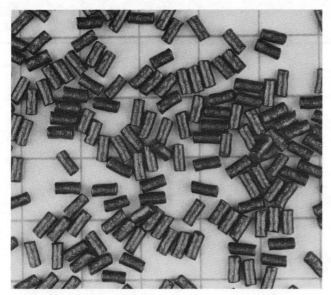

Accurate Arms MR3100—For use in medium cases with heavy bullets. Examples would be the .25/06 with the 120-grain bullet or .308 with the 180- or 200-grain projectile.

W/W 785—According to Winchester, a particularly good powder for the .243 Winchester. Slowest in the Olin line, it should never be used in reduced charge loadings.

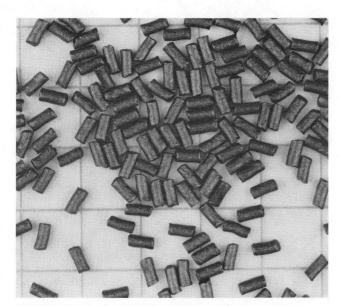

H-4831—Newly manufactured. Very popular in magnum applications. Use only loading data specified for this Hodgdon powder.

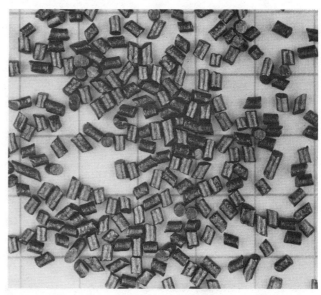

Norma MRP—Stands for Magnum Rifle Powder. Replaces the older N-205. Very slow burning. Ideal for huge magnum cases.

An Update on Propellants

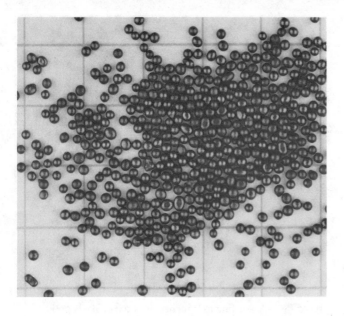

H-870—A slow burner. Best performance is attained in the larger or overbore cases to include the larger .300 Magnums.

Accurate Arms MR8700—Currently the slowest ball powder available on the open market. Applications would include the .300 H&H, .308 Norma Magnum or the .300 Weatherby or Winchester Magnums.

Chapter 7

At the Range

All your hard work at the loading bench will be rewarded at the range. There and only there is where theory turns into practical exercises; the proving ground, if you will.

Words like trajectory, ballistic coefficient or feet per second all come together in one form or another to substantiate or refute a handloader's ability to combine certain components in a cartridge capable of producing superior results at the target. It's an exciting time, for sure!

On the range, there are normally three ways to test pistol loads, and two for rifle loads. But before we break these down into subheadings, a suitable range must be found to do it the right way or a lot of preliminary efforts will be wasted.

Ninety percent of all shooters belong to a gun club with shooting facilities. Their dues entitle them to shoot in an area that should contain both short (pistol) and long (rifle) ranges. By short we mean a clear area of at least 25 yards, with 50 yards even better. For rifles, depending on which state you reside in, 100 to 300 yards is sufficient for most of your testing needs.

Quality facilities are very important. Shooting benches should be well made, comfortable and rock-steady. Good benches incorporate vertical stringers sunk in the ground past the frost line to prevent shifting. Cross and top member supports should be built from 2 × 10- or 2 × 12-inch lumber. In fact, when you walk up to the bench and try to shake it, all the power you can muster should not move the benchwork one millimeter! Believe me, it's that important. In addition, a chair or supporting member built at the right height will provide the shooter with the comfort he needs to complete his testing without undue strain. But before you even sit down at the bench, all safety factors have to be considered in relation to sight and sound.

Shatterproof glasses are a must to stop flying debris before it has a chance to cause damage. My general color preference is neutral gray, because on a bright, sunny day this color holds back roughly 70 percent of the available light, transmitting only 30 percent. Your needs on overcast days are just the opposite; you want a color to brighten and accent objects in view, so my choice here is haze yellow. In-

Shot from a rest, the resulting group is shown full size (insert). Only in this way can you actually see the full potential of your weapon.

cidentally, I keep a pair in my car. In a pouring rain, these yellow-colored glasses cut through the grayness making it easier to watch the road. With this color, about 80 percent of the light is allowed to pass through the lenses.

Hearing protection holds a top priority spot on my list of range equipment. Shooting muffs made by companies such as American Optical, Bilsom, David Clark or Wilson Products offer the bench rest shooter a choice of equipment tailored to his exact needs. There simply is no excuse not to wear them. In fact, those of you who have a "macho" complex and profess to be afraid of nothing, will soon hear exactly that—*nothing!*

For light pistol loads, tiny E-A-R plugs, which compress, then expand in your ear, will cancel out high-level frequencies. Heavier calibers dictate the use of the regular over-the-head muffs, and for

shooting the heavy, big-bore magnums, I find that combining both internal and external ear protection devices will tame sounds down to a mere whisper. Remember too, that as of a few years ago, by federal law, all hearing protection products must be labeled as to their Noise Reduction Rating. This is simply a basis for comparison so that the buyer can judge one product against the other. The rating relates to a decibel reading relevant to the particular product. Most ratings run in the mid-20s. One of my favorites, the Bilsom Viking, rates a comfortable 28.

Optional equipment would include a hat, spotting scope, possibly a chronograph, plus the usual assortment of cartridge boxes or travel containers. The hat should be the baseball type which allows the muffs to fit around the top of the head.

If you enjoy walking, and don't mind waiting until everyone on the range stops shooting, you don't need a spotting scope. However, with a scope available, you'll walk out once, tack up a bunch of targets, and that's it. A bench scope is not only a time saver, but an eye saver as well. Looking for .22-caliber holes at 100 yards with a pair of fixed binoculars or through your rifle scope cranked up to nine power will soon give you a severe case of eyestrain or worse yet, headaches.

My personal favorite is the Bushnell Trophy 50mm Armored rubber prismatic scope with a 16- to 32-power zoom eyepiece. Why a zoom? Because it fits right in with both pistol and rifle shooting, plus hunting. It is considered an ideal compromise. For me, any more magnification is hard to deal with. The slightest movement of the scope causes the image to shake and appear blurry, making the judging of game animals sometimes impossible, especially in bad weather. Other companies offering similar optics include Redfield, Tasco and Weatherby. Any spotting scope needs an adjustable stand for stability. Don't scrimp here. Get a good one.

A chronograph is next. Although very expensive and sometimes considered a luxury in days gone by, today's advances in technology have put these instruments within the reach of everyone.

Basically, a chronograph is nothing more than a highly sophisticated timer, with skyscreens acting as the on and off switches. When a bullet passes over the first screen, it turns the clock on; the projectile's shadow over the second skyscreen shuts the clock off. A very small inboard computer built into the chronograph processes these millisecond intervals into feet per second readings. All this happens in

The ultimate bench rest product for testing pistols. Shown here is how the Ransom Rest operates as the gun is fired.

Closeup of the Hoppe's pistol rest. The cloth protects the gun from the bare metal.

less than $1/10$ of a second—from the firing of the gun until a readout appears on the screen. And if you have a Oehler Model 33 Chronotach (under $300), it will give you high/low readings, averages, standard deviation and number of rounds fired.

Besides all this, you can use the chronograph to figure bullet drop—based on a true velocity reading, not estimated ballistics—comparing one gun against another, or different powders to see just exactly which one is the most efficient in your particular gun. If you are really serious about handloading, a chronograph is an investment, not just an accessory, for the man who demands the most out of his work.

Your specially tailored handloads should be kept in orderly fashion in cartridge boxes. You'll also need pistol cases and long, rigid rifle cases to help keep those precision scopes in check. All are readily available from such suppliers as Flambeau, MTM, Pachmayr or Protecto.

PISTOL RANGE TESTING

Because handguns are usually associated with short distances, unless your particular pistol is equipped with optical sights, 25 yards is considered the norm for all serious starting-load development. Then, if you are using one of the higher-powered cartridges for hunting, such as the .357 Magnum or Maximum, or the .41 or .44 Magnums, targets can and should be set up at 50, 75 or 100 yards to verify trajectory or group potential.

As mentioned earlier in this chapter, there are three ways to do your range testing: offhand, from the bench or with a machine rest. The first one, off-hand, is not a very precise approach for important work. While it might be acceptable for finding out if a certain brand of factory ammo could find its mark at defense distances of five to seven yards, no way can you hold the same sight picture by hand for shot after shot after shot.

Enter the stable bench rest position. For this you'll need either sandbags or a metal brace-type rest like the one marketed by Hoppe's. In either case, for consistent results, the gun's frame—and not the barrel or shroud—should rest on the bag or brace. In fact, the little reverse curve just in front of the trigger guard was seemingly made for that purpose. It not only gives you a reference mark on where to place the gun again after recoil, but also takes the strain off the barrel/frame connection and allows the barrel to vibrate at its own level. For small sidearms, (.25, .380 or 2-inch-barreled .38 Specials)

Testing rifles is usually done at 100 yards or more, so optics like this Bushnell spotting scope can save a lot of time and shoe leather.

both hands can hold the gun while it rests on top of the sandbag for good control.

Last would be the machine rest; the most popular type today being the Ransom Rest. Designed years ago by Chuck Ransom, the rest and its list of specialized grip inserts has continued to grow in popularity among rank and file pistol shooters. The original intent of this rest was slanted toward the target shooter; the bull's-eye shooter, if you please. But now with the economy the way it is, more and more handgunners are using this equipment (myself included) to get the most mileage from their loads with a minimum of fuss or bother.

The Ransom Rest is a device that not only compares loads with unmatched consistency, but also, and this is important, it eliminates human errors such as flinching, incorrect sighting, fatigue or trigger let-off problems. As soon as the rest demonstrates that the gun and its cartridge are doing their job, you'll shoot much more confidently with the gun out of the rest.

The rest itself ($245) comes in two parts which can be purchased separately or together as a unit. I recommend you buy both at the same time. One reason being that when you buy both at once, the rest and windage base ($105) are machined and finished at the same time, matched by number, then sent on to you. Also, the additional windage base makes sighting adjustments much, much easier.

As it stands now, the Ransom Company makes grip inserts ($32.50 each) for 57 different frame styles, plus a blank which you can carve yourself.

For safe transport to and from the range, plastic cases like these from MTM will keep all your test loads in order.

We talk about frame styles, but this does not include the various numbered models in a frame category, for example, the N insert for Smith & Wesson models 25, 27, 28, 29 and the 629. If we listed them all, we could mention 100 or more handguns.

In use, the Ransom Rest is first mounted on a board, then at the range is C-clamped to the shooting bench or other sturdy benchwork. The gun is inserted into the respective grip insert, tightened down, then aimed downrange.

With the gun *unloaded,* adjust the trigger release so it contacts about dead center on the trigger itself. Now you can get serious about sighting the gun on the target. Stand behind the gun and sight the piece in just as if you were holding it. After a good sight picture is established, you can fine tune the rest

and, in turn, the gun, by using the adjustments on the windage base.

When using the rest, establish a routine and follow it religiously. When firing a string of shots, follow a pattern. After charging the weapon, cock it, then place your thumb on the trigger bar. The other four fingers are positioned on the outboard side of the tension spring. Fire the gun. Then push it back down using the recoil lug which is cast into the rest frame for this purpose. Do not touch the weapon and never reset it by using the barrel as a lever. Repeat the procedure for each shot.

You might ask, exactly what constitutes a true picture of accuracy? A lot depends on the individual's parameters as well as the firearm in question. At 25 yards, a good, tuned target automatic should,

Out at the range, the Ransom Rest is bolted down, then the gun is sighted in to make sure each shot is striking the target. From then on in, the gun is tested with all loads.

The makers of the Ransom Rest have made provision for automatics, as this photo shows.

Here, the author is testing some loads from a Browning automatic not only for accuracy, but for functioning as well.

For rifle buffs, a new rest has hit the market. Called the Zero-One, it's made to cradle the rifle.

In this photo, the rifle butt must fit firmly into the rear of the rest.

Both elevation and windage adjustments are incorporated in the forend rest of the Zero-One.

with tested handloads, shoot several holes easily covered by a dime. With a wheelgun, using hunting or defense loads, the group size will be greater. At 50 yards, depending again on the ammo, 3½-inch groups or under with any handgun is good performance by my standards. Personal judgment is yet another aspect. Some fellows will work until they have exhausted the last possible fraction of an inch out of any group size; others will be happy with less. Actually seeing what is happening on the target, whether it be seven, 25 or even 50 yards away goes a long way to assure you of just what your gun is actually capable of doing. This will pay big dividends on the shooting end in the form of increased confidence.

RIFLE RANGE TESTING

The range testing of a scope-equipped rifle is based on an entirely different set of rules. For one thing, you are using optical sights, which many consider a must on today's high-powered and long-range rifles. Secondly, the distances are greater, which, in effect, magnifies errors. The slightest shift in the crosshairs is multiplied many times over out at 100 or 200 yards.

At this time, there are two acceptable or positive ways of bench-testing a rifle. The first is the new machine rest called Zero-One. The other is the time-proven method of supporting the gun on a set of sandbags.

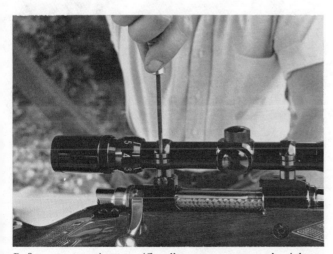

Before range testing any rifle, all scope screws must be tight.

The action screws must be tight.

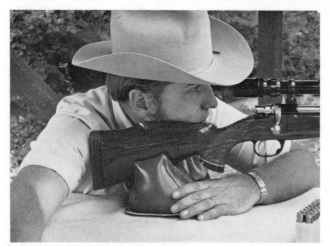

The rear bag is the steering part of the setup. Left or right for windage; back and forth for elevation.

The front sandbag should sit about two inches from the rear of the front swivel.

Of the two methods, I prefer the use of sandbags. Admittedly, I've had limited experience with the Zero-One, but it seems to me that too many variables enter into the picture with this machine rest. To start with, it must be bolted down to a solid rest to be effective, much like the Ransom Pistol Rest. Next, because of all the padding surrounding the firearm—around the forend and butt—you have to readjust the gun after every shot, because it will move. This is not very conducive to accuracy.

So on to the sandbags. You can buy sandbags or make your own. I bought mine years ago from Cole's, an outfit in New York specializing in such things, and they have served me well. Making your own is not out of the question either, but use a very tough material hand-sewn extra tight with nylon thread. The usual support combination is two or three sandbags plus a bench rest stand (also known as a rifle bed) to hold the forend. These stands are available from Freeland, Hoppe's and other manufacturers of shooting supplies.

With the equipment assembled, step up to the bench, lay out your rifle and related accessories, then settle down for serious work.

The bench rest stand goes in front, with a sandbag on it, if necessary. When in position, the gun should sit on the sandbag about two inches back from the front swivel, the theory being that at this

This is the correct position for accurate readings. Shooter is sitting very comfortably, gun is against the shoulder in a steady position, and left hand is making the final minute adjustments.

Careful preparation is a must for accurate testing and record keeping. Everything must be kept constant in order to compare one load against another.

particular point all stresses that may affect the stock or barrel are neutralized. One variable down, more to come.

The smaller bag goes under the rifle butt near the toe of the stock. This is the steering part of the arrangement; here lie all the tricks of the trade for consistency. It is also here that all major adjustments are made.

Now, with everything set up, let's run through a practice shooting. Sitting down at the bench, place your right hand—assuming that you are right-handed—on the grip of the stock with your index finger resting on the trigger guard.

Your left forearm should lie flat on the table so that the left hand is grasping the rear bag. While looking through the scope, slowly move the bag back and forth (for elevation) and left or right (for windage), getting a mental picture of what's going on. In effect, you control the sight picture from this point. Remember, forget the temptation to hold the rifle with your left hand. That simply adds another variable—something you're trying to avoid.

Your right hand, besides having the obvious duty of squeezing the trigger, also has the dubious honor of keeping the rifle up against your shoulder in the same position shot after shot. Trying to guide the weapon with this hand will only lead to lateral stringing on the target downrange. Keep your cheek pressure against the stock as constant as possible. This is yet another variable.

In summary, keep all forces equal: cheek, right hand, shoulder and remember to steer with the left. Check and double-check those factors enough times and you'll be surprised at what can be accomplished at the other end.

Photo shows the effect of the first bullet fired through an oiled bore. Always fire a few rounds to foul the bore before settling down to serious shooting. Other two targets show the effect of vertical or horizontal stringing.

Pressure signs should be checked to make sure the powder charges you have selected are not a possible overload. These primers indicate that all three have approached maximum status. The one on the left shows a blown primer; the middle, a flattened primer; the right, cratering is starting with the cartridge case beginning to bulge near the rim. If any of these signs appear, stop shooting at once, pull all bullets and lower your charge settings.

Chapter 8

American Centerfire Handgun Cartridges

American handloaders have never had it so good.

From its initial conception in the late 1800s, the reloadable centerfire cartridge of today has not only moved up into a world of high velocity, power and accuracy, but specialization as well.

Looking for a practical defense round? Try the 9mm, .38 Super or the .45 ACP. A target cartridge with a low recoil sensation? The .38 Special may be your cup of tea. Stopping power for hunting? The .44 Magnum. An excellent silhouette round? How about giving the .35 Remington a whirl.

Yes, there is something for everyone. In this chapter we have narrowed the field down to 20 centerfire cartridges, including the most popular calibers, plus some cartridges that are particularly interesting. Granted, there were others to be considered, but there have to be some limitations. At last count, there were some 78 different handgun rounds—both factory and wildcat—that could have been included. And, if you added in obsolete cartridges, you could go on forever!

But so be it. The cartridges discussed here relate to equipment used in the shooting or shooting tests, ballistics and modern handloading techniques. The guns used for the most part are over-the-counter specimens except for a very small number that were customized to my specs either for certain duties or article assignments. Favorite loads will be mentioned here and there, but please remember that these are recipes that have worked well in my tests, and more important, in *my guns*. Start about 5 to 6% below those listed, then work up gradually.

Handloading is a hobby regulated by tight guidelines. Keeping in those parameters will not only lead to satisfaction at the range, but will also contribute to safety and peace of mind.

And to me, that's what it's all about.

.22 REMINGTON JET

Introduced in May 1961, the Jet, also known as the .22 Center Fire Magnum, was a joint effort between Remington Arms (ammo) and Smith & Wesson (gun).

What started out to be a revelation in handgun cartridges actually turned into a big disappointment for its inventors. And, in my opinion, it was all due to a lack of commitment by the gun owners.

The trouble stemmed from cylinder lockups caused mainly by cartridge setback. Proper cleaning of the piece to alleviate any grease or oil in the cylinder charge holes could and will cancel this problem out. The lubricant on the inside of the charge holes prevented the cartridge from firmly gripping this area, therefore when the gun was fired, the case would move smartly to the rear. Proper instructions from the factory pointed out this fact, but apparently owners were reluctant to comply and the caliber died.

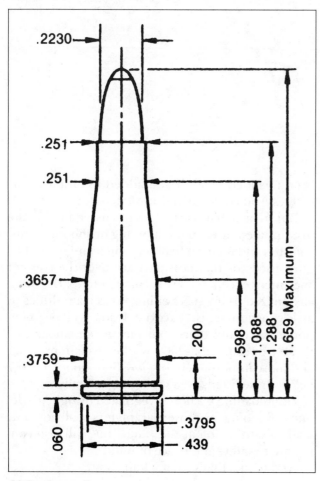

.22 Remington Jet.

In any event, for those of you who have one of these guns and know how to use and care for it, handloading for this cartridge can become a satisfying experience. Any popular powder in the Unique, H-110 or 2400 bracket can lead the shooter down the road to safe velocities in the 1400 to 1900 fps range by employing bullet weights in the 40- to 45-grain class.

Brass cases and factory ammunition are still available from Remington Arms. The handgun, if you can still find one, is Smith & Wesson's discontinued Model 53.

REMINGTON FIREBALL

The .221 Fireball is not a universally familiar cartridge, but nevertheless is very interesting in its own right.

Necked down from its parent, the .222 Remington, this particular round was introduced to the public in the early 1960s as a companion to Remington's modern rifle/pistol firearm called the XP-100. Incorporating a rifle action shortened to pistol dimensions, this handgun can be seen regularly in serious varmint hunting circles, especially when a scope is mounted on the barrel.

Although its water capacity only amounts to 20.8 grains, the Fireball can reach velocities bordering on 2700 fps with a 45-grain bullet. Used in a Thompson/Center Contender, velocities can reach 2900 fps, again with the 45-grain bullet and 2400 powder. For best success with the Fireball, the handloader must match a particular bullet to a good velocity. Too much power behind a lightweight bullet will cause the projectile to wobble on its way to the target, causing inaccuracy and frustration to the shooter. The same is true with a heavier slug moving too slowly.

Bullet weights that can be utilized with the XP-100 and the .221 include the previously mentioned 45-grain; then moving up we have the 50-, 52-, 53-, 55- and 60-grain bullets in styles ranging from the full metal-jacketed to soft points and hollow points for instant, one-shot kills on varmints like woodchucks. For propellants, IMR-4198 seems to rate top honors, followed by IMR-4227. Using a scoped gun, groups measuring 1 inch across are not hard to achieve if the handloader does his part.

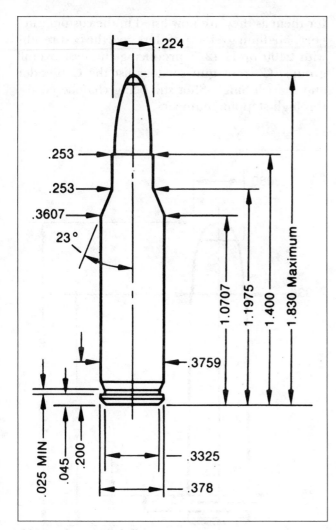

.221 Remington Fireball.

.25 ACP

This small cartridge just has too many things going against it to be very popular.

First, its very small case capacity can lead to loading problems. With powder charges running in the neighborhood of 1.1 to 1.7 grains, a deviation of as little as $1/10$ of a grain can change velocities to the point where pressure readings could skyrocket. Since autopistols depend on near maximum loadings to function properly, the loading tolerances become rather narrow.

Next, as of this writing bullet choices are very limited. Hornady, at present, is the only bullet maker to produce a true .251″ full metal-jacketed bullet, but we hear rumors that Speer may do the

same. Even so, being unable to choose from a variety of bullets is a definite handicap for a reloader.

Finally, there aren't many new .25 caliber handguns around. Skimming through various catalogs, we find that the number of .25 caliber pistols currently listed can be counted on two hands. Combining this with low energy figures, it's no wonder that most people who use this cartridge for back-up purposes just go ahead and buy over-the-counter commercial factory ammunition, and for their needs, it makes sense.

However, if you are a reloader who likes challenges, the Hornady bullets pushed with either Red Dot or Bullseye powder should do the trick. As with other autopistol cartridges, complete attention to detail is necessary during all phases of the loading operation to ensure trouble-free functioning.

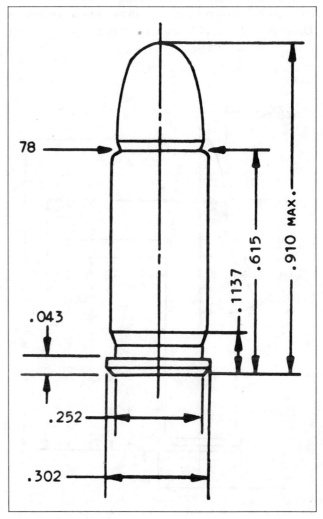

.25 ACP.

.256 WINCHESTER MAGNUM

If ever there was an apple in Bill Ruger's eye, his Hawkeye single-shot teamed with this cartridge could have been it. It's too bad the idea didn't work out.

Introduced in 1961, this joint effort between a handgun manufacturer and an ammo maker was intended to produce high velocity in a handgun to appeal to varmint shooters nationwide. However, the dream was short-lived as the pistol did not sell that well and was taken off the market in only a few months.

The cartridge, however, is a good one. It's not unusual to measure velocities of 2400 fps using a 60-grain bullet out of a Hawkeye. Heavier bullets will, of course, do less; closer to 2100 or 1800 fps with 75- or 87-grain bullets, respectively.

The cartridge case is nothing more than a .357 case necked down to .257, so brass is not a problem. Dies are still available but expect to pay a little more

for them as they are now listed in the custom category. Medium to slow powders give the best results with 2400 or H-4227 producing the best overall groups. Current gun catalogs list the Contender and Merrill Single-Shot still being chambered for this high-stepping number.

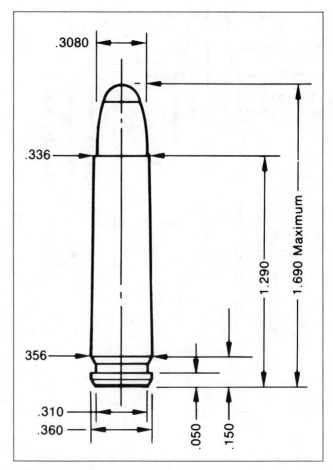

.30 Carbine (pistol).

.30 CARBINE

Those of us who remember falling in love with those lightweight .30 Carbine rifles in the Army years ago, now find ourselves doing it all over again, only this time in the pistol class.

While the .30 Carbine is not one of those high-velocity, big-recoiling handguns, it does have merit. The round is often used for dispatching furbearing animals humanely without damage to the pelts. A Ruger Blackhawk topped off with a scope makes for a handy field gun for such activities.

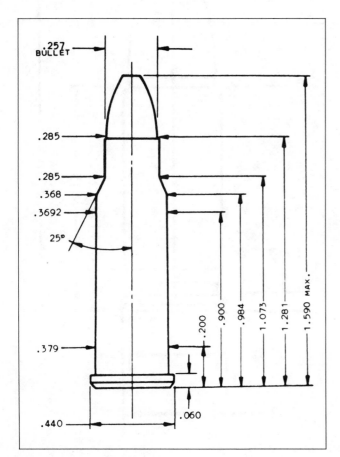

.256 Winchester Magnum.

With powders in the H-110 to 2400 range, velocities can be brought up safely to 1400 or 1450 fps. No barn burner to be sure, but in this age of high-performance cartridges, a real pleasure to shoot.

Limited to the use of 110-grain bullets, granted the cartridge is handicapped. While factory ammunition is available, it takes reloading of this particular cartridge to bring out its full potential.

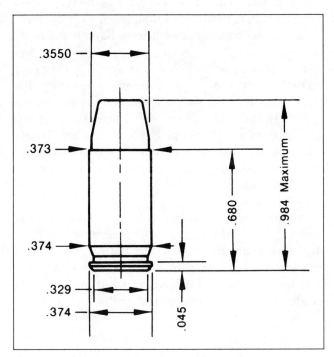

.380 Automatic.

.380 AUTOMATIC

The .380 cartridge, in the opinion of many, including yours truly, is the smallest practical round ever to be considered for personal defense work—and at that, only loaded in a high-volume automatic carrying 13 to 14 rounds.

While I am not advocating firepower over shooting accuracy, considering the energy of the round your best bet is to get plenty of them moving toward the target in a hurry. This is one way to build up energy levels at the terminal end. And with the .380 Automatic, this takes quantity.

Careful attention to detail during reloading is imperative; typical of any autopistol round. Constant monitoring of all loading procedures will ensure trouble-free operation in tight situations.

Bullets are available from all makers. When loading for defense, stick to the hollow-pointed designs. Neck tension must be tight to keep bullets from receding into the case, which will cause not only jams but pressure problems as well.

Small cases dictate fast powders, so propellants such as Bullseye, Olin 231 or 700X get the nod here. Small regular primers are used also. Case length for the .380 should never go above .680 inches.

9mm LUGER

In all probability this round is one of today's most talked about cartridges. With the U.S. armed forces thinking about switching over from the time-tested .45 ACP to the 9mm in a high-volume automatic, it's no wonder everyone in the business is coming out with new ideas on how a modern autopistol should look and function.

And that's good—good for competition, good for the services and good for the sports-minded consumer. Formerly scarce 9mm cartridge cases are now easier to find; ditto with components.

As of this writing, just about every bullet maker

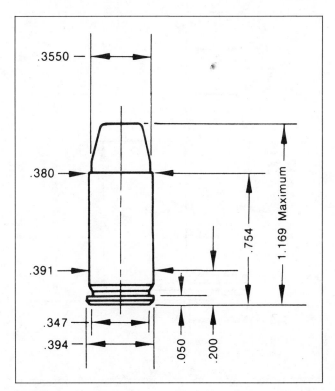

9mm Luger.

of note offers up to three different kinds of 9mm bullets. In soft points, hollow points or full metal-jacketed, they are all designed to feed or function perfectly in all autopistols.

Powder choices again run to the faster burning types. My choices tend toward Olin 231, Bullseye, and even Unique on occasion. In my Browning P-35 automatic, any one of the popular 115-grain bullets placed over 5.2 grains of Olin 231 give me velocities hovering around 1150 fps. And with good accuracy to boot!

Good handloading bench procedures are a must here. All rounds should be sized in a carbide die then cleaned with solvent or by tumbling. Because this case headspaces on the mouth, case length should be checked frequently. Depending on the gun, overall case length should also be gauged, then once a standard has been set—within that particular brand name—taper crimping should be employed instead of the roll-type crimp.

Choice of gun models is no problem with Smith & Wesson, Browning, Heckler and Koch, Llama and Beretta producing reliable firearms in this caliber. All are a pleasure to shoot. For defense or sport, you would never be shortchanged with a good modern autopistol chambered for the 9mm Luger.

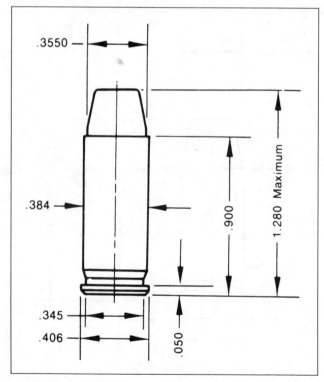

.38 Super.

.38 SUPER

Why this cartridge has not had a bigger influence on the American shooting public is a mystery to me. It has everything needed to be successful: power, velocity and a fantastic accuracy potential.

If you get the impression that it's one of my favorites, you are right. After years of playing with this round, I have had nothing but good results. In one weapon that really gets a lot of heavy use—a Crawford-modified, BoMar-sighted, Colt Government Model automatic—all tests have been more than gratifying.

Let me cite one particular example. Checking my records over the years, the single loading that stands out very tall over all the others starts with a Hornady full metal-jacketed flat nose bullet (FMJ/FN) weighing 124 grains. For a propellant, Hodgdon's HS-7, measured to exactly 9.0 grains, gives me just about 1200 fps. For the spark plug, CCI's standard 500 small pistol primer works very well with all loads.

All loads are worked up in new Remington nickeled cases, run through a carbide sizer before loading and charging. After the bullet is seated, I employ a taper crimp to hold the bullet in place, and for ease in feeding. Accuracy in my pistol averages $1\frac{1}{2}$-inch groups from a rest at 25 yards.

.38 SPECIAL

Of all the centerfire cartridges chambered for handguns, the .38 Special would definitely lead the pack in numbers; not in thousands or hundreds of thousands mind you, but in millions. Many millions! And, it's still the basic police caliber.

And it's not hard to see why. Easy reloadability, mild recoil and a tremendous selection of components make it a favorite of knowledgeable shooters everywhere.

For the target men, Smith & Wesson makes a semi-automatic .38 Special meant for shooting wadcutters. At 25 yards it will punch holes inside a 1-inch circle all day. The police use it in daily duties; hunters call upon it for clean kills on small game.

Jacketed bullets are available from all makers including Hornady, Sierra and Speer. Lead swaged bullets, for those of you who really don't enjoy slaving over a hot stove all day (myself included), are stocked by dealers under the brand names of Alberts, American Bullets, Green Bay and Zero.

Weightwise, .38 Special bullets are made in 95, 110, 125, 140, 150, 158, 160, 170 and 200 grains. Matching the proper powder—fast to medium burning rates—enables anyone from the novice to pro to produce a load suitable for almost any shooting sport.

For a person just starting out in pistol centerfire shooting or handloading, this is a good place to get your feet wet.

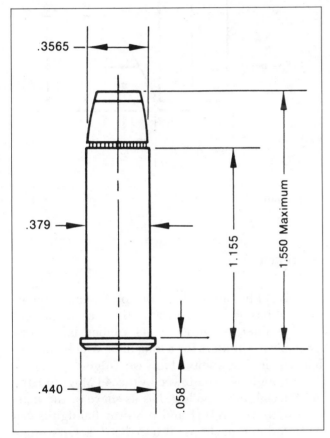

.38 Special.

.357 MAGNUM

Introduced in the 1930s, the .357 Magnum has steadily grown to where it now occupies a very strong place in the shooting world. It is based on the .38 Special case, and the original designers wisely decided to extend the case by a mere 1/10 of an inch to prevent the chambering of this cartridge in

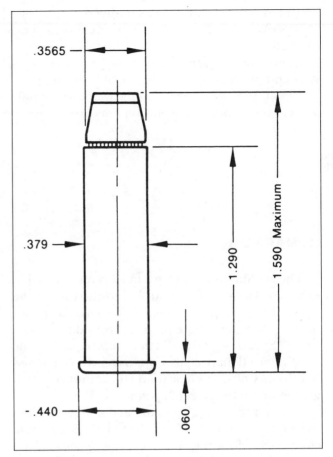

.357 Magnum.

weaker or older revolvers made especially for the .38 Special.

Again, like the .38 Special, this round is extremely versatile. Looking at my supply of bullets, my inventory of .357s is double the amount usually stocked in any other caliber. The caliber is easy to shoot compared to bigger magnums, and it is used more often in my own personal battery.

Checking my reloading records, powder choices for the .357 Mag range from medium to slow burning. This would include propellants such as Unique, H-4227, H-110 and 2400. Maximum loads should be approached with caution as this round operates at the 35,000 copper units of pressure level.

For defense, I'd opt for a 4-inch barrel over a 2½-incher. Muzzle blast is substantially reduced, accuracy is better and the extra 1½ inches of barrel is not going to hinder concealability one bit. Hunting calls for 6 inches or better; one of my all-time favorites in this caliber is a Ruger Blackhawk carrying a 6½-inch tube with a Leupold scope mounted on the frame. Realistically, this cartridge is effective only up to 100 yards, so plan your shots carefully.

Components, in the form of bullets, cases, powders and primers, are readily available in any sporting goods store catering to handloaders, which only adds to the popularity of this famous cartridge.

.41 MAGNUM

The .41 Magnum was born in 1964 and since that time has had a hard road uphill to success. At the onset, it was supposed to be the cure-all for police officers desiring a more powerful round to replace the .38 Special. But that did not come to pass. While most police departments were using the K-framed Smiths or Colts, this new powerful round required guns built on the larger N frame. Strike one.

Another discouraging note was the shooter's age-old nemesis—recoil. While the .41 does generate close to 850 foot pounds of energy in some cases, depending on the loading, it can be handled with practice and interest in the piece. But, apparently, in the police sector interest soon diminished.

Finally, in sporting circles, the .41 followed too closely on the heels of the by now famous and very popular .44 Magnum. And ballistically, there was a close similarity, with the two being kissing cousins in the feet per second and foot pounds of energy departments. Because of these factors, .41 Mag components are somewhat limited. Jacketed bullets are made in 170, 200, 210 and 220 grains in the usual hollow- or soft-pointed designs. Using Unique, H-100, 2400 or Blue Dot propellants, from a rest, groups tend to average in the 2- to 3-inch class at 25 yards.

As with any magnum, a tight bullet crimp is essential. Watch for pressure signs as you work up loads, such as cratered primers, hard extraction or erratic accuracy.

Regardless of what some people may think about the .41 Magnum, I consider it a good cartridge to load for. It offers a lot in terms of accuracy, power and firearms selection.

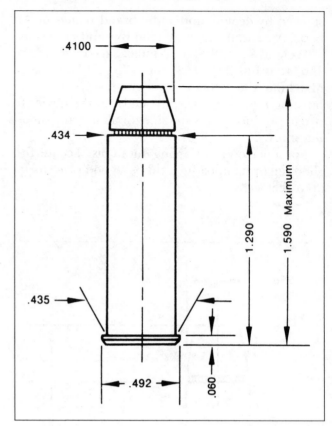
.41 Magnum.

.44 SPECIAL

This .44 has always been one of America's favorites and has been around since the turn of the century. Numerous guns in .44 caliber have been available to shooters for a long time, which only enhances the desirability of any cartridge.

Although overshadowed by the .44 Magnum, the .44 Special, nevertheless, has its share of the market. Many pre-WWII and post-war handguns can be found in gun shops even to this day. Up-to-date weapons would include the Charter Arms series of hideable Bulldog models in both carbon and stainless steel. This cartridge, like the .38 Special/.357 Magnum combo, can be used in handguns chambered for the .44 Magnum, but never conversely.

With the amount of .429 bullets around, loading is no problem. Propellants used in this cartridge range from Bullseye to 2400, depending upon the application. However, because of the case volume of the .44 Special, most shooters will settle on powders such as Unique, Herco and 231.

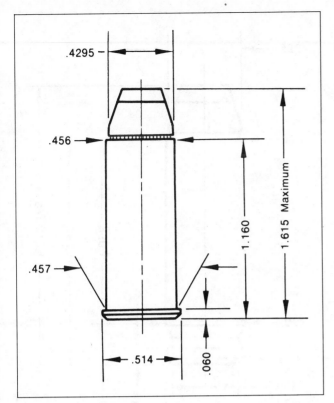

.44 Special.

.44 REMINGTON MAGNUM

With enough power to satisfy the most hardened shooter, the .44 Magnum is the most popular handgun cartridge for big game hunting and silhouette shooting.

Introduced in 1956 as a joint venture between Remington and Smith & Wesson, the popularity of this cartridge has grown to almost out of sight proportions. At one time the premium gun for this cartridge, Smith & Wesson's Model 29, was selling at inflated prices, even for used guns, because the guns were in short supply. The factory had to increase production on this one model by 300 percent to meet the demand.

In handloading circles, the .44 is considered a delight. Combining a big case with a bullet diameter of .429 inches, it is very forgiving, almost to the point of no matter what the propellant used, a fine load with tight groups will result. Over the years, handloading this cartridge for guns made by S&W, Ruger and Thompson/Center, an extra favorite gun of mine is the now discontinued Model 29 with the then standard 6¹/₂-inch barrel. Hunters who de-

mand a longer sight radius can choose between the new Ruger Redhawk with its 7¹/₂-inch tube or the Contender Super-14 with its long 14-inch barrel.

Bullet weights range from Sierra's hot 180-grain Jacketed Hollow Cavity to Speer's 240-grain hollow points. At 40,000 c.u.p., velocity is high; bullet expansion is violent or controlled depending on weight or design.

Delivering twice the muzzle energy of the .357, the .44 Mag is definitely a handgun to be mastered. Once this is accomplished, the .44 Magnum will be a favorite in your handgun battery, called upon for a multitude of chores.

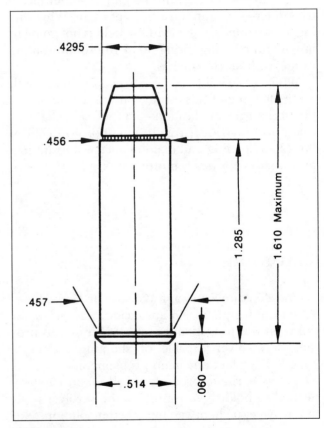

.44 Magnum.

.44 AUTO MAG

The .44 Auto Mag (Automatic Magnum) is to autopistols what the standard .44 Magnum is to wheelguns. But, unfortunately, it's an on again, off again proposition. On, when production of the gun is going great; off, after a limited number are made, prices rise and interest drops.

Basically, it's a good round, but plagued by unstable demand and supply. At one time there was a limited amount of factory ammunition available for shooting or reloading, but that, too, seems to have been exhausted.

Dyed-in-the-wool handloaders can fashion shootable brass from .30/06 rifle cases cut down to 1.300 inches in length. Then they have to ream out the mouth to a wall thickness of .015″. Next, the cases need to be trimmed to 1.296 to 1.298 inches. A lot of work, to be sure, but a real handloader's cartridge by any standard.

Velocities must be kept high in order for this pistol to function. In that vein, you can't consider this a dual purpose target/hunting gun. Another factor to ponder—the gun must be kept clean. While firing a few rounds at game in the field is not going to impair functioning, firing 50 to 100 rounds on the range, without cleaning, is.

While space is limited here to go into great depth on the loading of this round, various articles in national firearms publications can shed some light on this novel cartridge. Again, attention to detail in both handloading and maintenance will result in a gun suitable for heavy hunting tasks.

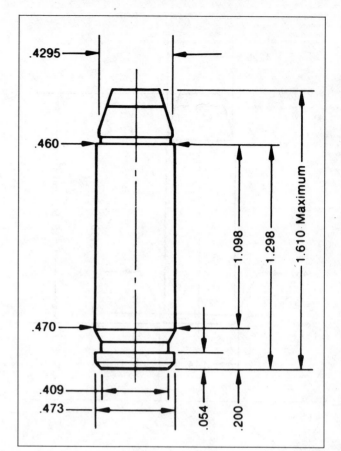

.44 Auto Mag.

.45 AUTO RIM

The .45 Auto Rim was a World War I expedient. When the supply of .45 automatics was lacking, a call went out to Colt and Smith & Wesson to produce a revolver capable of shooting the same round. They had one main problem. Since the .45 ACP was a rimless round, a half-moon clip was needed to hold these rounds in the revolver's cylinder. An expedient yes, but a better solution? No, not really.

Enter the Auto Rim, a .45 round made with a rim to fire and function in a revolver, without the need for a clip, and able to be ejected in a simultaneous six-round manner. Unlike its close relative the .45 ACP, it does not headspace on the mouth of the case, so crimping is allowed to prevent bullet movement during recoil.

While the .45 Auto Rim does not have a big following in these modern times, it is a good round to start out with. Today, only Smith & Wesson chambers a gun for it, but many good buys can still be had in the used gun department.

Experience has shown that about 7.0 grains of Unique with either the Sierra 185- or Speer 200-grain bullets will yield good accuracy at moderate ranges.

.45 ACP

At the present time, the .45 ACP (Automatic Colt Pistol) is enjoying a well-deserved rejuvenation. Not that it was ever failing, in the eyes of many shooters, but with the advent of practical shooting competitions across the country, this round is now going through some mild changes.

For one, many feel that lighter bullets are the way to go. And it may well be true, in certain cases. The standard bullet weight is the 230-grain hardball full metal-jacketed projectile. Now proponents feel that using the 200- or even the 185-grain pills will lead them down the road to success. Again, personal requirements always dictate the reasoning.

Personally, I still favor the 230-grain bullet in either a flat or round nose configuration. Combining this with standard primers and Winchester 231 powder, groups at 25 yards measure no more than 1 1/2 inches.

When turning out hundreds of rounds for practice or match use, one must still keep a constant vigil on proper reloading methods. Sort cases by maker or date to ensure unvarying inside case volume, which is very important to pinpoint accuracy. A tight grip plus a taper crimp on all cases is a definite must to eliminate bullet setback during the violent workings of the parent automatic pistol. Finally, trim length should be watched carefully as this case headspaces on the case mouth.

While hunting is not the mainstay of this particular cartridge, good results can be had by using lighter weight bullets driven at higher velocities. As always, monitor all steps when working near peak loadings.

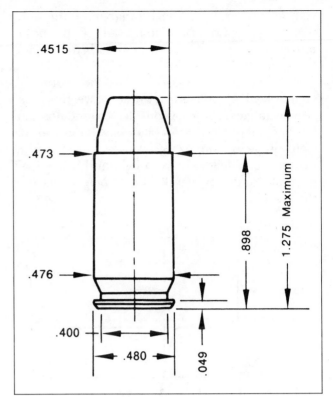

.45 ACP.

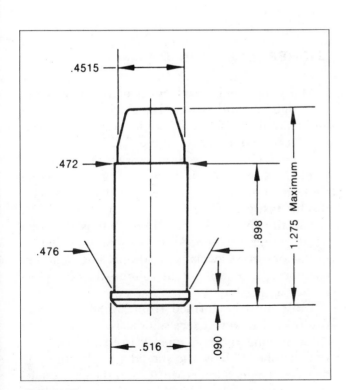

.45 Auto Rim.

.45 COLT

The .45 Long Colt is another round in the series of brought-back-to-life cartridges. In years past it was found only in guns reminiscent of the Old West—single-action army-type revolvers.

Smith & Wesson, just a few short years ago, finally put into production a modern double-action revolver in .45 Colt capable of great accuracy with the right loads. I ran a test on one of these Smiths a while back for *Guns* magazine. The gun had a 8³/₈-inch barrel and velocities could be brought up to safe levels without pressure problems. Please, whatever you do, forget about "magnumizing" this caliber. Several people (who really should know better) keep trying to do it, and although they are using the stronger Ruger single-actions or Contender single-shots, the results are not always pleasing. Split cases and erratic recoil sensations do not fit this easy going cartridge.

I've found that using one powder—Unique—could fill a multitude of shooting chores. With 8.6 grains of Unique, over 900 fps could be reached, with groups in the 2½-inch range more the norm than the exception. Developing 384 foot pounds of muzzle energy, this load was enough for me and this grand old round.

All major bullet companies produce both jacketed or lead .45 bullets in a variety of weights. For a real nostalgic feeling, try some lead round nose bullets in front of a charge of black powder in your old Colt Single Action Army pistol. As most loading manuals give loads for both light and heavy loadings, please double-check all data before charging the cases.

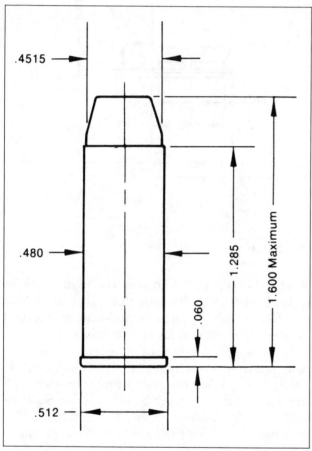

.45 Colt.

.35 REMINGTON

The concept of the Thompson/Center Contender single-shot pistol is to allow the shooter to be able to shoot numerous calibers economically by merely switching barrels. The idea has merit, and the pistol is extremely successful.

Some time back I tested and reported on this handgun chambered for a rifle cartridge—the .35 Remington. Long a favorite of eastern deer hunters, the .35 Remington has enough support to keep it from dying under the steady pressure from the modern magnums, which everyone seems to clamor for. It's reliable, accurate and relatively inexpensive as far as factory ammo goes.

Now take this round and chamber a handgun for it. Wow! Shooters' eyebrows rise, and conversations get hot and heavy on the merits of firing a hefty rifle cartridge in a handgun. Recoil, muzzle blast, sighting equipment—all are considered and weighed. The recoil is stout, so prepare for it. The muzzle blast is not that bad, but wear muffs anyway. As to sighting equipment, use a scope for dead-on accuracy.

In handloading for the .35/Contender combo, use new brass, full length resized. Rifle primers are used, remembering this is a *rifle* cartridge. Light loads can use the 158-grain .357″ diameter bullets. Heavier loadings demand the 170-grain .357″ or 200-grain .358″ bullet. For powders, H-4227, H-322 or Norma 200 top my list. Accuracy ranges from 1¾-inch groups with the lighter bullets, to 1-inch with the heavier 200- grainers.

If you are looking for a change of pace, this gun may be for you.

.357 HERRETT (Contender)

Many men who yearn for a high-performance cartridge that shoots well, is a challenge to reload and feels like a stick of dynamite going off in your hand, can find it all here in the .357 Herrett. After the .30 Herrett was well on its way, Steve Herrett wanted something a little bit stronger for taking western game larger than deer-sized animals. This was his answer.

For the interested out there, this is strictly a handloading situation. At the present time, there is no factory brass available, and only one handgun chambered for this potent round—the T/C Contender single-shot.

Brass must be formed from .30-30 cases, and fireformed to very exact standards. After cutting and trimming, the cases must be fired in a .357 Herrett chamber to blow the shoulder angle out to 30 degrees. To get a long case life and the greatest accuracy, the case should headspace on the shoulder, not the rim. Through every loading operation extra care has to be taken to ensure a close fit in the handgun. Too loose a fit will deform the case; too tight will impede the closing of the weapon. As with the .35 Remington, the best accuracy can be had by using powders in the H-4227, H-322 or Norma 200 class. The overall cartridge length will range from 2.100″ to 2.345″ depending upon the bullet weight.

For silhouette shooting or tough hunting requirements, consider this cartridge. Despite the extra work involved in getting to the finished product, the results are more than worth it.

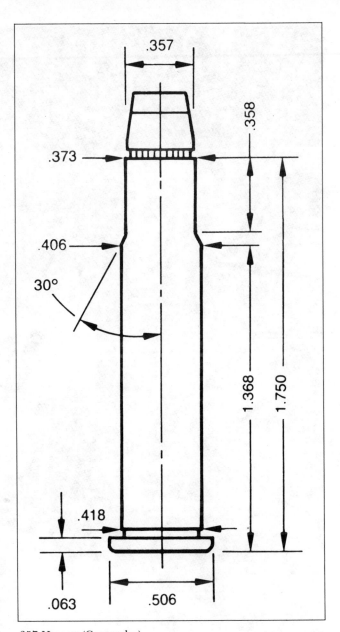

.357 Herrett (Contender).

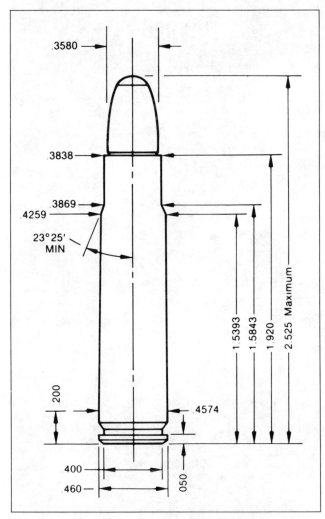

.35 Remington (Contender).

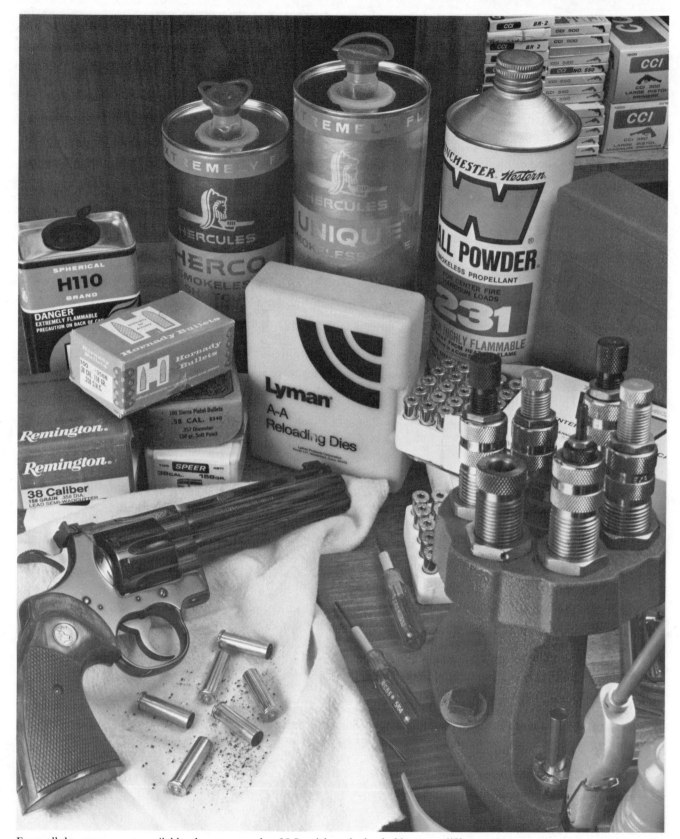

From all the components available, the ever-popular .38 Special can be loaded in many different ways.

Chapter 9

The Great .38 Special/.357 Magnum Combination

by Al Pickles

Unquestionably, the .38 Special cartridge enjoys the status of being the most popular of all centerfire handgun cartridges in the United States. The reasons go far beyond our national love affair with revolvers, perferring them over autoloaders. It's logical that a cartridge that is both easy for the tyro to control, while at the same time having the potential for accuracy without peer, would be a long-standing leader in a wide field of excellent handgun calibers.

The .38 Special was first introduced by Smith & Wesson in 1902 along with their then new round-butt S&W Model 1902 Military & Police revolver. It was their solution to the miserable performance of the previous military revolvers chambered for the .38 Long Colt, but was in no way a derivative of its impotent predecessor. At the time, the new cartridge was called .38 Smith & Wesson Special and was loaded with 20.6 grains of FFFg black powder. While it was an improvement over the older military round, it wasn't a significant improvement.

Rapid changes in powders and cartridge cases were taking place during that period. Black powder was giving way to smokeless, and cases progressed from the early folded-head type to a semi-balloon wherein the primer pocket was recessed into the powder cavity. The last case transition was, of course, to the modern solid head. The standard smokeless powder loading of the period was 3.6 grains of Bullseye behind a 158-grain round-nosed bullet, giving a velocity/energy rating of 860 feet per second/260 foot pounds of energy. Throughout this chapter, for the sake of simplicity, velocity/energy figures will read 860/260, for example.

In 1909, Colt came out with the .38 Colt Special which was identical in cartridge dimensions but sported a much improved bullet design over the earlier Smith & Wesson. The Colt bullet was also 158 grains in weight but had a flat nose, giving it some enhanced stopping power.

About 1930, a high-velocity round was introduced, again using a 158-grain bullet, but loaded to produce 1100/425 in a 6-inch-barreled, heavy frame revolver. Still later, a "Super Police" round was developed utilizing a 200-grain bullet with an extremely flat nose, only slightly beveled. The velocity/energy of this factory police loading was 730/237 but law enforcement experience demonstrated that stopping power was considerably increased, at least for a .38 Special. Also during this general period, references to Smith & Wesson and Colt were dropped in conversations and some writings, so the cartridge designation became simply .38 Special.

Very early in the game it probably became evident that the .38 Special was indeed something special in the accuracy department.With the possible exception of the .22 Long Rifle rimfire, the .38 Special is the best balanced handgun cartridge ever designed. It only naturally follows that over the years a wide variety of factory loads have been developed. Some of the most recent factory offerings have been the Hydra-Shok, the CCI Blazer line of non-reloadable aluminum cases, the super high-velocity +P loadings such as the Winchester Silvertip hollow points or the +P+ Treasury loads. All these, including the Blazer +P, are attempts to improve the .38 Special in one area where it has always been most needed—stopping power in a gun fight!

Stopping power is most important because not only is the .38 Special the gun most citizens maintain for home and personal defense, it is also the gun most often issued to and used by police departments throughout the nation. The reasons for its popularity are its controllability, by which we mean general lack of much perceived recoil in a medium-frame revolver, and its versatility in handling all the loadings developed for different purposes. Its popularity is therefore self-feeding and destined to continue long into the future.

Sure, there are better guns for police work and self-defense, but these more potent guns require a higher degree of training and self-discipline to master, and the majority of our police officers are not willing to truly master their sidearms, although their lives may depend on it. I would venture a good guess that the same problems existed with the Roman centurions; some were exceptional swordsmen but most were barely average. In any event, recent bullet and powder developments are improving the stopping power of the .38 Special and, coupled with all its other attributes, it is a truly great cartridge.

It naturally stands to reason that such a car-

Author Pickles range testing a revolver for accuracy.

tridge, being over 80 years old, has surrounded itself with an incredible amount of handloading data. There are more loads and bullet designs for the .38 Special than any other cartridge. Some old loading data is so good that it still stands today, an example being 2.7 grains of Bullseye behind a 148-grain lead wadcutter bullet. This target load is so hard to beat that I would unhesitatingly match it against any more modern target loading. While it's certainly fun to experiment in the art and science of handloading, you just can't argue with the accuracy displayed by this old load data, which alone will guarantee the continued production of Hercules Bullseye Powder.

One of the best target wadcutter bullet moulds available for casting is the Saeco .38/.357 146-grain #381. Since correct hardness of cast bullets, alloys and sources of lead are subjects worthy of an entire lengthy article, I will simply recommend that you obtain your lead from commercial establishments dealing in lead or bullet casting and guaranteeing uniform results. It does, indeed, make a difference.

Personally, for match target work with the .38 Special, I prefer purchasing swaged pure lead bullets from the Alberts Corporation. Pure lead presents no problems with barrel leading if velocities are kept low—and these same low velocities produce the best scores.

Alberts bullets are dry lubricated and of excellent uniformity while, surprisingly, being modestly priced. Their 148-grain Hollow Base WC is best matched with 2.7 grains of Hercules Bullseye, and is so recommended in their reloading sheet. Velocity in a 4-inch barrel is in the area of 700 fps, depending on the gun. Although energy figures are seemingly irrelevant in a match target load, the wadcutter is often used for a defensive load in little snubby revolvers such as the Charter Undercover and S&W Chief's Special Models 36 or 60. The energy is a misleading 161 fpe, or thereabouts, but the bullet shape, especially with ends reversed, makes it a better man-stopper than the still-standard police 158-grain lead round nose factory load.

The best defensive handload for the little snubby revolvers, so popular with police and civilians alike, again utilizes an Alberts bullet. This one is the Alberts Hydra-Shok, which they recommend for law enforcement only because of its tremendous expansion. Of course, such a recommendation only whets our appetite. The Hydra-Shok bullet design can probably best be described as a hollow point wadcutter with a cone inside the hollow. At easily controlled low velocities it will expand rather consistently to over .60 inch. While the Alberts loading data suggest 4.0 grains of Hercules Unique, as well as two other loads, I have found 3.0 grains of Bullseye to be exactly to my liking. Producing modest recoil, this load is accurate and the 146-grain bullet will expand to above .60 inch while penetrating to a depth of about four inches in flesh-like target media. That is just about optimum man-stopping power from a snubby .38 Special.

Progressing to the standard 4-inch barrel, medium frame service revolver, the best target load

If your forte is target shooting, these three examples from Hornady, Remington and Speer can fill the bill quite nicely.

still stands as aforementioned: 2.7 grains of Bullseye behind a 146- to 148-grain wadcutter bullet. For defense, the Alberts Hydra-Shok loads remain very good choices for close-in work. For all-round work the 160-grain lead semi-wadcutters, as designed by Elmer Keith, are very hard to beat. Moulds for this bullet are made by Saeco and Lyman, as well as others, or the bullets can be purchased from Speer in a modified and half-jacket form. It is, in my opinion, the best utility bullet for .38 Special revolvers with 4- to 6-inch barrels, and a wealth of loading data exists. With the Saeco cast lead bullet, I have enjoyed excellent results with 8.6 grains of Winchester 630-P powder, but I must caution you that this is a maximum load and must be worked up in increments using a strong modern revolver. It produces about 1000/355 (velocity/energy).

My favorite hunting load with the Speer 160-grain half jacket is 10 grains of Alcan AL-8 for a chronographed 1053/394. Again, this is a hot load devised for the purpose of hunting in a well-made gun. If you have doubts about your gun because of its age or it being a little-known brand, stick to factory ammo and by all means avoid the +P loadings. With that in mind, 9.5 grains of Hercules 2400 behind the Speer bullet makes a mild, controllable and accurate load at a true 850/257.

Probably the best general advice I could give regarding handloading is that you must work up your own loads tailored to your own gun for your own purposes. The loads I have mentioned have been

One of the author's favorite handguns, the Smith & Wesson Model 19 with a special Nitex finish.

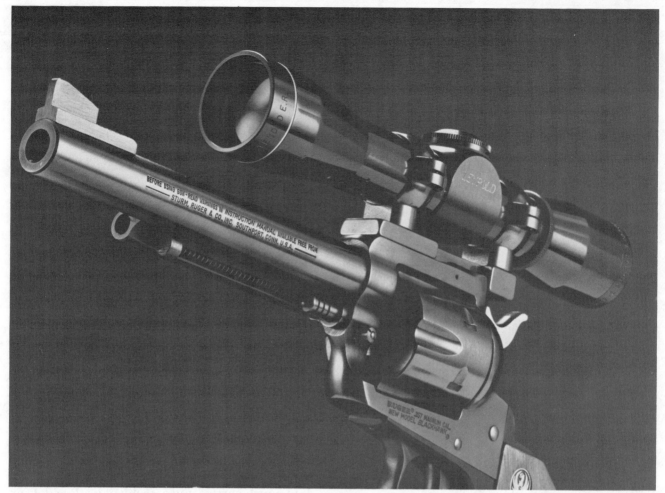

This Ruger Blackhawk coupled with a Leupold scope is an ideal handgun for hunting both small and big game with the .38 Special or .357 Magnum cartridge.

excellent in most of my .38 Special revolvers. They may work as well or better in your gun, or they may perform only marginally.

THE .357 MAGNUM

The .357 Magnum appeared on the scene in 1935, after 33 years of experimentation with the .38 Special by handloaders who wanted just a little bit more. It was developed, for the most part, by Douglas B. Wesson of Smith & Wesson, and Philip B. Sharpe, whose book, *The Complete Guide to Handloading*, is an all-time classic but, regrettably, is long out of print. Elmer Keith contributed much to the original bullet design.

The .357 Magnum cartridge differs in external appearance from the .38 Special in the length of its case, being about 1/10 of an inch longer. It is a more powerful cartridge generating heavier pressures and requiring stronger and better-made revolvers than many of the .38 Special light frame and medium frame guns. The extra length serves not only to allow more powder volume, but also prevents inadvertently chambering a .357 Magnum cartridge in a .38 Special revolver. The .357 was, until the advent of the .44 Magnum, the most powerful commercial handgun cartridge in the world.

In about 1957, this writer, as a law enforcement officer with several year's experience and a few gun incidents under his belt, switched from the S&W .38 Special Combat Masterpiece revolver to the relatively new S&W Model 19 .357 Magnum, more commonly known as the Combat Magnum.

I wanted more power and my personal shooting development was such that I was confident that I could handle it, an important factor indeed. Carrying a gun more powerful than you can handle is just as bad as carrying a gun with less power than you need. Actually, even for disinterested police officers, there is little sense in an officer, department or civilian purchasing .38 Special revolvers today when they can buy the same basic model chambered for the .357 for nearly the same price. The magnum revolvers will handle any .38 Special loads with the same excellent results and, should the individual develop in ability, he can start loading the bigger .357s in his sidearm. I have fired untold thousands of .38 Special loads through my Model 19 and experience no difficulty when switching to the magnums. I must admit, however, that there is an occasional and rare gun that will give extraction problems with .357 Magnum cases after digesting a large number of .38 Specials.

In any event, at that point in my police career I wanted a good all-round load for duty carry so,

quite naturally, I entered into correspondence with America's most outstanding handgunner, the late Elmer Keith. His recommendations were to use his 173-grain semi-wadcutter bullet design, moderately hard-cast, backed up by 13.5 grains of Hercules 2400 powder. Regular small pistol primers were used. In my gun this load delivered a velocity/energy figure of 1200/553 and accounted well for itself when the chips were down.

This load is, in my opinion, an all-time classic in that it is controllable in an experienced hand, is accurate far beyond the capabilities of most shooters, and offers an acceptable compromise between stopping power and penetration. Actually, during the early years of the California Police PPC Championships, I shot this load in competition when most others were using .38 Special target wadcutters. While I did not win first place, I did reasonably well with this load and easily made all the time limits, which attests to the load's controllability.

For law enforcement work, the .38 Special is both praised and damned in some circles for its lack of power. For all-round use, a low recoil sensation and the availability of guns, this cartridge will be around for quite a while.

The Great .38 Special/.357 Magnum Combination

An excellent .357 hunting load, but one that should be used only in a large frame revolver such as the Smith & Wesson Model 27, 28 or the Ruger single-action Blackhawks, is the Speer 160-grain half jacket bullet backed by 13 grains of Alcan AL-8. This load is listed in the older Speer Manual Number 8 and is a *maximum load*. I recommend that you work up to the listed charge with extreme caution and be alert for pressure signs, as with all loads. At 1288/590 it is both accurate and an excellent performer on medium-sized game such as deer if you prefer to use the .357 as opposed to the standard for big game—the .44 Magnum.

If I have not devoted too much time to the wide variety of hollow point bullets and loads available, it is for two reasons. With only one exception, I have not found any reload with a hollow point bullet that will give better expansion than the factory Winchester Silvertip, no matter whether you are shooting a .38 Special or .357 Magnum. When we are talking about service ammunition versus target ammo, I see no reason to reload unless I can improve on those loads offered by commercial ammunition makers.

The one reload that serves as an exception again utilizes the Alberts Hydra-Shok bullet. This 146-grain bullet design, previously described, loaded in a .357 case and backed by either 4.2 grains of Winchester 231 powder, or 4.5 grains of Hercules Unique, gives target accuracy, easy controllability and expansion to .65 inch without coming apart. It performs best in revolvers with barrel lengths from 2 to 4 inches.

The .38 Special has been with us for over 80 years and, almost unbelievably, the .357 Magnum is pushing 50 years. It is a certain bet that new and novel factory loads will be developed, along with updated powders, bullets and loading data. Being easy to shoot, as in the case of the .38 Special, and extremely versatile, as with the .357 Magnum, both cartridges are assured popularity—perhaps forever. While this author and shooter presently prefers larger caliber guns, the fact remains that I have fired more .38/.357 reloads than all centerfires combined and will probably continue to do so—if only just for the pure pleasure of it all.

As mentioned in the text, these bullets are favored by author Pickles for most of his work. From left to right: the Speer 160-grain half-jacket; the standard Hornady 148-grain wadcutter; and finally, for defense, the Alberts Hydra-Shok bullet.

Chapter 10

Care and Feeding of the Modern Automatic Pistol

Today's automatic pistols are very tough, very dependable and very accurate. They have to be, with more and more police departments switching over to high-capacity 9mms, and competitors using the big .45s in high-stakes matches.

Take the word tough. Law enforcement and military personnel, who have to be out in all sorts of weather and who may be faced with threatening situations day after day, need a gun able to take the punishment and still deliver the firepower when things get hairy.

Compared to a wheelgun, the automatic has a definite advantage in that it has less wear and tear per round thrust upon its mass than our time-tested revolver. Now, we are not going to start a revolver versus automatic debate right here, for, like death and taxes, the argument will never end. However, the point is still valid that, in proven tests, the wheelgun will not go the distance. Whereas, when the revolver starts to fade after 5,000 to 7,000 rounds, the auto is just starting to break in. It's not just a matter of physics; it's a matter of design.

But, and this is important, the automatic must be cared for. Plain and simple, the auto will only function so long as its owner takes care of it. The old excuse of blaming ammunition for malfunctions is no longer valid, for I have yet to see a misfire in factory ammunition, and never in home-brewed fodder if correct handloading procedures are followed.

Dependability is a major plus. With modern metallurgy, key parts in the top-grade autos are made with extra care and attention so as to avoid problems. When automatics first came on the scene many decades ago, parts such as slide stops, extractors, ejectors or even frames would develop stress fatigue, leading to cracks, then complete breakdown. In this present day and age, these problems have just about been wiped out. Sure it happens, but if you take that one part averaged out over all the pieces made, the percentage is very low. Very low indeed!

Accuracy? Sure, the auto has it. With carefully tailored handloaded ammo, my guns punch groups in paper at the 50-yard line measuring a scant 2½

Care and attention to both the gun and the loads is necessary to prevent smoke-stack jams. Here, an example was set up in a high-volume Steyr auto using an underpowered 9mm load. Situations like this can be very dangerous in combat or defense situations and must be avoided at all costs.

inches across. Granted, this was all done in a bolted-down machine rest, but it's not hard to realize the actual potential of semi-automatic weapons through such experiences.

Caring for, or the maintenance of your automatic, must be a top priority. There simply is no shortcut. The present-day autopistol is no harder to field strip than its rival, and one should not let parts such as springs, slides, barrels, barrel bushings or any other part deter him when he starts to get serious about cleaning his piece. Briefly then, before getting into the ammunition aspect of the automatic spectrum, let's go over proper maintenance to help illustrate the dos and don'ts of taking care of your weapon.

One of the first rules in cutting down maintenance time relates to the leather gear you wear when using your pistol. Never leave your gun in the holster while off duty or back from a hunting foray. Leather invites moisture. In fact, it's sponge-like. Those little beads of moisture will ruin the finish on the gun in short order, and water will find its way inside the piece and lie on the inner parts causing corrosion, possible failure, then breakage. This is one reason why many law enforcement agencies are pushing stainless steel guns. This is no bed of roses either. With stainless comes complacency. People think stainless steel is the best thing that ever came down the pike. But stainless will rust from neglect under the right conditions, so proper maintenance

procedures must be adhered to regardless of the gun's construction.

Some other rules: Don't tinker with the outer workings of the auto. That means don't fool with sight adjustments once they are set (unless of course you find a different or better load, then rezero), magazine release buttons or try to lap barrel bushings so they ride easier. All parts are made to minimum tolerances for a reason. Leave 'em alone!

For ordinary usage, autos tend to function very well with the field stripping method of weapon breakdown. This, in short, is what the manufacturer recommends in his instruction manual. To dive in any deeper will only get you into trouble and if this happens, you should have enough sense to acquire the services of a professional gunsmith.

In any event, after a range session, clear and double-check the weapon before bringing it into the close confines of your house. We have a strict policy at our homestead—no one, and that means no one—brings a loaded piece through the front door.

At your work station, disassemble the auto according to the maker's suggestions. Get out the Hoppe's #9 and go to work. Remove the grips, then run a fine film of the cleaner all over the weapon. Check all recesses for powder residue, then swab the barrel. If leading is prevalent, use a brass brush or a lead remover. Run a clean patch anointed with the Hoppe's through the barrel, then put the barrel aside for 24 hours in order for the cleaner to work.

Clean and check all the small parts, and lay them aside. The next day, rerun a clean patch through

For the average handgunner, this is as far as you will want to go to field strip an automatic pistol.

The most critical part of any automatic: the feed ramp area. For serious work, this part of the gun must work in concert with the ammunition chosen.

the barrel, then another and another until it comes out clean. A light coat of oil will keep those lands and grooves sparkling; ditto for the barrel exterior. Finish up by wiping the piece with a clean soft cloth, leaving just a trace of the Hoppe's on the internal parts of the slide and frame. This is enough to protect it from most of the moisture inside a normal dwelling; however, let the weather conditions in your area be your guide.

The whole key to faultless functioning of the auto is *minimal lubrication*. Soaking the slide rails, magazines or internal assemblies will only hinder the total operation of the gun. When a round goes off, various amounts of debris are scattered about which will cling to heavy lube concentrations; the consequences of which could be a slowing down of the action, resulting in a jam no matter how good the ammo is.

Autopistol Ammunition

Which leads us to the next subject—ammunition. While the method of loading pistol or rifle ammo follows general guidelines, when preparing handloads for semi-automatic weapons, words such as taper crimp, fast burning powder or full metal-jacketed bullets become very meaningful.

Handloading for an automatic takes time, patience and a thorough understanding of what happens to that cartridge when the gun is put into service. Depending on the model, most autos are made so the cartridge itself cycles or powers the action. This strips off another round from the maga-

zine forcing it into the chamber over the feed ramp, and ends up with the closing of the slide. With all this going on it becomes obvious that our ammunition must be impeccable; not at all difficult if one follows correct loading practices.

The first priority is to purchase brand new factory brass made by firms such as Federal, Remington and Winchester. Stay away from military surplus brass as some lots have sidewall dimension differences that could result in abnormal pressure readings. Avoid like the plague foreign bargain brands that incorporate Berdan priming pockets. Berdan primers are not only extremely hard to get in this country, but they are a real hassle to load or deprime as well.

Before you seat a bullet or load a charge run all brass through a reputable sizing die. A good idea here is to purchase a carbide die on the first go around. Good for a couple hundred thousand rounds, these die sets free you from the messy routine of lubing cases before placing them into the die.

After sizing, run a routine check on a random sampling of cases with a precision caliper or micrometer. Depending upon the caliber, attention should be given to overall length and the inside diameter of the case. As most autos headspace on the case mouth, too long a case could keep the slide from locking home; a definite problem in a stressful situation. The inside case diameter must be tight in relation to bullet diameter in order to keep the bul-

Even though this feed ramp was not highly polished, all ammunition tested in this Steyr went over the ramp with absolutely no problems—a tribute to fine engineering on their part.

For speed on the initial burst, the slide lock, safety levers and hammer are all located within easy reach.

Minimum lubrication is all that is necessary to ensure faultless functioning of any automatic. Over-lubrication will only catch dirt and debris, rendering the gun useless at perhaps the wrong time.

let from slipping into the case as it rides the feed ramp. If too large in the inside diameter section, a smaller expanding plug is needed as bullet push-back can bring on other problems including a drastic jump in pressure. If cases are found to be too long, a trimming session is necessary.

Priming and case flaring is next. With case capacities—in grains water—running from an average of 6.7 (.380 Auto) to about 14.5 (.45 ACP), standard pistol primers fill the bill very nicely. Since fast burning powders are used in these small cases, magnum primers should not even be considered in all but a very few instances. This would include cartridges like the .357 or .44 Auto Mag that may use

slower propellants such as Olin 630, IMR-4227 or the Hodgdon line of HS-5, 6 or 7.

The awareness of proper flaring or belling of the case mouth is a very important step in autopistol ammo reloading. Bullets used in today's automatics have a tendency to be lighter in weight than those of years past for one good reason—velocity. Because of this, bearing surfaces have been sacrificed to where case flare must be controlled to the point of minimum tolerance in order to have a tight hold on the projectile as it is seated into the case.

It's been my experience that when you reach the flaring stage in loading, ease the expander plug down toward the case very slowly. When it reaches

Six steps to producing topnotch autopistol reloads: (1) Use factory fresh or once-fired brass. (2) Create a very small flare to start the bullet home. (3) Seat the bullet on the neck of the case.

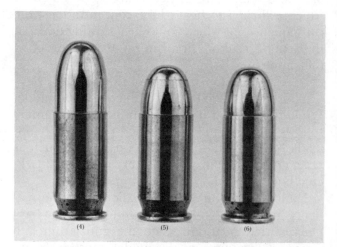

(4) Make sure the bullet is square on the neck before it enters the bullet seater. (5) Seat the bullet in place. (6) Finish with a taper crimp for perfect functioning.

Even the minor calibers like the .380, shown here with the Browning automatic, can be just the edge you need in a tense situation.

The Smith & Wesson Model 39, a forerunner to current models, is shown here with a tight grouping at 25 yards.

the case mouth, alternately raise the handle of the press as you screw in the plug very slowly no more than a half-turn at a time. As you get close to the "step" in the expander, resistance will increase. Watch your progress now, checking frequently for the beginning of the flare. While observing the case, as soon as you can seat a bullet on the mouth without its tipping, stop! You have reached minimum flare status.

Small auto cases demand the use of faster than normal powders. Propellants in the range of Bullseye, Unique and Olin 231 fill most of my autoloading needs. Again, as with primers, there are exceptions and generally they follow the same capacity cases as mentioned a few paragraphs earlier. Because fast powders do occupy less space than their medium to slower counterparts, all charged hulls should be checked for *double charges* before moving on.

After powder charging, bullet seating comes next, followed by crimping. Modern automatics thrive on perfect ammunition, so strive toward it. Not all bullets will work in all autos. Your job is to weed them out. For high-performance loads, fully jacketed bullets are a sure bet for absolute dependability. Stay away from lead bullets unless you are sure they function perfectly in *your* gun. For matches, where the foe is only a paper target, full metal-jacketed bullets are preferred. For serious work, where stopping power is essential, hollow points are the approved option. Don't forget, after bullet seating, a check should be made to make sure

A new generation automatic, this Smith & Wesson Model 469 is quite close to being the ideal hideout gun.

Care and Feeding of the Modern Automatic Pistol

your cartridge overall length is within the limits for that particular caliber and bullet style. Cartridge overall length combined with the right bullet ogive go a long way to ensure the shooter of trouble-free operation.

The crimping on autopistol rounds should be of the taper crimp variety, not the roll crimp usually associated with revolver or rifle cartridges. Dies that are honed inside to induce a gradual tapering of the case in the neck/bullet area are available from just about all makers. This tapering or coning keeps the bullet in place and aids in getting the completed cartridge to the chamber. This is a very important step in loading these rounds and should never be forgotten.

The final inspection of finished loads should be both visual and tactile (touch). Rolling a round between your fingers before you put it in the box will immediately sort the good from the bad. As a general practice at my loading bench, as soon as the top of the box is closed on a batch of handloaded ammo, a label must go on immediately. The label denotes the type of bullet, charge, powder, primer and the specific gun the rounds were loaded for. This is most important! As every gun is a law unto itself, accurate labeling is as important as loading the cases.

The proper care and feeding of your automatic is dependent on your attitude toward proper procedures. Anyone considering a high-capacity autopistol owes it to himself to do everything possible to ensure that his ammunition is flawless.

SELECTED AUTOPISTOL HANDLOADS

Gun	Caliber	Bullet	Bullet Weight (grains)	Powder	Powder Charge (grains)	Velocity (fps)
BHP	9mm	SP	100	231	5.6	1220
S&W	9mm	H	115	Bullseye	4.2	1050
BHP	9mm	R	115	231	5.2	1125
BHP	9mm	H	115	Unique	5.5	1200
BHP	9mm	H	124	Unique	5.5	1060
CGM	.38S	SP	100	Unique	7.0	1325
CGM	.38S	H	124	Blue Dot	8.7	1130
CGM	.38S	H	124	HS-7	9.0	1200
CC	.45ACP	SI	185	Bullseye	5.2	900
GC	.45ACP	SI	185	Unique	7.3	950
GC	.45ACP	SP	200	Bullseye	4.0	800
GC	.45ACP	H	230	231	5.7	750
GC	.45ACP	H	230	Unique	6.5	850

GUNS: BHP; Browning Hi-Power—S&W; Smith & Wesson Model 39—CGM; Colt Government Model—CC; Colt Commander—GC; Colt Gold Cup .45. BULLETS: H; Hornady—R; Remington—SI; Sierra—SP; Speer.

Chapter 11

Some Thoughts on Ballistics

by Mason Williams

Ballistics is an interesting subject which continually presents us with new challenges because in many instances things do not turn out as expected. This applies to both handgun and rifle ballistics. In order to understand how ballistics works it is necessary to divide the subject into three parts: internal ballistics, external ballistics and terminal ballistics.

Internal ballistics deals with what happens from the time the cartridge primer fires until the bullet leaves the muzzle of the gun. A lot can happen in that very short time. As we know, a cartridge is made up of a cartridge case, a primer, powder and a bullet. We must have all four components in order to have a complete cartridge. The primer acts as a spark plug shooting out a stream of flame that ignites the powder, which burns, creating gases that build up pressures which finally become so high that they force the bullet out of the case, into the barrel and through the barrel.

Many shooters do not realize that it is the cartridge that determines what happens when the bullet finally strikes the target. It is the selection of

components which make up the cartridge that controls the results at the target. The firearm is only a projectile launcher. It cannot basically affect what the bullet does when it strikes the target. As an example, if we do not put enough powder into the cartridge case we can still fire the cartridge but the bullet may only travel a hundred yards through the air and then fall to the ground.

Today, we have many different types of powders that burn with varying degrees of speed. Basically, fast burning powders should be used with lightweight bullets and short barrels. Heavy bullets require much slower burning powders to prevent too fast a build up of pressures within the cartridge case. The slower burning powders need resistance and a constantly maintained pressure curve in order to burn correctly and completely. (Unburned powder does not contribute to bullet velocity.) To work at peak efficiency, the slow burning powders must first have sufficient bullet weight to push against in order to build up pressure. And, the barrel, which acts as a burning chamber, must be long enough so that pressure can continue to push the bullet all the way through the barrel. If the barrel is too short, then bullet velocity will fall off because the powder has been unable to burn completely. Conversely, if the barrel is too long, then the powder may burn itself out before the bullet reaches the muzzle. Without gas pressure continually pushing the bullet down the barrel, friction will slow down bullet velocity.

These factors must be carefully considered when working up a load. The relationship between bullet weight, powder burning characteristics and barrel length will control velocity, bullet accuracy and terminal ballistics. As a result, the powder/bullet relationship is usually a compromise. Often, many different types of powders must be tried in order to achieve the desired velocity, safe pressures and accuracy at the target. A load that may be extremely accurate at 200 yards may fail to produce acceptable accuracy at 300 yards. There is also a definite relationship between velocity and the bullet used.

Once the cartridge has fired, driving the bullet out of the cartridge case into the barrel, the barrel lands and grooves grasp the bullet and force it to rotate. The speed of bullet rotation depends upon the twist of the barrel rifling and the bullet velocity. A barrel with a one in ten twist will rotate the bullet once in ten inches. A one in twelve twist will rotate the bullet once in twelve inches. This means that a bullet fired into a one in twelve twist barrel at a velocity of 3000 fps will leave the barrel turning at a speed of 15,000 rpms. In order to withstand this rotational force, bullets must be designed and constructed to hold together and to perform correctly at the target, whether it be paper or game.

It is essential that bullets rotate. If they were not turning they would probably tumble end over end in flight. Rotating the bullets keeps them flying true—point first. It is far better to have too fast a rifling twist than too slow a rifling twist. Basically, the longer the bullet in relation to its weight and caliber, the faster the twist should be. A 180-grain caliber .30/06 bullet works best with a barrel twist of around one in ten. A 125-grain .30/06 bullet calls for a barrel twist of approximately one in fourteen.

Shooters often create internal ballistics problems without realizing what they are doing. Heavy oil, light grease and similar substances, when left in the barrel and not removed prior to firing, can seriously affect the bullet and pressures. These shots often go wild, never striking the target. Other problems are dirt, snow, mud, sticks and similar debris that can get into barrels. In addition to affecting bullet performance, they can increase pressures to dangerous levels. Always check out the interior of the barrel before firing!

External Ballistics

Once the bullet emerges from the barrel muzzle we get into external ballistics. This deals with what the bullet does as it travels from the barrel muzzle to the target. Wind and gravity affect the bullet. We need not worry about gravity—rather, we must learn how to correct for the amount of wind pressure upon the bullet. This varies tremendously and only experience will teach us how to compensate correctly.

Even though the bullet has been correctly designed, built and rotated, it will usually yaw or not fly precisely point on for the first 50 to 60 yards. Often a bullet will travel well past 100 yards before it stabilizes and commences to fly absolutely true. As a result, groups at 100 yards can often be larger than groups out at 200 yards merely because the bullet is still yawing as it passes the 100-yard marker, but by the time it reaches the 200-yard marker it has settled down, or as they say, "gone to sleep." It is the rotational twist that puts the bullet to sleep.

Another factor that influences accuracy is velocity. If a bullet leaves the barrel muzzle at too slow a speed for that specific bullet it may never recover from yaw and it will slop around in the air striking far from the desired point of aim. Therefore, there is a definite and close relationship between velocity, barrel twist, accuracy, bullet weight and bullet construction. If a bullet is torn apart during its travel through the barrel it will emerge deformed and unable to fly accurately through the air. If the bullet is forced to exceed the velocities for which it was designed, it will also go to pieces in the air. If you need convincing, load a caliber .38 Special jacketed soft nose handgun bullet into a caliber .350 Remington Magnum case ahead of a full charge of rifle powder and fire it. The odds are you will be able to actually see the bullet self-destruct not too far past the rifle muzzle.

So far we have discussed some of the conditions that the shooter can control, but now let's get into factors that affect any bullets. If you are firing at a deer through brush you will have problems. How

A gun being sighted over the screens. Concentration is necessary here so you not only get accurate readings on the instrument, but you can check shooting accuracy as well.

serious these problems will be depends upon how thick the brush is, what bullet you are using and at what velocity the bullet is traveling. Usually a slow moving, heavy bullet will be a better brush buster than a high-velocity, lightweight bullet. Live, green twigs and branches can drastically change the bullet's path. A simple bush can cause a miss on game. Never try to shoot through anything in an attempt to down game. The odds are it will not work!

Hunters, and particularly target shooters, often need to know the velocities of their bullets in order to develop super-accurate loads for their firearms. Today, we have many fine, reasonably priced chronographs that do an excellent job of providing this information. The type of chronograph you need depends upon on how much work you will do with it and how often you will use it. Because of the

amount of testing that I do, I have settled on the Oehler Model 33 Chronotach. It's quite sophisticated and there are no tapes or wires to change. The machine uses light rays. This chronograph figures out all computations giving me instant readings for velocity, number of shots fired and averages, leaving me free to concentrate on firing. I can highly recommend it, if you plan to use a chronograph a great deal.

Another fine piece of equipment for handgunners is the Ransom Rest, which is an absolute necessity for the serious competitive shooter. It takes the guesswork and human element out of firing for accuracy, and tells you exactly what your loads are doing.

Terminal Ballistics

We now come to terminal ballistics, which deals with what the bullet does as it strikes the target and comes to rest. A bullet may strike a steel plate then fall to the ground. Another bullet may strike a wall, pass through it, ricochet off a refrigerator door and then glance into a wood door and remain embedded. Similarly, an incorrectly chosen bullet may strike a deer in precisely the right spot, down the deer but proceed on through the deer, pass through a small tree and veer off a rock to finally fall into a stream. Terminal ballistics vary tremendously and it is unfortunate that so many people fail to select the correct bullet for the job at hand.

When target shooting, bullet performance is not the key factor; accuracy is the key factor. We must assume, of course, that the bullets are caught in bullet traps or by backstops. In this phase of the shooting game the important and conclusive factor is bullet accuracy! However, we must not overlook metallic silhouette shooting where accuracy is possibly not quite as important as the bullet's ability to knock over the steel plates. In this example of competitive shooting, terminal ballistics are vital to winning matches.

In hunting, many new details enter into the terminal ballistics picture, not the least of which is the physical and mental condition of the game. If the game is excited and nervous, then one-shot kills are less frequent, and the mortally wounded animal may run off. Don't be too quick to blame the bullet if you fire, place the shot well and the game seems unaffected. Stop and think back. Try and evaluate the condition of the game at the moment when you fired. Many an excited, stimulated animal has run off carrying two or even three correctly placed shots, driven onward by the adrenalin pumping through its arteries, only to fall dead in mid-stride within seconds. The same animal standing quietly and undisturbed would likely drop on the spot when struck by one shot in a vital area.

Far too many shooters and hunters tend to lean too heavily upon tables, charts and other listings that have been drawn up to "prove this or to show that." Be wary of such things. They serve their purpose if used intelligently, but they can be terribly misleading if taken factually. Foot pounds of energy is a simple informative factor, yet, if not thoroughly understood, it will mislead many people. Regardless of what the tables show, it would be wrong to select a 110-grain .30/60 bullet for elk hunting. And yet, according to the tables, such a bullet could have sufficient foot pounds of energy (fpe) to equal the stopping power of a 180-grain projectile. However, the two different bullets are meant for two different purposes. Obviously, the latter bullet would be the one to use on elk; the 110-grain on varmints.

These tables assume that all of the potential energy inherent in a bullet moving at a specific velocity will be expended into and within the target. Such is not the case due to bullet construction, placement of the bullet and residual bullet velocity at the target. A bullet that is fully jacketed and designed not to expand, but to provide maximum accuracy at long ranges, cannot deliver its full potential of foot pounds into the game. Results would be drastically different. Bullet selection remains extremely important and must be matched to the job and the distances involved.

A bullet with a velocity of, say, 2175 fps, designed to open and expand when it hits a mule deer at 215 yards may do well under that distance, but when it strikes game out at 350 yards it may be moving so slowly that it won't mushroom, only wounding the animal. That bullet was stretched beyond its limits at the longer distance. All these factors must be kept in mind when considering and evaluating any foot pounds of energy table. They must be viewed as guides only.

Estimating Bullet Performance

It is possible to obtain a basic idea of what a bullet will do upon impact with the animal. Very little, if any, game is shot at muzzle velocity. Let's assume that you would like to know how well your bullet will perform at perhaps 250 yards. You are firing a

Jacketed, 125-grain, flat nose .38 Special bullet blew up the first container, smashed through the second and came to rest in the third.

.30/06 cartridge, using a 165-grain boat tail bullet ahead of 56.5 grains of 4350 powder. This loading will give you about 2850 fps. This is the muzzle velocity as the bullet leaves the gun.

Because you are interested in bullet velocity at 250 yards, go to a table in the Hornady or Sierra reloading manual and pick out the listing for a 165-grain 30-caliber bullet moving at 2900 fps muzzle velocity. But you want the velocity at 250 yards, so note the velocity given in the book for 300 yards. This runs 2303 fps.

Now look down to a muzzle velocity in the table of 2800 fps and note the 300-yard figure of 2217 fps. Add these figures together to get 4520 fps, then divide by two and the result is 2260. This is about what your velocity will be out at 250 yards.

Now, go back to your loading bench and, using a relatively fast burning powder like 4064, drop back down to around 42.0 or 43.0 grains. (Never attempt to load down with a slow burning powder similar to 4831, 4350, etc. Small amounts can cause detonations!) Load up a couple of cartridges using the reduced amounts of 4064 powder and fire the bullets into ordnance gelatin, Duxseal or ballistic putty. Extract the bullets and examine them. They should give you a rough idea of how much bullet performance you can expect from this specific bullet at velocities of around 2200 fps.

For the more casual shooter, I can highly recommend firing into water. Line up seven or eight half-gallon milk containers about one inch apart. Fill them to the top with water and fire handgun

Recovered .38 Special 125-grain, jacketed hollow point bullets from the milk carton test. Note uniform expansion.

bullets into them. For rifles, one-gallon milk containers work well but you will have to line up at least nine or ten, depending upon the cartridge and load you are using. Check out the accompanying photos. They will give you an idea of what to expect. Nothing can substitute for living flesh, but you can discover whether or not your bullet expands well enough to use in the field.

When firing at long ranges in the field, remember that your bullet was designed and constructed to perform well at reasonable distances. At close ranges it will often overperform and destroy a lot of meat due to the high velocity with which it strikes. Out at 300 yards expansion and penetration may be ideal. But when you try a shot at 400 to 500 yards, expansion may not be sufficient to put down game. On the other hand, bullet rotation keeps the bullet nose directly in line with the line of flight so that when the bullet strikes the game it will have a tendency to penetrate excessively due to lack of bullet nose expansion. When a bullet strikes and expands correctly the rapid increase in the diameter of the bullet nose slams the bullet to a stop within a short distance. This results in the bullet remaining within the animal. Without this nose expansion the bullet will often pass right through the animal at long distances. Unfortunately, there is no such thing as the perfect bullet—one that will perform perfectly at all ranges.

Heavy bullets such as the 180-, 200- and 220-grain caliber .30 bullets start off at lower velocities than lighter weight bullets but they will often retain far more wind bucking capabilities and produce more practical impact shock when they strike.

Today, many rifles are manufactured with short barrels to reduce weight and produce a light, fast-handling rifle. Many loads use the slower burning powders such as 4350, 4831, or H-205 in order to provide a slow, powerful push against the bullet base all the way through a conventional barrel. When we get down into 18-inch barrels these slow burning powders cannot burn completely. They require 24- and even 26-inch barrels in order to deliver their full potential. Because of this, if you plan to load for a short barrel rifle—or handgun for that matter—it is advisable to run tests using relatively fast burning powders. One of the advantages of a fine chronograph is that you can tailor loads to your specific rifle, thus obtaining maximum efficient velocity through utilizing the full potential of your powder/bullet/rifle barrel length relationship. As an example, let's say you have one of Remington's new Model 7 rifles in caliber .308—short barrel, light weight, fast and very handy.

Take a normal loading, either factory or handload, firing the 180-grain caliber .30 bullet. Fire five rounds and average out the velocity. The Oehler Model 33 does all this for you. Next, using the same bullet, turn to perhaps 4064 powder starting out in the mid-range of recommended loads. Again fire five shots for average velocity. Then gradually increase the powder charge by half-grain increments

The last stage of the testing includes the checking of stats on the chronograph, and recording them on forms that will come in handy later.

until you are just under maximum velocity. (Throughout any such test, always watch for and be guided by signs of excessive pressures). Keep checking the velocities.

You will discover that quite often these faster burning powders will give you higher velocities than you can obtain using conventional loads. The ideal situation that you are searching for is to have all of the powder burned just a moment before the bullet leaves the muzzle thereby eliminating all unburned powder. On the other hand, you do not want the powder to burn too rapidly allowing friction to slow down bullet velocity. A good chronograph will be of tremendous help in arriving at the right load. Try many different powders until you are completely satisfied.

The science of ballistics deals with projectiles. As we have seen, results can be confusing. They can also be instructive. There are few pat answers and the only way to learn about your specific firearm and its affinity for the nearly endless combinations of components is to try, try some more and then go at it again. Always keep in mind that what works for your firearm may not work for someone else's so be careful about recommending loads. Take care, test, shoot and enjoy it!

An ideal setup for machine resting a handgun. The Ransom Rest used with an Oehler 33 Chronotach. The pistol is a Viking undergoing accuracy and velocity tests.

Chapter 12

The Power of the Max

Not since the introduction of the famed .44 Magnum almost 30 years ago has one round stirred up as much controversy as the new .357 Remington Maximum.

For beginners, the .357 Max is a new cartridge, even though many claim it's just a variation on a theme. The theme being the .38 Special/.357 Magnum family. This could be true, but only up to a certain point. The point being that while the .357 Max uses the same bullets and similar powders as packed into the .38s or .357s, these old-timers never reach the same velocities or generate the same pressure readings as the Max.

Comparing velocities in standard length barrels, the .357 Magnum on its best day drives a 158-grain bullet approximately 1350 feet per second. The Max, on the other hand, hits the high side of 1625 from a 7^1/$_2$-inch barrel, roughly a 20% increase in velocity. In fact, range testing over a Oehler Model 33 Chronotach, actual factory velocities came in a little better than the quoted ballistics printed in catalogs and press releases. With my Ruger, equipped

with the 7^1/$_2$-inch tube, the Remington 158-grain offering averaged 1651 fps. High readings ran 1719; low, 1589. Federal's new entry, topped off with a 180-grain JHP bullet, hit 1512 on the average with 1566 on the high side; 1477, the low. But to do this, internal pressures have to be high, very high; in fact, in the neighborhood of 49,000 to 50,000 copper units of pressure.

The Federal brand had an extreme spread on the Chronotach of 89, versus Remington's 133. At 25 yards, Federal's .357SM punched holes grouping 1^1/$_4$ inches between centers. The Bridgeport brand, while coming in second, had done slightly poorer, at 2^1/$_2$ inches. To keep shooter effort to a minimum, a Ransom Rest was used to hold the pistol in a firm firing position.

Perhaps, before we proceed any further, a bit of history, stats and other pertinent information are called for to keep everything in proper perspective.

The project in total was started by Remington with their concept of the new cartridge. With silhouette shooting reaching new heights, this was going to be a round to match the game. Ruger was then approached (as Smith & Wesson was on the original .44 Magnum), which ultimately resulted in a new gun.

Ruger's new gun is basically a Super Blackhawk with a lengthened frame and a fluted cylinder. The lockwork is of the "New Model" ideal with the cylinder gap held to a tolerance of .002″. Actually, Sturm, Ruger is trying to hold it to .001″, and considering that the average off-the-line standard caliber revolver mikes .006″, this in itself is quite a feat.

Questions came up concerning the brass case. While some think it's just a .357 case stretched out, in reality it's not. The case itself, because of the new higher pressures generated, is built with extra strength in the head section. Remington takes a .223 case and in about the third draw stage, makes it a .357 Maximum—not a .223. The net result is a much stronger case than would be possible if it went the route of the regular .357 Magnum cartridge case.

If all this sounds exciting, it was for a while. I use the past tense because it seemed that as soon as the round hit the market, troubles started to brew in the wings, especially for the revolvers. Problems of flame cutting started to develop just above the cylinder gap on the top strap of the revolvers. With this, barrel erosion becomes another problem after only a few rounds are fired. To impede progress further, one manufacturer has put a halt on the production of the gun—although others have jumped in—and Federal has put its .357 Max ammunition on "hold" until further word from both the shooting public and the firearms industry in general.

Then why is this chapter included if everything seems gloomy for this particular cartridge? Because, my friends, there is an alternative which seems, so far, to eliminate all the problems mentioned above and makes the .357 Maximum a joy to shoot and reload.

It's called the Thompson/Center Contender. Single-shot in nature, there is no cylinder gap to contend with. Closed breeched guns eliminate that hyper jump of the bullet to the barrel, with no barrel erosion problems. So far. Also, barrel interchangeability with rugged scope mounts complete the picture for an all-round gun.

To try to exhaust all possibilities in reference to various barrel lengths and their effect on either velocity or accuracy, I ordered samples of the Con-

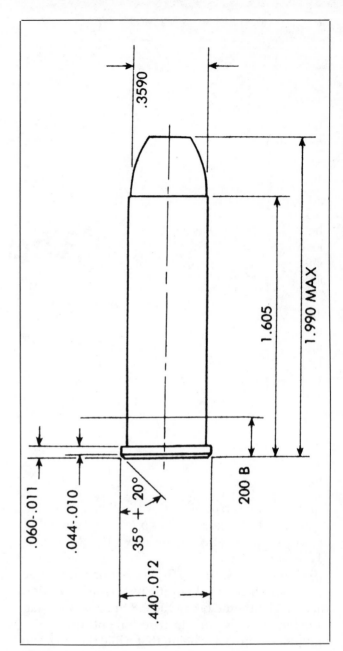

.357 Remington Maximum.

tender with the 10-inch and 14-inch (Super 14) barrels from Thompson/Center. Both guns were topped off with optical sights for accuracy testing. The 2.5 power scope went on the 10-incher; the 4 power was mounted on the longer tube. With the scopes cinched down and sealed with Loctite to keep the screws from backing out, my two test rigs were ready to go.

Handloading the .357 Max

For cartridge cases, I used some once-fired Remington brass and kept a careful check on it as the tests progressed. Also involved was some brand new Winchester .357 Maximum brass. Both were sized in Pacific/Hornady's die set made for the .38 Special/.357 Magnum/.357 Maximum, which incorporates a tungsten carbide die, expander and seater with three seating stems. These dies are now available at reloading suppliers.

Powders included H-110, Olin 296 and IMR-4227. Preliminary testing by myself and others in the field narrowed the choice down to these and possibly a few others, but for the sake of clarity combined with available time, these three proved to suit our needs just fine.

Bullets ran the gamut from 150 grains to 158, 160, 170 and included the newer 180-grain bullets made specifically for silhouette shooting. (Lighter bullets can be used, but it's my contention that for the best in knockdown power in terminal energy, stick with the heavier slugs.) All brands were represented including Hornady, Sierra and Speer.

To complete our list of components, all loads were sparked by Remington 7½ *small rifle primers*. Even though this is considered a pistol cartridge, *never, never*, use small *pistol* primers here. Because of the large quantities of powder used, the pistol primers will not do the job efficiently, effectively or safely.

All brass fully sized, it went into the Lyman Turbo Tumbler for cleaning. About two hours later we were finally ready to roll into the loading sequence. Then, before priming, cleaning and seating bullets, the overall length of each case was checked to be sure it did not exceed 1.610 inches. Priming was next with all cases getting the Remington 7½ *small rifle primers*. These are noted for helping to squeeze the last bit of accuracy out of bench rest calibers such as the .222 or .22-250, so figuring if they were good enough for those, they would be good enough for our .357 Max project.

Case flaring was done together with the priming of cases. With the Pacific expander die installed, the upstroke of the press flared the case for bullet acceptance; the downstroke primed it. The flare, or bell at the top of the case, was set very minimally to allow a good tight fit between bullet and case. This, combined later with a snug crimp, would ensure a good combustion ratio between powder and primer.

My RCBS 10-10 powder scale was zeroed and powder charging was started in earnest. Starting with Hodgdon's H-110, I then proceeded to load all the different charge weights. (The cans of other powders remained closed. In this way you can avoid switching powders by alternating loads which sometimes can lead to costly mistakes.) The H-110 flowed through my Lyman powder measure with ease, making it a pleasure to load.

As a matter of information, 21.0 grains filled the case to about five-eighths capacity. Twenty-four and a half grains approached three-quarters full with ease; 25.0 is a load that, with certain bullets, will level off at the bullet base. The performance was just about duplicated with the Olin 296 powder as its grain structure closely relates to H-110 in both size and volume in a cartridge case. With IMR-4227, the story changes somewhat. With 22.0 grains of this propellant, we had our first taste of com-

For an extensive testing program like the one involved with the .357 Maximum, attention to all details is imperative in order for all data to come out correctly. After changing barrels, the forend is tighted up to the correct torque.

Even though the brass is factory fresh, it never hurts to pass all the cases through the sizing die for uniformity.

case capacity would do best through the longer barrel. In reality, this was true. The Super 14 is the way to go for higher velocities—thus delivering more push downrange—and accuracy as well. Muzzle blast was more pronounced in some 10-inch loadings, which spewed a ball of fire roughly 6 to 8 inches in diameter out of the barrel. While this may be normal in some hi-per magnums, it can be somewhat disturbing to a silhouette shooter, for whom this cartridge was designed. With upwards of 25 grains of powder in a handgun cartridge, a longer barrel length is a definite plus.

The screen of the Chronotach showed that the Hodgdon H-110 propellant was the fastest of the bunch. This held true in all bullet weights including the heavier 180-grain silhouette bullets. And in some cases, the difference was as much as 200 to 300 feet per second. True to form, Olin 296 gave the next best readouts, followed by the slower IMR-4227. This also held true in the shorter barrel, but to a lesser degree.

With a moderate flair in the case mouth, the bullet is then inserted into the case for seating to the proper depth.

pressed loads. Nothing to be overly concerned with, but here I will again stress the need for heavy crimps for maximum performance.

All bullets listed in the chart were seated to the cannelure as they were to be fired in a single-shot pistol, hence no need to worry about cylinder gaps or cylinder rotational problems. All rounds checked out O.K. in the chambering department.

With the gun all secured in the Ransom Rest, sighting commenced at 25 yards, then firing for stats at 50 yards. (The shorter distance seems too close for a cartridge and gun this powerful. The longer distance is more appropriate for hunting. Also, it should be feasible to sight in and use this gun/scope combination at 100 yards without undue concern about bullet drop.)

Bracing myself for some surprises and disappointments, the range testing was started. I experienced both. In theory, I assumed that a cartridge of this magnitude in relationship to powder and

RANGE TEST RESULTS USING THE CONTENDER PISTOL

(Oehler 33 Chronotach. Screens placed 10 feet from muzzle. Temperature, 65 Degrees)

Bullet	Bullet Weight (grains)	Powder	Powder Charge (grains)	10-Inch Barrel Velocity (fps)	14-Inch Barrel Velocity (fps)	
Sierra	150	H-110	25.0	2057	2196	
Sierra	150	296	25.0	1977	2076	
Hornady	158	IMR4227	22.0	1700	1789	*
Hornady	158	H-110	24.5	1988	2087	
Hornady	160	H-110	24.5	1971	2057	
Hornady	160	296	24.5	1899	1993	
Sierra	170	IMR4227	21.0	1619	1721	
Sierra	170	296	22.5	1844	1954	*
Speer	180	H-110	21.0	1746	1841	*
Speer	180	296	21.0	1689	1804	
Hornady	180	H-110	21.0	1742	1801	*
Hornady	180	296	21.0	1733	1782	*
Remington Factory Load (158-grain bullet)				1808	1930	
Federal Factory Load (180-grain bullet)				1618	1705	

*Best potential for good accuracy.

In group size, the H-110 loadings led the pack in many instances. In three out of five sets, the bullet utilizing H-110 powder in the boiler room dominated the field, sometimes by as much as 25 to 50%! Case in point: Two loads using the Speer 180-grain bullets backed by 21.0 grains of powder (H-110 and Olin 296) gave groups that ran 1.25 inches with the former; 2.75 inches with the latter. Quite a difference. Of course, bullet construction and design do enter the picture, along with a thousand other variables. Seating a 180-grain Hornady bullet over 21.0 grains of H-110 brought home the bacon with a super 0.75-inch group. With the Olin 296 powder, we spread the group diameter to a solid one inch. Either one would satisfy me for hunting purposes. Comparing the 296 powder against the IMR-4227, we found the 296 the faster of the two. My personal powder choices for the .357 Max would be the H-110 and Winchester's 296.

It was also interesting to note that the smaller the velocity spread between shots, the tighter the group. On our two examples just mentioned, the H-110 showed 23 fps between shots; the 296, 42. And to top that off, one particular loading, a Hornady 160-grain offering, came up with 7 fps between all shots fired downrange. In this particular string, a 3-shot group was fired and the Chronotach came up with 2056, 2054 and 2061, averaging out to 2057 fps; a very nice velocity reading, and a good group as well. In theory, smaller velocity spreads should result in smaller groups. In actual shooting, during our testing, the theory proved correct.

Although the 10-inch barrel was shot as much as the 14-incher, I must admit I wasn't too terribly excited about it. For one thing, as mentioned, the muzzle blast that came forth from that tube was awesome with the handloads. The report was much like a solid punch, not the drawn out softness usually associated with the longer tube. In velocity, yes, there was a difference, as we expected. And, in groups sizes as well. Again citing our example of the Hornady 180-grain bullet, whereas the 14-inch barrel gave us groups of .075 and 1.00 inches, the shorter barrel delivered 1.25 and 1.50. Not much difference, granted, but enough to sway me over to the Super 14. Naturally, as in so many other instances, the choice is yours. If you want a gun for hunting and will carry it in a shoulder holster, by all means buy the shorter-barreled handgun. If your forte is silhouette shooting and higher velocities, then the longer, heavier gun is the one to use.

Case extraction was a problem with the 10-inch barrel. No, it wasn't pressure problems. Firing factory loads in the gun resulted in stuck cases which had to be charmed out of the chamber. The problem was caused by a tighter chamber. (We discovered this when we measured it later.) On the 14-inch barrel, the inside diameter was .382″; the 10-inch ran a tighter .377″. The problem can be solved in two ways. One, reduce the loads a wee bit to compensate for the expansion of the brass, or two, send the gun back to the factory for some minute reaming of the inside of the cylinder wall. I suggest the latter solution. If you can't get out of the gun what you put into it through careful handloading, it's of little use to you.

Special Preparations

The .357 Remington Maximum is a powerful handgun cartridge and it warrants much respect. For example, on the range eye and ear protection are mandatory, even when using a closed breeched gun like the Contender. Sponge inserts combined with outer ear muffs add needed comfort during extended range sessions. Gray-tinted sunglasses reduce eye strain by cutting down glare, especially on overly bright summer days, not to mention providing added protection against any flying debris. Scopes, rings and mounts must be anchored down securely, and this mandates the use of epoxy on all parts. Just three days before embarking for the range for some heavy testing, Loctite was used on all parts including mounting screws, clamping hex bolts and the base itself. To no avail. Halfway through the testing program all operations came to a complete halt as we had to take the scope off and retighten the mounting screws. And again, just before finishing, the scope mount developed a little more play. To keep things tight, clean all parts, use epoxy, then let it cure for a couple of extra days before heavy usage.

All handloading must be done with complete concentration and attention to detail. Remember, you are shooting a cartridge that generates upwards of 2000 fps at 50,000 copper units of pressure. You must be attentive to your duties at all times, and scrutinize your powder charges as they are dispensed. The Max is a good cartridge, but it requires effort on the shooter's part. With a wide range of components to choose from, time spent at the loading bench will prove rewarding and lead to a better understanding of this round.

After the smoke cleared and all the stats were in and compared, was this writer impressed? Yes, with some reservations. I would stick with the 14-inch barrel and handload for it. Results were more consistent with this length, accuracy far better, and it's a more comfortable gun to shoot.

Will the .357 Maximum continue to grow in popularity? This remains to be seen. Despite some problems with this round in the beginning, it's my opinion that eventually the .357 Max will find its place in line with the .35 Herrett or other high-velocity "handgun" rounds in a specialized sector using the T/C Contender. For the present though, this round needs a chance to settle down, be massaged a bit, then groomed into a formidable hunting or silhouette cartridge.

When this starts to happen, we'll all be a lot happier. I look forward to that time.

Chapter 13

The ABC's of Bullet Casting

by C. Kenneth Ramage

Who casts and shoots lead bullets? Had you asked that question a century ago, the answer would be, "everyone." It has only been since the turn of the century that a projectile superior to the lead/lead alloy bullet has been available to shooters. In fact, jacketed projectiles made their first serious inroads when, in 1898, the U.S. Government adopted the .30-40 Krag cartridge and rifle, thus replacing the venerable (and lead-bulleted) .45-70 trapdoor Springfield. Prior to said adoption in 1898, lead, cast into balls or drops of shot, was the only game in town.

Of course, the late 1890s didn't see many options of components or cartridge and rifle combinations. However, these items were soon to follow and many shooters, except muzzleloaders, turned to these newfangled jacketed bullets which, when used with recently developed smokeless powder, gave previously unheard of velocities and energies that delighted both hunters and target shooters alike. For years the jacketed bullet held sway over the American shooting sports, and those of the entire world for that matter.

Lately, though, an increasing number of shooters across the country have stepped back, pondered a while, and struck off in a new direction for at least some of their shooting. Did they continue further down the path of high velocity and high pressure? No. Instead, they turned to lead alloy bullets; especially the pistol shooters firing the practical pistol courses and the silhouette competitions.

Many factors contributed to this state of affairs, not the least of which was the discovery that guns were often even more fun to shoot when the loads were reduced. Cast bullets take to reduced loads like ducks take to water.

After a while it became clear that using cast bullet reloads provided another very tangible benefit—those reloads were a lot cheaper. Not only were the bullets themselves a fraction of the cost of jacketed bullets, but gun barrels were lasting much longer, too. Perhaps the most important benefit of all this shooting was that the shooters were improving their skills through more range time.

Bullet casting is sometimes overcomplicated by its more enthusiastic proponents, and draped in the

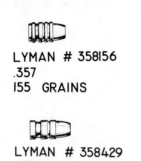

LYMAN # 358156
.357
155 GRAINS

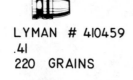

LYMAN # 410459
.41
220 GRAINS

LYMAN # 358429
.357
168 GRAINS

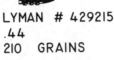

LYMAN # 429215
.44
210 GRAINS

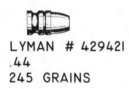

LYMAN # 410610
.41
215 GRAINS

LYMAN # 429244
.44
255 GRAINS

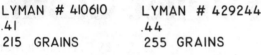

LYMAN # 429421
.44
245 GRAINS

Some typical cast-lead bullet sizes for handguns.

veils and mists of the occult arts by others. The truth lies at the opposite end of that spectrum. With proper, and easily obtainable, equipment and a reference library of only a few books, also easily obtainable, anyone reading this chapter can produce good, serviceable cast bullets at the first sitting.

Neophyte bullet casters who have the best results are those who enter the hobby willing to learn a few new things, while shooting their favorite firearms a lot more for a lot less. Those who accept the following basic guidelines do best:

1. The sized and lubricated cast bullet must slightly exceed the measured groove diameter of your gun barrel.

2. Cast bullet designs toward the heavy end of suitability for your caliber will tend to be the most accurate. Lighter bullets are often quite accurate, too, but best left until you have a bit of experience under your belt.

3. There is no all-round best bullet alloy. From harder to softer, they all produce a good quality, serviceable bullet. Success depends upon the caster, who must not drive the bullet beyond the limits of the alloy. More specifically, the softer the bullet metal, the lower the velocity.

4. Use the proper lubricant. For all but low-velocity pistol loads, I recommend the alox/beeswax lubricant sold by a number of companies, including Lyman, Lee and RCBS.

5. Buy the best equipment you can afford. Upgrade when you can. In bullet casting, as in everything else, you get what you pay for.

The key to an easy introduction is starting out with the proper equipment. The beginning caster needs a number of basic casting items for good results: mould and handles, melting pot, pouring ladle, ingot mould, casting mallet and a lubricator/sizer with the appropriate top punch and sizing die.

Your first mould purchase will probably depend upon how strongly you are committing yourself to casting. The Lee aluminum moulds, which include handles, are an inexpensive buy. However, they usually do not last nearly as long as the more expensive steel moulds offered by Lyman or RCBS. Talk to other casters, then make your choice.

You can economize on a melting pot if you wish. A simple iron pot capable of holding about eight pounds of metal is all you need. You can use it on the kitchen stove, which I don't recommend because of the smell. It's better to heat the pot on a camp stove outside. The mobility and versatility of the small pot can actually be a convenience. You're not tied to an electrical outlet. However, the electric pots offer a great deal more capacity and sophistication. With the bigger bottom-pour pots you can dip bullet metal with a ladle, or pour it from the bottom of the pot directly into the mould using the bottom-pour valve system. Additionally, the thermostat on these pots is calibrated with the scale on the control plate, so you can note temperature settings for future use. A handy option for the Lyman Mould Master XX is the mould gate. This device is attached to the furnace legs and serves to align and support mould blocks while casting from the bottom-pour valve.

The pouring ladle, or dipper, is a good, inexpensive item. These are offered by Lee, Lyman and RCBS. You should have a dipper on hand even if you buy one of the bottom-pour electric furnaces. Bullet casters are about equally divided between those who favor the dipper, and those who prefer a bottom-pour pot.

You'll need some sort of mallet with which to strike the mould's sprue plate to cut off the bullet's sprue. A hammer handle will do the job. Just be sure that you don't use any object that will mar or dent the mould. Lyman and RCBS offer a casting mallet which is weighted toward the striking end, and these work very well. Or, make your own.

The ingot mould is another important part of your basic casting equipment. Empty your pot or furnace into this mould at the end of a casting session and produce easily managed one-pound ingots which can be marked as to metal type, then stored. They're small enough to fit into all melting pots and furnaces.

Most experienced bullet casters agree that the sizer/lubricator is essential for perfectly finished bullets. For example, the tool not only swages the bullet to size, but will also put in a gas check (if needed) and lubricate the bullet. Thanks to the interchangeability of sizing dies and top punches, the Lyman or RCBS lube/sizers can handle just about any sizing chore, and produce clean, concentric cast bullets ready for loading.

For safety, every caster should wear stout safety garb. No casting should be done unless the caster is protected by sturdy gloves and safety glasses. Flying droplets of molten lead can cause very serious injuries to the eyes and face. The Lyman Safety Kit contains gloves, apron, safety glasses and other useful protective items.

Bullets can be cast and processed in the same area in which you reload—if you're very careful. All primers and propellants should be cleaned up and containers sealed and put away in the proper place. There are no special fixtures needed. A folded towel will cushion the bullets as they fall from the mould. An old box will serve to catch the sprue and rejects.

MELTING AND FLUXING BULLET METAL

To melt the lead you will, of course, need a suitable heat source capable of heating the metal to about 750 or 800 degrees Fahrenheit. A sturdy cast-iron pot to hold the metal, and a heat source such as a kitchen or camp stove, for instance, will suffice. An electric furnace is preferable, but may be financially unfeasible at first. The electric furnace is cleaner, safer and more convenient and its adjustable thermostat controls the temperature. The same melting and fluxing procedure is followed for blending alloys and casting actual bullets.

Heat the metal for about 20 minutes until it becomes a free-flowing liquid. Next comes fluxing to clean the metal of dirt and dross (impurities). One way to flux the metal is to drop a small bit of tallow, beeswax or bullet lubricant into the mixture. A smoky gas will rise from the top of the pot, which should be burned off immediately with a match. A much more pleasant fluxing procedure is to use a dry substance, such as Marvelux. This eliminates smoke and greasy fumes and produces a good flux. This method is preferable to the burn-the-smoky-gas technique.

Be sure to stir the mixture with the dipper regardless of the fluxing technique used. As you stir, hold the dipper as you would a soup spoon and lift it out of the molten metal with each stir. This seems to help the flux.

The surface of metal that has been properly fluxed will be almost mirror bright and flecked with small particles of black and brown impurities. These impurities should be skimmed off and discarded. Leave the dipper in the molten metal so it stays hot.

CASTING BULLETS

After the metal is hot enough to pour easily from the dipper, and has been fluxed, it is ready for casting. Keep a casting mallet or hardwood stick about ten inches long handy for opening the mould after casting. Also, pad an area of your bench or outside table with an old piece of toweling or carpet. This will soften the fall of the hot bullets as they drop from the mould and prevent them from being damaged. And, they won't roll around.

When it comes time for the actual casting, I suggest the following method: Half fill the dipper with metal and place the spout of the dipper against the pouring hole in the mould's sprue plate. Holding the mould and dipper together, slowly turn the mould upright while pouring with the dipper.

Casting via the bottom pour valve on an electric furnace will require a different technique. Instead of holding the mould tight against the external bottom pour valve and lifting the operating lever to release molten lead, it is often better to leave a little space between the mould and the valve, but no more than an inch. This latter method allows a good sprue puddle to form and, in some circum-

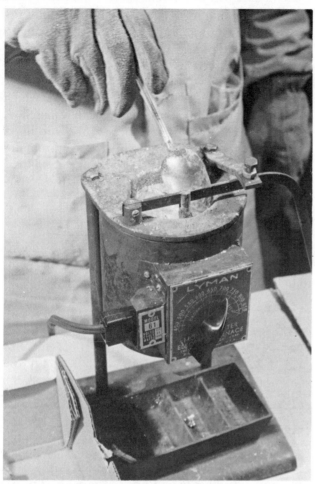

An old kitchen spoon makes a fine tool to use in cleaning the surface of the molten lead. The spoon's shape and size make its use a bit handier than a lead dipper.

stances, may enhance the escape of air from the mould as the molten lead pours in. By chance, if you find the lead is solidifying in the bottom pour valve, increase the pot temperature. Keep an ingot mould handy to catch drips.

The surplus metal that collects on the top of the mould is called sprue. After it hardens, which takes only seconds, pick up the hardwood stick and rap the sprue cutter sharply several times. This will cut the sprue free from the base of the bullet. Drop the sprue into a cardboard box or other receptacle. Separate the mould handles and let the bullet fall to the pad. If the bullet does not drop out readily, use the casting mallet or hardwood stick to tap the hinge pivot to shake the bullet loose. Never strike the mould blocks themselves, or the sprue cutter at this stage.

It is very important to have a generous amount of sprue. As the bullet cools, it contracts and draws down metal from the molten sprue above. If the sprue hardens first, or there isn't enough of it to cover the cavity opening, the bullet will form imperfectly. Conversely, cutting a still-molten sprue damages the base of the bullet and often creates a buildup of smeared alloy between the cutoff plate and mould blocks.

When you start with a cold mould, your first bullets will be imperfect. Repeating the casting process will bring the mould up to the proper temperature. Some casters prefer to preheat the mould by placing it on the rim of the furnace or alongside the lead pot on the stove.

Examine your first few batches of bullets for the following: Wrinkled bullets indicate that the mould, and/or metal, is too cool. Frosted bullets indicate that the mould, and/or metal is too hot. Good bullets should be clean, sharp and perfect replicas of the mould. Keep any imperfect bullets aside. Return these and the sprue to the melting pot after you've finished casting.

The pouring spout on the ladle and the pouring hole on the sprue cutter are designed to fit together closely.

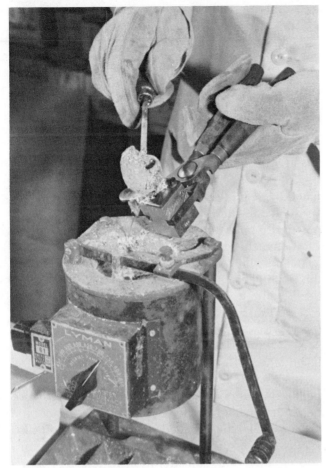

After the spout and mould are together snugly pour the lead into the mould by slowly rotating the block/ladle unit with the ladle on top. Experiment with your rate of pour to obtain the best results.

Weigh your best bullets on a reloading scale. This will reveal any air pockets that may have formed in the bullet, making it underweight or out of balance. The actual weight of your bullets will depend on the composition of the bullet metal, which may vary slightly from lot to lot. Rejected bullets can be saved and recast.

In casting for maximum accuracy, the byword is consistency. Know the materials and procedures with which you are dealing and be consistent in every aspect. In experimenting with the variables of alloy, lubricant and sized diameter, alter only one of these variables at a time. In this way, any changes in performance can be linked to their cause. (This same caution applies to cartridge cases, primers and propellants, and is covered elsewhere in this book.)

Over the years, many cast-bullet shooters who have been interested in pure accuracy experimentation have advocated the use of only single-cavity

blocks on the premise that multi-cavity blocks do not produce truly identical bullets from their individual cavities. It is my opinion that the vast majority of bullet casters are best served by well-made multi-cavity moulds—particularly double-cavity. The only shooters who might truly benefit from a single-cavity mould are those who are shooting state-of-the-art bench rest guns using advanced reloading techniques.

Sizing bullets is merely the process of swaging cast bullets to a diameter that corresponds to, or slightly exceeds, the groove diameter of your gun. Bullet sizing also ensures that the bearing bands of each bullet in the group are perfectly round. Because no metal is removed from the bullet during sizing, its weight remains unchanged.

Generally speaking, the less sizing a bullet requires, the more accurately it will shoot. According

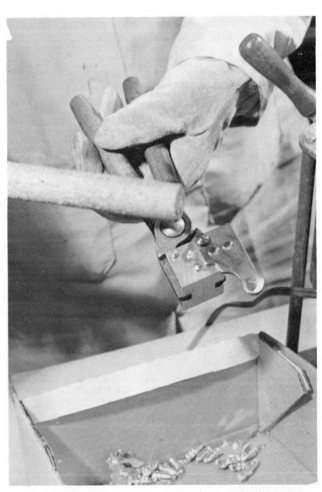

Hitting the hinge pin is the best way to shake loose a sticking bullet. Don't land random blows on the blocks or sprue cutter since this could cause deformation and affect the quality of the bullets.

to cast-bullet shooters, .002″ is the most a bullet can be sized and retain its accuracy. Whether .002″ is indeed that significant is only part of the overall question. The real criterion is the actual groove diameter of your gun's barrel. Rifle bores should be measured both at the muzzle and just forward of the chamber mouth. Handguns should receive the same bore measuring, and revolvers should have each chamber mouth measured as well. The results of these tests should indicate where to start in the sizing process.

These measurements are obtained by slugging; driving a pure lead slug into the barrel or chamber mouth. Revolver owners may want to use just one at the muzzle, because maneuvering around the frame to introduce that second slug is tough. Each chamber in a revolver's cylinder can be slugged with the bullets marked to match their corresponding chamber.

Normally, sizing will be to the diameter that will match, or slightly exceed, the groove diameter just ahead of the chamber. Sometimes revolver shooters may be confused when they see a groove diameter larger than that of their gun's chamber mouths. They should select their first sizing die on the basis of barrel, not chamber, dimension.

The production of moulds to a customer's specifications is the domain of the custom mould maker, and even then there are few (if any) who will guarantee a perfectly round cast bullet from their moulds. And, of course, the cost of such a custom mould is much greater than those produced for general use. Therefore, the bullets that drop from most moulds are intended to be reduced in diameter and trued up by the sizing process.

Sizing cast bullets has been done in a number of ways over the years. Today, all sizing dies feature tapered leads which allow excess metal to be swaged, rather than shaved, into dimensional conformity. This produces better bullets.

The lubricant, as applied to the grooved body of a given bullet design, provides a film between the bullet metal and the walls of the bore of the gun. This film greatly reduces friction as the bullet travels down the barrel, and either eliminates or minimizes leading. When this film breaks down, for whatever reason, leading occurs and reduced accuracy follows.

Demands on lubricant performance increased when black powder cartridges were developed in the late 1800s. The bullets in these cartridges were a groove-filling mechanical fit in the bore and thus needed greater protection from friction than projectiles fired from smooth-bore muskets. The velocities of these early cartridges were relatively low, to 1500 feet per second, and it wasn't too difficult to find satisfactory lubricants for those soft alloy or pure lead bullets. With the development of smokeless powder, and the resulting modern cartridges, ammunition companies started to use jacketed bullets in order to realize the performance potential of the new propellants. These jacketed bullets eliminated the leading problem and provided additional resistance in the bore which caused the smokeless powder to burn better.

Today, there are more sophisticated lubricants available. Many shooters feel that the Alox/beeswax mixture, when mixed 50/50 to the NRA formula, is the best high-velocity lubricant available. But before you purchase the product, make sure it states that it is made to the NRA formula, or that it is comprised of 50/50 Alox/beeswax. Otherwise you may be buying a different formula. This particular NRA formula can take cast bullets up to almost 3000 feet per second under optimum conditions, but it is not necessary on loads under 1000 fps and another type of lubricant may be used for these loads. It also should be noted that alloy hardness is an important, and equally vital, consideration in terms of lubricant performance.

The procedures for reloading cast bullets are the same as those for jacketed bullets, with two minor exceptions: Wipe all lubricant from each bullet base, and use the Lyman M expander die to flare the mouths of your cartridge cases.

Above all, relax and enjoy your new-found hobby. Don't worry about a few wrinkles here or there. The vast majority of shooters will not be hampered by minor projectile irregularities.

As a footnote, I should add that for the latest reports on bullet casting, particularly for rifle applications, you should join the Cast Bullet Association. This growing national organization is comprised of shooters keenly interested in the cast bullet and all the attendant pleasures and problems. The bimonthly newsletter, which is really a magazine, is always chock-full of interesting reading and sources for specialty equipment. For more information, contact:

The Cast Bullet Association, Director of Membership, 141 Van Doren Road, Manassas, VA 22111.

Chapter 14

Rifle Accuracy—Consistency is the Word

by Mike Venturino

Accuracy is the culmination of many factors working together: the quality of the gun, the quality of the ammunition, the weather conditions prevailing on the day the gun is used and not least in importance, the skill of the shooter. However, when handloaded ammunition enters the picture another factor of extreme importance to the quest for accuracy is involved—consistency.

Rifle shooting is already a variable-ridden pastime, but when home-reloaded ammunition is used we have variables upon the variables and, in some extreme instances, they could be countless. In essence then, to achieve success in the accuracy department with a rifle the variables must be kept to an absolute minimum. That is called consistency, and consistency means accuracy.

Let's start at the beginning. Say, for instance, that you have a new rifle that you want to begin testing for accuracy using several different bullets and powders. What is the first step in preparing good quality handloads that will use the full potential of that rifle?

Perhaps the most important steps, and certainly the most time-consuming ones involved in putting together the best possible handloads, are those needed to prepare the cartridges for reloading. Here's the way I do it.

First off, before resizing each case I give it a visual inspection. In doing this I am looking for any imperfections such as cracks, a bright ring in front of the case head or any other imperfection. At times a case will show only the slightest trace of a case mouth crack and I am often tempted to try to squeeze one more reload out of it. But, that is defeating my own purpose for upon firing, that crack will enlarge and introduce one more variable into my ammunition specifications. As for the bright ring in front of the case head, that is a sign of impending case separation. Most often this occurs with belted magnum cases when the reloading dies are not adjusted correctly. It can also be a sign of excessive headspace in rimless-type cases. Any cases discovered with such a bright ring should be discarded because they are in danger of splitting and when that happens the escaping gas can be dangerous to the shooter.

Another important factor can be mixed brands of cases in the same batch of reloads. It is quite easy to get different brands of brass in the same caliber mixed, and this will not help the accuracy of your handloads. On the surface, or to an inexperienced reloader, the act of mixing brass by brand does not seem to be such a big deal. After all, is not a .30/06 case a .30/06 case regardless of the brand? Sure, brass of the same caliber by different makers can be reloaded and fired safely, but it is not all alike. Brass of the same caliber from various manufacturers can differ in thickness, hardness and in minor dimensional details. It is not *exactly* the same!

Once a reloader has his cases sorted by brand and any defective ones discarded, he must decide exactly how he wishes to resize those good cases. It is commonly assumed by many shooters that the best accuracy may come with cases that were fired in one particular rifle and then are neck sized only and used always in that rifle. There may be some truth in that because the cases are form fitted to that rifle's chamber. However, this idea of fitting the brass to one gun must also be tempered with some common sense.

For example, do you have more than one gun in that caliber? Is this ammunition going to be used only for casual shooting, or will it be used during an expensive, long-awaited hunt to faraway Alaska, or even Africa? In terms of consistency we can look at full-length or neck-sized brass in two ways. The neck-sized brass is form fitted to one gun which makes it uniform in that respect, also. The only way to really determine for yourself is to test your own guns with cases resized both ways: full length and just neck sized.

One of the most crucial steps in preparing accurate rifle handloads, and the one step that I detest the most, is case trimming. Brass cases tend to flow forward erratically upon firing. In severity, this stretching is regulated by the design of the various cartridge cases. For instance, a long-sloping case like the .220 Swift is more prone to stretching than one with straight sidewalls and a sharp shoulder angle like the .300 Weatherby Magnum. In between those two extremes are most of our other case designs such as the .30/06, 7mm Remington or the popular .243 Winchester.

After the cartridge cases are prepared, the next step is seating the primer; and this is a very important operation in preparing consistently accurate ammunition. If the primer is not seated completely in the case, some of the firing pin's force is drained away in seating it deeper. That can cause erratic ignition because each primer does not give off exactly the same force. On the other hand, by seating a primer too deeply the priming pellet inside can be crushed or otherwise injured. This can also cause improper ignition. The remedy for either of the above problems is to seat the primers correctly in the first place.

No matter how much effort one puts into seating his primers correctly, it is wasted effort if the wrong primer is selected for the type of powder or the cartridge. In this country we now have four sizes of primers: large rifle; small rifle; large pistol; small pistol. They come in standard types, magnum types, dual purpose types, bench rest types and so forth. For many shooting applications the ordinary standard type of primer is fine, but if one is willing to experiment he will usually find one primer or another that will suit his purposes best. For instance, some powders are harder to ignite than others. Magnum-type primers will usually be best with those. Contrary to what many think, the term magnum primer does not indicate that these primers should be used in magnum calibers. It means that they give a longer, hotter flame upon ignition, which in turn causes the powder to burn more consistently. Since my work causes me to use a chronograph with most of my shooting, I have seen evidence of this many times over. I have loaded sample strings of identical handloads except that standard and magnum primers were each used in one half of the loads. Depending on the type of powder used, the velocity variation has shown how the primer affected the load. At times I have seen loads that were giving velocity variations in excess of 100 fps with standard primers drop to under 50 fps variation with the substitution of a hotter primer.

In working up handloads for all my rifles I have found that it is best to choose a range of powders for testing with every bullet weight. An example would be either the common .222 Remington or the .30/06. If beginning a loading project for the .222 Remington, I would choose such powders as IMR-4198, Reloder 7, H-322 or IMR-3031. On the other hand, if I happened to be starting a new loading project in .30/06, I would begin with powders in the range of Winchester 760, H-4350, IMR-4350 or IMR-4831.

Before loading any case, check for neck splits and other possible problem areas.

will find a charge that gives better results in your particular rifle than any other.

Previously, the care required in seating new primers was mentioned, and the same holds true in weighing out the powder and seating the bullets. Some extra care in those departments goes a long way toward preparing the most consistent handloads. Your patience will be rewarded.

For example, some handloaders adjust their powder measures for the correct charge and then weigh out hundreds of charges without ever again checking the measure. I consider this incorrect. The adjustments on the powder measures can loosen with use, and I have seen this happen to the point that the measure was throwing several grains off in either direction. Also, with a great many powder measure designs the amount of powder metered out can vary with the level of the powder in the hopper. As the weight of the powder in the hopper gets lighter, the amount of powder measured out can get lighter. I feel that every tenth charge metered out should be checked for accuracy on a powder scale, at least, if not more frequently.

Bullet seating and bullet seating depth are factors that greatly influence the accuracy of handloads. Most ordinary bullet seating dies do a creditable job of getting the bullets into the cases. However, in the field of rifle shooting nowadays most of the reloading manufacturers have special bullet seating dies that ensure the bullet is placed in the case neck as straight as possible. I have not run tests to determine if straight-line bullet seaters make a vast difference, but in order to hedge my bets I use them for all my reloading of cartridges to be used in scope-sighted, bolt action rifles.

Bullet seating depth is one of the more mysterious aspects of assembling the best possible reload. With many types of rounds, the bullet's seating depth is dictated by the maximum overall allowable length of the cartridge. With other calibers, where the only bullets available have crimping grooves and the particular design requires a crimp, there is no leeway. You must crimp in the furnished groove and that, simply, is the bullet seating depth you must use.

Without crimping restrictions, the bullet may be placed in the case neck at the reloader's whim, within certain limits, then most often the best accuracy is gotten with the bullet's ogive as close to the rifling as possible. However, this is not a hard and fast rule. Other very knowledgeable reloaders have

From past experiences I would just about bet that IMR-4350 would be the frontrunner both in terms of accuracy and velocity. The reason I feel that both the powders I have stressed here are good in those respective size cartridges is that they tend to fill up the case right to the base of a seated bullet. This leaves no air space, which would be another variable to contend with.

Then, sticking with only one type of primer and one bullet at a time, I would vary my powders and charges. If the rifle is an accurate one, somewhere along the way one of those powders and charges will give better results than the others. That is because I have happened on the combination that is consistent; meaning that the powder charge and type have mated with the primer's power and the bullet's weight and resistance. That is when the groups round out, and stay consistently good!

Even after deciding on the right powder or range of powders for a particular cartridge, the choices are not over yet. We must pick the right amount of that powder within its safe limits. In large volume cases I tend to go up and down in half-grain increments, but in the smaller cartridges I go by about two tenths of a grain. Somewhere in that testing you

A great many types of powders are available and a wide range should be tried in any particular rifle in order to find the best load.

reported good results with the bullets backed off from the rifling somewhat. This matter of bullet seating depth is certainly a variable. Personally, my reloads start with the bullet about $1/16$ inch from the rifling, and if this seating doesn't produce tight groups, I try experimenting with varied (ever so slight) bullet seating depths.

In order to find where the beginning of the rifling is, a bullet is purposely seated too long in the case and that test cartridge is run into the chamber. If the bullet touches the rifling, the die seating stem is turned down a touch and another test round is tried. This trial and error method is repeated until the cartridge chambers. Then the seating stem is turned down again another pinch for good measure and test shooting is started.

There are two final steps I always take to make sure that I arrive at the best possible handload for a particular rifle. The first is testing. One cannot rely on specific information gleaned from a magazine. Sure, some recommendations work, but you should test your own guns. All this requires is a shooting area, a good bench rest and some sandbags. Test fire your guns with groups of either three or five

shots, depending on the weight of your barrel. Personally, I like to shoot 5-shot groups from varmint rifles and 3-shot groups from big game rifles. However, one group is not enough. Go for averages in your testing. If time is available, my preference is for five 3-shot groups or three 5-shot groups at the minimum. That gives me an average of 15 rounds fired of that particular handload.

Next, I would urge all reloaders to keep careful records of their work. Nothing is more frustrating than to know you are on the right track and progressing, and be called off the job for some reason. If the project is left for any length of time, and careful records are not kept, you may as well go back to the beginning. Most members of society have their minds cluttered with all sorts of information, and it is easy to lose track of details in cartridge reloading. I know this is true from previous experience.

Handloading is like any other facet of life in general. You get out of it rewards directly in proportion to the efforts you put into it. If the rifle handloader appreciates consistency at the reloading bench, he will reap the rewards in tighter groups at the target.

With everything ready to go, the shots are fired from a steady rest for both accuracy and velocity readings.

Chapter 15

The Twenty-two Centerfires

by Dick Eades

At one time, reloading metallic cartridges was a universal practice. During the early stages of black powder cartridges, virtually everyone who used a gun reloaded. It simply wasn't practical to buy factory ammunition and discard the once-fired brass. Both price and convenience dictated reloading as a matter of course.

Gradually, as shooting became more of a pastime than a necessity, reloading dropped off and a far smaller percentage of shooters were also handloaders. Today, reloading is enjoying a renaissance. For most of the same reasons as their grandfathers', contemporary shooters are becoming reloaders.

Reloading is a bit more complicated than it was in the black powder era; you can't just scoop a case full of powder and stuff in a bullet and primer. There are many choices to be made regarding the type of powder, primer and bullet style. Modern reloaded ammunition is far more precise than yesteryear's.

Who reloads ammunition and why? Target shotgunners and pistol shooters who burn thousands of rounds per year reload for economy's sake. Big game hunters who may fire only a handful of cartridges in a year often handload because they have learned that tailoring a load to their firearm assures top accuracy and performance. Bench rest shooters are invariably reloaders since they cannot squeeze the last bit of accuracy from their rifles with factory ammunition.

Of all hunters, one fraternity is far more likely than any other to handload ammunition. Show me a varmint hunter and I'll show you a handloader. As a class, varminters are almost as fanatical about accuracy as are bench-resters. Add to that their concern with bullet performance at extreme ranges and you have about the most demanding shooter around. Many varminters won't even buy factory ammo to get brass. They start with virgin, unprimed brass and work up from there.

A half-century ago, reloading ammunition was looked upon as a risky business. Stuffing your own ammo was thought to be in the same category as going over Niagara Falls in a barrel—foolish and dangerous. A quarter-century ago, handloading was accepted as not necessarily dangerous, but just a method of producing inexpensive ammunition, which was still inferior to factory ammo of the day. Currently, handloading is accepted as the only way to obtain topflight accuracy and performance from any gun.

Today's reloader has the benefits of a vast array of bullets, powders, primers and equipment designed to make his handloads far superior to average factory-loaded fodder. To the varmint shooter, this means he can turn out ammunition capable of pinpoint accuracy at ranges greater than his father ever thought about.

Shooters who enjoy varmint hunting but have held back on reloading due to the cost of equipment and components haven't been keeping up with what's happened in the reloading market. Sure, you can spend a fortune on reloading equipment, but you can also get started for surprisingly little. Even the simplest reloading tools are capable of turning out excellent ammunition. It's possible to recover your entire investment through the savings realized after reloading just a few boxes of ammo.

Consider what is involved in reloading a metallic cartridge. First, after firing the factory round, the case must be saved and inspected. Provided there are no cracks or other defects, it can be reloaded.

Reloading consists of several steps, all of which are essential to production of high-quality handloads. Since the cartridge case expanded to fill the rifle's chamber when it was fired, exterior dimensions must be reduced so it will chamber easily after it is refilled. The spent primer must be removed from the primer pocket, a new primer inserted and propellant metered into the case. Finally, a new bullet must be seated.

My first reloading tool was manufactured by Lyman and sold, complete with dies, for less than $10. The same tool, the Lyman 310, is offered today but the price is about six times what I paid for my Lyman Ideal. Other important steps in handloading are case trimming, primer pocket cleaning, case mouth chamfering and the decision as to whether or not to crimp the bullet in place. All these procedures can be accomplished with either expensive, bench-mounted tools or small hand tools.

In addition to the basic loading tool and dies, the beginning reloader will need a few additional items. First, he must have a good quality powder scale unless he plans to stick with moderate loads which may be dipped or measured. Next, he will require a loading block to keep his cartridges upright and separated. A powder funnel is essential for placing charges in the cases. Various other accessories will be accumulated along the way.

Handloading for .22 centerfire rifles is an excellent way to determine if you have the aptitude and interest to expand your handloading facilities. Chances are, once you have tried, it, you will continue. If, for some reason, you decide to stay with factory ammunition, you will have a very small investment in one of the simpler hand tools.

Probably the most popular and certainly the least expensive hand tool on the market today is offered by Lee Precision. The Lee tool, complete to load a single caliber, is priced at around $16. Cartridge cases are forced into and out of the dies by use of a mallet and punch. Primer removal, primer seating and bullet placement are also accomplished by use of a mallet.

Other types of reloading tools accomplish exactly the same thing but they do it with a bit more ease. Bench tools provide greater leverage and require less effort than does the small Lee tool, but they cost many times as much, and make ammo that is not a bit better. Bench presses are offered in several forms, from the basic C to O types with optional accessories such as primer feeds, auto cartridge ejectors and other refinements which speed up the loading process. Turret-type tools hold a full set of dies and eliminate removal and replacement of dies while loading a single caliber. Some incorporate automatic indexing and automatic powder measuring. Such conveniences cost money.

For the loader who wants to turn out the greatest number of cartridges in a given time, progressive tools are the ultimate type. Progressive tools allow installation of a full set of dies that are used in rotation to turn out a loaded round. A progressive tool performs an operation on each of several cases with each handle stroke. After the turret or stage is filled, progressive tools will complete a loaded round with each stroke of the handle. Most progressives include both automatic primer feeding and powder metering and are therefore capable of loading hundreds of rounds per hour.

For purposes of this chapter, I borrowed three Sako rifles. In order to illustrate reloading of .22 centerfires, three types of tools were used to load for one rifle each. The three rifles were in calibers

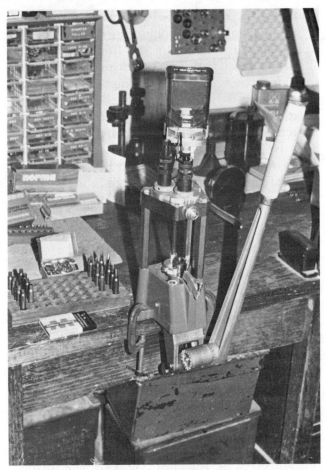
Lee's new Turret Press is a favorite tool with author Eades.

.222 Remington, .223 Remington and the .22-250.

Although all rifles were Sakos, each was a different model: the .222, a Sako Standard Model; the .223, a Sako Varmint Model; and the .22-250, a Sako Deluxe. (List prices for the guns vary from $435 to $525, but for complete specs on these fine products drop a line to Stoeger Industries, 55 Ruta Court, South Hackensack, NJ 07606.) To load for each of these guns, I decided to use a Lee Loader in the .223 caliber, a Bonanza Co-Ax press in .22-250 and a Lee turret press in the remaining .222. These three tools represent the various basic types available and provided a good opportunity to examine the workings of each.

Each rifle was fitted with a Simmons 3-9X variable scope on Sako mounts. The scopes were samples from the new line and, although each is different, all are well suited to varmint shooting. The scope on the .222 was a Model 1028 Wide Angle. The .223

had a standard Model 1010 and the .22-250 carried a Model 1038 Wide Angle with a 40mm objective lens. The entire Simmons line is new on the American market and includes optical goodies such as shooting glasses, spotting scopes and binoculars, as well as rifle scopes. All are top quality and reasonably priced.

Before starting reloading operations, I fired each rifle with an assortment of factory ammunition from Remington, Federal, Winchester, Frontier and Norma. Shooting factory loads served two purposes: it supplied me with empty brass for reloading; and records of accuracy for each rifle provided a standard for measuring the accuracy of my handloads.

Starting with the .223 and a Lee Loader, I selected Norma brass for my first box of reloads. Since I would use only the Lee Loader, I chose Hodgdon H-380 powder, which is recommended for the 1.9cc dipper furnished by Lee. A scoop of 1.9cc of H-380 will weigh approximately 27.5 grains and should propel a 50-grain .224 bullet from the muzzle at about 3000 fps.

After inspecting the brass cases, I ran them through the Lee decapping chamber and used a mallet and the furnished punch to deprime all the cases. Using the same mallet, I drove the first case into the tool with a series of short taps. Next, the locating ring was used to seat a primer by tapping on the priming rod.

The Lee tool was next placed on the decapping chamber and the priming rod used to tap the case free. At this point, the case had been neck sized and reprimed. Leaving the case in the tool and resting on the decapping chamber, I next added one level measure of powder.

A bullet was started into the case by dropping it into the open end of the Lee Loader. The bullet was fully seated by light taps from the mallet against the bullet seater, which is a hollowed rod attached to the priming chamber. After seating the bullet, the finished cartridge was removed from the Lee tool. The last six steps were repeated until the entire box of ammunition was reloaded. Although I am not accustomed to using the Lee Loader, this entire box of ammo was loaded in about a half-hour. With practice, I am certain additional speed could be developed. The accuracy of the load was checked later during a shooting session.

Turning next to my favorite press, a Bonanza

The Bonanza Co-Ax press, Model B-1, was used by the author to load all of his reloads in the .22-250.

Co-Ax Model B-1, which retails for about $100 less dies, I reloaded the first box of .22-250s. For this operation, I selected Winchester Ball Powder and 50-grain bullets from Sierra. Having no need for maximum velocity loads, I tried to duplicate factory velocities. I weighed each charge after measuring it from a Bonanza Bench Rest powder measure. Thirty-nine grains of W/W 760 powder gave a velocity of about 3650 fps. Each charge was dropped from the measure light, then scaled to correct weight.

Cartridges loaded on this press were set aside with the .223s for later accuracy tests. I'll have to admit to a slight edge with this load since I frequently use it in another .22-250. The time needed to produce a single box of cartridges with this press and scale was just about the same as that for the Lee Loader. When loading great numbers of rounds,

reloading speed should be better with the press but, for a single box, there is almost no difference.

Loading procedures for the Bonanza press are similar to those with any bench press. First, each cartridge case is run through the decapping/sizing die where it is full-length resized and deprimed. Next, I primed all brass using a Lee hand primer rather than the priming post located on the press. This use of a separate tool for priming is purely one of personal taste. I prefer to use a hand tool to retain a "feel" for primer seating, but the bench tool can be used for priming. After all brass was reprimed, I arranged it in a tray, upside down for powder metering.

Withdrawing one case at a time from the loading block, I used the Bonanza measure to drop a charge of powder into the scale pan, then used a powder trickler to bring the charge up to proper weight. A small funnel was used to pour the powder from the pan into the case. As each cartridge was replaced in the loading block, it was mouth up, filled with powder and ready to receive a bullet. A quick visual inspection proved that there were no grossly overweight powder charges and that each case did contain powder. It sounds impossible to miss a case when charging but strange things happen when reloading a large quantity of ammunition so the seconds involved in visual inspection are well spent.

Finally, bullets were seated with the bullet seating die and each cartridge wiped free of lubricant before being boxed. At the same time, a final inspection was made of each loaded round to eliminate any that didn't look right. Like the powder charge inspection, this final look is probably unnecessary, but I find it comforting and the time spent negligible. It's part of my standard procedure.

My only turret loading tool is a new Lee turret press with an Auto-Disk powder measure and an Auto-Index device. Intended primarily for high-volume production of handgun loads, the Lee press lends itself well to use with short, moderate capacity rifle cartridges. Lee Precision does not recommend this press for rifle cartridge loading and assumes no liability for mishaps that may occur. In inspecting the press, I find no reason for its not being used for rifle cartridges aside from the limited number of powder charge choices, and the fact that it would easily be possible to "outrun" the machine's ability to drop powder uniformly. With care, the Lee turret tool is an excellent device for loading rifle car-

SHOOTING RESULTS—.22 CENTERFIRES

Sako Standard .223 Remington. Temperature, 68 degrees. Relative humidity, 42%

Factory Ammo—best three-shot group

Winchester –	–	–	–	50-grain PSP	–	–	–	–	1.30 inches
Remington –	–	–	–	50-grain PSP	–	–	–	–	1.25 inches
Frontier –	–	–	–	50-grain PSP	–	–	–	–	1.18 inches

Handloads—best three-shot group

W/W case, Sierra 52-grain HP, 19.5 grs of RE-7	–	–	–	–	–	1.10 inches
RP case, Sierra 50-grain PSP, 26.0 grs of BLC-2	–	–	–	–	–	1.19 inches
RP case, Speer 50-grain PSP, 25.0 grs of H-335	–	–	–	–	–	1.20 inches

Sako Varminter .222 Remington. Temperature, 56 degrees. Relative humidity, 45%

Factory Ammo—best three-shot group

Norma	–	–	–	–	50-grain PSP	–	–	–	–	1.30 inches
Federal	–	–	–	–	50-grain PSP	–	–	–	–	1.15 inches
Remington –	–	–	–	50-grain PSP	–	–	–	–	1.20 inches

Handloads—best three-shot group

W/W case, Speer 52-grain HP, 26.0 grs of BLC-2	–	–	–	–	–	1.10 inches
Norma case, Sierra 50-grain PSP, 25.0 grs of BLC2	–	–	–	–	–	0.95 inches
Federal case, Sierra 52-grain HPBT, 25.0 grs of BLC2 –	–	–	–	–	0.90 inches

Sako Deluxe .22-250 Remington. Temperature, 60 degrees. Relative humidity, 56%

Factory Ammo—best three-shot group

Frontier	–	–	–	–	55-grain FMJ	–	–	–	–	1.20 inches
Norma	–	–	–	–	50-grain PSP	–	–	–	–	1.25 inches
Winchester –	–	–	–	50-grain PSP	–	–	–	–	1.25 inches

Handloads—best three-shot group

Frontier case, Sierra 52-gr HPBT, 37.0 grs of W/W760–	–	–	–	–	1.20 inches
W/W case, Sierra 50-gr PSP, 28.0 grs of RE-7 –	–	–	–	–	1.15 inches
Norma case, Speer 55-gr PSP, 37.0 grs of H-380	–	–	–	–	–	1.30 inches

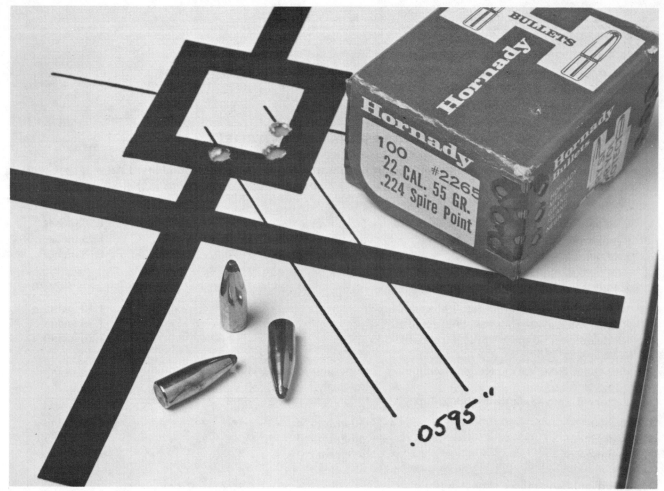

Today's modern .22 centerfires are capable of some really outstanding accuracy. This group was shot at 100 yards from a Weatherby .224 Varmintmaster.

tridges. It may be used with or without the automatic powder metering system and/or the automatic indexing provision. Many rifle ammo loaders prefer to use the tool without the extras.

In use, the Lee tool accepts a set of dies and powder measure, then rotates to bring each in turn over a case as the handle is pulled. In other words, three strokes are required to load a cartridge. Unlike some turret tools, the Lee was designed for strength, simplicity and price appeal.

Conventional loading dies were used on the Lee press, and powder was selected on the basis of an easy-metering powder that happened to match one of the powder disc apertures. My load was 19.5 grains of Hercules RelodeR 7 powder behind a 50-grain bullet. This load offers a velocity of approximately 3000 fps at safe operating pressures. The cases for the first box loaded on the Lee press were Winchester. The bullets were 50-grain Speer HPs.

A trip to the range with my new handloads quickly proved that each one was fully as accurate as a comparable factory load. Each rifle equalled or surpassed the accuracy obtainable with fresh factory ammunition. I was not surprised at this except in the case of the .223s, which were loaded on the Lee Loader. None of the powder used in these loads was weighed. Instead, it was measured with the dipper furnished with the loading tool.

After firing these reloads, I returned to the loading bench and checked several scooped charges by weighing each on a powder scale. To my surprise, variation from scoop to scoop was less than 0.3 grain, with most charges varying less than 0.2 grain. Although most reloaders attempt to keep their powder charges within a 0.1 grain tolerance, the slight additional difference caused by dipping had no apparent effect on accuracy.

Chapter 16

Just Starting Out? Try the .30/06 Springfield

Most rifle cartridges come and go depending on the mood of the shooting public. Old-line calibers such as the .257 Roberts, 7 × 57 Mauser and the .300 Holland and Holland were with us in full strength before the magnum age. Then "magnum mania" set in, which brought on the belted case and Monte Carlo and California stocks.

Not so with the .30/06 Springfield. This everlasting favorite has been with us since the turn of the century and is still going strong. Part of the reason is because it was a military cartridge. This meant that tons upon tons of surplus military brass came on the market, especially after a major war. But a big share of this cartridge's popularity is the fact that just about every rifle maker in this country chambers one model or another for the .30/06.

Officially, the handle given to this round by the armed forces is Caliber .30, Model 1906, Mark I. Briefly, from a historical standpoint, the military got the itch for a round that could top what they were using in the Krag rifle. A forerunner to the '06 was a rimless version dubbed the New Army

Rimless, Caliber .30, mentioned in a 1899 catalog. However, because of the powders available, velocity was disappointing, hardly much over the Krag, even with an improved version in 1903 loaded with a 220-grain bullet that traveled at 2300 feet per second. More was needed.

A few more years of experimenting brought on the lighter 150-grain bullet backed by a charge of Pyro-DG powder. This was an improvement over straight Pyro, which lacked the stabilizer diphenylamine. In 1914, the title was changed to Military Rifle Powder #20. But whatever the nomenclature, by war's end various plants were turning out close to a million pounds of it each day, seven days a week. Combining this powder with the 150-grain projectile edged the velocity up to 2700 fps.

From then on we have a success story just short of phenomenal. From rifles to loading equipment and everything in between, the .30/06 fan has never had it so good. All the famous names in "rifledom," starting with Alpine, BSA and Browning and ending with USRAC (Winchester) and Weatherby, all

Lining up the Oehler skyscreens so that they register every shot downrange.

produce fine bolt action rifles worthy of the inherent accuracy of this extraordinary cartridge. If you're not happy with the standard bolt-type, rifles can be procured in either single-shot, pump, automatic or high-priced custom grades.

Let's cite a few examples. I'll try to hit all of the popular makes, but don't feel slighted if I miss yours. The '06 is chambered by so many manufacturers that it would be easier to mention those that don't market the caliber.

We've already mentioned Alpine and BSA, so let's go on to Browning Arms. Many of us remember the fine turnbolts produced for Browning in Belgium a few years back. The mere mention of the Safari, Medallion or Olympian grades brings tears to my eyes because at the time my investment capitol was very low with raising a family and all, and owning one of these jewels was out of the question. An era passed.

But times change. Browning has brought on a new model called the Browning Lighting Bolt. Recently redesigned to get rid of a few bumps and bulges, this beauty has that famous Browning look, an aluminum channel in the forend to prevent warping and, of course, is chambered for the .30/06 Springfield. If an automatic is your choice, the famed Browning BAR is available in three grades to suit the most discriminating '06 user.

Chaplin is represented in the custom field, but at $4,600 plus per copy, it's not for everyone's gun rack. The Colt Sauer had been around for quite a while, is handsome and, with its novel bolting system, is very accurate. Still made in Germany, this baby retails at close to $1,200, depending on the caliber and options.

DuBiel makes a honey of a rifle, again custom-built and, after examining many samples, worth every penny, in my opinion. H&R's new centerfire

For range testing the .30/06, the author chose the Ruger M77 bolt action rifle with a Redfield 2-7X scope mounted on it.

model, the Model 340, is priced for the average hunter and has a classic style stock with a Mauser-type action. While on the Mauser action, the Mark X is marketed in this country by Interarms and is available in six models, all of which include the .30/06, except for the Alaskan. This one is for really big game—in .375 and .458 only!

Our oldest gunmaker, Remington Arms, offers quite a selection in this caliber. Heading the list in over-the-counter sales is the 700 BDL. Sporting a high gloss finish and super accuracy for an out-of-the-box sporter, it currently retails for a nickel under $422. Moving down the line one notch is the 700 ADL—same action, fewer frills. For the more conservative shooter, the Classic should fill the bill. To finish out the selection, all .30/06 entries are available in the pump series—Model Six and 7600, the automatics—Model Four and 7400, and super

Here, you can see why it is very important to size all cases before you load them. Note the difference in the necks from factory brass right out of the box (on the right).

Priming is very important. This is the Pacific Double 0-7 press with the novel 30-degree easy access opening.

custom grades made in the Custom Shop at Ilion, New York.

Close on the heels of the Remington for first place status is Ruger's fine Model 77. Classic in appearance, the rifles are finished in a soft satin sheen and hand-checkered. They go a long way in providing excellent quality for the money. One of my personal favorite 77s, and the subject of this handloading exercise, carries a 22-inch tube.

Sako and Savage are both old-line companies who pride themselves on fine workmanship and value to the consumer. Sako, whose rifles are imported from Finland, offers a variety of models in plain and fancy grades. Savage, of course, has been providing the American shooter with hard-working tools of the sport for decades.

United States Repeating Arms Company (US-RAC) has made a grand entry into the field after taking over the old Winchester line. Still licensed to use the Winchester name, the company has three

models chambered for the ought six. One is the new Featherweight, weighing in around 6 ¾ pounds, with real cut checkering and a deep bluing on all metal parts. The other two are the Model 70 Westerner, and the Model 70 XTR Sporter complete with the not-often-found 24-inch barrel.

No list would be complete without the mention of Weatherby products. Long a favorite of American shooters, the strong Mark V rifle is available in the .30/06 chambering. Featuring a 54-degree bolt lift, extra fancy stocks and combining excellent accuracy due to the hammer-forged barrels, this rifle is hard to beat in all departments. Another grade in the Weatherby line is Vanguard, a medium-priced rifle in three models. Although two Vanguard models have slightly heavier barrels than most, nevertheless, with very little attention, they will group very nicely all day long.

Other .30/06 rifle designs would include the single-shot, pump or slide, semi-automatic, drilling and double rifle. A visit to your local gun dealer will reveal a broad selection to meet your needs and desires. Keep a tight grip on your charge card.

Commercial ammunition is yet another slice of the '06 pie. A random sampling from ammo makers such as Federal, Frontier, Norma, PMC, Remington and Winchester shows that right now approximately 29 commercial loadings are available for over-the-counter sales. From the little Accelerators, on to 100-, 130-, 150-, 165-, 180-, 200- and 220-grain loadings, the .30/06 of today is made to take on anything from mice to moose.

Handloading possibilities will tax your imagina-

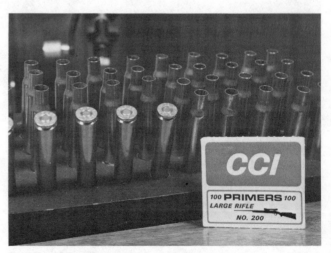

For all powders in the testing program, the author found the standard CCI 200 primers to perform faultlessly.

Lot numbers have a high priority when it comes to shooting tight groups over the long haul. Always purchase enough brass with the same code for good test results.

fer, as well as makes, plus you have to contend with removing that military crimp around the primer. For consistent results, brass turned out from the mills of Federal, Remington or Winchester serve the task very well. All are drawn from top-quality brass yielding cartridge cases of uncompromisingly good quality.

It doesn't really matter what brand you buy, as long as it's all the same brand. Purchase a minimum of six boxes for the initial range testing and subsequent loading sessions. Five boxes (100 rounds) are always used in one bunch, making sure you keep these especially for this particular rifle. The reasoning behind this will be mentioned later. The last or sixth box are spares. These are called on in the event of loss or die damage, which sometimes happens in the neck or shoulder area. One last reminder when purchasing brass: Buy the same lot number. This is the number or prefix stamped on the inside of the box denoting the run or date manufactured. Inside volume can differ between lot numbers, affecting test stats later.

For priming the '06, my own experiences with this round and the powders it uses only confirm my strong opinion of the CCI 200 standard primers. If you show a preference for slow powders in the IMR-4831 or MRP ranges, or possibly frequently hunt in very cold weather, by all means change to the magnum types. But if you go this route, please remember to drop your charge weights a bit, then watch for pressure signs on the buildup.

Before you even think about priming or charging cases, size all the cases first. Dies made by Lyman, Pacific or RCBS fill the bill nicely here. This

tion! With enough time on your hands, even in one lifetime, exhausting all the combinations would, in short order, put you in the funny farm halfway through your experiments. With firms such as Hornady, Nosler, Sierra and Speer grinding out bullets in basically the same weight structure as the factory offerings, plus others, the possible combinations of powders, primers, velocities, bullets and cases number into the thousands. Perhaps more!

Let's cite just one example using a rifle and some loads from the books, and record the results.

The rifle is a Ruger Model 77 in .30/06 with a 22-inch barrel. A regular production model, it is equipped with a 2–7X Redfield scope in Ruger rings. For all intents and purposes, nothing fancy, yet a rifle that suits my style of shooting to a "T."

As in any other handloading exercise, fresh brass is a definite asset. Military brass may be acceptable for some purposes, but remember that lots will dif-

To find one best hunting load, you will have to go through a large assortment of bullet weights.

The Hornady 180-grain bullet produced this grouping at 100 yards; a nice tight 1.25 inches.

not only squares up all the cases but brings them into one common denominator. They will all be the same dimension in the shoulder area, a very important factor.

Picking an average load in the manuals, load up the 100 cases with a mid-range powder in the 4320 to 4350 class, and fire them all in only one particular rifle. After the initial firing, the sizing die should be set so that it just touches the case shoulder. This technique was described in Chapter 5 complete with photos to further illustrate this step. With this system you not only guarantee case concentricity in the chamber, but headspacing, too, is kept to a minimum level, thus retarding any movement of the case, which often leads to incipient separation.

Powders play an important role in the life of any cartridge, the .30/06 being no exception. My preference is for the mid-range propellants, as already mentioned: IMR 4320 or IMR-4350. They not only

suit my requirements but deliver remarkable accuracy as well. You may want to go even slower or faster, but prior experience shows that a slower powder will yield lower velocities in some cases, ditto for too fast a propellant. Case volume also affects performance. While 60 grains of a slower powder like IMR-4831 fills the case to near compressed levels, my two favorites top out in the shoulder area. The net result here is increased velocities plus excellent accuracy.

Let's talk about 30-caliber bullets. The .30/06 is blessed with a choice unrivaled in many other calibers. As of this printing we can count in the neighborhood of 55 different styles or shapes of projectiles suited to hunting with this cartridge. Not included would be the needle-nosed match bullets, available to the target shooters in weights equal to the big game projectiles.

For our testing I settled on bullets of 150, 165

After the smoke has cleared, careful analysis of all groups will show which combination of components is the better handload.

For the advanced hobbyist, these components can be called on to produce even better results if you have the time and patience.

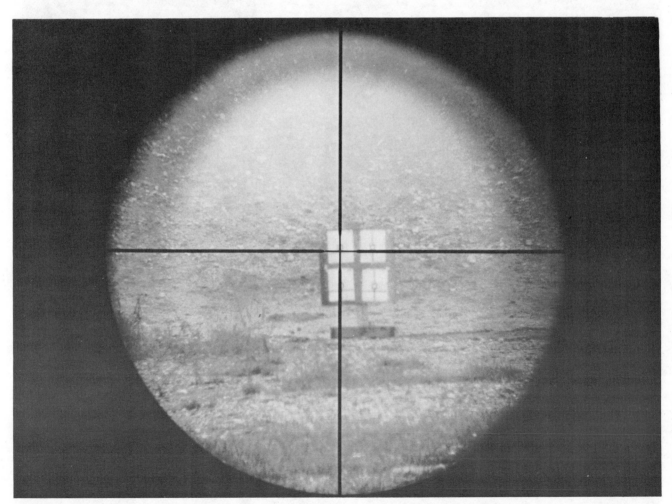

Shown here is what a target looks like at 100 yards seen through a scope. The smallest square you can see measures a scant 1.5 inches across.

RESULTS OF RANGE TESTING THE .30/60 SPRINGFIELD

Bullet	Bullet Weight (grains)	Powder	Powder Charge (grains)	OVAL	Velocity (fps)	Group
Speer	150	IMR-4320	51.1	3.300"	2740	1.00 inches
Speer	150	IMR-4320	52.1	3.300"	2756	2.50 inches
Hornady	150	IMR-4320	51.1	3.250"	2720	1.25 inches
Nosler	150	IMR-4320	51.1	3.275"	2710	1.25 inches
Speer	165	IMR-4350	55.0	3.300"	2595	1.75 inches
Speer	165	IMR-4350	55.0	3.200"	2628	1.00 inches
Hornady	165	IMR-4350	55.0	3.250"	2629	1.50 inches
Hornady	165	IMR-4350	56.0	3.250"	2689	2.00 inches
Nosler	165	IMR-4350	55.0	3.275"	2629	2.50 inches
Speer	180	IMR-4350	54.0	3.300"	2527	2.00 inches
Hornady	180	IMR-4350	54.0	3.250"	2573	1.25 inches

REDUCED .30/06 LOADS—SHOT FOR ACCURACY AT 50 YARDS

Bullet	Bullet Weight (grains)	Powder	Powder Charge (grains)	OVAL	Velocity (fps)	Group
Hornady	150	Unique	12.0	3.250"	1273	1.25 inches
Speer	150	SR-4759	24.0	3.300"	1967	0.75 inches

Notes:
OVAL—Overall cartridge length with bullet.
Primers—CCI 200

and 180 grains. This would be the middle-of-the-road selections with weights of 100-130 on the lower end, and 190-220 on the upper. Speer, Hornady and Nosler were represented.

Going through the manuals and picking the velocities that would fit my plans, I calculated an average powder charge that would fall under *maximum loads*. As with most cartridges, the most accurate and consistent loads were not maximum charges, but loads a few grains under. After charging, the bullets were then seated in accordance with the inner dimensions of the Ruger's chamber and leade (the "throat," or origin of the rifling).

At the range all testing went forward without any problems. Groups, as well as various combinations of powder and bullet pairings, started to fall into place. In all, looking back over my notes, roughly 36 different blocs of components were necessary to get a dozen decent loads that could be considered for serious hunting chores.

Noting the chart, in the 150-grain range, the Speer product came in with the goods with an almost perfect 1-inch group. Clocking over the screens at 2740 fps (don't forget, we are using a 22-inch barrel here), this, combined with a calculated muzzle energy of 2501 foot pounds of energy, will provide any field hunter with a load paralleling that of the famous 130-grain .270 Winchester selection.

In the 165-grain weight class, your regular over-the-counter Hornady with 55.0 grains of 4350 led the pack producing a group held in a neat one and a half inches. The Speer Grand Slam—a specialized controlled expansion bullet—narrowed that down to an inch.

If I were hitting the game fields in pursuit of elk, caribou or the larger bears, the 180-grain Hornady spiced with 54.0 grains of IMR-4350 would go along. At 2573 fps, this little number generates approximately 2641 pounds of muzzle energy. Consulting our trajectory charts, we find that zeroing in this load at 300 yards will allow us to shoot dead on up to this point, then allow for a 14.6-inch drop at 400.

Want more versatility? Try reduced loads for plinking or small game hunting. Twenty-four (24.0) grains of SR-4759 will show 1967 fps on the Chronotach; 12.0 grains of Unique, 1273 fps. All propellants are under a 150-grain bullet, with recoil so mild it's hardly worth mentioning.

So there you have it. The .30/06 Springfield has been with us now since the turn of the century. In its time it has been proven in war, taken game from antelope to zebra, and has won more titles in competition than its true magnum brothers.

For the man on a budget, the old .30/06 is very efficient with just two powders: Du Pont's IMR-4320 and 4350.

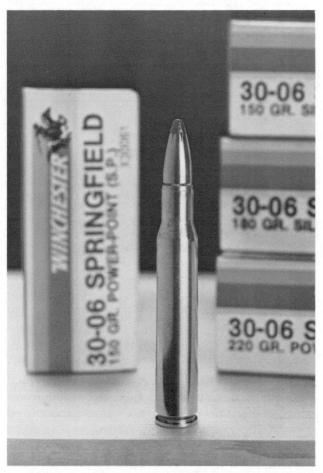

In many commercial forms, the .30/06 is a super performer.

Bullets shown here represent major brands, including Speer, Hornady and Nosler, with weights in the 150-, 165- and 180-grain class.

Chapter 17

A Rebounding Cartridge—the
7mm Mauser

The 7×57mm started its life in the early 1890s. First developed for a limited run of German Mausers, this round finally hit paydirt when an improved version of the Mauser chambered for this round was introduced in about 1893. The Spanish liked it and turned it into a government issue for all their troops.

The Americans got wind of this rifle/caliber combination when the Spanish-American War broke out in 1898. The rifle offered decent accuracy and mild recoil, and the Spanish seemed to be doing very well with it. The Yanks, on the other hand, were still hefting the .30-40 Krag, and in some cases the older single-shot .45-70s, which led to some disastrous results for our side.

About this time, the Americans started their search for a new military cartridge, which eventually led to our present-day .30/06. It doesn't take long to realize that by stretching the 7mm Mauser case a mere 5 millimeters, then opening up the neck to .308, you have a .30/06 Springfield. At the onset it was called the .30-03. Later, minute design changes in the neck area, followed by a bullet loading of 150 grains, gave us the .30/06 that we are so familiar with today.

In any event, after the war, hunters started to look at the 7×57 with an eye toward big game hunting. The famous W.D.M. Bell used this round almost exclusively on elephants, knocking down a thousand of them with precise brain shots. Now, I'm not advocating clearing the north forty of rogue elephants with the 7×57, but it does fuel the one man, one gun theory. Later, greats like Major Jim Corbett and Jack O'Connor would find favor with this particular 7mm. The former used it in India from 1920 to 1940; the latter, worldwide on his hunts for sable, gemsbok and zebra. Both often remarked on its inherent accuracy and pleasantness to shoot.

I agree wholeheartedly. In fact, I think so much of the cartridge that I had Bishop build a custom rifle for me in this caliber complete with all the trimmings, and equipped with a long 24-inch barrel. The gun is a sweetheart to shoot and considering

Author Trzoniec thought so much of the 7mm Mauser cartridge that he had Bishop Stocks make a rifle for him based on the trusted Mauser action. That's a Leupold 6X scope topping off the rig.

the two feet of cold steel sticking out front, still handles great in the field.

But of late new things have been popping up all around us in the firearms business. Take, for example, the slow trend toward shorter barrels. You see it everywhere. While years ago we had 24- and 26-inch tubes (and still do), today's shooter can get standard barrel lengths in the form of 22 or even 20 inches, if he wants.

Now that last one really turned me on! Especially since it was available in a real favorite of mine—a Ruger Number One International. This gun is Mannlicher-stocked in straight-grained American walnut, single-shot by design, carries the above-mentioned 20-inch barrel and weighs in at around 7¼ pounds, depending of course on the density of the wood, minus scope. It comes with open sights, but I favor the optical kind, so on went a Redfield 4X scope cinched down in Ruger rings.

For testing purposes on this rifle, I tried to keep the technicalities to sort of a simple ABC type of loading program by using one brand of bullets (although the weights would differ), primers and brass. Powders were three in number: H-4895 for the light weights; Olin 760 for the in-betweens; followed by IMR-4064 for the heavier 175-grain projectiles. They turned out to be good choices.

As for bullets, Hornady's lineup of 7mm offerings got the nod. Starting off with the 100-grainer, we went on to include the bullet weights of 120, 139, 154, 162 and 175 grains. All of them, with the exception of the 175-grain round nose (if you use this in lieu of the spire points we were loading here), are bullets engineered with ballistic coefficients of .340 plus, with our 162-grain boat-tailed hollow point grabbing the ring at .560! In layman's terms, it simply means bullets that are designed to knife through the air with less resistance than ever be-

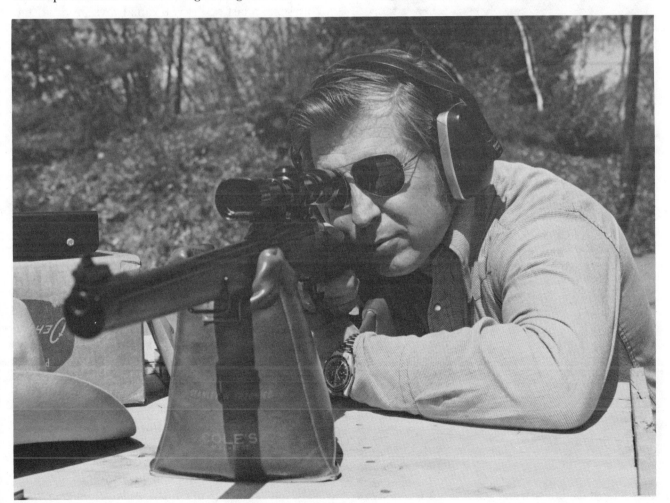

For testing this old-line cartridge, the author picked a brand new modern rifle, the Ruger International, sporting a 20-inch barrel. Topped off with a Redfield 4X scope, it makes an excellent big game rig.

A Rebounding Cartridge—the 7mm Mauser

After each batch was fired, brass was checked for tightness of fit in the chamber as well as for obvious pressure signs.

Filed by order, all loads were carefully gone over to ensure accuracy all the way down the line.

fore. The advantages are numerous, but the two that are most important to any rifleman are flatter trajectory and good accuracy.

By sticking with one brand of bullet, and using that company's whole lineup of 7mm pills, we could cover all possible shooting requirements. For example, the 100- and 120-grain bullets can be used on varmints or other small game; the 139, 154 and 162 for medium eastern or plains game; concluding with the 175 for larger animals at moderate distances. That's variety.

For brass, a large quantity of Remington cartridge cases was procured from Dick Dietz, my product information friend at Remington Arms. However, he has since informed me that his company has stopped producing this brass as a separate component. From now on if you want 7×57 brass, you'll have to turn to Winchester. Federal does have it from time to time, but again, on a limited basis. Of course, as a last resort you can always shoot off factory ammunition as a source of brass. A trifle expensive for sure, but if things get desperate it is an outlet. Finishing off our list, Federal 210 primers were our spark plugs.

After the initial fireforming ritual, cases were resized and recharged for serious testing. After sizing, all the cases were minutely flared for ease of bullet entry on the upstroke with Lyman's M die, then primed on the return with Federal 210 primers. As already mentioned, all the bullets were Hornadys, of recent manufacture and miked .284″ in diameter.

HORNADY 100-GRAIN HOLLOW POINT #2800

The propellant choice here was H-4895 because of prior experience with this powder in similar capacity cases. Looking a lot like IMR-4320, it meters the same with a minimum of grain cutting as it runs through the measure. Because of this, however, experience showed some uneven drops, so trickling was necessary to bring each charge up to par. A dose of 45.4 grains almost filled the case to the neck line; 47.2 did make it to this juncture. Cartridge overall length with the bullet came to 2.950″ which chambered easily in the Ruger Number One.

Range testing proved this bullet to be very accurate, especially with the first powder charge. With an extreme spread of only 17 fps between rounds,

Shown here in closeup are three fired cases on the left, brand new cases on the right. Note the difference in the neck and shoulder area after the round has conformed to the rifle's chamber.

1-inch groups were very common. The next loading increased our velocity about 200 fps but also expanded group size. Overall, a handy combination for varmint or small game hunting.

HORNADY 120-GRAIN SPIRE POINT—SOFT POINT #2810

This was the first of four to be loaded with Olin's 760 Ball Powder. This powder is noted for its easy flow characteristics, making it tempting to use the measure only, but please weigh each and every charge of 760 for exact confirmation in grains metered to the cartridge case.

While the book quoted 3000 fps with 53.3 grains in a 22-inch barrel, in our shorter 20-incher, 2943 was more realistic. A charge of 54.9 grains produced 2995 fps on my Chronotach, with a compressed charge in the case. The bullet was seated out for an overall length of 3.000″.

An ideal choice for small game, this load is easy to shoot and generated between 2300 and 2400 foot pounds of muzzle energy. Both loads were accurate, with the second selection coming in just a hair better.

HORNADY 139-GRAIN BOAT TAIL—SOFT POINT #2825

For all practical purposes, this bullet weight could be the ideal compromise for the average one-load, one-gun hunter. Topping out at 2869 fps and developing roughly 2542 foot pounds of energy, this particular entry is not only accurate, but has the potential of being deadly on game as well.

With the cartridge overall length at 2.980", the bullet is right at the cannelure line. When this round is fired in a single-shot, crimping is not necessary as long as you maintain a tight neck tension. With 50.4 grains of the Olin 760 you start approaching the shoulder-neck area in the case; 52.4 grains raised the charge up into the neck, enough to be considered a mildly compressed charge.

Compared to the Federal factory load with the 140-grain bullet, we did better by about 300 fps and 500 fpe in the power department. For light game—antelope or deer—this would be a good choice.

HORNADY 154-GRAIN SPIRE POINT—SOFT POINT #2830

One of the most popular bullet weights in the 7mm series, this 154-grain soft point combines good weight retention with a decent trajectory for the taking of medium game in the deer/caribou class. Like the preceding 120- and 139-grain Hornadys, this weight was loaded with Olin 760 propellant, then seated to 3.000" overall length.

While it doesn't quite match the popular 150-grain 7mm Remington Magnum loading in performance, driving a bullet at 2766 fps, it does offer the shooter a good combination for general hunting. The trajectory sighted in for a 300-yard zero was as follows:

Cases can be smoked with a candle to show when the die barely touches the shoulder. This is minimum headspacing, which in turn will lead to the best accuracy and fit in any one particular rifle.

100 yards	+4.7 inches
200 yards	+5.6 inches
300 yards	0.0 inches
400 yards	−13.3 inches

With groups averaging 1½ inches all around, this load is a definite asset to the 7mm Mauser.

HORNADY 162-GRAIN BOAT TAIL—SOFT POINT #2845

Sporting the highest ballistic coefficient out of all the bullets used, this streamlined baby was the last of the series to use the Olin 760 powder. Again, there were no problems in weighing accurate charges with this powder. Seating the bullet was a snap thanks to its pronounced boat tail design. The overall length with the bullet was 3.000″.

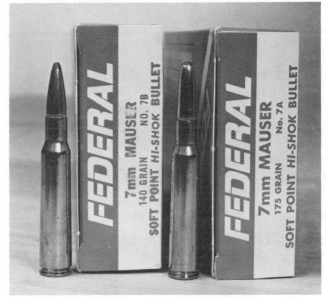

For a basis of comparison, these two Federal loads were shot alongside the handloads in the Ruger International.

RANGE TESTING THE 7 × 57 MAUSER IN THE RUGER INTERNATIONAL NUMBER ONE

All loads used Hornady bullets, Remington brass, Federal 210 primers, and were clocked over a Oehler Model 33 Chronotach. Temperature, about 65 degrees.

Bullet Weight (grains)	Powder	Powder Charge (grains)	Book Velocity (fps)	Range Velocity (fps)	Muzzle Energy (fpe)	Comments
100	H-4895	45.4	3200	3085	2116	1″
100	H-4895	47.2	3300	3241	2326	Warm!
120	760	53.3	3000	2943	2302	Accurate
120	760	54.9	3100	2995	2400	
139	760	50.4	2800	2781	2385	Nice
139	760	52.4	2900	2869	2542	
154	760	49.5	2700	2708	2493	Good Load
162	760	47.7	2600	2580	2394	1½″
162	760	49.4	2700	2668	2564	
175	IMR4064	40.9	2400	2424	2275	
175	IMR4064	42.4	2500	2515	2467	1″
140	Federal Factory		2660	2571	2053	
175	Federal Factory		2440	2356	2164	

When starting out, please reduce all loads by at least 5 to 6% in your particular firearm, watching for pressure signs as you work up!

Moving up into the heavyweights, this selection comes pretty close to matching some competitive loads in the .308 class. Overall performance was really good averaging 1- to 1½-inch groups or better at 100 yards. At 2668 fps, the shoulder starts to feel the tingle of over 2500 fpe. Although not a threat to good shooting, the recoil does let you know you are firing a big-bore rifle. The 162-grain bullet has the edge over the 154-grain bullet, as far as better terminal ballistics are concerned, thus producing extra knockdown power for shooters looking for a little more punch from their 7×57 rifles.

HORNADY 175-GRAIN SPIRE POINT—SOFT POINT #2850

While Hornady does make a round nose and a spire-pointed bullet in this weight, my choice here is the latter. If you want to compare figures, the round nose has a ballistic coefficient of .260; the spire point, .506! In trajectory language this amounts to the following, for a 300-yard zero:

	.260 Round Nose	.506 Spire Point
100 yards	+ 7.2	+ 5.7
200 yards	+ 8.6	+ 6.6
300 yards	0.0	0.0
400 yards	− 22.0	− 15.2
500 yards	− 61.7	− 40.2

Both the round nose and the spire point bullets were computed at 2515 feet per second, with 2467 foot pounds of muzzle energy.

We seated the 175-grainers over IMR-4064, a stick powder just a little faster than the previously used 760. It turned out to be a good choice because

Here is what the cartridge case looks like after it emerges from the sizing die. Note how the neck has been touched by the die, the shoulder only slightly. For one rifle and one rifle only, this is the way to go in sizing all cases.

For both lead or jacketed bullets, the Lyman M die is just the ticket for a minimum flare without disturbing the inner neck dimensions. It also aids in bullet insertion, thus reducing the problem of collapsed necks during the same operation.

loading 42.4 grains of propellant produced groups in one-minute-of-angle clusters. This round has enough power, certainly more than marginal, for bigger game animals. And, in the Ruger 20-inch barrel, its great for close in hunting for deer and bear.

Again, we edged out the factory loading by about 7% in velocity and 14% in muzzle energy. And we did it safely and without pressure problems. The overall length of the case with bullet came to 2.970".

Concluding this chapter on the 7×57, we find that it can be both accurate and powerful enough to serve many of our needs. Granted, the cartridge is overshadowed by some of the bigger 7mm's, but in all the testing this sort of comparison never came to mind. I was very happy with all the results, including the final stats from the shorter 20-inch barrel. I accept the 7×57 on its own merits and advantages, especially in a gun like the Ruger International. Those of you who are not the excitable type when it comes to seeing game and can calmly squeeze off an unhurried round will probably find the 7×57 to your liking.

In any event, don't sell it short! It's still a darn good cartridge.

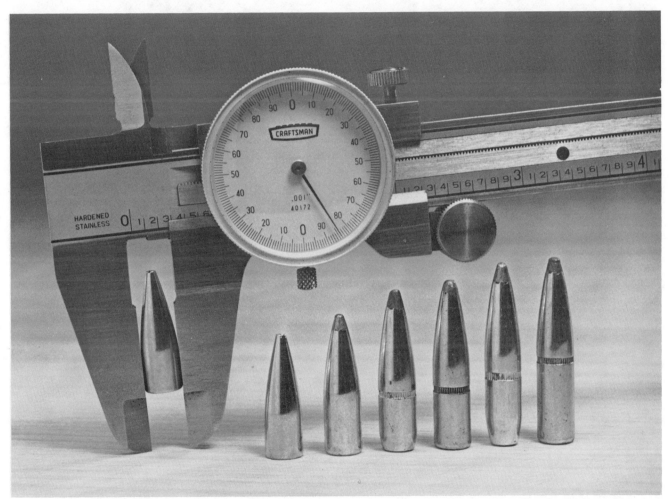

One maker's lineup of bullets for the 7mm Mauser. Shown here from left to right: Hornady's 100-, 120-, 139-, 154-, 162- and 175-grained bullets. Note the exact measurement on the dial calipers of .284 inches.

A Rebounding Cartridge—the 7mm Mauser

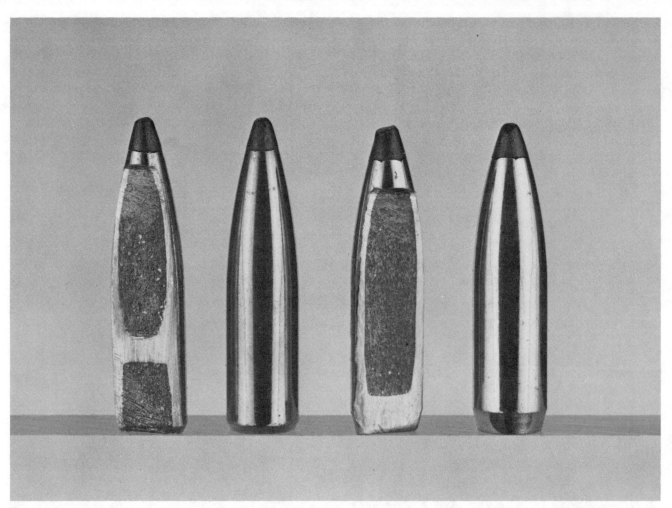

Shown in a closeup of cutaway bullets are the Nosler Partition bullet (left) and the Nosler solid base (right). In hunting, the Partition bullet will peel back only to the solid wall about three-fourths of the way down. Thus expanded when it hits an animal, it transfers its energy more positively, stays in the animal and kills more humanely.

Chapter 18

Additional Handloading Equipment

Sooner or later, in addition to the normal everyday equipment you purchased for loading metallic cartridges, you're going to need something extra. It's inevitable.

Aside from making your work a lot easier in some instances, most of this equipment has a specialized task. You may need something out of the ordinary to help shrink those groups downrange. Or possibly you may want a piece of gear not directly associated with handloading, yet important from a convenience standpoint.

The equipment shown in this chapter represents only a small segment of the entire industry. Going through catalogs of the various manufacturers I've picked out products that have a lot of user appeal. They are not only popular in terms of sales, but also very useful to handloaders in general.

For the home bullet caster making small runs, Lee offers a great lineup of inexpensive equipment to complete the task.

For the man who likes to prime his cases in a separate operation, the RCBS automatic priming tool may be the answer. It comes complete with all the attachments to load both small and large American-type Boxer primers.

Using a Lyman Turbo Tumbler is a fast way to remove case lube or powder residue from your cartridge cases. In two hours all your cases will have a factory-new appearance.

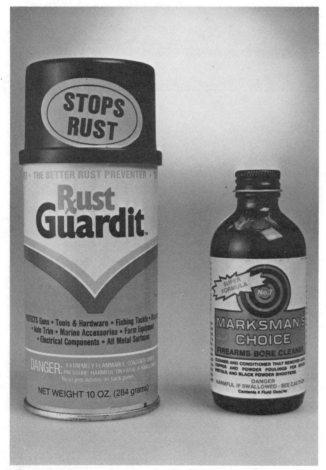

Maintenance of equipment, whether firearms or presses, is essential if you plan to receive the full benefit from your investment. For protection against rust, Rust-Guardit is a good product; for cleaning your firearms, turn to Marksman's Choice.

If you feel adventurous, by all means get into bullet swaging. You can make your own jacketed bullets. The master of this game is Dave Corbin. He has tons of information available and sells equipment to fill every swaging need.

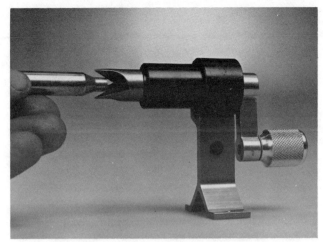

A departure from the norm, this deburring tool can be mounted in a fixture made by Forster. An excellent idea, this tool can also be mounted permanently to your bench.

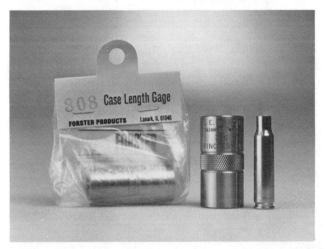

For checking case length, products from Forster or Wilson are available at a very modest cost.

Wilson Products makes a complete line of precision equipment for the advanced handloader.

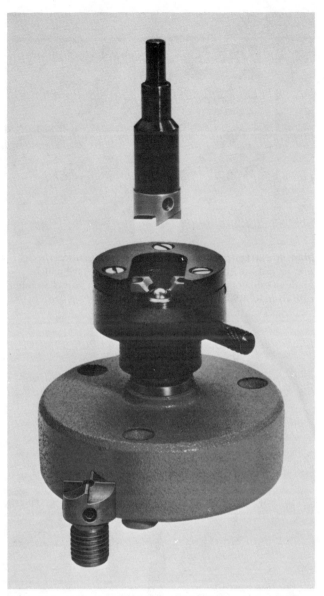

Brought back by popular demand, the drill press case trimmer is just the ticket for large-volume ammo loaders.

Made to extremely close tolerances, the Competition Die Set may be just the thing you need to take a 1000-yard match. Made in calibers from .222 to .308, it comes in its own wooden case from RCBS.

Using a trim die is a quick way to check for overlength cases. If they are, just file them down to proper specs. Heat treated to prevent wear to the die, they are available in five pistol and 15 rifle calibers from RCBS.

For the best possible accuracy potential, loaded rounds can be checked for bullet runout on this Bonanza Co-Ax Indicator.

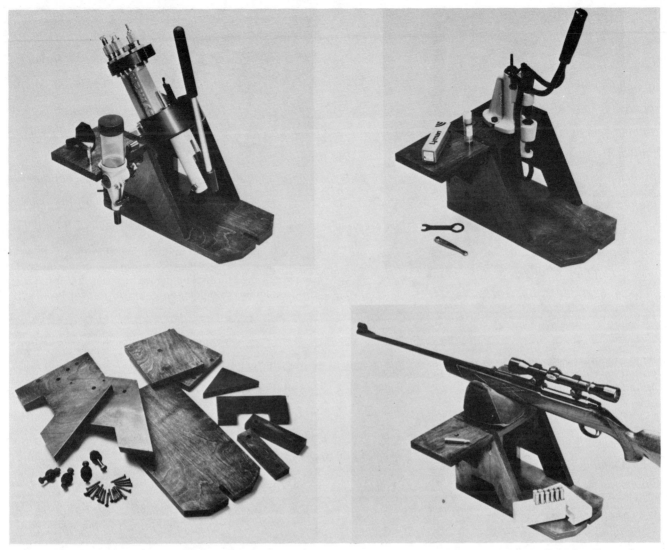

In Chapter 1 we talked about the apartment dweller's biggest problem—space. This could be the answer. Made by Lyman, under $50, and put together in a few minutes, the Organizer can be set up a number of different ways to accommodate all kinds of equipment.

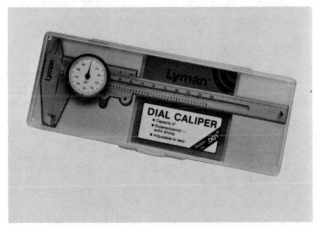

For checking overall length of cartridge cases, a dial caliper is a wise investment. From Lyman, and under $30.

Tired of changing shell holders every time you switch calibers? This could be the solution. It's a self-adjusting shell holder from Quinetics.

Additional Handloading Equipment

179

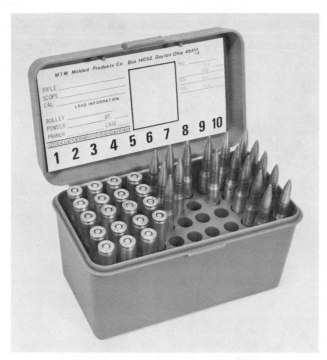

Being organized at the range is just as important as it is at the loading bench. From MTM, this box holds 50 rounds of centerfire rifle ammo.

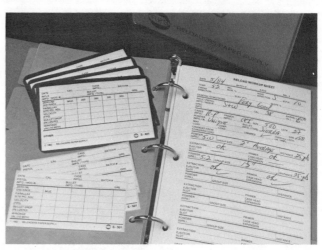

Record-keeping is a very important step of loading ammunition. Reloaders Paper Supply has made the job easier with pre-printed forms. For about $10, you get the forms, dividers, ammo box holders and a tough vinyl notebook.

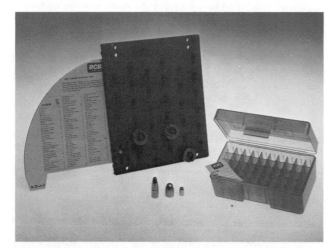

Two recent products from RCBS include a bench-mountable shell holder with reference chart and plastic see-thru cartridge boxes. In the foreground are some new bullet entries from Speer, including .25 and .45 ACPs.

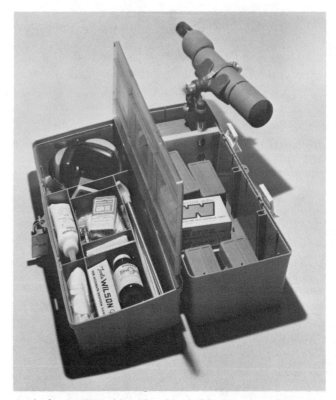

Again from MTM, this gadget box holds enough equipment and ammo for a full day of range testing. Added features include a lockable top and a spotting scope divider.

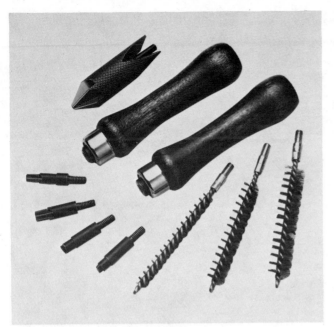

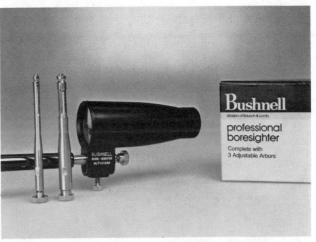

Nobody likes to save ammo costs more than a handloader, so before you shoot a round out of that newly scoped rifle, boresight it with this Bushnell product. It comes complete with a case and three arbors for easy field carry.

Case preparation is the key to good handloads, and this kit from Lyman includes a nice assortment of neat attachments. The two handles accept a deburring/chamfering tool, primer pocket cleaners and inside neck brushes for .25, .38 and .45 calibers.

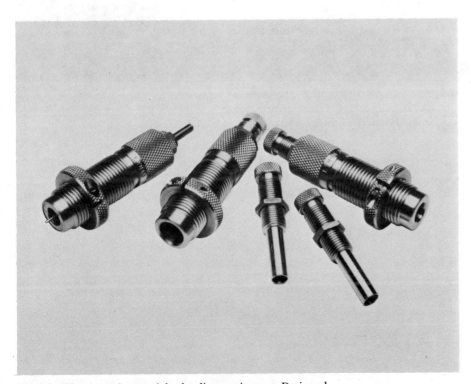

Special calibers require special reloading equipment. Designed especially for the new high-powered .357 Maximum, this Lyman set includes a tungsten carbide die and extra seating stems to compensate for different bullet ogives.

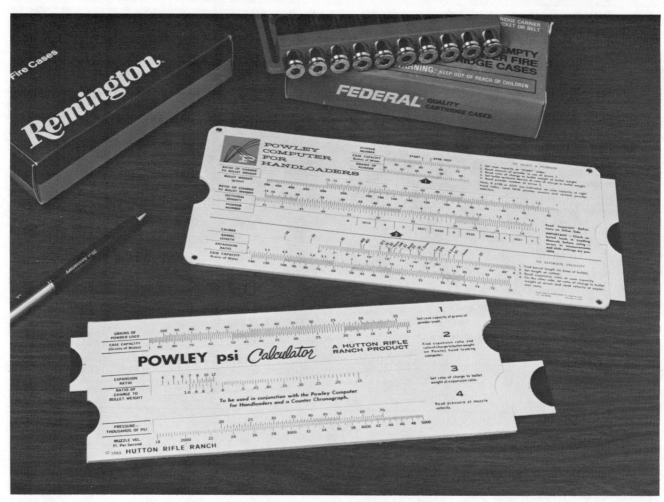

When you get to the point of calculating pressure in your rifle
or what powder is going to be the most efficient, these
"slapsticks" from Marian Powley are a must.

Chapter 19

Favorite Loads from American Gun Writers

KEVIN E. STEELE

Kevin Steele has been actively involved with guns and hunting since the age of five, when his father presented him with a custom-stocked Mossberg .22 rifle. He has served the shooting industry as Editor of Guns *magazine for five years, as Associate Editor of* The American Handgunner *for three years and as Shotgun Editor of* Guns *for two years. Kevin is currently a Managing Editor with the Omega Group Ltd., Publishers of* Soldier of Fortune *and* Survive *magazines.*

For the past four years, I have successfully hunted with the .308 Winchester round in the Heckler & Koch 770 semi-automatic rifle. The 770 is known as an extremely accurate autoloader, and I optimized the rifle's inherent accuracy with a handload consisting of the .308″ 180-grain Hornady Interlock soft point bullet #3070 over 48.0 grains of 760 Ball Powder. This load uses the Federal 210 primer and Frontier brass, and generates 2600 fps velocity at the muzzle of the 770.

I have taken several varieties of tough big game with this rifle/load combo including an aoudad ram, a trophy-class fallow buck and a 410-pound Russian boar, at ranges from 60 to 220 yards. All were one-shot kills. The Hornady Interlock bullet performed marvelously on all game encountered. Both the fallow deer and the boar dropped in their tracks, and the aoudad, hit high in the lung, ran about 100 yards before collapsing.

I consider this handload capable of taking all but the largest North American big game out to ranges of 250 yards. In the HK770 rifle, this load holds $1/2$ minute of angle 3-shot groups from the bench. I should advise that this load is near maximum, and is ideal for the heavy recoil required to operate the 770's massive action. In your own rifle, start out slow, and work your way up, being ever cognizant of excess pressure indicators.

My handgun shooting concerns itself primarily with IPSC-style events where accuracy ranks equally with time. To that end, the load must be accurate, yet generate sufficient power to rank on the

Kevin Steele and an aoudad ram.

pendulum. Another factor is that excessive recoil will hinder your time when engaging multiple targets, so a compromise must be reached.

After considerable trial and error, I arrived at a handload which provided me with the compromise I was searching for. This load consists of the .451″ Speer 200-grain .45 ACP lead semi-wadcutter over 5.6 grains of Unique, in W/W brass powered by the CCI large pistol primer. This handload generates 740 fps from my John Spilborghs custom 6-inch .45 automatic. From the offhand position, modified Weaver stance, I can routinely shoot 2- to 2 ½-inch 7-shot groups at 25 yards. Bear in mind that the Spilborghs .45 pistol is highly modified, and groups of this nature are far from the norm when using "factory" guns.

J.D. JONES

"J.D." is president of SSK Industries, which deals in high-velocity, big-bore handguns and modifications thereof. He is a recipient of the Outstanding American Handgunner Award. When he is not in the game fields, you can find him at the range or at home hard at work penning articles for major firearms publications. He also has many wildcat cartridges to his credit, including the much-publicized .375 JDJ.

Asking for my favorite rifle and pistol load out of the thousands I've worked with equates to, "If I had to get by with two cartridges and loads, what would they be?" This restatement of the question makes the job a lot simpler, particularly since I primarily view the subject from the standpoint of a hunter.

I would unhesitatingly select the SSK Custom Contender in .375 JDJ loaded with the Federal 215 primer, 46.5 grains of H-4895 and the 270-grain Hornady spire point. This gives about 1950 fps and 2280 foot pounds of energy from a 14-inch barrel, with outstanding accuracy and superb penetration. It's quite a handgun.

In a rifle, my choice would be the .30/06 in this load: Federal 215 primer, 57.0 grains of IMR-4350 (or maybe a little more depending on case capacity) and 180-grain bullets. If I had to choose one bullet

J.D. Jones with a record book Kudu.

it would probably be the Nosler Partition although I would certainly like to be able to switch bullets for various jobs.

My selection of the Federal 215 primer is due to the fact that it is the hottest primer currently available and delivers exceptional cold temperature velocities. Be cautious when using this primer, however, as I believe it can raise pressures substantially if used indiscriminately instead of milder primers in maximum loads.

Good Shootin!

DICK METCALF

Presently on the staff of Shooting Times *magazine, Dick is known in a wide circle of shooting activities. He is on the board of the Smith & Wesson Collector's Association and was a nominee for the 1983 Outstanding American Handgunner Award. Dick is also a federally licensed firearms consultant/expert, deputy sheriff and legislative consultant for the National Rifle Association.*

Like most shooters who use a variety of types and calibers of guns, I have a favored handload for each, depending on its individual character. It's hard to pick just one favorite handload for rifle or handgun, just as it's hard to pick a single favorite gun. But, if I consider the handloads that I use the most and that have been the most generally productive over the years, I'd have to reduce them down to these: one for the .308 Winchester and one for the .44 Magnum.

For the .308 Winchester, I regularly load the Speer 150-grain boat tail bullet over 48.0 grains of Winchester 748 propellant. I use Federal brass from factory Premium cartridges, and CCI BR-2 bench rest primers. This load is tailored to my Smith & Wesson Model 1500 Varmint heavy-barreled rifle, and with the aid of a Leupold 3-9X

Dick Metcalf with a turkey gobbler.

scope, it will give me .87-inch 3-shot average groups at 100 meters from a bench rest under range conditions. The 150-grain bullet is more than enough for deer, and has sufficient accuracy for woodchuck-sized varmints out to 250 yards. It is as close to an all-round centerfire handload as I have come up with.

For the .44 Magnum handgun, the best all-round useful handload for me remains the one that the late Elmer Keith came up with long, long ago: 22.0 grains of 2400 behind a cast 240-grain lead semi-wadcutter; specifically, the Lyman #429421 that Keith designed. When loading .44 Magnum handloads for handguns, I have found that specific choice of brass and primers makes little apparent difference in measurable accuracy or velocity, with the reservation that I never use magnum primers.

They have always given me more erratic results than so-called standard primers of any make. I use this load in all types of .44 Magnum handguns, from 5-inch revolvers to 14-inch scoped T/C Contenders. I have taken all types of North American game with it, from wild turkey to black bear. Its average accuracy varies from gun to gun, but in a 7 1/2-inch Ruger Super Blackhawk fitted with a Leupold M8-2X EER scope, it averages 2.25-inch 5-shot groups from a sandbag rest at 50 meters. That's good enough for me.

NICK SISLEY

Nick shares the same pastime as the author of this Guide. We both like varmint hunting. He is a true out-

Nick Sisley with a varmint rifle.

doorsman involved in varied activities including fishing, hunting and outdoor writing; traveling the world for story material. Nick has six books to his byline, is an editor for a couple of quarterlies, has written for over 40 different magazines at one time or another and currently writes a syndicated weekly column published in 30 Pennsylvania newspapers.

I have many favorite varmint loads, but the cartridge I load most is the .223 Remington. The last several summers I've fired over 3,000 rounds of .223 reloads at prairie dogs in South Dakota.

I use two different powders, but in my .223s both loads strike at the same point of impact. One utilizes 21.5 grains of IMR-4198, the other 26.0 grains of Accurate Arms MR-223 ball powder. The latter is less expensive, if readers can find it. Like all ball powders, Accurate Arms MR-223 throws extremely consistent charges.

It's important to use the Remington 7½ small rifle primer with both loads. The bullet to select with the above is the Sierra 55-grain Blitz. This bullet should not be driven any faster than .223 velocities, but it's literally dynamite on smallish varmints like prairie dogs. Performance on woodchucks is also excellent with this load.

Velocity is over 3100 fps, and accuracy is excellent out of either my 788 Remington or my Thompson/Center Contender single-shot; some groups register under an inch at 100 yards. One doesn't need accuracy any better than this for varmint shooting at ranges at which the .223 is effective, say, under 225 yards. Of course, it is possible to pop an occasional "dog" or "chuck" at slightly longer ranges.

For whitetail hunting, a special favorite is a fast-expanding bullet like the 100-grain Winchester Power Point or the 100-grain Sierra HP in .264 Winchester Magnum. My rifle is a Winchester Model 70. A couple of Alabama friends also love this cartridge and this load. They have specially built Savage 110s in .264 and they often kill 40 whitetail bucks a season with the above-mentioned 100-grain bullets. Of course, Alabama has a long, one-buck-a-day season.

In the big .264 case you can't beat Hodgdon's H-4831. My load of 68.0 grains is near *maximum,* so readers should work up to it slowly, miking case bases to determine that expansion is minimal (if I get more than .002″ expansion after firing, I simply back off on any powder charge). They should also scrutinize primers for excessive flattening. That 68.0-grain load of H-4831 behind the 100-grain bullet results in velocities near 3500 fps. Accuracy in my Model 70 is under 2 inches. This is one of the most lethal deer loads I've ever used. Hunters must refrain from taking shots when they are unsure of bullet placement, however. Few lung-shot deer will die on the spot when hit with most any other cartridge or bullet, but this is one load that will consistently produce those types of results.

DON ZUTZ

Don has been active in gun writing since 1965. He was a former state skeet shooting champion in 12 and 20 gauge, and experiments extensively with all types of sporting arms to determine reload performances. He is Gun Editor of Fur-Fish-Game; *Reloading Editor of* Guns and Shooting Industry; *Contributing Editor of* Trap and

Don Zutz tests a load at the range.

Field; *and Author of* Handloading for Hunters *and* The Double Shotgun.

My favorite rifle/cartridge pairing is the Remington M725 in .280 Remington. This rifle from the late 1950s and early 1960s was button-rifled, not hammer-forged, and the barrels were of a different steel than today's 700s. They were superbly accurate for hunting rifles, and the .280 is a very versatile cartridge that uses 7mm bullets with their excellent exterior ballistics. All loads given reach 1 minute of angle.

In this gun I use the 115-grain Speer HP over 50.0 grains of IMR-4064 for varmints. For open country antelope or deer, the 130-grain Speer spitzer boat tail over 61.0 grains of H-4831 fills the bill nicely. Finally, for basic big game, I use the Hornady 154-grain round nose or spire point with 58.5 grains of H-4831, or the Speer Mag-Tip or Grand Slam using 55.5 grains of IMR-4831.

As for handguns, the 9mm Browning P-35 with adjustable sights and factory grips feels just right in my hand. Here, I use the 115-grain Sierra HP over 5.0 grains of PB powder. This was a Du Pont pub-lished maximum load some years ago, but I note that in a recent factory listing Du Pont has cut that back to 4.8 grains of PB as the recommended maximum. This load has produced 1½-inch 5-shot groups at 25 yards, seldom straying beyond 2 inches.

BOB BELL

Bob is a very personable guy. I first met him at Remington Farms and shared a blind with him. If you want to know all about scopes, contact Bob. He is the Editor of Pennsylvania Game News *and has hunted this country from Maine to California. Bob also has over 500 articles and stories to his credit, including a yearly assignment for* Gun Digest, *on, you guessed it, scopes. His writing is based on many years of experience.*

In 1947 I bought a 150-pound keg of World War II surplus 4895 powder from Hodgdon. Over the next eight or ten years I shot up all of this except a few pounds that I saved for some nebulous reason.

Bob Bell out after woodchucks.

Most of it was burned in a .219 Donaldson Wasp, a .22-250 (then a wildcat) and a .222 Remington, all varmint rifles. Since then, I've used a lot of the IMR-4895 in cartridges as different as the .222 Remington and the .458 Magnums. It isn't the optimum in some, but it's as good as anything in a number of medium-capacity cases, and it would be hard to beat if a shooter were restricted to one powder for everything from the .222 Remington up.

In the late '40s, some .22-250 shooters were using as much as 38.0 grains of the 4895 with a 55-grain bullet, so I figured 36.0 grains would be a reasonable starting place. An early adjustment of my powder measure happened to give 36.2, so I tried it—and used it in about three-quarters of the 15,000 rounds or so I've put through five .22-250s. With good barrels and bullets, less than inch-groups for 5 shots at 100 yards were common, and often the 200-yard groups weren't a lot larger. Many friends used 34 grains with similar results.

Current manuals listing IMR-4895 loads are more conservative than those early maximums with the GI stuff. Today's suggestions are usually about 34.0 or 35.0 grains, for a velocity of 3600 to 3700 fps with the 55-grain bullet. My favorite load in the heavy barrel Model 700 I'm now shooting is the 53-grain Sierra bench rest bullet and 35.3 grains of the

above powder in concert with the Remington 9½ primer, loaded in Remington brass. This load produces a velocity of 3611 fps at 7½ feet over Oehler skyscreens.

On the big game side, which here refers to deer, my favorite rifle for some years was a 98 Mauser barreled for the .284 Winchester cartridge, now pretty much an orphan, unfortunately. With it I killed 15 whitetails with 16 shots, one bullet blowing up on an ice-covered branch before it got to the deer. I've never had better results with any big game rifle.

My favorite deer load is a tossup between the 139-grain Hornady and 50 grains of 4895, velocity 2946 fps from the 22-inch barrel; and the 145-grain Speer with 56.0 grains of 4350, velocity 2916. Both group in about 1½ minutes, and that will handle deer at any sensible range. In thick country where a high percentage of the shots might be angling away, I'd take the 140-grain Nosler Partition, for perhaps more consistent penetration. I wouldn't hesitate to go into elk country with this bullet, which moves at 2900 fps. The 150-grain Nosler Partition might be a trifle better on elk, and in my rifle 57.0 grains of 4350 and the 120 Winchester primer give me 2882 fps. I often wonder why the .284 has become a forgotten cartridge.

Stan Trzoniec with a caribou.

STAN TRZONIEC

Besides writing most of this publication, Stan is also Special Projects Editor of Guns *magazine, has contributed articles to all major firearms publications, is author of a book,* Modern American Centerfire Handguns, *is a competitor in IPSC and PPC matches and travels the continent in search of big game.*

When I asked some of my colleagues to choose their favorite loads for this chapter, I never realized it would be so tough, until it was my turn. Picking just two loads out of the many I've tested and hunted with over the years was a struggle. Now I know what they went through. Thank you, my friends. Finally, after much deliberation, here are my two votes.

For handguns, I guess deep down the .38 Super in a customized Dick Crawford Colt Government Model is my number one load. Dick installed BoMar sights on this gun, trimmed the trigger

down to very acceptable levels and in general made the gun a joy to shoot. My choice of bullets is Hornady's 124-grain flat nose full metal-jacketed (FN/FMJ). I use Remington cases. The powder is 9.0 grains of Hodgdon's HS-7, sparked by CCI 500 primers. I taper crimp this load to 1.230″ and it moves smartly out of the muzzle at a true 1194 fps. In a rest it will shoot holes at 25 yards circling an inch.

Rifles are another matter. Here, I like shorter tubes and I work up loads until I can get the maximum out of them without problems. Such is the case with my Remington Classic bolt action rifle in .270 Winchester. Using the Remington "Core-Lokt" 130-grain bullet, 57.0 grains of IMR-4831 and a CCI 250 magnum primer, I reach an honest 3029 fps in the 22-inch barrel. It is a very efficient load, because the extreme spread between rounds fired is only 29 fps! Seated to an overall length of 3.240″, half-inch groups at 100 yards are the norm, rather than the exception.

Chapter 20

Questions and Answers

Samples of typical, frequently asked questions concerning handloading, guns, calibers and related topics.

QUESTION: With so many different styles and bullet weights in the popular .30/06 cartridge, is it possible to narrow down the field for all-round hunting use?

ANSWER: For most North American game, yes, it is possible to narrow the field, with a few exceptions. If there was only one choice, I would opt for the 165-grained projectile in either a spire point or partition style. This bullet carries enough mass to do the job if proper bullet placement is achieved. Loaded to velocities in the 2900 fps range, with powders such as IMR-4350, IMR-4831 or Norma MRP, groups at 100 yards should measure 1½ inches or less. For eastern or western plains game, the 165-grain bullet, when zeroed at 300 yards, rises approximately 4.1 inches at 100, 4.9 at 200, then drops 11.4 inches below the point of aim at 400 yards. The only exceptions noted would be that if I was going exclusively for antelope, I'd use the 150-grain; for elk, the 180-grain bullet.

Any hunting trip deserves careful planning: game, terrain and probable shooting distances. Study your game plan thoroughly. In the end I think you'll find the 165-grain bullet to your liking.

QUESTION: I have looked around for a good automatic pistol that suits my particular style and settled on the Colt Automatic chambered in the .38 Super. Any comments on loading or bullets to use?

ANSWER: The .38 Super is a fine automatic cartridge and one of my favorites as it fits in between the 9mm and .45 ACP. Introduced in 1929, the .38 Super never reached the popularity it deserves, which is a mystery to those who like the round. As of this writing, it would very well be that the lack of availability of handguns chambered for this round has kept it in relative obscurity, as only Colt produces a pistol for it in this country. However, a few

European makers export guns of this caliber. There are several to choose from.

Many claim that poor accuracy and loading troubles have plagued this round. Both accusations are false. In an extensive loading program I found powders in the range of Unique, Blue Dot or Hodgdon's HS-7 gave excellent results, with the HS-7 nudging out the other two by a fair margin. In fact, with the gun in a Ransom Rest, groups averaged 1 to 1½ inches at 25 yards! Muzzle velocity was a true 1287 fps calculated 8 feet from the muzzle, with a 124-grain projectile.

As with any other auto cartridge, attention to detail is required on your part to ensure trouble-free functioning of the weapon. New brass, jacketed bullets and taper crimps are the way to go in cartridge makeup, especially if you're going to use the .38 Super as a defense weapon.

QUESTION: Being a rifle fan for many years, I have now started to enjoy handgun shooting. Now that I am proficient with a .22 rimfire, what would be the next step into centerfire cartridges with a slight leaning towards eventual handloading on a modest scale?

ANSWER: Making the transition from rimfire to centerfire is an easy one and I recommend the .38 Special as your number-one choice for several reasons. The round is extremely popular.

Consider gun availability. Every major firearms manufacturer produces a gun (or many guns) in the .38 Special. But don't just buy a .38 Special. Purchase a handgun chambering both the .38 Special and the .357 Magnum. While both take .357 inch bullets, the .357 will deliver them at a higher velocity with more punch. Discuss this with your dealer before you make a decision.

Consider the .38 Special and handloading. Scanning the loading manuals of Hornady, Sierra, Speer and other bullet makers reveals a great number of load combinations among bullet, primer and powders for the .38. For general practice or target shooting you can use lead wadcutter-type projectiles with velocities as low as 700 fps. And the recoil produced is hardly more than if you were shooting a .22 rimfire. Moving up, you can load 110-, 125-, 150- or 158-grain bullets to around 900 fps; perfect for small game gathering or vermin. Later, as you progress, you can make the jump to the full .357 Mag loads.

In short, that's what makes the .38 so great—versatility and accuracy combined with reasonable shooting costs. Have fun!

QUESTION: If you had to, could you get along with just three powders? My limited budget dictates that I ask this question.

ANSWER: Probably given this choice, I would have to pick Unique for my handgun loads; IMR-4320 and IMR-4350 (or the Hodgdon equivalents) for rifle shooting.

Unique has been around since the turn of the century and has proved itself to be a very versatile powder. In handguns, from the 9mm on up and including the heavy hitters—.357, .41 and .44 Magnums—Unique will fill most of the gaps with no reservations. Granted, it may not be as efficient in some calibers as in others, but if you are budget conscious you'll have to compromise somewhere. Overall, however, your shooting will not suffer if you choose Unique.

IMR-4320 will serve you well in the smaller rifle cartridges because it is faster burning than IMR-4350. We have an overlap here. For cartridges up to about the .30/06, IMR-4320 is a very efficient and accurate powder. When cases start gaining in volume—7mm Remington or .300 Winchester Magnums—I'd start looking toward the IMR-4350.

QUESTION: On the subject of primers, can you please straighten me out on the proper usage of each. I am talking now of both pistol and rifle applications.

ANSWER: The selection of primers must be made with the same considerations allotted to bullets or powders. The kind of shooting, the caliber, the burning properties of the powder, even the weather can determine the proper primer. While every primer manufacturer has his particular code for these ignitors, basically they are classified as small rifle, large rifle, small pistol, large pistol—along with magnum and match or bench rest types.

In general terms, small rifle and pistol cases are those that take the .175″ diameter primers. Large rifle and pistol cases accept the .210″ primers. Regular primers are designed for powders and powder charges of normal volume. Magnum primers give a longer burning cycle thus making them more suitable for large doses of slower burning propellants. They can also be used in colder weather for medium burning powders. Last, match or bench rest primers are carefully made and controlled to deliver absolute consistency to those shooters whose whole crusade in life is to place ten shots in one small hole.

QUESTION: *Considering all the loading manuals on the shelves these days, how do I go about finding a load that will be both safe and accurate in my pet rifle?*

ANSWER: To start out, buy three different manuals. Look up average charge weights for your caliber, or any caliber for that matter. But let's cite an example so you can follow along. In fact, this is how I arrived at a very accurate load in my .270.

Looking at the Sierra, Speer and Hornady manuals, for the .270 130-grain spire-pointed bullet, the listings ran 55.4, 55.0 and 55.8 grains of IMR-4831 for an average *starting point* of 55.4 grains of propellant. The velocity readings were just under the 3000 feet-per-second mark; something I wanted for the utmost in trajectory for this all-round bullet weight.

Using this as a starting point, I then loaded six cases of each with 55.5, 56.0, 56.5 and 57.0 grains. While accuracy was good with 55.5 and 56.0 grains, it started looking better as I approached 56.5, with spectacular groups coming in around one minute of angle with the 57.0 loading. No pressure problems were in evidence and over my Oehler Chronotach I was getting an honest 3029 fps from a 22-inch barrel. Over the years I have found this particular load ideal for my kinds of hunting. From Montana to northern Canada this load has served me faithfully on all accounts.

One last tip. The calculations mentioned here were computed from *under* the *maximum* loads listed in all manuals. Never start at the *maximum* and work up from there. Always start lower and work up.

QUESTION: *How often should I trim my cartridge cases and what equipment do I need?*

ANSWER: The need for case trimming depends on the amount of shooting you do, the loads and the caliber. In most instances, all factories produce new brass close to or below SAAMI specs. Most brass will lengthen after repeated use. In general terms, usually about every fifth reload of a case will involve a routine trimming. When it is needed, always trim cases ten thousandths under normal length. For example, the overall length of .25/06 brass is 2.494 inches; trim it back to 2.484 inches.

As for equipment, every reloading company makes a case trimmer resembling a miniature lathe. Pop the case in, set up the machine for the amount of brass to be taken off, trim, take it out of the trimmer, measure it with a micrometer, and if everything's in order trim the rest of that batch of brass. Besides case trimmers, trim dies are available which allow you to use a file instead of a rotary trimmer. Again, personal preference will dictate equipment choice.

QUESTION: *Many of my friends have warned me about the problems in handloading for modern autopistols. If you are not careful you wind up with jams or feeding problems. I've been a revolver shooter for years. Can you shed some light on this for me?*

ANSWER: If you are looking for one word to summarize autopistol handloading, it would have to be *conscientious*. For all the details, read Chapter 10 on the care and feeding of modern automatics. If you put these suggestions into practice you should never have any problems with any automatic pistol.

QUESTION: *Looking through the various catalogs, there seems to be a wide assortment of loading dies. Should I consider the regular or more costly bench rest die sets?*

ANSWER: For ninety percent of all your shooting needs the regular line of reloading dies will suffice with plenty of features to spare. They are made to last a lifetime if properly maintained. Tolerances are close and the metal has been hardened to take constant use.

Bench rest or competition sets are made to even more exacting standards, and this is reflected in the purchase price—almost double and sometimes triple the cost, depending on the brand name. For instance, hardened expander balls for ease of decapping are almost a standard feature, as is absolute concentricity of all internal parts, ensuring a true round after assembly. Most brands are even equipped with a top micrometer to allow the user to seat bullets to within .001".

If you feel you have one pet rifle that you think would be fun to work with in the accuracy department, by all means invest in a set of the high-priced dies. Once in a while it's worth the extra cost to go off on a tangent if only for the sake of doing it another way, or a better way. These dies are available in the popular bench rest calibers of .222, .223 and .22/250. RCBS also makes them for hunters who prefer the .243, .270, 7mm/08, 7mm Remington Magnum, .30/06 and .308.

QUESTION: *There has been a lot of talk lately on the subject of "magnumizing" the .45 Colt in Ruger or Contender handguns. Any truth to this?*

ANSWER: My advice to you is to forget you ever heard such talk. While it is possible to increase the old .45 Colt in velocity from 900 fps to over 1300 fps in modern Rugers or Contenders, there is no reason to put the additional strain on both the cartridge case and the gun itself.

The .45 Colt is a very old, very popular and mild cartridge to shoot. Boosting this round upwards only takes the pleasure away from shooting it. You don't have to have the feeling of dynamite going off in your hand with every round you shoot downrange. If you absolutely, positively feel you want to give a lift to the .45 Colt, please shoot it only in a closed breeched weapon like the T/C Contender. Sturm, Ruger has taken its Blackhawk chambered for the .45 Colt off the market, and I have this deep, dark feeling it was because of this "magnumizing" effort by some people who really should know better, and then putting such notions in print.

Leave the .45 Colt in its original form. For more power go to the pure magnums in .41, .44 or .45 Winchester.

QUESTION: *Help! After a very careful analysis of 7mm rifle cartridges, I am undecided between the 7×57, 7mm/08 or the 7mm twins from Remington and Weatherby. Any advice?*

ANSWER: They are all good cartridges, and I guess what it really boils down to is your feeling about use, power and available guns.

The 7×57 Mauser is an old-line cartridge dating back to the turn of the century. I personally think it's a grand cartridge (see Chapter 17) deserving of much more shooter appeal. The newer 7mm/08 is nothing more than a .308 necked down to 7mm for use in short-actioned rifles. Its use would be on medium-sized game or silhouette matches. Only the future will tell on this round as the newness is yet to wear off, hence future shooter appeal is uncertain at this date.

The bigger 7mms—both Remington's and Weatherby's entries—are the upper limit of this pleasant cartridge. The Remington rifle, which was introduced in the 1960s, and Roy Weatherby's 1944 surprise, are on equal footing when it comes to accuracy, power and long-range potential.

Pick your needs, then the cartridge and finally the gun.

QUESTION: *As a beginner in handloading, lately I am getting case shoulders that seem to collapse as I full length resize them. If this weren't enough, I just had a case get stuck in the same die. Any suggestions?*

ANSWER: You are having lubrication problems. Too much lube on the lube pad, which is then transferred to the case before entry into the die, will cause the shoulder to collapse. On the other question, you either didn't lube the case enough or you just forgot to roll it over the pad.

When applying case lube to the pad use it sparingly. Remember, each case that passes through the die will only add lube to the inner parts of the die leading to a buildup, causing problems. When you can just feel the lube on the cases, that's enough. A final tip: When running the cases on the pad, keep them flat. In this way you will keep excess lube off the sensitive shoulder area.

QUESTION: *Are there any benefits in handloading for the magnums that I don't get by purchasing over-the-counter factory ammunition for my pistols?*

ANSWER: Yes, I call it versatility. In no way will factory loads ever match your ability to mix or match components. Commercial ammo is average-loaded for a mass shooting audience, but you can literally customize your handloads for any game or use you have in mind.

Take, for instance, the ever-popular .44 Magnum. While current factory loadings include the 180- and 240-grain loads, you can utilize bullet weights of 180, 200, 240 or 265 grains, plus numerous lead bullets if you have your own bullet casting facilities.

Aside from bullet selections, velocity increases are another big plus. Taking the 240-grain hunting round, current factory specs list it traveling at 1180 fps. Careful handloading can increase this figure by almost 30% to 1500 fps. On the other hand, you can also downgrade this cartridge to .44 Special levels—750 to 800 fps—thus making practice sessions a real joy.

QUESTION: *In a heated discussion lately my buddy and I were talking about the merits (or demerits) of the Weatherby line of proprietary cartridges. I like the idea of the increased range a hunter would gain by using handloaded* or factory ammo in these guns. My friend claims that doesn't justify the horrendous recoil the shooter has to endure with these cartridges. Who is right?

ANSWER: You both are, to a point. On the increased range part, yes. Because of the added velocity of the Weatherby calibers, you can increase the distance between you and the game animal. However, this doesn't matter if the hunter is a poor shot. My own self-imposed limit is 300 yards with a .270 Winchester and even then conditions have to be just right.

Recoil sensations are very subjective. One shooter will claim one gun is a real hard kicker, while another may totally disagree. Many fellows who shoot a .30 caliber Springfield regularly will wince at the thought of firing a 7mm Remington Magnum. Yet, both calibers are similar in measured recoil in guns of the same weight. Rifle weight and stock design have a lot to do with perceived recoil.

Just recently I was testing a gun chambered for the .270 Winchester and one in .270 Weatherby. With the former, velocities reached 3000 fps; the Weatherby brand hit 3281. Both fired the 130-grain bullet and, when computed out, the Winchester loading came in with 19.2 foot pounds of recoil energy; the Weatherby, 26.5.

In the end, you will be the sole judge.

QUESTION: Of late I have noticed a return to the older, or perhaps I should say, the nostalgic cartridges of yesteryear. Any problems with these older cartridges blending into this modern era?

ANSWER: Not at all. In fact, with the advent of modern powders, they are performing better today than ever before.

Browning, Remington, Ruger and Winchester are chambering rifles for the .257 Roberts, .250-3000 Savage and the .300 Holland and Holland. This means shooters have an opportunity to try these rounds in current, reasonably priced guns. We all know the great Winchester Model 70's of forty years ago and the collector prices they bring now—$1,000 is not unusual for a mint, original model 70 chambered in .257 Roberts. But at $400 a copy for a modern weapon, many more of us can enjoy these cartridges today.

All the calibers mentioned exhibit excellent accuracy, good striking power and are easy on the shoulder. These old-timers are enjoying a renewed loyal following, and with good reason.

QUESTION: Any tips on maintaining my loading equipment? This would include dies, presses and related gear.

ANSWER: For the most part, rely on common sense. Heavy-duty equipment such as presses need a certain amount of lube on the ram for smooth operation. Moderation is the word here for too much lube will only attract powder or primer residue. This can prevent the press from keeping close tolerances on critical bullet seating operations.

I have found that keeping a can of air around, and using it often reduces most problems of dust on these machines. Primer tubes should have dry air blown through them to get rid of any primer dust buildup leading to a possible detonation later.

New dies require attention in the form of a good cleaning before actual use. Preservatives applied at the factory must be cleaned off with a mild solvent. Check your press and dies periodically to ensure all is clean inside, especially around primer punches and neck expanders. After a while you will get to know your dies with regard to frequency of use. Some calibers are not used as often as others and can stand a light coat of oil on outer and inner surfaces. Others, like tungsten carbide dies, may require less attention. In any event, plan ahead and work out a maintenance program.

QUESTION: Since I am trying to squeeze the last bit of velocity out of my .25/06, do I dare exceed the maximum loadings imposed on me by the various loading manuals?

ANSWER: Never! Under no circumstances should you ever exceed the maximum loads in the manuals without the proper equipment at your disposal. Since the majority of shooters don't have access to professional chronographs, pressure barrels or scientific data, stay at or below maximum loads.

The one saving grace of this hobby is that if you don't like being held back by one cartridge, go to another. You can gain about 200 fps by going from the .25/06 to the .257 Weatherby, but you really have to be committed to this before switching. The target at 250 yards will never appreciate the extra 200 fps, so is it really worth it?

My advice is to jump up a caliber to the .270 or .308. Bullet weight will increase as will velocity in most cases, enabling you a decent increase in striking power without damage to yourself or others around you. Enjoy the great .25/06 as it is.

QUESTION: *Name a few common problems to look out for when loading cartridge cases.*

ANSWER: After a shooting session and before you actually start to run a case through any die, check for scratches or longitudinal splits. Scratches can come from the host firearm and could indicate trouble in the feeding or chamber area. Case side splitting can be cause for concern as this signals weak brass either from too much use or case life coming to an end.

Neck splits are another sure sign of age. Also a possibility here is that you may be inner chamfering too much after trimming. A light touch with the deburring tool can help save this area for extended use.

Corrosion is a minor occurrence taking place in humid climates or caused by leaving cartridges in leather gear for extended periods. After a hunt or varmint foray, remove all brass cartridge cases from the belt. Police personnel should rotate all their ammunition frequently depending on where they live. A cop in Phoenix won't have the same brass corrosion problems as one in New Orleans.

Aside from always monitoring case length after resizing, check primer pockets for foreign debris. Another area most people neglect is inspecting all cases after using the newer tumbling machines. Walnut or corn kernels can fill primer pockets to where they can and will break decapping pins during the resizing cycle.

QUESTION: *Being an avid eastern deer hunter I favor the old, but faithful .35 Remington cartridge in my Marlin 336. Now I see I can get the same round chambered in a Thompson/Center Contender handgun. While it would be extremely handy to carry such a weapon in a shoulder holster, are there any other advantages to the pistol over a rifle?*

ANSWER: You hit upon the only one—that of convenience. A while back I was intrigued with this possibility. The deer hunting here in New England is probably similar to your situation. Walking the woods with nothing more than a handgun strapped to my shoulder seemed like a really nice way to hunt.

Ballistics tests showed not much difference between rifle and pistol. Using the Sierra 200-grain bullet, the parent company claims close to 2000 fps with a Marlin 336 rifle equipped with a 20-inch barrel. In a Contender Super-14 an honest 2000 fps

was listed, but the chronograph gave different results. I came out with 1906 using Norma 200 powder. Hodgdon's H322 did a little better—2246 fps—but at the expense of pressure problems, coupled with hard extraction, bad accuracy and compressed charges.

While there is a certain amount of pride in taking big game with a handgun, if you're looking for a tradeoff, I'm sorry, you won't find it here. In this particular case I think you'd be better off sticking with the Marlin 336.

QUESTION: *This long winter is getting to me. Can I shoot safely indoors with my .38 caliber handgun and reduced loads?*

ANSWER: You can and with very little trouble. Some people use reduced loads or wax bullets, but the best method I know of is to shoot the plastic bullets marketed by Speer.

According to their manual and my personal experience, these little bullets zip along at around 400 fps and are powered by primers only, no powder. Accuracy is fair, but at 20 feet or less. However, the fun involved more than offsets the absence of one-hole groups. While they function best in revolvers, you can fire them in automatic pistols if you load these plastic bullets one at a time. They don't generate enough recoil to work the action of an auto.

Depending on the load used, you will need a suitable backstop unless you want your neighbor to start shooting back at you. For plastic bullets, a cardboard box with rubber baffles will suffice. Real target loads—complete with powder—need real backstops.

As a passing note, did you ever consider .22 shorts for indoor practice? Recoil is extremely mild, a heavy steel backstop is not needed and accuracy is on a par with the best of guns. But whatever your choice, please remember one important factor: *safety.*

QUESTION: *Partitions, Spire Points, Grand Slams, Hollow Points. Why so many bullet choices?*

ANSWER: Why does General Motors produce Chevrolets, Pontiacs, Oldsmobiles, Buicks and Cadillacs? There is something for everyone.

You will find that the more you handload, the more your horizons will widen concerning the products around you. While Hornady Interlocks may work well in one gun in the hunting fields with regard to expansion and accuracy, it is possible another brand may not, leaving you to track a wounded animal.

Speer Grand Slams or the famous Nosler Partitions seem to lead the way in big game hunting. Soft or hollow points are good all-round game getters, but again much depends on the gun, the rifling, the load and, of course, the shooter.

In answer to your question, I recommend you read all you can on outdoor lore and hunting practices, run your own private survey, then try a few brands. Only then will you be completely satisfied.

QUESTION; The competition bug has bitten me and to prove it I just plunked down a hefty pile of hard-earned cash for a Smith & Wesson Model 52. With so much practice needed to keep up good scores, should I see a progressive loader in my future?

ANSWER: I do. And with good reason.

First, to practice more you have to shoot more. While this is not earth-shaking news in itself, to accomplish this with the least strain on you and your budget, a progressive loader is indeed one way to go. The Dillon or Hornady Pro-7 will do the job of turning out hundreds of reloads per hour with a consistency that is almost scary!

In concert with this, you might want to consider bullet casting. By scrounging around for lead and casting your own 148-grain wadcutter bullets, costs will start to come down very fast.

The Smith & Wesson Model 52 is a real honey of a pistol that shoots better than you (or I) can offhand. My Model 52 is amazingly accurate. Held in a rest and shooting just about any 148-grain wadcutters, it'll put all the shots through one hole. Best of luck on the competition circuit.

QUESTION: I'm a woman, love the outdoors and would like to go varmint hunting with my spouse. Do you have any particular rifle caliber preference that would suit a woman's slighter body frame and lesser physical strength, as opposed to a man's? I'd like to surprise my husband with my new-found knowledge of the sport.

ANSWER: For woodchucks, the .22 Hornet or .222 Remington are good bets. Both are easy on the shoulder and remarkably accurate. The Kimber Classic rifle is a real dandy in the Hornet, a cartridge that will hit the mild side of 2500 fps with just 9.5 grains of 2400 powder behind a 40-grain bullet. Since you didn't mention just what type of varmint hunting, the Hornet can be loaded with 45-, 50- and 55-grain bullets. The .222 takes over where the Hornet leaves off, extending your range another 100 yards or more.

All-round cartridges like the .243 Winchester, 6mm Remington or .250 Savage are good choices if you think a deer hunt with your husband may be in your future. They, too, have a mild recoil and can be loaded down; another joint venture the both of you can share, that of handloading.

QUESTION: For an upcoming hunting trip can you please give me trajectory tables on the following three bullet weights: 150, 180 and 220 grains, with velocities approaching 3300, 3000 and 2600 fps. The cartridge is the .300 Winchester Magnum.

ANSWER: Sure thing. Since you didn't mention the exact bullets you would be using, I chose Hornady's brand of 150-, 180- and 220-grain bullets. Fed into my Apple IIe with a DataTech Ballistics Program, I came up with the following table—with a zero of 300 yards on the first two; 100 yards on the heavier 220-grainer. The height of the scope was computed at 1.5 inches, the average for scope-equipped rifles. But before you take these figures as gospel, I would suggest you try them at the various distances in your gun just to confirm my findings.

	150 gr./3300 fps	180 gr./3000 fps	220 gr./2600 fps
50 yds.	+ 1.3 in.	+ 1.7 in.	0.0 in.
100 yds.	+ 3.1 in.	+ 3.9 in.	0.0 in.
150 yds.	+ 4.1 in.	+ 4.9 in.	− 1.8 in.
200 yds.	+ 3.9 in.	+ 4.6 in.	− 5.7 in.
250 yds.	+ 2.6 in.	+ 3.0 in.	− 12.1 in.
300 yds.	0.0 in.	0.0 in.	− 21.6 in.
350 yds.	− 4.0 in.	− 4.6 in.	—
400 yds.	− 9.6 in.	− 10.9 in.	—

The table also shows some interesting things about bullet trajectory. Note in the first example how on departure from the muzzle, the bullet rises out to 150 yards, then begins a gradual descent as it approaches the zero base. Now you can see why a zero at 300 yards is just about right for fast-stepping magnum calibers. With absolutely no holdover on your part, groups will be in roughly an 8-inch circle ($+4''$ $-4''$) all the way out to 350 yards.

QUESTION: With all the .22 centerfires so popular today, which do you prefer for varmint hunting: the .223, .22/250 or the .224 Weatherby? Naturally, I am a handloader.

ANSWER: That's a real toughie as I hate to foster my opinions on anyone else, but here goes.

Out of the three you mentioned—.223, .22/250 and the .224 Weatherby—the last one happens to be my own particular favorite. And it boils down to just three things: a well-proportioned rifle, superb accuracy and good, long-range velocity potential. Please remember, these results reflect *my* findings in *my* rifles with regards to velocity readings yielding the best accuracy. You may come up with

different results; again, this is what makes handloading so darned interesting.

First, the rifle. Weatherby makes a honey of a varmint rifle they call the Varmintmaster. Because I live in New England I like a light rifle for "chuckin." We hunt them here by roving from field to field instead of just sitting on a hilltop with a bull-barreled rifle and waiting for the little critters to pop up. In any event, the Varmintmaster checks in at around 7 to 7½ pounds, depending on the density of the wood, and has the smooth Weatherby action all nestled in a stock much shorter than its bigger brother, the Mark V.

For comparison, let's make up a chart showing results at the range. Again, while I know the .22/250 can be brought up in velocity, the best groups came in at these readings. With any .22 centerfire, I use a 200-yard zero and a bullet weight of 55 grains.

As for accuracy, my Weatherby will print groups in the quarter- and half-minute of angle at 100 yards if I do my part with 31.9 grains of IMR-4895, BR-2 primers and Hornady 55-grain spire point bullets. As always, for you first-timers trying this load in your rifle, please start at least 8 to 10% under my loading charge.

	.223 @ 3200 fps	.22/250 @3400 fps	.224 @ 3600 fps
100 yds.	+ 1.5 in.	+ 1.2 in.	+ 1.0 in.
200 yds.	0.0 in.	0.0 in.	0.0 in.
300 yds.	− 7.8 in.	− 6.7 in.	− 5.8 in.
400 yds.	− 23.9 in.	− 20.7 in.	− 17.0 in.

REFERENCE SECTION

Alberts Corp., P.O. Box 157, Franklin Lakes, NJ 07417—**LEAD BULLETS**

B-Square Co., Box 11281, Fort Worth, TX 76610—**GUNSMITH SUPPLIES**

Bear Reloaders, Inc., 2110 1st National Tower, Akron, OH 44308—**RELOADING TOOLS**

Belding and Mull, 100 North 4th Street, Philipsburg, PA 16866—**RELOADING EQUIPMENT**

Bonanza Sports, 412 Western Avenue, Faribault, MN 55021—**RELOADING EQUIPMENT**

Brass Extrusion Labs, 800 West Maple Lane, Bensenville, IL 60106—**SPECIAL RUN BRASS CASES FOR OLDER CALIBERS**

C'Arco, (Ransom Rest) P.O. Box 2043, San Bernardino, CA 92406—**PISTOL REST, RELOADING EQUIPMENT**

C-H Tool and Die, 106 North Harding, Owen, WI 54461—**RELOADING EQUIPMENT**

Camdex Inc., 2228 Fourteen Mile Road, Warren, MI 48092—**RELOADING EQUIPMENT**

Corbin Mfg., P.O. Box 758, Phoenix, OR 97535—**BULLET SWAGING EQUIPMENT**

DataTech Software Systems, 19312 E. Eldorado Drive, Aurora, CO 80013—**BALLISTICS PROGRAMS FOR MOST COMPUTERS**

Dillon Precision Products, 7755 E. Gelding Drive, Scottsdale, AZ 85260—**PROGRESSIVE RELOADERS**

Du Pont Powder Sales, Wilmington, DE 19898—**MODERN GUNPOWDER**

Federal Cartridge Co., 2700 Foshay Tower, Minneapolis, MN 55402—**AMMUNITION AND COMPONENTS**

Flambeau Products Corp., Middlefield, OH 44062—**RANGE PRODUCTS FOR THE HANDLOADER**

Forster Products, 82 East Lanark Ave., Lanark, IL 61046—**PRECISION RELOADING PRODUCTS**

Frontier Cartridge, Box 1848, Grand Island, NE 68801—**AMMUNITION**

Godfrey Reloading Supply, R.R. #1, Box 688, Brighton, IL 62012—**RELOADING EQUIPMENT**

Gopher Shooter's Supply, Box 278, Faribault, MN 55021—**RELOADING EQUIPMENT**

Green Bay Bullets, 233 North Ashland, Green Bay, WI 54303—**BULLETS**

Hensley and Gibbs, Box 10, Murphy, OR 97533—**BULLET MOULDS**

Hercules Inc., 910 Market Street, Wilmington, DE 19899—**MODERN GUNPOWDER**

Hodgdon Powder Co., 7710 W. 63rd St., Shawnee Mission, KS 66202—**MODERN GUNPOWDER**

Hornady Mfg., Box 1848, Grand Island, NE 68801—**RELOADING EQUIPMENT, BULLETS, LEAD SHOT**

Huntington's Die Specialities, P.O. Box 991, Oroville, CA 95965—**CUSTOM DIES**

Jet-Aer Corp., 100 Sixth Avenue, Paterson, NJ 07524—**CHEMICALS FOR THE SHOOTER AND HANDLOADER**

Lee Precision, Inc., 4275 Highway U, Hartford, WI 53027—**RELOADING EQUIPMENT**

Lyman Products, Route 147, Middlefield, CT 06455—**RELOADING EQUIPMENT**

MTM Molded Products, 5680 Webster Street, Dayton, OH 45414—**CARTRIDGE BOXES AND RANGE PRODUCTS**

Marquart Precision Co., Box 1740, Prescott, AZ 86302—**RELOADING EQUIPMENT**

Mayville Engineering, 715 South Street, Mayville, WI 53050—**SHOTSHELL RELOADING PRESSES**

Mequon Reloading Corp., 46 East Jackson, Hartford, WI 53027—**RELOADING EQUIPMENT**

Nosler Bullets, P.O. Box 688, Beaverton, OR 97005—**RIFLE BULLETS**

Oehler Research, Inc., P.O. Box 9135, Austin, TX 78766—**CHRONOGRAPHS**

Pacific Tool, Ordnance Plant Road, Grand Island, NE 68801—**RELOADING EQUIPMENT**

Pak-Tool Co., 4411 South West 100th, Seattle, WA 98146—**HAND-HELD RELOADING TOOLS**

Ponsness-Warren, P.O. Box 8, Rathdrum, ID 83858—**RELOADING EQUIPMENT**

Marian Powley, Petra Lane, R.R.#1, Eldridge, IA 52748—**"SLAPSTICKS"**

Quinetics Corp., Box 29007, San Antonio, TX 78229—**RELOADING EQUIPMENT**

RCBS, P.O. Box 1919, Oroville, CA 95965—**RELOADING EQUIPMENT**

Redding, 114 Starr Road, Cortland, NY 13045—**RELOADING EQUIPMENT**

Remington Arms Co., P.O. Box 1939, Bridgeport, CT 06602—**AMMUNITION, COMPONENTS**

SAECO, P.O. Box 778, Carpenteria, CA 93013—**BULLET MOULDS**

SSK Industries, Route One, Della Drive, Bloomingdale, OH 43910—**CUSTOM HANDGUNS AND LOADING EQUIPMENT FOR SAME**

Sierra Bullets, 10532 South Painter Ave., Santa Fe Springs, CA 90670—**PISTOL AND RIFLE BULLETS**

Speer Bullets, Box 896, Lewiston, ID 83501—**PISTOL AND RIFLE BULLETS**

Star Machine Works, 418 10th Avenue, San Diego, CA 92101—**RELOADING EQUIPMENT**

Texan Reloaders, 444 Cip Street, Watseka, IL 60970—**RELOADING EQUIPMENT**

Vibra-Tek, 2200 Bott Street, Colorado Springs, CO 80904—**BULLET CLEANING EQUIPMENT**

Weatherby Inc., 2781 Firestone Blvd., South Gate, CA 90280—**AMMUNITION FOR WEATHERBY CALIBERS, LOADING DIES**

Wilson, Box 324, Cashmere, WA 98815—**RELOADING EQUIPMENT**

Winchester-Western, New Haven, CT 06504—**AMMUNITION, COMPONENTS, MODERN GUNPOWDER**

Zero Bullets, P.O. Box 1188, Cullman, AL 35055—**BULLETS**

CCI AMMUNITION

22 RIMFIRE

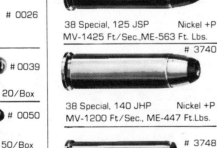

0030
Mini-Mag Long Rifle

0034
Mini-Mag Long Rifle
50 pack paper

0031
Mini-Mag Long Rifle
Hollow Point

0032
Mini-Group Long Rifle

0029
Mini-Mag Long

0027
Mini-Mag Short

0028
Mini-Mag Short
Hollow Point

0037
Mini-Group
Short Target

0038
Mini-Mag CB Long

0026
Mini-Cap CB

0039
Mini-Mag Shotshell
20/Box

0050
Stinger, Long Rifle
Hollow Point   50/Box

0023
Maxi-Mag WMR
Solid   50/Box

0024
Maxi-Mag WMR
Hollow Point   50/Box

0025
Maxi-Mag WMR
Shotshell   20/Box

380 AUTO

#3605
380 88JHP
MV1000Ft/Sec.   ME-195 Ft. Lbs.

9mm LUGER

3610
9mm Luger,100 JHP   Brass
MV-1315 Ft/Sec. ME-384 Ft. Lbs.

3620
9mm Luger, 125 JSP   Brass
MV-1120Ft/Sec., ME-348 Ft. Lbs.

38 SPECIAL

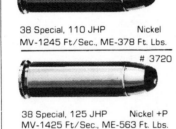

3710
38 Special, 110 JHP   Nickel
MV-1245 Ft/Sec., ME-378 Ft. Lbs.

3720
38 Special, 125 JHP   Nickel +P
MV-1425 Ft/Sec., ME-563 Ft. Lbs.

3725
38 Special, 125 JSP   Nickel +P
MV-1425 Ft/Sec.,ME-563 Ft. Lbs.

3740
38 Special, 140 JHP   Nickel +P
MV-1200 Ft/Sec., ME-447 Ft.Lbs.

3748
38 Special,148 HBWC   Brass
MV-825 Ft/Sec.,ME-223 Ft. Lbs.

3752
38 Special, 158 SWC   Nickel
MV—975 Ft/Sec.,ME-333 Ft. Lbs.

3758
38 Special, 158 RN   Nickel
MV-975 Ft/Sec.,ME-333 Ft. Lbs.

3759
38 Special, 158 JSP   Nickel +P
MV-1025 Ft/Sec., ME-368 Ft. Lbs.

3760
38 Special, 158 JHP   Nickel+P
MV-1025 Ft/Sec.,ME-368 Ft. Lbs.

3708
38/357 Shotshell
#9 Shot 50/Box

3709
38/357 Shotshell   Nickel
#9 shot 10/Box
MV-1150 Ft/Sec.,ME-308 Ft. Lbs.

357 MAGNUM

3910
357 Magnum, 110 JHP   Nickel
MV-1700 Ft/Sec., ME-705 Ft. Lbs.

3920
357 Magnum, 125 JHP   Nickel
MV-1900 Ft/Sec. ME-1001 Ft. Lbs.

3925
357 Magnum, 125 JSP   Nickel
MV-1900 Ft/Sec.,ME-1001 Ft. Lbs.

3940
357 Magnum, 140 JHP   Nickel
MV-1780 Ft/Sec. ME-984 Ft. Lbs.

3959
357 Magnum, 158 JSP   Nickel
MV-1625 Ft/Sec.,ME-926 Ft. Lbs.

3960
357 Magnum, JHP   Nickel
MV-1625 Ft/Sec., ME-926 Ft. Lbs.

44 MAGNUM

3972
44 Magnum, 200 JHP   Brass   25/Box
MV-1675 Ft/Sec.,ME-1246 Ft. Lbs.

3974
44 Magnum, 240 JSP   Brass   25/Box
MV-1650 Ft/Sec. ME-1450 Ft. Lbs.

44 Magnum Shotshell   # 3978
#9 shot 25/Box   Brass

44 Magnum Shotshell   # 3979
#9 Shot 10/Box   Brass
MV-1200 Ft/Sec., ME-494 Ft. Lbs.

45 AUTO

3965
45 Auto, 200 JHP   Brass
MV-1025 Ft/Sec.,ME-466 Ft.Lbs.

BLAZER CENTERFIRE
50 Pak 25 AUTO
3501   25 Auto-50-FMJ
9mm
3509   9mm-115-FMJ
38 SPECIAL
3514   38 + P-125-JHP
3517   38-148-HBWC
3519   38 + P-150-FMJ
3522   38-158-RNL
3523   38 + P-158-SWC HP
3526   38 + P-158-JHP
357 MAGNUM
3532   357-125-JHP
3542   357-158-JHP

FEDERAL CENTERFIRE AMMUNITION

NO.	CALIBER	WT. GRS.	BULLET STYLE	FACTORY PRIMER NO.
222A	222 Remington	50	Soft Point	205
222B	222 Remington	55	Metal Case Boat-tail	205
22250A	22-250 Remington	55	Soft Point	210
22250C	22-250 Remington	40	Hollow Point	
223A	223 Remington (5.56mm)	55	Soft Point	205
223B	223 Remington (5.56mm)	55	Metal Case Boat-tail	205
223C	223 Remington (5.56mm)	55	Hollow Point	
6A	6mm Remington	80	Soft Point	210
6B	6mm Remington	100	Hi-Shok Soft Point	210
243A	243 Winchester	80	Soft Point	210
243B	243Winchester	100	Hi-Shok Soft Point	210
2506A	25-06 Remington	90	Hollow Point	210
2506B	25-06 Remington	117	Hi-Shok Soft Point	210
270A	270 Winchester	130	Hi-Shok Soft Point	210
270B	270 Winchester	150	Hi-Shok Soft Point	210
7A	7mm Mauser	175	Hi-Shok Soft Point	210
7B	7mm Mauser Hi-S SP		Hi-Shok Soft Point	
7RA	7mm Remington Magnum	150	Hi-Shok Soft Point	215
7RB	7mm Remington Magnum	175	Hi-Shok Soft Point	215
30CA	30 Carbine	110	Soft Point	205
30CB	30 Carbine	110	Metal Case	205
3030A	30-30 Winchester	150	Hi-Shok Soft Point	210
3030B	30-30 Winchester	170	Hi-Shok Soft Point	210
3030C	30-30 Winchester	125	Hollow Point	210
3006A	30-06 Springfield	150	Hi-Shok Soft Point	210
3006B	30-06 Springfield	180	Hi-Shok Soft Point	210
3006C	30-06 Springfield	125	Soft Point	210
3006D	30-06 Springfield	165	Soft Point Boat-tail	210
3006E	30-06 Springfield	200	Soft Point Boat-tail	210
300A	300 Savage	150	Hi-Shok Soft Point	210
300B	300 Savage	180	Hi-Shok Soft Point	210
300WB	300 Winchester Magnum	180	Hi-Shok Soft Point	215
308A	308 Winchester	150	Hi-Shok Soft Point	210
308B	308 Winchester	180	Hi-Shok Soft Point	210
8A	8mm Mauser	170	Hi-Shok Soft Point	210
32A	32 Winchester Special	170	Hi-Shok Soft Point	210
35A	35 Remington	200	Hi-Shok Soft Point	210
44A	44 Remington Magnum	240	Hollow Soft Point	150
4570A	45-70 Government	300	Hollow Soft Point	210

RIFLE CARTRIDGES

NO.	CALIBER	WT. GRS.	BULLET STYLE	PRIMER NO.
25AP	25 Auto Pistol (6.35mm)	50	Metal Case	100
32AP	32 Auto Pistol (7.65mm)	71	Metal Case	100
380AP	380 Auto Pistol	95	Metal Case	100
380BP	380 Auto Pistol	90	Jacketed Hollow Point	100
9AP	9mm Luger Auto Pistol	123	Metal Case	100
9BP	9mm Luger Auto Pistol	115	Jacketed Hollow Point	100
38A	38 Special (Match)	148	Lead Wadcutter	100
38B	38 Special	158	Lead Round Nose	100
38C	38 Special	158	Lead Semi-Wadcutter	100
38D	38 Special (High Vel + P)	158	Lead Round Nose	200
38E	38 Special (High Vel + P)	125	Jacketed Hollow Point	200
38F	38 Special (High Vel + P)	110	Jacketed Hollow Point	200
38G	38 Special (High Vel + P)	158	Lead Semi-Wad Cutter Hollow Point	200
38H	38 Special (High Vel + P)	158	Lead Semi-Wadcutter	200
38J	38 Special (High Vel + P)	125	Jacketed Soft Point	200
357A	357 Magnum	158	Jacketed Soft Point	200
357B	357 Magnum	125	Jacketed Hollow Point	200
357C	357 Magnum	158	Lead Semi-Wadcutter	200
357D	357 Magnum	110	Jacketed Hollow Point	200
357E	357 Magnum	158	Jacketed Hollow Point	200
357G	357 Magnum		Jacketed Hollow Point	
357SM	357 Magnum		Jacketed Hollow Point	
44SA	S & W Special	200	Semi-Wadcutter Hollow Point	150
44B	44 Remington Magnum		Jacketed Hollow Point	150
45A	45 Automatic (Match)	230	Metal Case	150
45B	45 Automatic (Match)	185	Metal Case S.W.C.	150
45C	45 Automatic	185	Jacketed Hollow Point	150
45LCA	45 Colt	225	Lead Semi-Wad Cutter Hollow Point	150

PISTOL CARTRIDGES

HORNADY FRONTIER CARTRIDGES

RIFLE AMMUNITION

■ 222 REM.
50 gr. SX .... #8010
55 gr. SX .... #8015

■ 223 REM.
55 gr. SP .... #8025
55 gr. FMJ .... #8027

■ 22-250 REM.
53 gr. HP .... #8030
55 gr. SP .... #8035
55 gr. FMJ .... #8037
NEW 60 gr. SP .... #8039

■ 220 SWIFT
55 gr. SP .... #8120
60 gr. HP .... #8122

■ 243 WIN.
75 gr. HP .... #8040
80 gr. FMJ .... #8043
100 gr. BTSP .... #8046

■ 270 WIN.
110 gr. HP .... #8050
130 gr. SP .... #8055
140 gr. BTSP .... #8056
150 gr. SP .... #8058

■ 7mm REM. MAG.
NEW 139 gr. BTSP .... #8059
154 gr. SP .... #8060
175 gr. SP .... #8065

■ 30 M1 CARBINE
*110 gr. RN .... #8070
*110 gr. FM .... #8077

■ 30-30 WIN.
150 gr. RN .... #8080
170 gr. FP .... #8085

■ 308 WIN.
150 gr. SP .... #8090
165 gr. SP .... #8095
165 gr. BTSP .... #8098
168 gr. BTHP (Match) .... #8097

■ 30-06 SPRINGFIELD
150 gr. SP .... #8110
165 gr. BTSP .... #8115
168 gr. BTHP (Match) .... #8117
180 gr. SP .... #8118

■ 300 WIN. MAG.
180 gr. SP .... #8200
NEW 190 gr. BTSP .... #8220

PISTOL AMMUNITION

■ 25 AUTO
*50 gr. FMJ-RN .... #9000

■ 380 AUTO
*90 gr. JHP .... #9010
*100 gr. FMJ .... #9015

■ 9MM LUGER
*90 gr. JHP .... #9020
*100 gr. FMJ .... #9023
*115 gr. JHP .... #9025
*124 gr. FMJ-FP .... #9027
NEW *124 gr. RN .... #9029

■ 38 SPECIAL
*110 gr. JHP .... #9030
*125 gr. JHP .... #9032
*125 gr. JFP .... #9033
NEW *140 gr. JHP .... #9035
*148 gr. HBWC (Match) .... #9043
*158 gr. JHP .... #9036
*158 gr. JFP .... #9038
*158 gr. LRN .... #9045
*158 gr. SWC .... #9046

■ 357 MAG.
*125 gr. JHP .... #9050
*125 gr. JFP .... #9053
NEW *140 gr. JHP .... #9055
*158 gr. JHP .... #9056
*158 gr. JFP .... #9058
*158 gr. SWC .... #9065

■ 44 REM. MAG.
200 gr. JHP .... #9080
240 gr. JHP .... #9085
240 gr. SWC .... #9087

■ 45 ACP
185 gr. JHP .... #9090
185 gr. Target SWC .... #9095
200 gr. SWC .... #9110
200 gr. FMJ-C/T (Match) .... #9111
230 gr. FMJ-RN .... #9097
230 gr. FMJ-FP .... #9098

*Packed 50 per box. All others packed 20 per box.

NORMA CENTERFIRE RIFLE AMMO

NO.	WT. GRAINS	BULLET STYLE
220 SWIFT:		
15701	50	Soft Point Semi Pointed
222 REMINGTON:		
15711	50	Soft Point Semi Pointed
15712	**50**	**Full Jacket**
15714	53	Soft Point Semi Pointed Match Spitzer
22-250		
15733	53	Soft Point Semi Pointed Match Spitzer
22 SAVAGE HIGH POWER: (5.6x52 R):		
15604	71	Soft Point Semi Pointed
15605	71	Full Jacketed Semi Pointed
243 WINCHESTER:		
16002	100	Full Jacketed Semi Pointed
16003	100	Soft Point Semi Pointed
6.5 JAP:		
16531	139	Soft Point Semi Pointed Boat Tail
16532	156	Soft Point Round Nose
6.5 x 55:		
16557	139	Plastic Pointed "Dual-Core"
16552	156	Soft Point Round Nose
6.5 CARCANO:		
16535	156	Soft Point Round Nose
16536	139	Plastic Pointed "Dual-Core"
270 WINCHESTER:		
16902	130	Soft Point Semi Pointed Boat Tail
16903	150	Soft Point Semi Pointed Boat Tail
7 x 57 (7MM MAUSER):		
17002	150	Soft Point Semi Pointed Boat Tail
7MM REM. MAGNUM:		
17021	150	Soft Point Semi Pointed Boat Tail

NO.	WT. GRAINS	BULLET STYLE
7.5 x 55 SWISS:		
17511	180	Soft Point Semi Pointed Boat Tail
30 U.S. CARBINE:		
17621	110	Soft Point Round Nose
7.62 x 39 SHORT RUSSIAN:		
17672	**125**	**Soft Point**
7.62 RUSSIAN:		
17634	180	Soft Point Semi Pointed Boat Tail
30-06 SPRINGFIELD:		
17640	130	Soft Point Semi Pointed Boat Tail
17643	150	Soft Point Semi Pointed Boat Tail
17648	180	Soft Point Round Nose
17653	180	Plastic Pointed "Dual-Core"
30-30 WINCHESTER:		
17630	150	Soft Point Flat Nose
17631	170	Soft Point Flat Nose
308 WINCHESTER:		
17623	130	Soft Point Semi Pointed Boat Tail
17624	150	Soft Point Semi Pointed Boat Tail
17628	180	Plastic Pointed "Dual-Core"
308 NORMA MAGNUM:		
17638	180	Plastic Pointed "Dual-Core"
7.65 ARGENTINE:		
17701	150	Soft Point Semi Pointed
303 BRITISH:		
17712	150	Soft Point Semi Pointed
17713	180	Soft Point Semi Pointed Boat Tail
7.7 JAP:		
17721	130	Soft Point Semi Pointed
17722	180	Soft Point Semi Pointed Boat Tail
8 x 57 JS (8 MM MAUSER):		
18003	196	**Soft Point Round Nose**

NORMA CENTERFIRE PISTOL AMMUNITION

NO.	WT. GRAINS	BULLET STYLE
30 LUGER:		
17612	93	Full Jacketed Round Nose
32 ACP:		
17614	77	Full Jacketed Round Nose
9MM LUGER:		
19021	115	Hollow Point
19026	116	Soft Point Flat Nose
38 SPECIAL:		
19114	158	Full Jacketed Semi-Wad Cutter
19119	110	Jacketed Hollow Point Magnum
19110	148	Lead Wad Cutter
19112	158	Lead Round Nose

NO.	WT. GRAINS	BULLET STYLE
38 SPECIAL:		
19124	158	Soft Point Flat Nose
19125	158	Hollow Point
357 MAGNUM:		
19101	158	Hollow Point
19106	158	Full Jacketed Semi-Wad Cutter
19107	158	Soft Point Flat Nose
44 MAGNUM:		
11103	240	Power Cavity (Box of 50)

REMINGTON CENTERFIRE PISTOL & REVOLVER CARTRIDGES
with "KLEANBORE" PRIMING

22 Remington "Jet" Magnum

No.	Bullet weight	Bullet style	Wt. case, lbs.
R22JET	40 gr.	Soft Point	12

50 in a box, 500 in a case.

32 Short Colt

No.	Bullet weight	Bullet style	Wt. case, lbs.
R32SC	80 gr.	Lead	10

50 in a box, 500 in a case.

221 Remington "Fire Ball"

No.	Bullet weight	Bullet style	Wt. case, lbs.
R221F	50 gr.	PTd. Soft Point	12

20 in a box, 500 in a case.

32 Long Colt

No.	Bullet weight	Bullet style	Wt. case, lbs.
R32LC	82 gr.	Lead	10

50 in a box, 500 in a case.

25 (6.35mm) Auto. Pistol

No.	Bullet weight	Bullet style	Wt. case, lbs.
R25AP	50 gr.	Metal Case	28

50 in a box, 2,000 in a case.

32 (7.65mm) Auto. Pistol

No.	Bullet weight	Bullet style	Wt. case, lbs.
R32AP	71 gr.	Metal Case	36

50 in a box, 2,000 in a case.

32 S & W

No.	Bullet weight	Bullet style	Wt. case, lbs.
R32SW	88 gr.	Lead	41

50 in a box, 2,000 in a case.

32 S & W Long

No.	Bullet weight	Bullet style	Wt. case, lbs.
R32SWL	98 gr.	Lead	46

50 in a box, 2,000 in a case.

357 Magnum

No.	Bullet weight	Bullet style	Wt. case, lbs.
R357M7	110 gr.	Semi-Jacketed Hollow Point	63
R357M1	125 gr.	Semi-Jacketed Hollow Point	71
R357M2	158 gr.	Semi-Jacketed Hollow Point	77
R357M3	158 gr.	Soft Point	77
R357M4	158 gr.	Metal Point	77
R357M5	158 gr.	Lead	77
R357M6	158 gr.	Lead (Brass Case)	77

50 in a box, 2,000 in a case.

9mm Luger Auto. Pistol

No.	Bullet weight	Bullet style	Wt. case, lbs.
R9MM1	115 gr.	Jacketed Hollow Point	54
R9MM2	124 gr.	Metal Case	56

50 in a box, 2,000 in a case.

38 S & W

No.	Bullet weight	Bullet style	Wt. case, lbs.
R38SW	146 gr.	Lead	63

50 in a box, 2,000 in a case.

(+P) Ammunition with (+P) on the case headstamp is loaded to higher pressure. Use only in firearms designated for this cartridge and so recommended by the gun manufacturer.

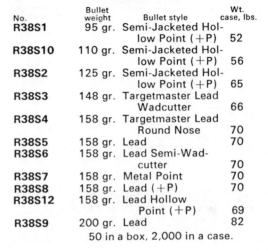

38 Special

No.	Bullet weight	Bullet style	Wt. case, lbs.
R38S1	95 gr.	Semi-Jacketed Hollow Point (+P)	52
R38S10	110 gr.	Semi-Jacketed Hollow Point (+P)	56
R38S2	125 gr.	Semi-Jacketed Hollow Point (+P)	65
R38S3	148 gr.	Targetmaster Lead Wadcutter	66
R38S4	158 gr.	Targetmaster Lead Round Nose	70
R38S5	158 gr.	Lead	70
R38S6	158 gr.	Lead Semi-Wad-cutter	70
R38S7	158 gr.	Metal Point	70
R38S8	158 gr.	Lead (+P)	70
R38S12	158 gr.	Lead Hollow Point (+P)	69
R38S9	200 gr.	Lead	82

50 in a box, 2,000 in a case.

38 Short Colt

No.	Bullet weight	Bullet style	Wt. case, lbs.
R38SC	125 gr.	Lead	14

50 in a box, 500 in a case.

38 Super Auto. Colt Pistol

Adapted only for 38 Colt Super and Colt Commander Automatic Pistols.

No.	Bullet weight	Bullet style	Wt. case, lbs.
R38SUI	115 gr.	Jacketed Hollow Point (+P)	56
R38SUP	130 gr.	Metal Case (+P)	62

50 in a box, 2,000 in a case.

38 Auto. Colt Pistol

Adapted only for 38 Colt Sporting, Military and Pocket Model Automatic Pistols.

No.	Bullet weight	Bullet style	Wt. case, lbs.
R38ACP	130 gr.	Metal Case	62

50 in a box, 2,000 in a case.

REMINGTON CENTERFIRE CARTRIDGES
PISTOL/REVOLVER

380 Auto. Pistol

No.	Bullet weight	Bullet style	Wt. case, lbs.
R380A1	88 gr.	Jacketed Hollow Point	45
R380AP	95 gr.	Metal Case	45

50 in a box, 2,000 in a case.

41 Magnum

No.	Bullet weight	Bullet style	Wt. case, lbs.
R41MG1	210 gr.	Soft Point	52
R41MG2	210 gr.	Lead	49

50 in a box, 1,000 in a case.

44 S&W Special

No.	Bullet weight	Bullet style	Wt. case, lbs.
R44SW	246 gr.	Lead	25

50 in a box, 500 in a case.

44 Remington Magnum

No.	Bullet weight	Bullet style	Wt. case, lbs.
R44MG1	240 gr.	Lead, Gas-Check	57
R44MG4	240 gr.	Lead	57

50 in a box, 1,000 in a case.

No.	Bullet weight	Bullet style	Wt. case, lbs.
R44MG2	240 gr.	Soft Point	29
R44MG3	240 gr.	Semi-Jacketed Hollow Point	29
R44MG5	180 gr.	Semi-Jacketed Hollow Point	29

20 in a box, 500 in a case.

45 Colt

No.	Bullet weight	Bullet style	Wt. case, lbs.
R45C	250 gr.	Lead	26

50 in a box, 500 in a case.

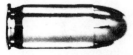

45 Auto.

No.	Bullet weight	Bullet style	Wt. case, lbs.
R45AP1	185 gr.	Targetmaster Metal Case Wadcutter	43
R45AP2	185 gr.	Jacketed Hollow Point	43
R45AP4	230 gr.	Metal Case	49

45 Auto. Rim

No.	Bullet weight	Bullet style	Wt. case, lbs.
R45AR	230 gr.	Lead	27

50 in a box, 500 in a case.

REMINGTON CENTER FIRE BLANK

No.	Caliber	No. in case	Wt. case, lbs.
R32BLNK	32 S & W	5,000	37
R38SWBL	38 S & W	2,000	25
R38BLNK	38 Special	2,000	28

50 in a box.

RIFLE

17 Remington

No.	Bullet weight	Bullet style	Wt. case, lbs.
R17REM	25 gr.	Hollow Point "Power-Lokt"	12

20 in a box, 500 in a case.

22 Hornet

No.	Bullet weight	Bullet style	Wt. case, lbs.
R22HN1	45 gr.	Pointed Soft Point	9
R22HN2	45 gr.	Hollow Point	9

50 in a box, 500 in a case.

222 Remington

No.	Bullet weight	Bullet style	Wt. case, lbs.
R222R1	50 gr.	Pointed Soft Point	27
R222R4	55 gr.	Metal Case	27
R222R3	50 gr.	Hollow Point "Power-Lokt"	27

20 in a box, 1,000 in a case.

222 Remington Magnum

No.	Bullet weight	Bullet style	Wt. case, lbs.
R222M1	55 gr.	Pointed Soft Point	15
R222M2	55 gr.	Hollow Point "Power-Lokt"	15

20 in a box, 500 in a case.

22-250 Remington

No.	Bullet weight	Bullet style	Wt. case, lbs.
R22501	55 gr.	Pointed Soft Point	42
R22502	55 gr.	Hollow Point "Power-Lokt"	42

20 in a box, 1,000 in a case.

(*) May be used in rifles chambered for .244 Remington.

REMINGTON CENTERFIRE RIFLE CARTRIDGES

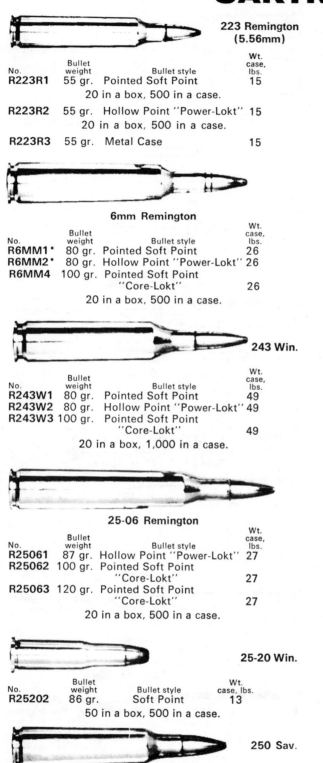

223 Remington (5.56mm)

No.	Bullet weight	Bullet style	Wt. case, lbs.
R223R1	55 gr.	Pointed Soft Point	15
		20 in a box, 500 in a case.	
R223R2	55 gr.	Hollow Point "Power-Lokt"	15
		20 in a box, 500 in a case.	
R223R3	55 gr.	Metal Case	15

6mm Remington

No.	Bullet weight	Bullet style	Wt. case, lbs.
R6MM1*	80 gr.	Pointed Soft Point	26
R6MM2*	80 gr.	Hollow Point "Power-Lokt"	26
R6MM4	100 gr.	Pointed Soft Point "Core-Lokt"	26
		20 in a box, 500 in a case.	

243 Win.

No.	Bullet weight	Bullet style	Wt. case, lbs.
R243W1	80 gr.	Pointed Soft Point	49
R243W2	80 gr.	Hollow Point "Power-Lokt"	49
R243W3	100 gr.	Pointed Soft Point "Core-Lokt"	49
		20 in a box, 1,000 in a case.	

25-06 Remington

No.	Bullet weight	Bullet style	Wt. case, lbs.
R25061	87 gr.	Hollow Point "Power-Lokt"	27
R25062	100 gr.	Pointed Soft Point "Core-Lokt"	27
R25063	120 gr.	Pointed Soft Point "Core-Lokt"	27
		20 in a box, 500 in a case.	

25-20 Win.

No.	Bullet weight	Bullet style	Wt. case, lbs.
R25202	86 gr.	Soft Point	13
		50 in a box, 500 in a case.	

250 Sav.

No.	Bullet weight	Bullet style	Wt. case, lbs.
R250SV	100 gr.	Pointed Soft-Point	24
		20 in a box, 500 in a case.	

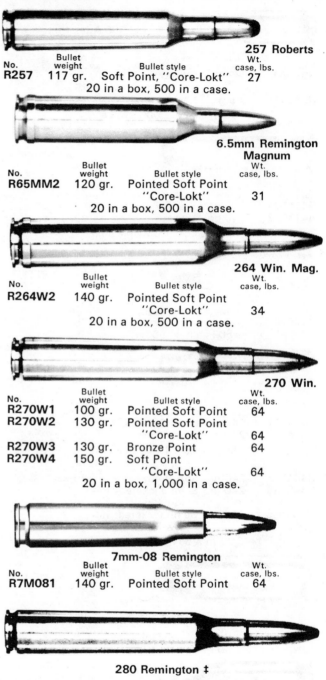

257 Roberts

No.	Bullet weight	Bullet style	Wt. case, lbs.
R257	117 gr.	Soft Point, "Core-Lokt"	27
		20 in a box, 500 in a case.	

6.5mm Remington Magnum

No.	Bullet weight	Bullet style	Wt. case, lbs.
R65MM2	120 gr.	Pointed Soft Point "Core-Lokt"	31
		20 in a box, 500 in a case.	

264 Win. Mag.

No.	Bullet weight	Bullet style	Wt. case, lbs.
R264W2	140 gr.	Pointed Soft Point "Core-Lokt"	34
		20 in a box, 500 in a case.	

270 Win.

No.	Bullet weight	Bullet style	Wt. case, lbs.
R270W1	100 gr.	Pointed Soft Point	64
R270W2	130 gr.	Pointed Soft Point "Core-Lokt"	64
R270W3	130 gr.	Bronze Point	64
R270W4	150 gr.	Soft Point "Core-Lokt"	64
		20 in a box, 1,000 in a case.	

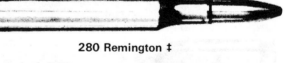

7mm-08 Remington

No.	Bullet weight	Bullet style	Wt. case, lbs.
R7M081	140 gr.	Pointed Soft Point	64

280 Remington ‡

No.	Bullet weight	Bullet style	Wt. case, lbs.
R280R1	150 gr.	Pointed Soft Point "Core-Lokt"	33
R280R2	165 gr.	Soft Point "Core-Lokt"	34
		20 in a box, 500 in a case.	

‡ Interchangeable with 7mm "Express" Rem.

REMINGTON CENTERFIRE RIFLE CARTRIDGES

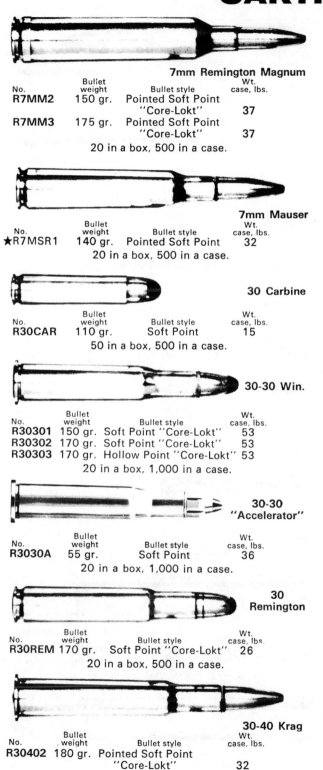

7mm Remington Magnum

No.	Bullet weight	Bullet style	Wt. case, lbs.
R7MM2	150 gr.	Pointed Soft Point "Core-Lokt"	37
R7MM3	175 gr.	Pointed Soft Point "Core-Lokt"	37

20 in a box, 500 in a case.

7mm Mauser

No.	Bullet weight	Bullet style	Wt. case, lbs.
★R7MSR1	140 gr.	Pointed Soft Point	32

20 in a box, 500 in a case.

30 Carbine

No.	Bullet weight	Bullet style	Wt. case, lbs.
R30CAR	110 gr.	Soft Point	15

50 in a box, 500 in a case.

30-30 Win.

No.	Bullet weight	Bullet style	Wt. case, lbs.
R30301	150 gr.	Soft Point "Core-Lokt"	53
R30302	170 gr.	Soft Point "Core-Lokt"	53
R30303	170 gr.	Hollow Point "Core-Lokt"	53

20 in a box, 1,000 in a case.

30-30 "Accelerator"

No.	Bullet weight	Bullet style	Wt. case, lbs.
R3030A	55 gr.	Soft Point	36

20 in a box, 1,000 in a case.

30 Remington

No.	Bullet weight	Bullet style	Wt. case, lbs.
R30REM	170 gr.	Soft Point "Core-Lokt"	26

20 in a box, 500 in a case.

30-40 Krag

No.	Bullet weight	Bullet style	Wt. case, lbs.
R30402	180 gr.	Pointed Soft Point "Core-Lokt"	32

20 in a box, 500 in a case.

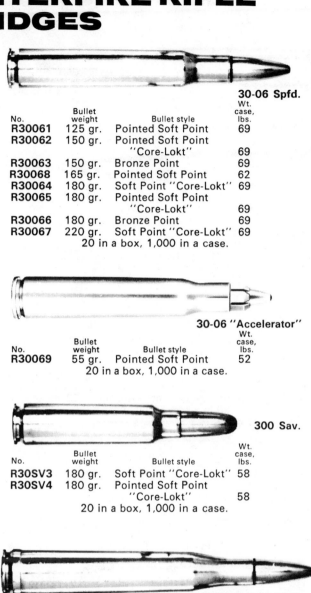

30-06 Spfd.

No.	Bullet weight	Bullet style	Wt. case, lbs.
R30061	125 gr.	Pointed Soft Point	69
R30062	150 gr.	Pointed Soft Point "Core-Lokt"	69
R30063	150 gr.	Bronze Point	69
R30068	165 gr.	Pointed Soft Point	62
R30064	180 gr.	Soft Point "Core-Lokt"	69
R30065	180 gr.	Pointed Soft Point "Core-Lokt"	69
R30066	180 gr.	Bronze Point	69
R30067	220 gr.	Soft Point "Core-Lokt"	69

20 in a box, 1,000 in a case.

30-06 "Accelerator"

No.	Bullet weight	Bullet style	Wt. case, lbs.
R30069	55 gr.	Pointed Soft Point	52

20 in a box, 1,000 in a case.

300 Sav.

No.	Bullet weight	Bullet style	Wt. case, lbs.
R30SV3	180 gr.	Soft Point "Core-Lokt"	58
R30SV4	180 gr.	Pointed Soft Point "Core-Lokt"	58

20 in a box, 1,000 in a case.

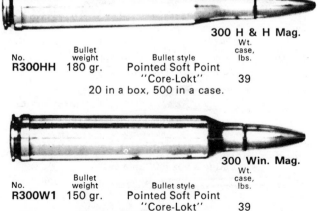

300 H & H Mag.

No.	Bullet weight	Bullet style	Wt. case, lbs.
R300HH	180 gr.	Pointed Soft Point "Core-Lokt"	39

20 in a box, 500 in a case.

300 Win. Mag.

No.	Bullet weight	Bullet style	Wt. case, lbs.
R300W1	150 gr.	Pointed Soft Point "Core-Lokt"	39
R300W2	180 gr.	Pointed Soft Point "Core-Lokt"	39

20 in a box, 500 in a case.

REMINGTON CENTERFIRE RIFLE CARTRIDGES

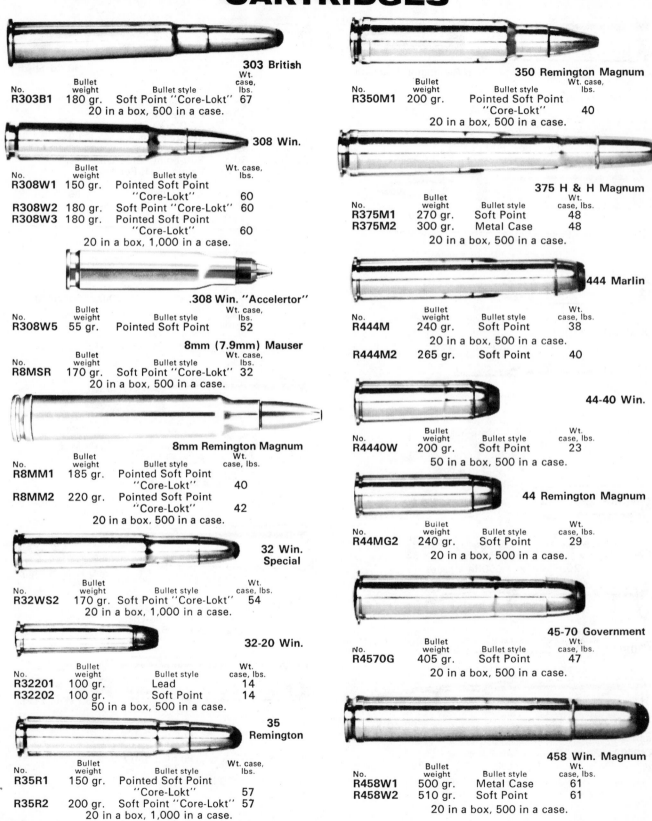

303 British

No.	Bullet weight	Bullet style	Wt. case, lbs.
R303B1	180 gr.	Soft Point "Core-Lokt"	67

20 in a box, 500 in a case.

308 Win.

No.	Bullet weight	Bullet style	Wt. case, lbs.
R308W1	150 gr.	Pointed Soft Point "Core-Lokt"	60
R308W2	180 gr.	Soft Point "Core-Lokt"	60
R308W3	180 gr.	Pointed Soft Point "Core-Lokt"	60

20 in a box, 1,000 in a case.

.308 Win. "Accelertor"

No.	Bullet weight	Bullet style	Wt. case, lbs.
R308W5	55 gr.	Pointed Soft Point	52

8mm (7.9mm) Mauser

No.	Bullet weight	Bullet style	Wt. case, lbs.
R8MSR	170 gr.	Soft Point "Core-Lokt"	32

20 in a box, 500 in a case.

8mm Remington Magnum

No.	Bullet weight	Bullet style	Wt. case, lbs.
R8MM1	185 gr.	Pointed Soft Point "Core-Lokt"	40
R8MM2	220 gr.	Pointed Soft Point "Core-Lokt"	42

20 in a box, 500 in a case.

32 Win. Special

No.	Bullet weight	Bullet style	Wt. case, lbs.
R32WS2	170 gr.	Soft Point "Core-Lokt"	54

20 in a box, 1,000 in a case.

32-20 Win.

No.	Bullet weight	Bullet style	Wt. case, lbs.
R32201	100 gr.	Lead	14
R32202	100 gr.	Soft Point	14

50 in a box, 500 in a case.

35 Remington

No.	Bullet weight	Bullet style	Wt. case, lbs.
R35R1	150 gr.	Pointed Soft Point "Core-Lokt"	57
R35R2	200 gr.	Soft Point "Core-Lokt"	57

20 in a box, 1,000 in a case.

350 Remington Magnum

No.	Bullet weight	Bullet style	Wt. case, lbs.
R350M1	200 gr.	Pointed Soft Point "Core-Lokt"	40

20 in a box, 500 in a case.

375 H & H Magnum

No.	Bullet weight	Bullet style	Wt. case, lbs.
R375M1	270 gr.	Soft Point	48
R375M2	300 gr.	Metal Case	48

20 in a box, 500 in a case.

444 Marlin

No.	Bullet weight	Bullet style	Wt. case, lbs.
R444M	240 gr.	Soft Point	38

20 in a box, 500 in a case.

| R444M2 | 265 gr. | Soft Point | 40 |

44-40 Win.

No.	Bullet weight	Bullet style	Wt. case, lbs.
R4440W	200 gr.	Soft Point	23

50 in a box, 500 in a case.

44 Remington Magnum

No.	Bullet weight	Bullet style	Wt. case, lbs.
R44MG2	240 gr.	Soft Point	29

20 in a box, 500 in a case.

45-70 Government

No.	Bullet weight	Bullet style	Wt. case, lbs.
R4570G	405 gr.	Soft Point	47

20 in a box, 500 in a case.

458 Win. Magnum

No.	Bullet weight	Bullet style	Wt. case, lbs.
R458W1	500 gr.	Metal Case	61
R458W2	510 gr.	Soft Point	61

20 in a box, 500 in a case.

WINCHESTER
PISTOL/REVOLVER CARTRIDGES

WINCHESTER SYMBOL	CARTRIDGE	CASE CONTAINS M's	BOXES PER CASE	CASE WT. LBS.
	218 Bee			
•X218B	46 gr. Hollow Point SUPER-X	½	10	10
	22 Hornet			
•X22H1	45 gr. Soft Point SUPER-X	½	10	9
•X22H2	46 gr. Hollow Point SUPER-X	½	10	9
	22-250 Remington			
X222501	55 gr. Pointed Soft Point SUPER-X	1	50	44
	222 Remington			
X222R	50 gr. Pointed Soft Point SUPER-X	1	50	31
X222R1	55 gr. Full Metal Case SUPER-X	1	50	32
	223 Remington			
X223R	55 gr. Pointed Soft Point SUPER-X	½	25	18
X233R1	55 gr. Full Metal Case SUPER-X	½	25	18
X223RH	53 gr. Hollow Point **NEW**	½	25	16
	225 Winchester			
X2251	55 gr. Pointed Soft Point SUPER-X	1	50	42
	243 Winchester (6mm)			
X2431	80 gr. Pointed Soft Point SUPER-X	1	50	50
X2432	100 gr. Power-Point (S.P.) SUPER-X	1	50	53
	6mm Remington			
X6MMR1	80 gr. Pointed Soft Point SUPER-X	½	25	27
X6MMR2	100 gr. Pointed Soft Point SUPER-X	½	25	27
	25-06 Remington			
X25061	90 gr. Positive Expanding Point SUPER-X.	½	25	30
X25062	120 gr. Positive Expanding Point SUPER-X.	½	25	32
	25-20 Winchester			
•X25202	86 gr. Soft Point	½	25	12
	25-35 Winchester			
X2535	117 gr. Soft Point SUPER-X	1	50	49
	250 Savage			
X2501	87 gr. Pointed Soft Point SUPER-X	½	25	26
X2503	100 gr. Silvertip Expanding SUPER-X.	½	25	27
	256 Winchester Magnum			
•X2561P	60 gr. Hollow Point SUPER-X	2	100	49
	257 Roberts + P			
X257P2	100 gr. Silvertip Expanding SUPER-X + P	½	25	27
X257P3	117 gr. Power-Point (S.P.) SUPER-X + P	½	25	28
	264 Winchester Magnum			
X2641	100 gr. Pointed Soft Point SUPER-X	½	25	32
X2642	140 gr. Power-Point (S.P.) SUPER-X	½	25	35
	270 Winchester			
X2701	100 gr. Pointed Soft Point SUPER-X	1	50	58
X2705	130 gr. Power-Point (S.P.) SUPER-X	1	50	63
X2703	130 gr. Silvertip Expanding SUPER-X	1	50	63
X2704	150 gr. Power-Point (S.P.) SUPER-X	1	50	64
	284 Winchester			
X2842	150 gr. Power-Point (S.P.) SUPER-X	1	50	63
	7mm Mauser (7 x 57)			
X7MM	175 gr. Soft Point SUPER-X	½	25	33
	7mm Remington Magnum			
X7MMR3	125 gr. Power-Point (S.P.) SUPER-X	½	25	33
X7MMR1	150 gr. Power-Point (S.P.) SUPER-X	½	25	35
X7MMR2	175 gr. Power-Point (S.P.) SUPER-X	½	25	37
	30 Carbine			
•X30M1	110 gr. Hollow Soft Point	1	20	29
•X30M2	110 gr. Full Metal Case	1	20	29
	30-30 Winchester			
X30301	150 gr. Hollow Point SUPER-X	1	50	55
X30306	150 gr. Power-Point (S.P.) SUPER-X	1	50	55
X30302	150 gr. Silvertip Expanding (S.P.) SUPER-X	1	50	55
X30303	170 gr. Power-Point (S.P.) SUPER-X	1	50	57
X30304	170 gr. Silvertip Expanding SUPER-X.	1	50	57

•50 Per Box—All Others 20 Per Box   (S.P.) = Soft Point
+ P = Ammunition with (+ P) on the case head stamp is loaded to higher pressure.
Use only in firearms designated for this cartridge and so recommended by the gun manufacturer.

WINCHESTER CENTERFIRE RIFLE CARTRIDGES

CENTERFIRE RIFLE

Symbol No.	Cartridge	Wt. Grs.	Type of Bullet
•X218B	218 Bee	46	HP
•X22H1	22 Hornet	45	SP
•X22H2	22 Hornet	46	HP
X222501	22-250 Remington	55	PSP
X222R	222 Remington	50	PSP
X222R1	222 Remington	55	FMC
X223R	223 Remington	55	PSP
X223R1	223 Remington	55	FMC
X2251	225 Winchester	55	PSP
X2431	243 Win. (6mm)	80	PSP
X2432	243 Win. (6mm)	100	PP (SP)
X6MMR1	6 mm Remington	80	PSP
X6MMR2	6 mm Remington	100	PSP
X25061	25-06 Remington	90	PEP
X25062	25-06 Remington	120	PEP
•X25202	25-20 Winchester	86	SP
X2535	25-35 Winchester	117	SP
X2501	250 Savage	87	PSP
X2503	250 Savage	100	ST Exp
•X2561P	256 Win. Magnum	60	HP
X2572	257 Roberts	100	ST Exp
X2573	257 Roberts	117	PP (SP)
X257P2	257 Roberts + P new	100	ST Exp
X257P3	257 Roberts + P new	117	PP (SP)
X2641	264 Win. Magnum	100	PSP
X2642	264 Win. Magnum	140	PP (SP)
X2701	270 Winchester	100	PSP
X2705	270 Winchester	130	PP (SP)
X2703	270 Winchester	130	ST Exp
X2704	270 Winchester	150	PP (SP)
X2842	284 Winchester	150	PP (SP)
X7MM	7 mm Maus.(7x57)	175	SP
X7MMR1	7 mm Rem. Mag.	150	PP (SP)
X7MMR2	7 mm Rem. Mag.	175	PP (SP)
X7MMR3	7 mm Rem. Mag.	125	PP (SP)
•X30M1	30 Carbine	110	HSP
•X30M2	30 Carbine	110	FMC
X30301	30-30 Winchester	150	HP
X30306	30-30 Winchester	150	PP (SP)
X30302	30-30 Winchester	150	ST Exp
X30303	30-30 Winchester	170	PP (SP)
X30304	30-30 Winchester	170	ST Exp
X30060	30-06 Springfield	110	PSP
X30062	30-06 Springfield	125	PSP
X30061	30-06 Springfield	150	PP (SP)
X30063	30-06 Springfield	150	ST Exp
X30064	30-06 Springfield	180	PP (SP)
X30066	30-06 Springfield	180	ST Exp
X30068	30-06 Springfield	220	PP (SP)
X30069	30-06 Springfield	220	ST Exp
X30401	30-40 Krag	180	PP (SP)
X30403	30-40 Krag	180	ST Exp
X30WM1	300 Win. Magnum	150	PP (SP)
X30WM2	300 Win. Magnum	180	PP (SP)
X30WM3	300 Win. Magnum	220	ST Exp
X300H2	300 H & H Mag.	180	ST Exp
X3001	300 Savage	150	PP (SP)
X3003	300 Savage	150	ST Exp

CENTERFIRE RIFLE [Continued]

Symbol No.	Cartridge	Wt. Grs.	Type of Bullet
X3004	300 Savage	180	PP (SP)
X3005	300 Savage	180	ST Exp
X3032	303 Savage	190	ST Exp
X303B1	303 British	180	PP (SP)
X3075	307 Win. New	150	PP (SP)
X3076	307 Win. New	180	PP (SP)
X3081	308 Winchester	110	PSP
X3087	308 Winchester	125	PSP
X3085	308 Winchester	150	PP (SP)
X3082	308 Winchester	150	ST Exp
X3086	308 Winchester	180	PP (SP)
X3083	308 Winchester	180	ST Exp
X3084	308 Winchester	200	ST Exp
X32WS2	32 Win. Special	170	PP (SP)
X32WS3	32 Win. Special	170	ST Exp
•X32201	32-20 Winchester	100	L
•X32202	32-20 Winchester	100	SP
W3240JW	32-40 Winchester John Wayne Commemorative	165	SP
X8MM	8 mm Mauser (8x57, 7.9)	170	PP (SP)
X3381	338 Win. Magnum	200	PP (SP)
X3383	338 Win. Magnum	225	SP
X3482	348 Winchester	200	ST Exp
X35R1	35 Remington	200	PP (SP)
X35R3	35 Remington	200	ST Exp
•X351SL2	351 Win. S.L.	180	SP
X3561	356 Win. new	200	PP (SP)
X3563	356 Win. new	250	PP (SP)
X3581	358 Win. (8.8mm)	200	ST Exp
X375W	375 Winchester	200	PP (SP)
X375W1	375 Winchester	250	PP (SP)
X375H1	375 H & H Mag.	270	PP (SP)
X375H2	375 H & H Mag.	300	ST Exp
X375H3	375 H & H Mag.	300	FMC
•X3840	38-40 Winchester	180	SP
X3855	38-55 Winchester	255	SP
•X44MP	44 Rem. Mag. SX	240	L (GC)
X44MHSP	44 Rem. Mag. SX	240	HSP
X4440	44-40 Winchester	200	SP
X4570H	45-70 Govt.	300	JHP
X4580	458 Win. Magnum	500	FMC
X4581	458 Win. Magnum	510	SP

CENTERFIRE PISTOL & REVOLVER

Symbol No.	Cartridge	Wt. Grs.	Type of Bullet
•X25AXP	25 Auto (6.35mm)	45	EP
•X25AP	25 Auto (6.35mm)	50	FMC
•X2561P	256 Win. Magnum	60	HP
•X30LP	30 Luger (7.65mm)	93	FMC
•X32ASHP	32 Automatic	60	STHP
•X32AP	32 Automatic	71	FMC
•X32SWP	32 S & W	85	L
•X32SWLP	32 Smith & Wesson (Colt New Police) Long	98	L
•X32SCP	32 Short Colt	80	L
•X32LCP	32 Long Colt	82	L
	32 Colt New Police - See 32 S & W Long		
•X32201	32-20 Winchester	100	L
•X32202	32-20 Winchester	100	SP

CENTERFIRE PISTOL & REVOLVER [Continued]

Symbol No.	Cartridge	Wt. Grs.	Type of Bullet
•X3573P	357 Magnum SX	110	JHP
•X3576P	357 Magnum SX	125	JHP
•X357SHP	357 Magnum	145	STHP
•X3571P	357 Magnum SX	158	L
•X3574P	357 Magnum SX	158	JHP
•X3575P	357 Magnum SX	158	JSP
•X9MMJSP	9mmLuger(Par) + P	95	JSP
•X9LP	9mm Luger (Par)	115	FMC
•X9MMSHP	9mm Luger (Par)	115	STHP
•X38SWP	38 S & W	145	L
•X38WCPSV	38 Special	158	SWC
•X38S1P	38 Special	158	L
•X38S2P	38 Special	158	MP
•38S3P	38 Special	200	L
•X38SSHP	38 Spec. SX + P	95	STHP
•X38S6PH	38 Spec. SX + P	110	JHP
•X38S7PH	38 Spec. SX + P	125	JHP
•38SPD	38 Spec. SX + P	158	HP
•X38WCP	38 Spec. SX + P	158	SWC
•X38S4P	38 Spec. SX + P	150	L
•X38SMRP	38 Special Mid-Range	148	(Sharp Corner) Match
•X38SMP	38 Special SM	158	L
•X38SCP	38 Short Colt	130	L
•X38LCP	38 Long Colt	150	L
•X38ASHP	38 Automatic SX (For use only in 38 Colt Super and Colt Commander Automatic Pistols) + P	125	STHP
•X38A1P	38 Automatic SX (For use only in 38 Colt Super and Colt Commander Automatic Pistols) + P	125	FMC
•X38A2P	38 Automatic (For all 38 Colt Automatic Pistols)	130	FMC
•X380ASHP	380 Automatic	85	STHP
•X380AP	380 Automatic	95	FMC
•X3840	38-40 Winchester	180	SP
•X41MP	41 Rem. Mag. SX	210	L
•X41MJSP	41 Rem. Mag. SX	210	JSP
•X41MHP	41 Rem. Mag. SX	210	JHP
•X44SP	44 S & W Special	246	L
•X44STHPS	44 S&W Spec. new	200	STHP
•X44MP	44 Rem. Mag. SX	240	L (GC)
X44MHSP	44 Rem. Mag. SX	240	HSP
•X4440	44-40 Winchester	200	SP
•X45CSHP	45 Colt	225	STHP
•X45CP	45 Colt	255	L
•X45A1P	45 Automatic	230	FMC
X45ASHP	45 Automatic	185	STHP
•X45AWCP	45 Automatic SM Clean Cutting	185	FMC
•X45WM	45 Win. Mag. SX Not for arms chambered for standard 45 Automatic	230	FMC

CENTERFIRE BLANK CARTRIDGES

•32BL1P	32 S & W (No Bullet) Smokeless		
•32BL2P	32 S & W (No Bullet) Black Powder		
•38BLP	38 S & W (No Bullet) Smokeless		
•38SBLP	38 Special (No Bullet) Smokeless		

+ P = Ammunition with a (+ P) on the case head stamp is loaded to higher pressure. Use only in firearms designated for this cartridge and so recommended by the gun manufacturer.

• Packed 50 in a box, all others 20 in a box.

EP—Expanded Point	JHP—Jacketed Hollow Point	PEP—Positive Expanding Point	Spgfld.—Springfield
FMC—Full Metal Case	L—Lead	PP—Power-Point	SM—Super-Match
GC—Gas Check	Mag.—Magnum	Rem.—Remington	STHP—Silvertip Hollow Point
HV—High Velocity	Met. Pierc.—Metal Piercing	SL—Self-Loading	SWC—Semi-Wad Cutter
HP—Hollow Point	MP—Metal Point	ST Exp—Silvertip Expanding	SX—Super-X
HSP—Hollow Soft Point	MR—Mid-Range	SP—Soft Point	Win.—Winchester
JSP—Jacketed Soft Point	OPE—Open Point Expanding	PSP—Pointed Soft Point	

Conversion Factors and Tables

Common inch calibers converted to metric
.25 inch = 6.35mm
.256 inch = 6.5mm
.270 inch = 6.858mm
.280 inch = 7.11mm
.297 inch = 7.54mm
.300 inch = 7.62mm
.301 inch = 7.62mm
.303 inch = 7.696mm
.308 inch = 7.82mm
.311 inch = 7.899mm
.312 inch = 7.925mm
.380 inch = 9.65mm
.400 inch = 10.16mm
.402 inch = 10.21mm
.450 inch = 11.43mm
.455 inch = 11.557mm
.500 inch = 12.7mm
.550 inch = 13.97mm
.577 inch = 14.65mm
.600 inch = 15.24mm
.661 inch = 16.79mm

Pressure

1 kg per sq cm = 14.223 lb per sq inch
1 kg per sq cm =   0.0063493 tons per sq inch
1 kg per sq cm =   0.968 Atmospheres
1 Atmosphere = 14.7 lb. per sq inch
1 Atmosphere =   0.00655 tons per sq inch

1 ton per sq inch = 152.0 Atmospheres
1 lb per sq inch =   0.0680 Atmospheres
1 Atmosphere   =   1.03 kg per sq cm
1 lb per sq inch =   0.070309 kg per sq cm
1 ton per sq inch = 157.49 kg per sq cm

Energy
1 m.kg = 7.2331 foot lb
1 foot lb = 0.13825 m.kg

Velocity
1 meter per second = 3.2809 feet per second
1 foot   per second = 0.30479 meters per second

Weight

1 gram = 15.432 grains
1 grain = 0.0648 grams
1 oz   = 28.349 grams

Linear
1 meter = 1.0936 yards
1 meter = 3.2808 feet
1 yard = 0.91438 meters
1 foot = 0.30479 meters
1 inch = 25.4mm
¼ inch = 6.35mm
½ inch = 12.7mm
¾ inch = 19.05mm
⅛ inch = 3.175mm
⅜ inch = 9.525mm
⅝ inch = 15.875mm
⅞ inch = 22.225mm
 1/16 inch = 1.5875mm
 3/16 inch = 4.7625mm
 5/16 inch = 7.9375mm
 7/16 inch = 11.1125mm
 9/16 inch = 14.2875mm
11/16 inch = 17.4625mm
13/16 inch = 20.6375mm
15/16 inch = 23.8125mm

FEDERAL BALLISTICS

25AP 32AP 380AP 9AP 9BP 38B 38D 38C 38G 38H 38E 38F 38J 357A 357B 357D 357E 44SA 45A 45B

Automatic Pistol Ballistics (Approximate)

Federal Load No.	Caliber	Bullet Style	Bullet Weight in Grains	Velocity in Feet Per Second		Energy in Foot/Lbs.		Mid-range Trajectory 50 yds.	Test Barrel Length
				Muzzle	50 yds.	Muzzle	50 yds.		
25AP	25 Auto Pistol (6.35mm)	Metal Case	50	760	730	64	59	1.8"	2"
32AP	32 Auto Pistol (7.65mm)	Metal Case	71	905	855	129	115	1.4"	4"
380AP	380 Auto Pistol	Metal Case	95	955	865	190	160	1.4"	3¾"
380BP	380 Auto Pistol	Jacketed Hollow Point	90	1000	890	200	160	1.4"	3¾"
9AP	9mm Luger Auto Pistol	Metal Case	123	1120	1030	345	290	1.0"	4"
9BP	9mm Luger Auto Pistol	Jacketed Hollow Point	115	1160	1060	345	285	0.9"	4"
9CP	9mm Luger Auto Pistol	Jacketed Soft Point	95	1350	1140	385	275	0.7"	4"
45A	45 Automatic (Match)	Metal Case	230	850	810	370	335	1.6"	5"
45B	45 Automatic (Match)	Metal Case, S.W.C.	185	775	695	247	200	2.0"	5"
45C	45 Automatic (Match)	Jacketed Hollow Point	185	950	900	370	335	1.3"	5"

Revolver Ballistics (Approximate)

	Federal Load No.	Caliber	Bullet Style	Bullet Weight in Grains	Velocity in Feet Per Second		Energy in Foot/Lbs.		Mid-range Trajectory 50 yds.	Test Barrel Length*
					Muzzle	50 yds.	Muzzle	50 yds.		
	32LA	32 S & W Long	Lead Wadcutter	98	780	630	130	85	2.2"	4"
	32LB	32 S & W Long	Lead Round Nose	98	705	670	115	98	2.3"	4"
New	32HRA	32 H & R Magnum	Lead Semi-Wadcutter	95	1030	940	225	190	1.1"	4⅝"
	38A	38 Special (Match)	Lead Wadcutter	148	710	634	166	132	2.4"	4" -V
	38B	38 Special	Lead Round Nose	158	755	723	200	183	2.0"	4" -V
	38C	38 Special	Lead Semi-Wadcutter	158	755	723	200	183	2.0"	4" -V
▲	38D	38 Special (High Velocity + P)	Lead Round Nose	158	890	855	278	257	1.4"	4" -V
▲	38E	38 Special (High Velocity + P)	Jacketed Hollow Point	125	945	898	248	224	1.3"	4" -V
▲	38F	38 Special (High Velocity + P)	Jacketed Hollow Point	110	995	926	242	210	1.2"	4" -V
▲	38G	38 Special (High Velocity + P)	Semi-Wadcutter Hollow Point	158	890	855	278	257	1.4"	4" -V
▲	38H	38 Special (High Velocity + P)	Lead Semi-Wadcutter	158	890	855	278	257	1.4"	4" -V
▲	38J	38 Special (High Velocity + P)	Jacketed Soft Point	125	945	898	248	224	1.3"	4" -V
	357A	357 Magnum	Jacketed Soft Point	158	1235	1104	535	428	0.8"	4" -V
	357B	357 Magnum	Jacketed Hollow Point	125	1450	1240	583	427	0.6"	4" -V
	357C	357 Magnum	Lead Semi-Wadcutter	158	1235	1104	535	428	0.8"	4" -V
	357D	357 Magnum	Jacketed Hollow Point	110	1295	1094	410	292	0.8"	4" -V
	357E	357 Magnum	Jacketed Hollow Point	158	1235	1104	535	428	0.8"	4" -V
	357G	357 Magnum	Jacketed Hollow Point	180	1090	980	475	385	1.0"	4" -V
	357SM	357 Maximum	Jacketed Hollow Point	180	1550	1305	960	680	0.6"	10½"
New	41A	41 Rem. Magnum	Jacketed Hollow Point	210	1300	1130	790	595	0.7"	4" -V
	44SA	44 S & W Special	Semi-Wadcutter Hollow Point	200	900	830	360	305	1.4"	6½"-V
	44A	44 Rem. Magnum	Jacketed Hollow Point	240	1180	1081	741	623	0.9"	6½"-V
**	44B	44 Rem. Magnum	Jacketed Hollow Point	180	1610	1365	1045	750	0.5"	6½"-V
	44C	44 Rem. Magnum	Metal Case Profile	220	1390	1260	945	775	0.6"	6½"-V
	45LCA	45 Colt	Semi-Wadcutter Hollow Point	225	900	860	405	369	1.6"	5½"

*"V" indicates vented barrels to simulate service conditions.   **The 44B may be used in either handguns or rifles, however it is accurate only in handguns.   ▲ This "+ P" ammunition is loaded to a higher pressure. Use only in firearms so recommended by the manufacturer.   Pistol and revolver cartridges packed 50 rounds per box, 20 boxes per case. Exception: 44A packed 20 rounds per box.

FEDERAL BALLISTICS

Premium™ Centerfire Cartridge Ballistics
(Approximate)

Federal Load No.	Caliber	Bullet Wgt. in Grains	Bullet Style	Factory Primer	Velocity In Feet Per Second						Energy In Foot/Pounds					
					Muzzle	100 yds	200 yds	300 yds	400 yds	500 yds	Muzzle	100 yds	200 yds	300 yds	400 yds	500 yds
P22250B	22-250 Remington	55	Boat-tail H.P.	210	3680	3280	2920	2590	2280	1990	1655	1315	1040	815	630	480
P243C	243 Winchester	100	Boat-tail S.P.	210	2960	2760	2570	2380	2210	2040	1950	1690	1460	1260	1080	925
P243D		85	Boat-tail H.P.	210	3320	3070	2830	2600	2380	2180	2080	1770	1510	1280	1070	890
P270C	270 Winchester	150	Boat-tail S.P.	210	2850	2660	2480	2300	2130	1970	2705	2355	2040	1760	1510	1290
P270D		130	Boat-tail S.P.	210	3060	2830	2620	2410	2220	2030	2700	2320	1980	1680	1420	1190
P270E		150	Nosler Partition	210	2850	2590	2340	2100	1880	1670	2705	2225	1815	1470	1175	930
P7RD	7mm Remington Magnum	150	Boat-tail S.P.	215	3110	2920	2750	2580	2410	2250	3220	2850	2510	2210	1930	1690
P7RE		165	Boat-tail S.P.	215	2860	2710	2560	2420	2290	2160	3000	2690	2410	2150	1920	1700
P7RF		160	Nosler Partition	215	2950	2730	2520	2320	2120	1940	3090	2650	2250	1910	1600	1340
New P3030D	30-30 Winchester	170	Nosler Partition	210	2200	1900	1620	1380	1190	1060	1830	1355	990	720	535	425
P3006D	30-06 Springfield	165	Boat-tail S.P.	210	2800	2610	2420	2240	2070	1910	2870	2490	2150	1840	1580	1340
P3006F		180	Nosler Partition	210	2700	2470	2250	2040	1850	1660	2910	2440	2020	1670	1360	1110
P3006G		150	Boat-tail S.P.	210	2910	2690	2480	2270	2070	1880	2820	2420	2040	1710	1430	1180
P308C	308 Winchester	165	Boat-tail S.P.	210	2700	2520	2330	2160	1990	1830	2670	2310	1990	1700	1450	1230
P300WC	300 Winchester Magnum	200	Boat-tail S.P.	215	2830	2680	2530	2380	2240	2110	3560	3180	2830	2520	2230	1970
P338A	338 Winchester Magnum	210	Nosler Partition	215	2830	2590	2370	2150	1940	1750	3735	3130	2610	2155	1760	1435

Ballistic specifications were derived from test barrels 24 inches in length.

Hi-Power Centerfire Cartridge Ballistics
(Approximate)

Federal Load No.	Caliber	Bullet Wgt. in Grains	Bullet Style	Factory Primer	Velocity In Feet Per Second						Energy In Foot/Pounds					
					Muzzle	100 yds	200 yds	300 yds	400 yds	500 yds	Muzzle	100 yds	200 yds	300 yds	400 yds	500 yds
222A	222 Remington	50	Soft Point	205	3140	2600	2120	1700	1350	1110	1095	750	500	320	200	135
222B		55	Metal Cs. Boat-T.	205	3020	2740	2480	2230	1990	1780	1115	915	750	610	485	385
22250A	22-250 Remington	55	Soft Point	210	3680	3140	2660	2220	1830	1490	1655	1200	860	605	410	270
New 22250C		40	Hollow Point	210	4000	3320	2720	2200	1740	1360	1420	980	660	430	265	165
223A	223 Remington	55	Soft Point	205	3240	2750	2300	1910	1550	1270	1280	920	650	445	295	195
223B		55	Metal Cs. Boat-T.	205	3240	2950	2670	2410	2170	1940	1280	1060	875	710	575	460
223C		55	Boat Tail H.P.	205	3240	2880	2550	2240	1950	1680	1280	1010	790	610	460	345
6A	6mm Remington	80	Soft Point	210	3470	3060	2690	2350	2040	1750	2140	1665	1290	980	735	540
6B		100	Hi-Shok S.P.	210	3100	2830	2570	2330	2100	1890	2135	1775	1470	1205	985	790
243A	243 Winchester	80	Soft Point	210	3350	2960	2590	2260	1950	1670	1995	1550	1195	905	675	495
243B		100	Hi-Shok S.P.	210	2960	2700	2450	2220	1990	1790	1945	1615	1330	1090	880	710
2506A	25-'06 Remington	90	Hollow Point	210	3440	3040	2680	2340	2030	1750	2365	1850	1435	1100	825	610
2506B		117	Hi-Shok S.P.	210	2990	2730	2480	2250	2030	1830	2380	1985	1645	1350	1100	885
270A	270 Winchester	130	Hi-Shok S.P.	210	3060	2800	2560	2330	2110	1900	2700	2265	1890	1565	1285	1045
270B		150	Hi-Shok S.P.	210	2850	2500	2180	1890	1620	1390	2705	2085	1585	1185	870	640
7A	7mm Mauser	175	Hi-Shok S.P.	210	2440	2140	1860	1600	1380	1200	2315	1775	1340	1000	740	565
7B		140	Hi-Shok S.P.	210	2660	2450	2260	2070	1890	1730	2200	1865	1585	1330	1110	930
7RA	7mm Remington Magnum	150	Hi-Shok S.P.	215	3110	2830	2570	2320	2090	1870	3220	2670	2200	1790	1450	1160
7RB		175	Hi-Shok S.P.	215	2860	2650	2440	2240	2060	1880	3180	2720	2310	1960	1640	1370
*†30CA	30 Carbine	110	Soft Point	205	1990	1570	1240	1040	920	840	965	600	375	260	210	175
*†30CB		110	Metal Case	205	1990	1600	1280	1070	950	870	970	620	400	280	220	185
3030A	30-30 Winchester	150	Hi-Shok S.P.	210	2390	2020	1680	1400	1180	1040	1900	1355	945	650	460	355
3030B		170	Hi-Shok S.P.	210	2200	1900	1620	1380	1190	1060	1830	1355	990	720	535	425
3030C		125	Hollow Point	210	2570	2090	1660	1320	1080	960	1830	1210	770	480	320	260
3006A	30-'06 Springfield	150	Hi-Shok S.P.	210	2910	2620	2340	2080	1840	1620	2820	2280	1825	1445	1130	875
3006B		180	Hi-Shok S.P.	210	2700	2470	2250	2040	1850	1660	2915	2435	2025	1665	1360	1105
3006C		125	Soft Point	210	3140	2780	2450	2140	1850	1600	2735	2145	1660	1270	955	700
3006D		165	Boat Tail S.P.	210	2800	2610	2420	2240	2070	1910	2870	2490	2150	1840	1580	1340
3006E		200	Boat Tail S.P.	210	2550	2400	2260	2120	1990	1860	2890	2560	2270	2000	1760	1540
300WB	300 Winchester Magnum	180	Hi-Shok S.P.	215	2960	2750	2540	2340	2160	1980	3500	3010	2580	2195	1860	1565
300A	300 Savage	150	Hi-Shok S.P.	210	2630	2350	2100	1850	1630	1430	2305	1845	1460	1145	885	685
300B		180	Hi-Shok S.P.	210	2350	2140	1940	1750	1570	1410	2205	1825	1495	1215	985	800
308A	308 Winchester	150	Hi-Shok S.P.	210	2820	2530	2260	2010	1770	1560	2650	2140	1705	1345	1050	810
308B		180	Hi-Shok S.P.	210	2620	2390	2180	1970	1780	1600	2745	2280	1895	1555	1270	1030
**8A	8mm Mauser	170	Hi-Shok S.P.	210	2360	1970	1620	1330	1120	1000	2100	1465	995	670	475	375
32A	32 Winchester Special	170	Hi-Shok S.P.	210	2250	1920	1630	1370	1180	1040	1910	1395	1000	710	520	410
35A	35 Remington	200	Hi-Shok S.P.	210	2080	1700	1380	1140	1000	910	1920	1280	840	575	445	370
*††357G	357 Magnum	180	Hollow S.P.	100	1550	1160	980	860	770	680	960	535	385	295	235	185
*†44A	44 Remington Magnum	240	Hollow S.P.	150	1760	1380	1090	950	860	790	1650	1015	640	485	395	330
*4570A	45-'70 Government	300	Hollow S.P.	210	1880	1650	1430	1240	1110	1010	2355	1815	1355	1015	810	680

Unless otherwise noted, ballistic specifications were derived from test barrels 24 inches in length. †Test Barrel Length 20 Inches. ††Test Barrel Length 18 Inches. *Without Cartridge Carrier. **Only for use in barrels intended for .323 inch diameter bullets. Do not use in 8mm Commission Rifles (M1888) or sporting arms of similar bore diameter.
Rifle cartridges packed 20 rounds per box, 25 boxes per case. Exception: 357G packed 50 rounds per box. Velocity figures rounded off to nearest "10". Energy figures rounded off to nearest "5".

Premium™ Centerfire Cartridge Ballistics
(Approximate)

Bullet Drop — In Inches From Bore Line
Drift — In Inches In 10 mph Crosswind

Height of Trajectory
Inches above line of sight if sighted in at ⊕ yards. For sights .9" above bore.
Trajectory figures show the height of bullet impact above or below the line of sight at the indicated yardages. Aim low indicated amount for + figures and high for − figures. Zero ranges indicated by circled crosses.

Bullet Drop					Drift					Height of Trajectory												
100	200	300	400	500	100	200	300	400	500	50	100	150	200	250	300	100	150	200	250	300	400	500
yds	yds	yds	yds	yds	yds	yds	yds	yds	yds	yds	yds	yds	yds	yds	yds	yds	yds	yds	yds	yds	yds	yds
1.4	6.0	14.7	28.7	49.4	0.8	3.6	8.4	15.8	26.3	+0.1	+0.5	⊕	−1.4	−3.8	−7.3	+2.0	+2.3	+1.6	⊕	−2.8	−12.5	−28.9
2.0	8.5	20.3	38.2	63.2	0.6	2.6	6.1	11.3	18.4	+0.2	⊕	−0.9	−3.1	−6.5	−11.4	+1.5	+1.4	⊕	−2.7	−6.8	−19.7	−39.7
1.6	6.9	16.5	31.2	52.1	0.7	2.7	6.3	11.6	18.8	−0.1	⊕	−0.9	−2.8	−5.8	−9.9	+1.4	+1.2	⊕	−2.3	−5.8	−16.6	−33.6
2.2	9.4	22.3	41.7	68.8	0.7	2.7	6.3	11.6	18.9	+0.6	+0.9	⊕	−2.2	−5.9	−11.0	+2.0	+1.7	⊕	−3.1	−7.7	−22.0	−43.9
2.0	8.2	19.6	37.0	61.4	0.7	2.8	6.6	12.1	19.7	+0.4	+0.8	⊕	−1.9	−5.1	−9.7	+1.7	+1.4	⊕	−2.7	−6.8	−19.6	−39.5
2.3	9.8	23.7	45.5	77.2	0.9	3.9	9.2	17.3	28.5	+0.6	+1.0	⊕	−2.4	−6.4	−12.2	+2.2	+1.8	⊕	−3.4	−8.6	−25.0	−51.4
1.8	7.6	18.0	33.6	55.2	0.5	2.2	5.1	9.3	15.0	+0.4	+0.7	⊕	−1.8	−4.7	−8.8	+1.6	+1.3	⊕	−2.5	−6.2	−17.6	−35.0
2.0	8.8	20.9	38.8	63.4	0.5	2.1	4.8	8.7	14.0	+0.2	+0.7	⊕	−1.9	−5.1	−9.7	+1.6	+1.4	⊕	−2.7	−6.9	−19.7	−39.1
2.1	8.8	20.9	40.2	66.5	0.8	3.3	7.7	14.1	23.4	+0.5	+0.8	⊕	−2.3	−5.9	−11.1	+1.8	+1.6	⊕	−3.1	−7.7	−22.4	−44.7
4.0	17.7	44.8	90.3	160.2	1.9	8.0	19.4	36.7	59.8	+0.6	⊕	−3.0	−8.9	−18.0	−31.1	+2.0	⊕	−4.8	−13.0	−25.1	−63.6	−126.7
2.2	9.5	22.7	42.8	71.0	0.7	2.8	6.6	12.3	19.9	+0.5	⊕	−1.1	−4.2	−8.8	−14.3	+2.1	+1.8	⊕	−3.0	−8.0	−22.9	−45.9
2.5	10.8	25.9	49.4	83.2	0.9	3.7	8.8	16.5	27.1	+0.2	⊕	−1.6	−4.8	−9.7	−16.5	+2.4	+2.0	⊕	−3.7	−9.3	−27.0	−54.9
2.0	8.9	21.4	40.7	68.0	0.7	3.0	7.1	13.4	22.0	+0.2	⊕	−1.0	−3.3	−7.0	−12.3	+1.7	+1.5	⊕	−2.9	−7.3	−21.4	−43.6
2.4	10.2	24.5	46.3	76.8	0.7	3.0	7.0	13.0	21.1	+0.1	⊕	−1.3	−4.0	−8.4	−14.4	+2.0	+1.7	⊕	−3.3	−8.4	−24.3	−48.9
2.1	9.0	21.4	39.9	65.3	0.5	2.2	5.0	9.2	14.9	+0.2	+0.7	⊕	−2.0	−5.3	−10.1	+1.7	+1.5	⊕	−2.8	−7.1	−20.3	−40.4
2.3	9.8	23.5	44.8	75.3	0.8	3.5	8.3	15.4	25.4	+0.6	+1.0	⊕	−2.4	−6.3	−11.9	+2.1	+1.8	⊕	−3.3	−8.4	−24.3	−49.5

NOTE: Ballistic specifications were derived from test barrels 24 inches in length. These trajectory tables were calculated by computer using a modern scientific technique to predict trajectories from available data for each round. Each trajectory is expected to be reasonably representative of the behavior of the ammunition at sea level conditions, but shooters are cautioned that trajectories may differ because of variations in ammunition, rifles, and atmospheric conditions.

Hi-Power Centerfire Cartridge Ballistics
(Approximate)

Bullet Drop — In Inches From Bore Line
Drift — In Inches In 10 mph Crosswind

Height of Trajectory
Inches above line of sight if sighted in at ⊕ yards. For sights .9" above bore.
Trajectory figures show the height of bullet impact above or below the line of sight at the indicated yardages. Aim low indicated amount for + figures and high for − figures. Zero ranges indicated by circled crosses.

Bullet Drop					Drift					Height of Trajectory												
100	200	300	400	500	100	200	300	400	500	50	100	150	200	250	300	100	150	200	250	300	400	500
yds	yds	yds	yds	yds	yds	yds	yds	yds	yds	yds	yds	yds	yds	yds	yds	yds	yds	yds	yds	yds	yds	yds
2.0	9.2	24.3	51.6	98.2	1.7	7.3	18.3	36.4	63.1	+0.5	+0.9	⊕	−2.5	−6.9	−13.7	+2.2	+1.9	⊕	−3.8	−10.0	−32.3	−73.8
2.0	8.6	21.0	40.8	68.2	0.9	3.4	8.5	16.8	26.3	+0.5	+0.8	⊕	−2.1	−5.4	−10.8	+1.9	+1.6	⊕	−2.8	−7.7	−22.7	−45.3
1.4	6.4	16.4	33.5	61.2	1.2	5.2	12.5	24.4	42.0	+0.2	+0.5	⊕	−1.6	−4.4	−8.6	+2.3	+2.6	+1.9	⊕	−3.4	−15.8	−38.6
1.2	5.7	14.8	31.3	59.2	1.3	5.7	14.0	27.9	49.2	+0.1	+0.4	⊕	−1.4	−4.0	−8.0	+2.0	+2.4	+1.8	⊕	−3.2	−15.5	−39.3
1.8	8.4	21.5	44.4	81.8	1.4	6.1	15.0	29.4	50.8	+0.4	+0.8	⊕	−2.2	−6.0	−11.8	+1.9	+1.6	⊕	−3.3	−8.5	−26.7	−59.6
1.8	7.5	18.2	34.8	58.8	1.8	3.3	7.8	14.5	24.0	+0.3	+0.7	⊕	−1.8	−4.8	−9.1	+1.6	+1.3	⊕	−2.5	−6.4	−18.9	−38.7
1.8	7.8	19.2	37.6	65.2	1.0	4.2	10.0	19.1	32.0	+0.4	+0.7	⊕	−1.9	−5.1	−9.9	+1.7	+1.4	⊕	−2.8	−7.0	−21.1	−44.3
1.6	6.9	17.0	33.4	58.3	1.0	4.1	9.9	18.8	31.6	+0.3	+0.6	⊕	−1.6	−4.5	−8.7	+2.4	+2.7	+1.9	⊕	−3.3	−14.9	−35.0
1.9	8.2	19.8	37.7	63.6	0.8	3.3	7.9	14.7	24.1	+0.4	+0.8	⊕	−1.9	−5.2	−9.9	+1.7	+1.5	⊕	−2.8	−7.0	−20.4	−41.7
1.7	7.4	18.3	36.0	63.0	1.0	4.3	10.4	19.8	33.3	+0.3	+0.7	⊕	−1.8	−4.9	−9.4	+2.6	+2.9	+2.1	⊕	−3.6	−16.2	−37.9
2.1	9.0	21.7	41.6	70.2	0.9	3.6	8.7	15.7	25.8	+0.5	+0.9	⊕	−2.2	−5.8	−11.0	+1.9	+1.6	⊕	−3.1	−7.8	−22.6	−46.3
1.6	7.0	17.2	33.8	58.9	1.0	4.1	9.8	18.7	31.3	+0.3	+0.6	⊕	−1.7	−4.5	−8.8	+2.4	+2.7	+2.0	⊕	−3.4	−15.0	−35.2
2.1	8.8	21.2	40.5	68.2	0.8	3.4	8.1	15.1	24.9	+0.5	+0.8	⊕	−2.1	−5.7	−10.8	+1.9	+1.6	⊕	−3.0	−7.6	−22.3	−45.8
2.0	8.4	20.1	38.3	64.3	0.8	3.2	7.6	14.2	23.3	+0.4	+0.8	⊕	−2.0	−5.3	−10.1	+1.8	+1.5	⊕	−2.8	−7.1	−20.6	−42.0
2.3	10.3	25.5	50.6	89.2	1.2	5.3	12.8	24.5	41.3	+0.7	+1.0	⊕	−2.6	−7.1	−13.6	+2.3	+2.0	⊕	−3.8	−9.7	−29.2	−62.2
3.1	13.7	34.1	62.8	119.3	1.5	6.2	15.0	28.7	47.8	+0.4	⊕	−2.2	−6.6	−13.4	−23.0	+1.5	⊕	−3.6	−9.7	−18.6	−46.8	−92.8
2.7	10.9	26.3	50.0	81.9	1.3	3.2	8.2	15.4	23.4	+0.4	⊕	−1.5	−4.6	−9.9	−16.4	+2.4	+2.1	⊕	−3.2	−9.6	−27.3	−53.5
1.9	8.2	19.7	37.8	63.9	0.8	3.4	8.1	15.1	24.9	+0.4	+0.8	⊕	−1.9	−5.2	−9.9	+1.7	+1.5	⊕	−2.8	−7.0	−20.5	−42.1
2.2	9.5	22.5	42.5	70.8	0.7	3.1	7.2	13.3	21.7	+0.6	+0.9	⊕	−2.3	−6.0	−11.3	+2.0	+1.7	⊕	−3.2	−7.9	−22.7	−45.8
5.2	24.8	67.2	142.0	257.6	3.4	15.0	35.5	63.2	96.7	+0.9	⊕	−4.5	−13.5	−28.3	−49.9	⊕	−4.5	−13.5	−28.3	−49.9	−118.6	−228.1
5.1	24.1	64.5	135.1	244.1	3.1	13.7	32.6	58.7	90.3	+0.9	⊕	−4.3	−13.0	−26.9	−47.4	+2.9	⊕	−7.2	−19.7	−38.7	−100.4	−200.5
3.4	15.4	39.9	82.3	149.8	2.0	8.5	20.9	40.1	66.1	+0.5	⊕	−2.6	−7.7	−16.0	−27.9	+1.7	⊕	−4.3	−11.6	−22.7	−59.1	−120.5
4.0	17.7	44.8	90.3	160.2	1.9	8.0	19.4	36.7	59.8	+0.6	⊕	−3.0	−8.9	−18.0	−31.1	+2.0	⊕	−4.8	−13.0	−25.1	−63.6	−126.7
3.0	14.2	38.0	81.0	148.7	2.2	10.1	25.4	49.4	81.6	+0.1	⊕	−2.0	−7.3	−15.8	−28.1	+3.2	+2.4	⊕	−5.5	−15.8	−51.7	−112.3
2.2	9.5	23.2	44.9	76.9	1.0	4.2	9.9	18.7	31.2	+0.6	+0.9	⊕	−2.3	−6.3	−12.0	+2.1	+1.8	⊕	−3.3	−8.5	−25.0	−51.8
2.5	10.8	25.9	49.4	83.2	0.9	3.7	8.8	16.5	27.1	+0.2	⊕	−1.6	−4.8	−9.7	−16.5	+2.4	+2.0	⊕	−3.7	−9.3	−27.0	−54.9
1.9	8.3	20.6	40.6	70.7	1.1	4.5	10.8	20.5	34.4	+0.4	+0.8	⊕	−2.1	−5.6	−10.7	+1.8	+1.5	⊕	−3.0	−7.7	−23.0	−48.5
2.2	9.5	22.7	42.8	71.0	0.7	2.8	6.6	12.3	19.9	+0.5	⊕	−1.1	−4.2	−8.8	−14.3	+2.1	+1.8	⊕	−3.0	−8.0	−22.9	−45.9
2.6	11.2	26.6	59.7	81.6	0.6	2.6	6.0	11.0	17.7	+0.5	⊕	−2.0	−6.0	−12.4	−18.8	+2.3	+1.8	⊕	−4.1	−9.0	−25.8	−51.3
2.1	8.8	20.9	39.4	65.3	0.7	2.8	6.6	12.3	20.0	+0.5	+0.8	⊕	−2.1	−5.5	−10.4	+1.9	+1.6	⊕	−2.9	−7.3	−20.9	−41.9
2.7	11.7	28.7	55.8	96.1	1.1	4.8	11.6	21.9	36.3	+0.3	⊕	−1.8	−5.4	−11.0	−18.8	+2.7	+2.2	⊕	−4.2	−10.7	−31.5	−65.5
3.4	14.3	34.7	66.4	112.3	1.1	4.6	10.9	20.3	33.3	+0.4	⊕	−2.3	−6.7	−13.5	−22.8	+1.5	⊕	−3.6	−9.6	−18.2	−44.1	−84.2
2.3	10.1	24.8	48.0	82.4	1.0	4.4	10.4	19.7	32.7	+0.2	⊕	−1.5	−4.5	−9.3	−15.9	+2.3	+1.9	⊕	−3.6	−9.1	−26.9	−55.7
2.7	11.5	27.6	52.7	88.8	0.9	3.9	9.2	17.2	28.3	+0.2	⊕	−1.8	−5.2	−10.4	−17.7	+2.6	+2.1	⊕	−4.0	−9.9	−28.9	−58.8
3.5	11.1	42.1	87.8	161.0	2.1	9.3	22.9	43.9	71.7	+0.5	⊕	−2.7	−8.2	−17.0	−29.8	+1.8	⊕	−4.5	−12.4	−24.3	−63.8	−130.7
3.8	17.1	43.7	88.9	159.3	1.9	8.4	20.3	38.6	63.0	+0.6	⊕	−2.9	−8.6	−17.6	−30.5	+1.9	⊕	−4.7	−12.7	−24.7	−63.2	−126.9
4.6	21.5	56.9	118.9	215.6	2.7	12.0	29.0	53.3	83.3	+0.8	⊕	−3.8	−11.3	−23.5	−41.2	+2.5	⊕	−6.3	−17.1	−33.6	−87.7	−176.3
8.9	42.2	107.8	NA	NA	5.8	21.7	45.2	76.1	NA	⊕	−4.0	−14.2	−31.5	−56.8	−91.2	⊕	−8.2	−23.4	−46.8	−79.1	NA	NA
6.7	32.4	87.0	179.8	319.6	4.2	17.8	39.8	68.3	102.5	⊕	−2.7	−10.2	−23.6	−44.2	−73.3	⊕	−6.1	−18.1	−37.4	−65.1	−150.3	−282.5
4.3	21.5	57.2	112.8	NA	1.7	7.6	18.6	35.7	NA	⊕	−2.4	−8.2	−17.6	−31.4	−51.5	⊕	−4.6	−12.8	−25.4	−44.3	95.5	NA

NOTE: These trajectory tables were calculated by computer and are given here unaltered. The computer used a standard modern scientific technique to predict trajectories from the best available data for each round. Each trajectory is expected to be reasonably representative of the behavior of the ammunition at sea level conditions, but the shooter is cautioned that trajectories differ because of variations in ammunition, rifles, and atmospheric conditions.

NORMA BALLISTICS

Caliber / Bullet weight / Ref.	Velocity - Feet per sec.				Energy - Foot pounds				Sight at yards	Line of sights 1½ above center of bore. + indicates point of impact in inches above, - in inches below sighting point.					
	Muzzle	100 yards	200 yards	300 yards	Muzzle	100 yards	200 yards	300 yards		25 yards	50 yards	100 yards	150 yards	200 yards	300 yards
22 Hornet 45 gr/2.9 g Ref. 15601	2428	1896	1451	1135	589	360	210	129	100	−0.4	+0.2	O	−2.6	−8.4	−33.1
									150	±0	+1.1	+1.8	O	−4.9	−27.8
									200	+0.6	+2.3	+4.2	+3.7	O	−20.5
220 Swift 50 gr/3.2 g Ref. 15701	4110	3611	3133	2681	1877	1448	1090	799	100	−0.9	−0.5	O	−0.2	−1.2	−5.9
									180	−0.8	−0.3	+0.4	+0.4	−0.4	−4.7
									200	−0.8	−0.2	+0.6	+0.7	O	−4.1
222 Rem. 50 gr/3.2 g Ref. 15711	3200	2650	2170	1750	1137	780	520	340	100	−0.8	−0.3	O	−0.9	−3.2	−12.9
									180	−0.5	+0.3	+1.2	+0.8	−0.9	−9.4
									200	−0.4	+0.5	+1.6	+1.5	O	−8.2
222 Rem. 50 gr/3.2 g Ref. 15712	3200	2610	2080	1630	1137	756	480	295	100	−0.7	−0.2	O	−1.1	−3.7	−15.7
									180	−0.4	+0.5	+1.4	+1.0	−1.0	−11.6
									200	−0.3	+0.7	+1.9	+1.7	O	−10.1
222 Rem. 50 gr/3.2 g Ref. 15713	2790	2235	1755	1340	863	554	341	199	100	−0.6	±0	O	−1.7	−5.8	−23.4
									180	−0.1	+1.0	+2.1	+1.5	−1.5	−17.1
									200	+0.1	+1.4	+2.9	+2.6	O	−14.8
222 Rem. 50 gr/3.2 g Ref. 15715	3200	2610	2080	1630	1137	756	480	295	100	−0.7	−0.2	O	−1.1	−3.7	−15.7
									180	−0.4	+0.5	+1.4	+1.0	−1.0	−11.6
									200	−0.3	+0.7	+1.9	+1.7	O	−10.1
222 Rem. 53 gr/3.4 g Ref. 15714	3117	2670	2267	1901	1142	838	604	425	100	−0.7	−0.2	O	−1.0	−3.5	−14.0
									180	−0.4	+0.4	+1.3	+0.9	−0.9	−10.1
									200	−0.3	+0.6	+1.7	+1.6	O	−8.7
22-250 53 gr/3.4 g Ref. 15733	3707	3192	2741	2332	1616	1198	883	639	100	−0.9	−0.4	O	−0.5	−1.9	−8.6
									180	−0.7	−0.1	+0.7	+0.5	−0.6	−6.6
									200	−0.6	+0.1	+1.0	+1.0	O	−5.7
5.6x52 R 71 gr/4.6 g Ref. 15604	2790	2329	1955	1640	1226	855	603	424	100	−0.6	−0.1	O	−1.5	−4.8	−18.6
									180	−0.2	+0.8	+1.8	+1.2	−1.2	−13.2
									200	O	+1.1	+2.4	+2.1	O	−11.4
5.6x52 R 71 gr/4.6 g Ref. 15605	2790	2329	1955	1640	1226	855	603	424	100	−0.6	−0.1	O	−1.5	−4.8	−18.6
									180	−0.2	+0.8	+1.8	+1.2	−1.2	−13.2
									200	O	+1.1	+2.4	+2.1	O	−11.4
243 Win. 100 gr/6.5 g Ref. 16002	3070	2790	2540	2320	2090	1730	1430	1190	100	−0.7	−0.2	O	−0.9	−2.9	−10.6
									180	−0.5	+0.3	+1.1	+0.7	−0.7	−7.4
									200	−0.4	+0.5	+1.4	+1.3	O	−6.3
243 Win. 100 gr/6.5 g Ref. 16003	3070	2790	2540	2320	2090	1730	1430	1190	100	−0.7	−0.2	O	−0.9	−2.9	−10.6
									180	−0.5	+0.3	+1.1	+0.7	−0.7	−7.4
									200	−0.4	+0.5	+1.4	+1.3	O	−6.3
6.5 Jap. 139 gr/9.0 g Ref. 16531	2362	2185	2021	1867	1722	1473	1260	1076	100	−0.6	−0.1	O	−2.3	−6.4	−20.9
									130	−0.3	+0.4	+1.0	−0.9	−4.4	−17.9
									200	+0.2	+1.2	+3.2	+2.4	O	−11.3
6.5 Jap. 156 gr/10.1 g Ref. 16532	2065	1871	1692	1529	1481	1213	992	810	100	−0.3	+0.4	O	−2.9	−8.5	−29.2
									130	−0.1	+0.9	+1.1	−1.2	−6.3	−26.0
									200	+0.8	+2.5	+4.3	+3.5	O	−16.4
6.5 Carcano 139 gr/9 g Ref. 16536	2576	2379	2192	2012	2046	1745	1481	1249	100	−0.6	±0	O	−1.5	−4.7	−16.6
									180	−0.1	+0.9	+1.8	+1.1	−1.1	−11.3
									200	±0	+1.2	+2.3	+2.0	O	−9.6
6.5 Carcano 156 gr/10.1 g Ref. 16535	2430	2208	2000	1800	2046	1689	1386	1123	100	−0.5	+0.1	O	−1.9	−5.7	−20.2
									180	±0	+1.2	+2.2	+1.4	−1.3	−13.7
									200	+0.2	+1.5	+2.9	+2.4	O	−11.7
6.5x55 77 gr/5.0 g Ref. 16550	2725	2362	2030	1811	1271	956	706	562	100	−0.6	−0.1	O	−1.5	−4.8	−18.1
									180	−0.2	+0.8	+1.8	+1.2	−1.2	−12.7
									200	O	+1.1	+2.4	+2.1	O	−10.9
6.5x55 80 gr/5.2 g Ref. 16528	3002	2398	1886	1499	1604	1023	633	400	100	−0.7	−0.2	O	−1.4	−4.7	−19.3
									180	−0.3	+0.7	+1.7	+1.2	−1.2	−14.2
									200	±0	+1.0	+2.3	+2.1	O	−12.3
6.5x55 139 gr/9.0 g Ref. 16551	2854	2691	2533	2370	2512	2233	1978	1732	100	−0.7	−0.2	O	−1.0	−2.3	−12.3
									180	−0.6	+0.4	+1.3	+0.8	−0.8	−8.6
									200	−0.2	+0.5	+1.7	+1.5	O	−7.4
6.5x55 139 gr/9.0 g Ref. 16557	2790	2630	2470	2320	2402	2136	1883	1662	100	−0.7	−0.2	O	−1.1	−3.7	−13.3
									180	−0.3	+0.5	+1.4	+0.9	−0.9	−9.2
									200	−0.2	+0.8	+1.8	+1.6	O	−7.8
6.5x55 156 gr/10.1 g Ref. 16552	2495	2271	2062	1867	2153	1787	1473	1208	100	−0.7	+0.2	O	−1.7	−5.3	−18.8
									180	±0	+1.0	+2.0	+1.3	−1.3	−12.7
									200	+0.1	+1.3	+2.6	+2.2	O	−10.9
270 Win. 130 gr/8.4 g Bullet 16902	3140	2884	2639	2404	2847	2401	2011	1669	100	−0.8	−0.3	O	−0.8	−2.7	−10.7
									180	−0.5	+0.2	+1.0	+0.7	−0.7	−7.7
									200	−0.4	+0.4	+1.4	+1.3	O	−6.6
270 Win. 150 gr/9.7 g Ref. 16903	2800	2616	2436	2262	2616	2280	1977	1705	100	−0.7	−0.2	O	−1.1	−3.6	−13.1
									180	−0.3	+0.5	+1.4	+0.9	−0.9	−9.0
									200	−0.2	+0.7	+1.8	+1.6	O	−7.7
7x57 150 gr/9.7 g Ref. 17002	2755	2539	2331	2133	2530	2148	1810	1516	100	−0.7	−0.1	O	−1.2	−3.9	−14.3
									180	−0.3	+0.6	+1.5	+1.0	−1.0	−9.8
									200	−0.2	+0.9	+2.0	+1.7	O	−8.4
7x57 R 150 gr/9.7 g Ref. 17005	2690	2476	2270	2077	2411	2042	1717	1437	100	−0.6	−0.1	O	−1.3	−4.2	−15.2
									180	−0.2	+0.7	+1.6	+1.1	−1.0	−10.4
									200	−0.1	+1.0	+2.1	+1.8	O	−8.9
7 mm Rem. M. 150 gr/9.7 g Ref. 17021	3250	2960	2690	2440	3519	2919	2410	1983	100	−0.8	−0.3	O	−0.7	−2.4	−9.5
									180	−0.6	+0.1	+0.9	+0.6	+0.6	−6.8
									200	−0.5	+0.3	+1.2	+1.1	O	−5.8
7x64 150 gr/9.7 g Ref. 17013	2890	2625	2375	2165	2779	2295	1879	1561	100	−0.7	−0.2	O	−1.0	−3.3	−12.5
									180	−0.4	+0.4	+1.2	+0.9	−0.8	−8.8
									200	−0.3	+0.6	+1.7	+1.5	O	−7.5
7x64 175 gr/11.3 g Ref. 17015	2725	2533	2369	2238	2884	2493	2181	1946	100	−0.7	−0.1	O	−1.2	−3.6	−12.7
									180	−0.3	+0.6	+1.4	+0.9	−0.9	−8.5
									200	−0.2	+0.8	+1.8	+1.6	O	−7.2
280 Rem. 150 gr/9.7 g Ref. 17050	2900	2683	2475	2277	2802	2398	2041	1727	100	−0.7	−0.2	O	−1.0	−3.4	−12.4
									180	−0.4	+0.4	+1.2	+1.1	−0.8	−8.6
									200	−0.3	+0.7	+1.7	+1.5	O	−7.4
7.5x55 Swiss 180 gr/11.6 g Ref. 17511	2650	2461	2277	2106	2807	2420	2072	1773	100	−0.6	−0.1	O	−1.4	−4.3	−15.3
									180	−0.2	+0.7	+1.6	+1.1	−1.0	−10.4
									200	−0.1	+0.9	+2.1	+1.8	O	−8.9
30 US Carbine 110 gr/7.1 g Ref. 17621	1970	1595	1300	1090	948	622	413	290	100	−0.1	+0.6	O	−4.1	−12.4	−45.7
									130	+0.3	+1.4	+1.5	−1.8	−9.3	−41.1
									200	+1.4	+3.7	+6.2	+5.2	O	−27.0

NORMA BALLISTICS

Caliber Bullet weight Ref.	Velocity - Feet per sec.				Energy - Foot pounds				Sight at yards	Line of sights 1½ above center of bore. + indicates point of impact in inches above, − in inches below sighting point.					
	Muzzle	100 yards	200 yards	300 yards	Muzzle	100 yards	200 yards	300 yards		25 yards	50 yards	100 yards	150 yards	200 yards	300 yards
7.62 Russian 180 gr/11.6 g Ref. 17634	2575	2382	2211	2041	2650	2268	1954	1665	100 180 200	−0.6 −0.1 ±0	±0 +0.9 +1.2	○ +1.7 +2.3	−1.5 +1.1 +2.0	−4.6 −1.1 ○	−16.5 −11.2 −9.5
30–06 130 gr/8.4 g Ref. 17640	3205	2876	2561	2263	2966	2388	1894	1479	100 180 200	−0.8 −0.5 −0.4	−0.3 +0.2 +0.4	○ +1.0 +1.4	−1.5 +0.7 +1.3	−2.7 −0.7 ○	−10.8 −7.8 −6.7
30–06 130 gr/8.4 g Ref. 17658	2900	2466	2071	1717	2427	1754	1238	850	100 180 200	−0.7 −0.3 −0.1	−0.1 +0.7 +0.9	○ +1.6 +2.2	−1.3 +1.1 +1.9	−4.3 −1.1 ○	−16.9 −12.0 −10.4
30–06 150 gr/9.7 g Ref. 17643	2970	2680	2402	2141	2943	2393	1922	1527	100 180 200	−0.7 −0.4 −0.3	−0.2 +0.4 +0.6	○ +1.3 +1.7	−1.0 +0.9 +1.5	−3.4 −0.9 ○	−12.9 −9.1 −7.8
30–06 180 gr/11.6 g Ref. 17648	2700	2493	2297	2106	2914	2484	2109	1773	100 180 200	−0.6 −0.3 −0.1	−0.1 +0.7 +0.9	○ +1.6 +2.1	−1.3 +1.0 +1.8	−4.1 −1.7 ○	−14.9 −10.2 −8.7
30–06 180 gr/11.6 g Ref. 17649	2700	2513	2336	2152	2914	2524	2181	1851	100 180 200	−0.6 −0.3 −0.1	−0.1 +0.7 +0.9	○ +1.5 +2.0	−1.3 +1.0 +1.8	−4.1 −1.0 ○	−14.8 −10.2 −8.7
30–06 180 gr/11.6 g Ref. 17653	2700	2513	2336	2152	2914	2524	2181	1851	100 180 200	−0.6 −0.3 −0.1	−0.1 +0.7 +0.9	○ +1.5 +2.0	−1.3 +1.0 +1.8	−4.1 −1.0 ○	−14.8 −10.2 −8.7
30–30 Win. 150 gr/9.7 g Ref. 17630	2329	1998	1722	1486	1806	1330	988	735	100 130 200	−0.4 −0.3 +0.5	+0.2 +0.9 +2.1	○ −1.1 +3.8	−2.6 −5.8 +3.3	−7.6 −5.8 ○	−28.3 −25.6 −16.8
30–30 Win. 170 gr/11.0 g Ref. 17631	2133	1808	1555	1342	1717	1234	913	680	100 130 200	−0.3 ±0 +0.8	+0.4 +0.9 +2.6	○ +1.1 +4.5	−3.0 −1.3 +3.7	−8.9 −6.8 ○	−32.1 −28.6 −18.7
308 Win. 130 gr/8.4 g Ref. 17623	2900	2590	2300	2030	2428	1937	1527	1190	100 180 200	−0.7 −0.4 −0.2	−0.2 +0.5 +0.8	○ +1.4 +1.9	−1.1 +1.0 +1.7	−3.7 −0.9 ○	−14.2 −10.0 −8.6
308 Win. 130 gr/8.4 g Ref. 17674	2854	2424	2033	1683	2350	1695	1192	817	100 130 200	−0.7 −0.5 −0.1	−0.1 +0.1 +1.0	○ +0.5 +2.3	−1.4 −0.6 +2.0	−4.5 −3.5 ○	−17.5 −16.1 −10.7
308 Win. 150 gr/9.7 g Ref. 17624	2860	2570	2300	2050	2725	2200	1760	1400	100 180 200	−0.7 −0.3 −0.2	−0.2 +0.6 +0.8	○ +1.4 +1.9	−1.2 +1.0 +1.7	−3.8 −1.0 ○	−14.2 −10.0 −8.5
308 Win. 180 gr/11.6 g Ref. 17628	2610	2400	2210	2020	2725	2303	1952	1631	100 180 200	−0.6 −0.2 ±0	−0.1 +0.8 +1.1	○ +1.7 +2.3	−1.4 +1.1 +1.9	−4.5 −1.1 ○	−16.2 −11.0 −9.4
308 Win. 180 gr/11.6 g Ref. 17635	2610	2400	2210	2020	2725	2303	1952	1631	100 180 200	−0.6 −0.2 ±0	−0.1 +0.8 +1.1	○ +1.7 +2.3	−1.4 +1.1 +1.9	−4.5 −1.1 ○	−16.2 −11.0 −9.4
308 Win. 180 gr/11.6 g Ref. 17636	2610	2393	2185	1988	2725	2287	1906	1578	100 180 200	−0.6 −0.2 ±0	±0 +0.8 +1.1	○ +1.7 +2.3	−1.4 +1.1 +2.0	−4.6 −1.1 ○	−16.5 −11.3 −9.6
308 Norma M. 180 gr/11.6 g Ref. 17638	3020	2815	2618	2435	3646	3167	2739	2370	100 180 200	−0.8 −0.5 −0.4	−0.3 +0.2 +0.4	○ +1.0 +1.3	−0.8 +0.7 +1.2	−2.6 −0.7 ○	−10.1 −7.1 −6.1
7.65 Argentine 150 gr/9.7 g Ref. 17701	2789	2533	2290	2067	2591	2137	1747	1423	100 180 200	−0.7 −0.3 −0.2	−0.1 +0.6 +0.9	○ +1.5 +2.0	−1.3 +1.0 +1.7	−4.1 −1.0 ○	−14.8 −10.1 −8.7
303 British 150 gr/9.7 g Ref. 17712	2720	2440	2170	1930	2465	1983	1569	1241	100 180 200	−0.6 −0.2 −0.1	−0.1 +0.7 +1.0	○ +1.7 +2.2	−1.4 +1.1 +1.9	−4.4 −1.1 ○	−16.3 −11.3 −9.7
303 British 180 gr/11.6 g Ref. 17713	2540	2340	2147	1965	2579	2189	1843	1544	100 130 200	−0.6 −0.4 ±0	±0 +0.3 +1.2	○ +0.6 +2.4	−1.6 −0.7 +2.1	−4.9 −3.7 ○	−17.3 −15.6 −10.0
7.7 Jap. 130 gr/8.4 g Ref. 17721	2950	2635	2340	2065	2513	2004	1581	1231	100 180 200	−0.7 −0.4 −0.3	−0.2 +0.5 +0.7	○ +1.3 +1.8	−1.1 +0.9 +1.6	−3.5 −0.9 ○	−13.5 −9.5 −8.2
7.7 Jap. 180 gr/11.6 g Ref. 17722	2495	2292	2101	1922	2484	2100	1765	1477	100 130 200	−0.6 −0.4 +0.1	±0 +0.3 +1.3	○ +0.6 +2.6	−1.7 −0.8 +2.2	−5.2 −3.9 ○	−18.1 −16.3 −10.4
8x57 J 196 gr/12.7 g Ref. 17901	2525	2195	1894	1627	2778	2097	1562	1152	100 130 200	−0.6 −0.4 +0.2	±0 +0.4 +1.5	○ +0.7 +2.9	−1.8 −0.8 +2.5	−5.8 −4.4 ○	−21.4 −19.3 −12.7
8x57 JS 108 gr/7.0 g Ref. 18009	2976	2178	1562	1129	2122	1137	585	305	100 150 200	−0.6 −0.4 −0.1	−0.1 +0.5 +1.5	○ +1.2 +3.1	−1.8 ○ +4.0	−6.1 −3.8 ○	−27.1 −23.5 −17.9
8x57 JS 196 gr/12.7 g Ref. 18003	2525	2195	1894	1627	2778	2097	1562	1152	100 130 200	−0.6 −0.4 +0.2	±0 +0.4 +1.5	○ +0.7 +2.9	−1.8 −0.8 +2.5	−5.8 −4.4 ○	−21.4 −19.3 −12.7
8x57 JS 196 gr/12.7 g Ref. 18007	2525	2195	1894	1627	2778	2097	1562	1152	100 130 200	−0.6 −0.4 +0.2	±0 +0.4 +1.5	○ +0.7 +2.9	−1.8 −0.8 +2.5	−5.8 −4.4 ○	−21.4 −19.3 −12.7
9.3x57 154 gr/10.0 g Ref. 19304	2526	1987	1528	1186	2186	1353	800	481	100 150 200	−0.5 −0.1 +0.4	+0.1 +0.9 +2.0	○ +1.6 +3.8	−2.3 ○ +3.3	−7.5 −4.4 ○	−29.9 −25.2 −18.6
9.3x57 286 gr/18.5 g Ref. 19302	2065	1818	1595	1404	2714	2099	1616	1252	100 130 200	−0.3 ±0 +0.9	+0.4 +1.0 +2.7	○ +1.1 +4.6	−3.1 −1.3 +3.8	−9.1 −6.8 ○	−32.0 −28.5 −18.3
9.3x57 286 gr/18.5 g Ref. 19303	2065	1818	1595	1404	2714	2099	1616	1252	100 130 200	−0.3 ±0 +0.9	+0.4 +1.0 +2.7	○ +1.1 +4.6	−3.1 −1.3 +3.8	−9.1 −6.8 ○	−32.0 −28.5 −18.3
9.3x62 154 gr/10.0 g Ref. 19316	2854	2275	1769	1346	2790	1772	1072	621	100 150 200	−0.6 −0.4 ±0	−0.1 +0.5 +1.2	○ +1.1 +2.6	−1.6 ○ +2.3	−5.2 −3.1 ○	−22.0 −18.8 −14.2
9.3x62 286 gr/18.5 g Ref. 19314	2360	2088	1815	1592	3544	2769	2092	1609	100 180 200	−0.5 +0.1 +0.3	+0.1 +1.4 +1.8	○ +2.5 +3.3	−2.1 +1.6 +2.8	−6.5 −1.6 ○	−23.5 −16.0 −13.7
9.3x62 286 gr/18.5 g Ref. 19315	2360	2088	1815	1592	3544	2769	2092	1609	100 180 200	−0.5 +0.1 +0.3	+0.1 +1.4 +1.8	○ +2.5 +3.3	−2.1 +1.6 +2.8	−6.5 −1.6 ○	−23.5 −16.0 −13.7

REMINGTON CENTERFIRE RIFLE BALLISTICS

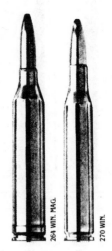

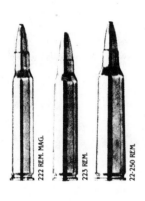

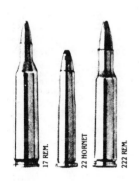

Remington Ballistics

CALIBERS	REMINGTON Order No.	BULLET		
		Wt.-Grs.	Style	Primer No.
17 REM.	R17REM	25*	Hollow Point Power-Lokt*	7½
22 HORNET	R22HN1	45*	Pointed Soft Point	6½
	R22HN2	45	Hollow Point	6½
222 REM.	R222R1	50	Pointed Soft Point	7½
	R222R3	50*	Hollow Point Power-Lokt	7½
	R222R4	55	Metal Case	7½
222 REM. MAG.	R222M1	55*	Pointed Soft Point	7½
	R222M2	55	Hollow Point Power-Lokt	7½
223 REM.	R223R1	55	Pointed Soft Point	7½
	R223R2	55*	Hollow Point Power-Lokt	7½
	R223R3	55	Metal Case	7½
22-250 REM.	R22501	55*	Pointed Soft Point	9½
	R22502	55	Hollow Point Power-Lokt	9½
243 WIN.	R243W1	80	Pointed Soft Point	9½
	R243W2	80*	Hollow Point Power-Lokt	9½
	R243W3	100	Pointed Soft Point Core-Lokt*	9½
6mm REM.	R6MM1	80**	Pointed Soft Point	9½
	R6MM2	80**	Hollow Point Power-Lokt	9½
	R6MM4	100*	Pointed Soft Point Core-Lokt	9½
25-20 WIN.	R25202	86‡	Soft Point	6½
250 SAV.	R250SV	100*	Pointed Soft Point	9½
257 ROBERTS	R257	117*	Soft Point Core-Lokt	9½
25-06 REM.	R25061	87	Hollow Point Power-Lokt	9½
	R25062	100*	Pointed Soft Point Core-Lokt	9½
	R25063	120	Pointed Soft Point Core-Lokt	9½
6.5mm REM. MAG.	R65MM2	120*	Pointed Soft Point Core-Lokt	9½M
264 WIN. MAG.	R264W2	140*	Pointed Soft Point Core-Lokt	9½M
270 WIN.	R270W1	100	Pointed Soft Point	9½
	R270W2	130*	Pointed Soft Point Core-Lokt	9½
	R270W3	130	Bronze Point	9½
	R270W4	150	Soft Point Core-Lokt	9½
7mm MAUSER	R7MSR1	140*	Pointed Soft Point	9½
7mm-08 REM.	R7M081	140*	Pointed Soft Point	9½
280 REM.††	R280R2	165*	Soft Point Core-Lokt	9½
7mm EXPRESS REM.††	R7M061	150*	Pointed Soft Point Core-Lokt	9½
7mm REM. MAG.	R7MM2	150*	Pointed Soft Point Core-Lokt	9½M
	R7MM3	175	Pointed Soft Point Core-Lokt	9½M
30 CARBINE	R30CAR	110*	Soft Point	6½
30 REM.	R30REM	170*	Soft Point Core-Lokt	9½
30-30 WIN. "ACCELERATOR"	R3030A	55*	Soft Point	9½
30-30 WIN.	R30301	150*	Soft Point Core-Lokt	9½
	R30302	170	Soft Point Core-Lokt	9½
	R30303	170	Hollow Point Core-Lokt	9½

†† 280 Rem. and 7mm Express Rem. are interchangeable.
‡ Subject to stock on hand.
* Illustrated.
** Interchangeable in 244 Rem.
+ Inches above or below line of sight. Hold low for positive numbers, high for negative numbers.

Cartridges not shown in actual size.
Specifications are nominal.
Ballistics figures established in test barrels.
Individual rifles may vary from test-barrel specifications.

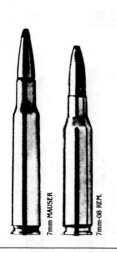

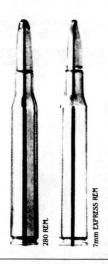

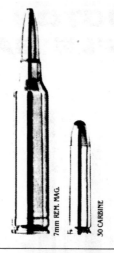

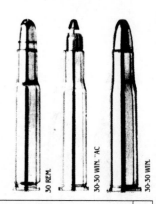

7mm MAUSER · 7mm-08 REM. · 280 REM. · 7mm EXPRESS REM. · 7mm REM. MAG. · 30 CARBINE · 30 REM. · 30-30 WIN. "AC" · 30-30 WIN.

TRAJECTORY† 0.0 Indicates yardage at which rifle was sighted in.

SHORT RANGE — Bullet does not rise more than one inch above line of sight from muzzle to sighting-in range.
LONG RANGE — Bullet does not rise more than three inches above line of sight from muzzle to sighting-in range.

VELOCITY FEET PER SECOND Muzzle	100 Yds.	200 Yds.	300 Yds.	400 Yds.	500 Yds.	ENERGY FOOT-POUNDS Muzzle	100 Yds.	200 Yds.	300 Yds.	400 Yds.	500 Yds.	SHORT RANGE 50 Yds.	100 Yds.	150 Yds.	200 Yds.	250 Yds.	300 Yds.	LONG RANGE 100 Yds.	150 Yds.	200 Yds.	250 Yds.	300 Yds.	400 Yds.	500 Yds.	BARREL LENGTH
4040	3284	2644	2086	1606	1235	906	599	388	242	143	85	0.1	0.5	0.0	-1.5	-4.2	-8.5	2.1	2.5	1.9	0.0	-3.4	-17.0	-44.3	24"
2690	2042	1502	1128	948	840	723	417	225	127	90	70	0.3	0.0	-2.4	-7.7	-16.9	-31.3	1.6	0.0	-4.5	-12.8	-26.4	-75.6	-163.4	24"
2690	2042	1502	1128	948	840	723	417	225	127	90	70	0.3	0.0	-2.4	-7.7	-16.9	-31.3	1.6	0.0	-4.5	-12.8	-26.4	-75.6	-163.4	
3140	2602	2123	1700	1350	1107	1094	752	500	321	202	136	0.5	0.9	0.0	-2.5	-6.9	-13.7	2.2	1.9	0.0	-3.8	-10.0	-32.3	-73.8	24"
3140	2635	2182	1777	1432	1172	1094	771	529	351	228	152	0.5	0.9	0.0	-2.4	-6.6	-13.1	2.1	1.8	0.0	-3.6	-9.5	-30.2	-68.1	
3020	2562	2147	1773	1451	1201	1114	801	563	384	257	176	0.6	1.0	0.0	-2.5	-7.0	-13.7	2.2	1.9	0.0	-3.8	-9.9	-31.0	-68.7	
3240	2748	2305	1906	1556	1272	1282	922	649	444	296	198	0.4	0.8	0.0	-2.2	-6.0	-11.8	1.9	1.6	0.0	-3.3	-8.5	-26.7	-59.5	24"
3240	2773	2352	1969	1627	1341	1282	939	675	473	323	220	0.4	0.8	0.0	-2.1	-5.8	-11.4	1.8	1.6	0.0	-3.2	-8.2	-25.5	-56.0	
3240	2747	2304	1905	1554	1270	1282	921	648	443	295	197	0.4	0.8	0.0	-2.2	-6.0	-11.8	1.9	1.6	0.0	-3.3	-8.5	-26.7	-59.6	24"
3240	2773	2352	1969	1627	1341	1282	939	675	473	323	220	0.4	0.8	0.0	-2.1	-5.8	-11.4	1.8	1.6	0.0	-3.2	-8.2	-25.5	-56.0	
3240	2759	2326	1933	1587	1301	1282	929	660	456	307	207	0.4	0.8	0.0	-2.1	-5.9	-11.6	1.9	1.6	0.0	-3.2	-8.4	-26.2	-57.9	
3730	3180	2695	2257	1863	1519	1699	1235	887	622	424	282	0.2	0.5	0.0	-1.5	-4.3	-8.4	2.2	2.6	1.9	0.0	-3.3	-15.4	-37.7	24"
3730	3253	2826	2436	2079	1755	1699	1292	975	725	528	376	0.2	0.5	0.0	-1.4	-4.0	-7.7	2.1	2.4	1.7	0.0	-3.0	-13.6	-32.4	
3350	2955	2593	2259	1951	1670	1993	1551	1194	906	676	495	0.3	0.7	0.0	-1.8	-4.9	-9.4	2.6	2.9	2.1	0.0	-3.6	-16.2	-37.9	24"
3350	2955	2593	2259	1951	1670	1993	1551	1194	906	676	495	0.3	0.7	0.0	-1.8	-4.9	-9.4	2.6	2.9	2.1	0.0	-3.6	-16.2	-37.9	
2960	2697	2449	2215	1993	1786	1945	1615	1332	1089	882	708	0.5	0.9	0.0	-2.2	-5.8	-11.0	1.9	1.6	0.0	-3.1	-7.8	-22.6	-46.3	
3470	3064	2694	2352	2036	1747	2139	1667	1289	982	736	542	0.3	0.6	0.0	-1.6	-4.5	-8.7	2.4	2.7	1.9	0.0	-3.3	-14.9	-35.0	24"
3470	3064	2694	2352	2036	1747	2139	1667	1289	982	736	542	0.3	0.6	0.0	-1.6	-4.5	-8.7	2.4	2.7	1.9	0.0	-3.3	-14.9	-35.0	
3130	2857	2600	2357	2127	1911	2175	1812	1501	1233	1004	811	0.4	0.7	0.0	-1.9	-5.1	-9.7	1.7	1.4	0.0	-2.7	-6.8	-20.0	-40.8	
1460	1194	1030	931	858	797	407	272	203	165	141	121	0.0	-4.1	-14.4	-31.8	-57.3	-92.0	0.0	-8.2	-23.5	-47.0	-79.6	-175.9	-319.4	24"
2820	2504	2210	1936	1684	1461	1765	1392	1084	832	630	474	0.2	0.0	-1.6	-4.7	-9.6	-16.5	2.3	2.0	0.0	-3.7	-9.5	-28.3	-59.5	24"
2650	2291	1961	1663	1404	1199	1824	1363	999	718	512	373	0.3	0.0	-1.9	-5.8	-11.9	-20.7	2.9	2.4	0.0	-4.7	-12.0	-36.7	-79.2	24"
3440	2995	2591	2222	1884	1583	2286	1733	1297	954	686	484	0.3	0.6	0.0	-1.7	-4.8	-9.3	2.5	2.9	2.1	0.0	-3.6	-16.4	-39.1	24"
3230	2893	2580	2287	2014	1762	2316	1858	1478	1161	901	689	0.4	0.7	0.0	-1.9	-5.0	-9.7	1.6	1.4	0.0	-2.7	-6.9	-20.5	-42.7	
3010	2749	2502	2269	2048	1840	2414	2013	1668	1372	1117	902	0.5	0.8	0.0	-2.1	-5.5	-10.5	1.9	1.6	0.0	-2.9	-7.4	-21.6	-44.2	
3210	2905	2621	2353	2102	1867	2745	2248	1830	1475	1177	929	0.4	0.7	0.0	-1.8	-4.9	-9.5	2.7	3.0	2.1	0.0	-3.5	-15.5	-35.3	24"
3030	2782	2548	2326	2114	1914	2854	2406	2018	1682	1389	1139	0.5	0.8	0.0	-2.0	-5.4	-10.2	1.8	1.5	0.0	-2.9	-7.2	-20.8	-42.2	24"
3480	3067	2690	2343	2023	1730	2689	2088	1606	1219	909	664	0.3	0.6	0.0	-1.6	-4.5	-8.7	2.4	2.7	1.9	0.0	-3.3	-15.0	-35.2	24"
3110	2823	2554	2300	2061	1837	2791	2300	1883	1527	1226	974	0.4	0.7	0.0	-2.0	-5.3	-10.0	1.7	1.5	0.0	-2.8	-7.1	-20.8	-42.7	
3110	2849	2604	2371	2150	1941	2791	2343	1957	1622	1334	1087	0.4	0.7	0.0	-1.9	-5.1	-9.7	1.7	1.4	0.0	-2.7	-6.8	-19.9	-40.5	
2900	2550	2225	1926	1653	1415	2801	2165	1649	1235	910	667	0.6	1.0	0.0	-2.3	-6.8	-13.1	2.2	1.8	0.0	-3.6	-9.3	-28.1	-59.7	
2660	2435	2221	2018	1827	1648	2199	1843	1533	1266	1037	844	0.2	0.0	-1.7	-5.0	-10.0	-17.0	2.5	2.0	0.0	-3.8	-9.6	-27.7	-56.3	24"
2860	2625	2402	2189	1988	1798	2542	2142	1793	1490	1228	1005	0.6	0.9	0.0	-2.3	-6.11	-11.6	2.1	1.7	0.0	-3.2	-8.1	-23.5	-47.7	24"
2820	2510	2220	1950	1701	1479	2913	2308	1805	1393	1060	801	0.2	0.0	-1.5	-4.6	-9.5	-16.4	2.3	1.9	0.0	-3.7	-9.4	-28.1	-58.8	24"
2970	2699	2444	2203	1975	1763	2937	2426	1989	1616	1299	1035	0.5	0.9	0.0	-2.2	-5.8	-11.0	1.9	1.6	0.0	-3.1	-7.8	-22.8	-46.7	24"
3110	2830	2568	2320	2085	1866	3221	2667	2196	1792	1448	1160	0.4	0.8	0.0	-1.9	-5.2	-9.9	1.7	1.5	0.0	-2.8	-7.0	-20.5	-42.1	24"
2860	2645	2440	2244	2057	1879	3178	2718	2313	1956	1644	1372	0.6	0.9	0.0	-2.3	-6.0	-11.3	2.0	1.7	0.0	-3.2	-7.9	-22.7	-45.8	
1990	1567	1236	1035	923	842	967	600	373	262	208	173	0.9	0.0	-4.5	-13.5	-28.3	-49.9	0.0	-4.5	-13.5	-28.3	-49.9	-118.6	-228.2	20"
2120	1822	1555	1328	1153	1036	1696	1253	913	666	502	405	0.7	0.0	-3.3	-9.7	-19.6	-33.8	2.2	0.0	-5.3	-14.1	-27.2	-69.0	-136.9	24"
3400	2693	2085	1570	1187	986	1412	886	521	301	172	119	0.4	0.8	0.0	-2.4	-6.7	-13.8	2.0	1.8	0.0	-3.8	-10.0	-15.0	-84.4	24"
2390	1973	1605	1303	1095	974	1902	1296	858	565	399	316	0.5	0.0	-2.7	-8.2	-17.0	-30.0	1.8	0.0	-4.6	-12.5	-24.6	-65.3	-134.9	24"
2200	1895	1619	1381	1191	1061	1827	1355	989	720	535	425	0.6	0.0	-3.0	-8.9	-18.0	-31.1	2.0	0.0	-4.8	-13.0	-25.1	-63.6	-126.7	
2200	1895	1619	1381	1191	1061	1827	1355	989	720	535	425	0.6	0.0	-3.0	-8.9	-18.0	-31.1	2.0	0.0	-4.8	-13.0	-25.1	-63.6	-126.7	

REMINGTON CENTERFIRE RIFLE BALLISTICS

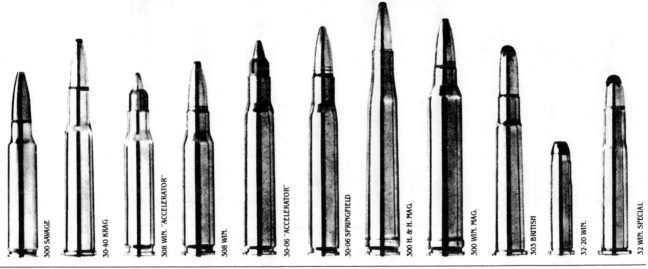

300 SAVAGE · 30-40 KRAG · 308 WIN. "ACCELERATOR" · 308 WIN. · 30-06 "ACCELERATOR" · 30-06 SPRINGFIELD · 300 H. & H. MAG. · 300 WIN. MAG. · 303 BRITISH · 32-20 WIN. · 32 WIN. SPECIAL

Remington Ballistics

CALIBERS	REMINGTON Order No.	BULLET Wt.-Grs.	BULLET Style	Primer No.	Muzzle	100 Yds.	200 Yds.	300 Yds.	400 Yds.	500 Yds.
300 SAVAGE	R30SV1	150	Soft Point Core-Lokt	9½	2630	2247	1897	1585	1324	1131
	R30SV3	180	Soft Point Core-Lokt	9½	2350	2025	1728	1467	1252	1098
	R30SV4	180*	Pointed Soft Point Core-Lokt	9½	2350	2137	1935	1745	1570	1413
30-40 KRAG	R30402	180*	Pointed Soft Point Core-Lokt	9½	2430	2213	2007	1813	1632	1468
308 WIN. "ACCELERATOR"	R308W5	55*	Pointed Soft Point	9½	3770	3215	2726	2286	1888	1541
308 WIN.	R308W1	150	Pointed Soft Point Core-Lokt	9½	2820	2533	2263	2009	1774	1560
	R308W2	180	Soft Point Core-Lokt	9½	2620	2274	1955	1666	1414	1212
	R308W3	180	Pointed Soft Point Core-Lokt	9½	2620	2393	2178	1974	1782	1604
30-06 "ACCELERATOR"	R30069	55*	Pointed Soft Point	9½	4080	3485	2965	2502	2083	1709
30-06 SPRINGFIELD	R30061	125	Pointed Soft Point	9½	3140	2780	2447	2138	1853	1595
	R30062	150	Pointed Soft Point Core-Lokt	9½	2910	2617	2342	2083	1843	1622
	R30063	150	Bronze Point	9½	2910	2656	2416	2189	1974	1773
	R3006B	165*	Pointed Soft Point Core-Lokt	9½	2800	2534	2283	2047	1825	1621
	R30064	180	Soft Point Core-Lokt	9½	2700	2348	2023	1727	1466	1251
	R30065	180	Pointed Soft Point Core-Lokt	9½	2700	2469	2250	2042	1846	1663
	R30066	180	Bronze Point	9½	2700	2485	2280	2084	1899	1725
	R30067	220	Soft Point Core-Lokt	9½	2410	2130	1870	1632	1422	1246
300 H. & H. MAG.	R300HH	180*	Pointed Soft Point Core-Lokt	9½M	2880	2640	2412	2196	1990	1798
300 WIN. MAG.	R300W1	150	Pointed Soft Point Core-Lokt	9½M	3290	2951	2636	2342	2068	1813
	R300W2	180*	Pointed Soft Point Core-Lokt	9½M	2960	2745	2540	2344	2157	1979
303 BRITISH	R303B1	180*	Soft Point Core-Lokt	9½	2460	2124	1817	1542	1311	1137
32-20 WIN.	R32201	100	Lead	6½	1210	1021	913	834	769	712
	R32202	100*	Soft Point	6½	1210	1021	913	834	769	712
32 WIN. SPECIAL	R32WS2	170*	Soft Point Core-Lokt	9½	2250	1921	1626	1372	1175	1044
8mm MAUSER	R8MSR	170*	Soft Point Core-Lokt	9½	2360	1969	1622	1333	1123	997
8mm REM. MAG.	R8MM1	185*	Pointed Soft Point Core-Lokt	9½M	3080	2761	2464	2186	1927	1688
	R8MM2	220	Pointed Soft Point Core-Lokt	9½M	2830	2581	2346	2123	1913	1716
35 REM.	R35R1	150	Pointed Soft Point Core-Lokt	9½	2300	1874	1506	1218	1039	934
	R35R2	200*	Soft Point Core-Lokt	9½	2080	1698	1376	1140	1001	911
350 REM. MAG.	R350M1	200*	Pointed Soft Point Core-Lokt	9½M	2710	2410	2130	1870	1631	1421
375 H. & H. MAG.	R375M1	270*	Soft Point	9½M	2690	2420	2166	1928	1707	1507
	R375M2	300	Metal Case	9½M	2530	2171	1843	1551	1307	1126
44-40 WIN.	R4440W	200*	Soft Point	2½	1190	1006	900	822	756	699
44 REM. MAG.	R44MG2	240	Soft Point	2½	1760	1380	1114	970	878	806
	R44MG3	240	Semi-Jacketed Hollow Point	2½	1760	1380	1114	970	878	806
444 MAR.	R444M	240	Soft Point	9½	2350	1815	1377	1087	941	846
	R444M2	265*	Soft Point	9½	2120	1733	1405	1160	1012	920
45-70 GOVERNMENT	R4570G	405*	Soft Point	9½	1330	1168	1055	977	918	869
458 WIN. MAG.	R458W1	500	Metal Case	9½M	2040	1823	1623	1442	1237	1161
	R458W2	510*	Soft Point	9½M	2040	1770	1527	1319	1157	1046

Reference Section

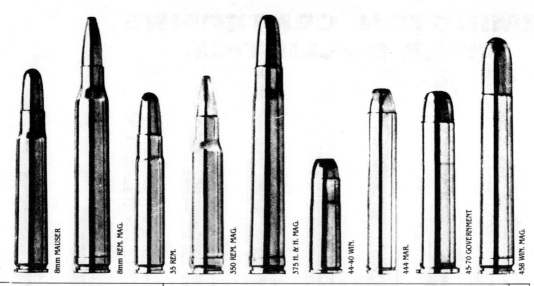

8mm MAUSER · 8mm REM. MAG. · 35 REM. · 350 REM. MAG. · 375 H. & H. MAG. · 44-40 WIN. · 444 MAR. · 45-70 GOVERNMENT · 458 WIN. MAG.

TRAJECTORY† 0.0 Indicates yardage at which rifle was sighted in.

	ENERGY FOOT-POUNDS					SHORT RANGE — Bullet does not rise more than one inch above line of sight from muzzle to sighting-in range.						LONG RANGE — Bullet does not rise more than three inches above line of sight from muzzle to sighting-in range.							BARREL LENGTH
Muzzle	100 Yds.	200 Yds.	300 Yds.	400 Yds.	500 Yds.	50 Yds.	100 Yds.	150 Yds.	200 Yds.	250 Yds.	300 Yds.	100 Yds.	150 Yds.	200 Yds.	250 Yds.	300 Yds.	400 Yds.	500 Yds.	
2303	1681	1198	837	584	426	0.3	0.0	-2.0	-6.1	-12.5	-21.9	1.3	0.0	-3.4	-9.2	-17.9	-46.3	-94.8	
2207	1639	1193	860	626	482	0.5	0.0	-2.6	-7.7	-15.6	-27.1	1.7	0.0	-4.2	-11.3	-21.9	-55.8	-112.0	
2207	1825	1496	1217	985	798	0.4	0.0	-2.3	-6.7	-13.5	-22.8	1.5	0.0	-3.6	-9.6	-18.2	-44.1	-84.2	24"
2360	1957	1610	1314	1064	861	0.4	0.0	-2.1	-6.2	-12.5	-21.1	1.4	0.0	-3.4	-8.9	-16.8	-40.9	-78.1	24"
1735	1262	907	638	435	290	0.2	0.5	0.0	-1.5	-4.2	-8.2	2.2	2.5	1.8	0.0	-3.2	-15.0	-36.7	24"
2648	2137	1705	1344	1048	810	0.2	0.0	-1.5	-4.5	-9.3	-15.9	2.3	1.9	0.0	-3.6	-9.1	-26.9	-55.7	
2743	2066	1527	1109	799	587	0.3	0.0	-2.0	-5.9	-12.1	-20.9	2.9	2.4	0.0	-4.7	-12.1	-36.9	-79.1	24"
2743	2288	1896	1557	1269	1028	0.2	0.0	-1.8	-5.2	-10.4	-17.7	2.6	2.1	0.0	-4.0	-9.9	-28.9	-58.8	
2033	1483	1074	764	530	356	0.4	1.0	0.9	0.0	-1.9	-5.0	1.8	2.1	1.5	0.0	-2.7	-12.5	-30.5	24"
2736	2145	1662	1269	953	706	0.4	0.8	0.0	-2.1	-5.6	-10.7	1.8	1.5	0.0	-3.0	-7.7	-23.0	-48.5	
2820	2281	1827	1445	1131	876	0.6	0.9	0.0	-2.3	-6.3	-12.0	2.1	1.8	0.0	-3.3	-8.5	-25.0	-51.8	
2820	2349	1944	1596	1298	1047	0.6	0.9	0.0	-2.2	-6.0	-11.4	2.0	1.7	0.0	-3.2	-8.0	-23.3	-47.5	
2872	2352	1909	1534	1220	963	0.7	1.0	0.0	-2.5	-6.7	-12.7	2.3	1.9	0.0	-3.6	-9.0	-26.3	-54.1	24"
2913	2203	1635	1192	859	625	0.2	0.0	-1.8	-5.5	-11.2	-19.5	2.7	2.3	0.0	-4.4	-11.3	-34.4	-73.7	
2913	2436	2023	1666	1362	1105	0.2	0.0	-1.6	-4.8	-9.7	-16.5	2.4	2.0	0.0	-3.7	-9.3	-27.0	-54.9	
2913	2468	2077	1736	1441	1189	0.2	0.0	-1.6	-4.7	-9.6	-16.2	2.4	2.0	0.0	-3.6	-9.1	-26.2	-53.0	
2837	2216	1708	1301	988	758	0.4	0.0	-2.3	-6.8	-13.8	-23.6	1.5	0.0	-3.7	-9.9	-19.0	-47.4	-93.1	24"
3315	2785	2325	1927	1583	1292	0.6	0.9	0.0	-2.3	-6.0	-11.5	2.1	1.7	0.0	-3.2	-8.0	-23.3	-47.4	24"
3605	2900	2314	1827	1424	1095	0.3	0.7	0.0	-1.8	-4.8	-9.3	2.6	2.9	2.1	0.0	-3.5	-15.4	-35.5	
3501	3011	2578	2196	1859	1565	0.5	0.8	0.0	-2.1	-5.5	-10.4	1.9	1.6	0.0	-2.9	-7.3	-20.9	-41.9	24"
2418	1803	1319	950	687	517	0.4	0.0	-2.3	-6.9	-14.1	-24.4	1.5	0.0	-3.8	-10.2	-19.8	-50.5	-101.5	24"
325	231	185	154	131	113	0.0	-6.3	-20.9	-44.9	-79.3	-125.1	0.0	-11.5	-32.3	-63.8	-106.3	-230.3	-413.3	
325	231	185	154	131	113	0.0	-6.3	-20.9	-44.9	-79.3	-125.1	0.0	-11.5	-32.3	-63.6	-106.3	-230.3	-413.3	24"
1911	1393	998	710	521	411	0.6	0.0	-2.9	-8.6	-17.6	-30.5	1.9	0.0	-4.7	-12.7	-24.7	-63.2	-126.9	24"
2102	1463	993	671	476	375	0.5	0.0	-2.7	-8.2	-17.0	-29.8	1.8	0.0	-4.5	-12.4	-24.3	-63.8	-130.7	24"
3896	3131	2494	1963	1525	1170	0.5	0.8	0.0	-2.1	-5.6	-10.7	1.8	1.6	0.0	-3.0	-7.6	-22.5	-46.8	
3912	3254	2688	2201	1787	1438	0.6	1.0	0.0	-2.4	-6.4	-12.1	2.2	1.8	0.0	-3.4	-8.5	-24.7	-50.5	24"
1762	1169	755	494	359	291	0.6	0.0	-3.0	-9.2	-19.1	-33.9	2.0	0.0	-5.1	-14.1	-27.8	-74.0	-152.3	
1921	1280	841	577	445	369	0.8	0.0	-3.8	-11.3	-23.5	-41.2	2.5	0.0	-6.3	-17.1	-33.6	-87.7	-176.4	24"
3261	2579	2014	1553	1181	897	0.2	0.0	-1.7	-5.1	-10.4	-17.9	2.6	2.1	0.0	-4.0	-10.3	-30.5	-64.0	20"
4337	3510	2812	2228	1747	1361	0.2	0.0	-1.7	-5.1	-10.3	-17.6	2.5	2.1	0.0	-3.9	-10.0	-29.4	-60.7	
4263	3139	2262	1602	1138	844	0.3	0.0	-2.2	-6.5	-13.5	-23.4	1.5	0.0	-3.6	-9.8	-19.1	-49.1	-99.5	24"
629	449	360	300	254	217	0.0	-6.5	-21.6	-46.3	-81.8	-129.1	0.0	-11.8	-33.3	-65.5	-109.5	-237.4	-426.2	24"
1650	1015	661	501	411	346	0.0	-2.7	-10.0	-23.0	-43.0	-71.2	0.0	-5.9	-17.6	-36.3	-63.1	-145.5	-273.0	
1650	1015	661	501	411	346	0.0	-2.7	-10.0	-23.0	-43.0	-71.2	0.0	-5.9	-17.6	-36.3	-63.1	-145.5	-273.0	20"
2942	1755	1010	630	472	381	0.6	0.0	-3.2	-9.9	-21.3	-38.5	2.1	0.0	-5.6	-15.9	-32.1	-87.8	-182.7	
2644	1768	1162	791	603	498	0.7	0.0	-3.6	-10.8	-22.5	-39.5	2.4	0.0	-6.0	-16.4	-32.2	-84.3	-170.2	24"
1590	1227	1001	858	758	679	0.0	-4.7	-15.8	-34.0	-60.0	-94.5	0.0	-8.7	-24.6	-48.2	-80.3	-172.4	-305.9	24"
4620	3689	2924	2308	1839	1469	0.7	0.0	-3.3	-9.6	-19.2	-32.5	2.2	0.0	-5.2	-13.6	-25.8	-63.2	-121.7	
4712	3547	2640	1970	1516	1239	0.8	0.0	-3.5	-10.3	-20.8	-35.6	2.4	0.0	-5.6	-14.9	-28.5	-71.5	-140.4	24"

† Subject to stock on hand.
* Illustrated.
‡ Inches above or below line of sight. Hold low for positive numbers, high for negative numbers.

Cartridges not shown in actual size.
Specifications are nominal.
Ballistics figures established in test barrels.
Individual rifles may vary from test-barrel specifications.

REMINGTON BALLISTICS

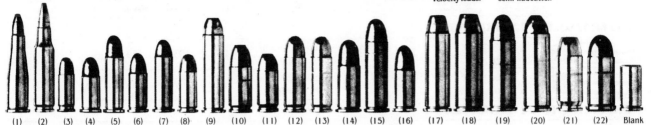

Semi-Jacketed Hollow Point, for maximum expansion.

Soft Point, for deeper penetration than SJHP.

Metal Case ensures positive functioning in autoloaders.

Wadcutter, solid lead for precision target shooting.

Metal Point, jacketed for best penetration.

Lead Gas-Check, minimizes lead fouling in higher-velocity loads.

Lead, our general-purpose bullet, in both round nose and semi-wadcutter.

(1) (2) (3) (4) (5) (6) (7) (8) (9) (10) (11) (12) (13) (14) (15) (16) (17) (18) (19) (20) (21) (22) Blank

Remington Ballistics

CALIBER	REMINGTON Order No.	Primer No.	Wt.-Grs.	BULLET Style	VELOCITY (FPS) Muzzle	50 Yds.	100 Yds.	ENERGY (FT LB) Muzzle	50 Yds.	100 Yds.	TRAJECTORY 50 Yds.	100 Yds.	BARREL LENGTH
(1) 22 REM. "JET" MAG.	R22JET	6½	40*	Soft Point	2100	1790	1510	390	285	200	0.3"	1.4"	8⅜"
(2) 221 REM. "FIRE BALL"	R221F	7½	50*	Pointed Soft Point	2650	2380	2130	780	630	505	0.2"	0.8"	10½"
(3) 25 (6.35mm) AUTO. PISTOL	R25AP	1½	50*	Metal Case	810	755	700	73	63	54	1.8"	7.7"	2"
(4) 32 S. & W.	R32SW	5½	88*	Lead	680	645	610	90	81	73	2.5"	10.5"	3"
(5) 32 S. & W. LONG	R32SWL	1½	98*	Lead	705	670	635	115	98	88	2.3"	10.5"	4"
(6) 32 SHORT COLT	R32SC	1½	80*	Lead	745	665	590	100	79	62	2.2"	9.9"	4"
(7) 32 LONG COLT	R32LC	1½	82*	Lead	755	715	675	100	93	83	2.0"	8.7"	4"
(8) 32 (7.65mm) AUTO. PISTOL	R32AP	1½	71*	Metal Case	905	855	810	129	115	97	1.4"	5.8"	4"
(9) 357 MAG. Vented Barrel	R357M7	5½	110	Semi-Jacketed H.P.	1295	1094	975	410	292	232	0.8"	3.5"	4"
	R357M1	5½	125	Semi-Jacketed H.P.	1450	1240	1090	583	427	330	0.6"	2.8"	4"
	R357M2	5½	158*	Semi-Jacketed H.P.	1235	1104	1015	535	428	361	0.8"	3.5"	4"
	R357M3	5½	158	Soft Point	1235	1104	1015	535	428	361	0.8"	3.5"	4"
	R357M4	5½	158	Metal Point	1235	1104	1015	535	428	361	0.8"	3.5"	4"
	R357M5	5½	158	Lead	1235	1104	1015	535	428	361	0.8"	3.5"	4"
	R357M6	5½	158	Lead (Brass Case)	1235	1104	1015	535	428	361	0.8"	3.5"	4"
(10) 9mm LUGER AUTO. PISTOL	R9MM1	1½	115*	Jacketed H.P.	1110	1030	971	339	292	259	1.0"	4.1"	4"
	R9MM2	1½	124	Metal Case	1115	1047	971	341	2	241	0.9"	3.9"	4"
(11) 380 AUTO. PISTOL	R380AP	1½	95	Metal Case	955	865	785	190	160	130	1.4"	5.9"	4"
	R380A1	1½	88*	Jacketed H.P.	990	920	868	191	165	146	1.2"	5.1"	4"
(12) 38 AUTO. COLT PISTOL	R38ACP	1½	130*	Metal Case	1040	980	925	310	275	245	1.0"	4.7"	4½"
(13) 38 SUPER AUTO. COLT PISTOL	R38SU1	1½	115*	Jacketed H.P. (+P)†	1300	1147	1041	431	336	277	0.7"	3.3"	5"
	R38SUP	1½	130	Metal Case (+P)†	1280	1140	1050	475	375	320	0.8"	3.4"	5"
(14) 38 S. & W.	R38SW	1½	146*	Lead	685	650	620	150	135	125	2.4"	10.0"	4"
(15) 38 SPECIAL Vented Barrel	R38S1	1½	95	Semi-Jacketed H.P. (+P)†	1175	1044	959	291	230	194	0.9"	3.9"	4"
	R38S10	1½	110	Semi-Jacketed H.P. (+P)†	1020	945	887	254	218	192	1.1"	4.9"	4"
	R38S2	1½	125	Semi-Jacketed H.P. (+P)†	945	898	858	248	224	204	1.3"	5.4"	4"
	R38S3	1½	148	"Targetmaster" Lead W.C.	710	634	566	166	132	105	2.4"	10.8"	4"
	R38S4	1½	158	"Targetmaster" Lead	755	723	692	200	183	168	2.0"	8.3"	4"
	R38S5	1½	158*	Lead (Round Nose)	755	723	692	200	183	168	2.0"	8.3"	4"
	R38S6	1½	158	Semi-Wadcutter	755	723	692	200	183	168	2.0"	8.3"	4"
	R38S7	1½	158	Metal Point	755	723	692	200	183	168	2.0"	8.3"	4"
	R38S8	1½	158	Lead (+P)†	915	878	844	294	270	250	1.4"	5.6"	4"
	R38S12	1½	158	Lead H.P. (+P)†	915	878	844	294	270	250	1.4"	5.6"	4"
	R38S9	1½	200	Lead	635	614	594	179	168	157	2.8"	11.5"	4"
(16) 38 SHORT COLT	R38SC	1½	125*	Lead	730	685	645	150	130	115	2.2"	9.4"	6"
(17) 41 REM. MAG. Vented Barrel	R41MG1	2½	210*	Soft Point	1300	1162	1062	788	630	526	0.7"	3.2"	4"
	R41MG2	2½	210		965	898	842	434	376	331	1.3"	5.4"	4"
(18) 44 REM. MAG. Vented Barrel	R44MG5	2½	180*	Semi-Jacketed H.P.	1610	1365	1175	1036	745	551	0.5"	2.3"	6"
	R44MG1	2½	240	Lead Gas Check	1350	1186	1069	971	749	608	0.7"	3.1"	4½"
	R44MG2	2½	240	Soft Point	1180	1081	1010	741	623	543	0.9"	3.7"	4½"
	R44MG3	2½	240	Semi-Jacketed H.P.	1180	1081	1010	741	623	543	0.9"	3.7"	4½"
	R44MG4	2½	240	Lead (Med. Vel.)	1000	947	902	533	477	433	1.1"	4.8"	4½"
(19) 44 S. & W. SPECIAL	R44SW	2½	246*	Lead	755	725	695	310	285	265	2.0"	8.3"	6½"
(20) 45 COLT	R45C	2½	250*	Lead	860	820	780	410	375	340	1.6"	6.6"	5½"
(21) 45 AUTO.	R45AP1	2½	185	Metal Case Wadcutter	770	707	650	244	205	174	2.0"	8.7"	5"
	R45AP2	2½	185*	Jacketed H.P.	940	890	846	363	325	294	1.3"	5.5"	5"
	R45AP4	2½	230	Metal Case	810	776	745	335	308	284	1.7"	7.2"	5"
(22) 45 AUTO. RIM	R45AR	2½	230*	Lead	810	770	730	335	305	270	1.8"	7.4"	5½"
38 S. & W.	R38SWBL	1½	- *	Blank	-	-	-	-	-	-	-	-	-
32 S. & W.	R32BLNK	5½	-	Blank	-	-	-	-	-	-	-	-	-
38 SPECIAL	R38BLNK	1½	-	Blank	-	-	-	-	-	-	-	-	-

†Ammunition with (+P) on the case headstamp is loaded to higher pressure. Use only in firearms designated for this cartridge and so recommended by the gun manufacturer.
*Illustrated (not shown in actual size).

REMINGTON RIMFIRE BALLISTICS

		Remington Order No.	Wt. Grs.	Bullet Style	Velocity— Ft. Per Second		Energy— Foot-Pounds		Mid-Range Trajectory
					Muzzle	100 Yds.	Muzzle	100 Yds.	100 Yds. inches
"HYPER VELOCITY" 22 CARTRIDGES									
	22 Long Rifle "Viper"	1922	36	Truncated Cone, Solid	1410	1056	159	89	3.1
	22 Long Rifle "Yellow Jacket"	1722	33	Truncated Cone, Hollow Point	1500	1075	165	85	2.8
"HIGH VELOCITY" 22 CARTRIDGES									
	22 Long Rifle	1522 1500†	40	Lead	1255	1017	140	92	3.6
		1622 1600†	36	Hollow Point	1280	1010	131	82	3.5
	22 Long	1322	29	Lead	1240	962	99	60	3.9
	22 Short	1022	29	Lead	1095	903	77	52	4.5
		1122	27	Hollow Point	1120	904	75	49	4.4
"TARGET" STANDARD VELOCITY 22 CARTRIDGES									
	22 Long Rifle	6122 6100†	40	Lead	1150	976	117	85	4.0
	22 Short	5522	29	Lead	1045	872	70	49	4.8

WEATHERBY BALLISTICS

Note: Any load having an average breech pressure of over 55,000 p.s.i. should not be used, and is shown for reference only. All ballistic data were compiled using Weatherby cartridge cases, Hornady or Nosler bullets and powder and primers as indicated. Loads shown with Norma powder are factory-equivalent loads. Other powders shown are DuPont IMR 3031, 4350 and 4064, and Hodgdon 4831. Velocities from 24″ barrels for all calibers are approximately 90 fps less than those listed.

.224 WEATHERBY MAGNUM VARMINTMASTER

Primer: Federal #215 Overall cartridge length: 2⁵/₁₆″

Charge	Powder	Bullet	Muzzle Velocity in 26″ Barrel	Avg. Breech Pressure	Muzzle Energy in Foot-Pounds
29.5 grs	3031	50 gr	3500-FPS	45,700-PSI	1360
30.0 grs	3031	50 gr	3560	47,500	1410
30.5 grs	3031	50 gr	3620	50,000	1455
31.0 grs	3031	50 gr	3670	52,000	1495
31.5 grs	3031	50 gr	3695	52,600	1515
32.0 grs	3031	50 gr	3740	55,200	1550
29.0 grs	3031	55 gr	3390	46,700	1405
29.5 grs	3031	55 gr	3450	48,000	1455
30.0 grs	3031	55 gr	3470	49,100	1470
30.5 grs	3031	55 gr	3525	53,200	1520
31.0 grs	3031	55 gr	3580	56,200	1570

WEATHERBY BALLISTICS

.240 WEATHERBY MAGNUM

Primer: Federal #215   Overall cartridge length: 3¹/₁₆″

Charge	Powder	Bullet	Muzzle Velocity in 26″ Barrel	Avg. Breech Pressure	Muzzle Energy in Foot-Pounds
53 grs	4350	70 gr	3684	48,530	2110
54 grs	4350	70 gr	3732	50,440	2163
55 grs	4350	70 gr	3780	52,270	2221
56 grs	4350	70 gr	3842	54,840	2293
55 grs	4831	70 grs	3533	44,680	1937
56 grs	4831	70 gr	3598	47,630	2011
57 grs	4831	70 gr	3708	52,070	2136
58.3 grs	Norma MRP	70 gr	3850	53,790	2304
54.1 grs	Norma MRP	87 gr	3500	53,420	2366
50 grs	4350	90 gr	3356	48,970	2246
51 grs	4350	90 gr	3424	51,270	2340
52 grs	4350	90 gr	3507	54,970	2453
53 grs	4831	90 gr	3325	48,630	2205
54 grs	4831	90 gr	3395	50,860	2299
55 grs	4831	90 gr	3451	52,410	2374
54.0 grs	Norma MRP	100 gr	3395	52,900	2560
49 grs	4350	100 gr	3223	50,680	2302
50 grs	4350	100 gr	3308	53,400	2425
51 grs	4350	100 gr	3367	56,190	2512
51 grs	4831	100 gr	3157	48,850	2208
52 grs	4831	100 gr	3222	50,950	2297
53 grs	4831	100 gr	3268	51,760	2370
54 grs	4831	100 gr	3362	54,740	2502

.257 WEATHERBY MAGNUM

Primer: Federal #215   Overall cartridge length: 3¹/₄″

Charge	Powder	Bullet	Muzzle Velocity in 26″ barrel	Avg. Breech Pressure	Muzzle Energy in Foot-Pounds
68 grs	4350	87 gr	3698	51,790	2644
69 grs	4350	87 gr	3715	53,270	2666
70 grs	4350	87 gr	3831	56,120	2835
69 grs	4831	87 gr	3521	44,750	2390
71 grs	4831	87 gr	3617	48,140	2532
73 grs	4831	87 gr	3751	52,470	2717
75 grs	4831	87 gr	3876	57,910	2901
74.1 grs	Norma MRP	87 gr	3825	50,700	2825
65 grs	4350	100 gr	3450	52,860	2638
66 grs	4350	100 gr	3520	54,860	2747
67 grs	4350	100 gr	3588	57,130	2857
66 grs	4831	100 gr	3315	43,640	2435
68 grs	4831	100 gr	3418	48,190	2593
70 grs	4831	100 gr	3543	53,410	2786
71 grs	4831	100 gr	3573	55,690	2833
71.3 grs	Norma MRP	100 gr	3555	51,730	2806
62 grs	4350	117 gr	3152	50,020	2573
64 grs	4350	117 gr	3262	54,860	2755
63 grs	4831	117 gr	3152	46,650	2573
65 grs	4831	117 gr	3213	48,520	2679
67 grs	4831	117 gr	3326	53,930	2867
67.1 grs	Norma MRP	117 gr	3300	53,050	2830

WEATHERBY BALLISTICS

.270 WEATHERBY MAGNUM

Primer: Federal #215   Overall cartridge length: 3¼″

Charge	Powder	Bullet	Muzzle Velocity in 26″ Barrel	Avg. Breech Pressure	Muzzle Energy in Foot-Pounds
70 grs	4350	100 gr	3636	49,550	2934
72 grs	4350	100 gr	3764	54,540	3148
74 grs	4350	100 gr	3885	58,200	3353
74 grs	4831	100 gr	3492	43,800	2700
76 grs	4831	100 gr	3594	47,790	2865
77 grs	4831	100 gr	3654	50,940	2966
78 grs	4831	100 gr	3705	52,890	3048
77.2 grs	Norma MRP	100 gr	3760	51,400	3139
65 grs	4350	130 gr	3184	46,780	2922
66 grs	4350	130 gr	3228	49,130	3006
67 grs	4350	130 gr	3286	52,120	3108
68 grs	4350	130 gr	3345	55,210	3224
68 grs	4831	130 gr	3076	43,320	2730
70 grs	4831	130 gr	3178	47,600	2913
71 grs	4831	130 gr	3242	51,150	3024
72 grs	4831	130 gr	3301	52,980	3138
73 grs	4831	130 gr	3335	54,350	3206
74 grs	4831	130 gr	3375	56,520	3283
73.3 grs	Norma MRP	130 gr	3375	50,260	3285
65 grs	4350	150 gr	3085	52,120	3167
67 grs	4350	150 gr	3150	57,560	3299
66 grs	4831	150 gr	2920	46,470	2840
67 grs	4831	150 gr	2971	48,380	2939
68 grs	4831	150 gr	3014	50,580	3027
69 grs	4831	150 gr	3069	53,720	3140
70 grs	4831	150 gr	3124	56,960	3246
68.5 grs	Norma MRP	150 gr	3245	51,800	3508

7MM WEATHERBY MAGNUM

Primer: Federal #215   Overall cartridge length: 3¼″

Charge	Powder	Bullet	Muzzle Velocity in 26″ Barrel	Avg. Breech Pressure	Muzzle Energy in Foot-Pounds
68 grs	4350	139 gr	3250	51,930	3254
69 grs	4350	139 gr	3308	54,310	3375
70 grs	4350	139 gr	3373	57,960	3500
72 grs	4831	139 gr	3147	45,990	3047
73 grs	4831	139 gr	3233	49,700	3223
74 grs	4831	139 gr	3291	52,570	3335
75 grs	4831	139 gr	3328	54,520	3417
74.1 grs	Norma MRP	139 gr	3300	50,300	3360
66 grs	4350	154 gr	3055	49,960	3191
67 grs	4350	154 gr	3141	54,500	3365
68 grs	4350	154 gr	3175	55,210	3439
70 grs	4831	154 gr	3013	46,940	3109
71 grs	4831	154 gr	3066	49,160	3212
72 grs	4831	154 gr	3151	53,010	3387
73 grs	4831	154 gr	3183	53,520	3462
71.0 grs	Norma MRP	154 gr	3160	51,250	3414
71.8 grs	Norma MRP	160 gr Nosler	3150	53,700	3525
71.0 grs	Norma MRP	*175 gr	3070	53,350	3662
63 grs	4350	*175 gr	2828	46,900	3112
65 grs	4350	*175 gr	2946	53,830	3369
68 grs	4831	*175 gr	2852	49,470	3157
69 grs	4831	*175 gr	2885	49,930	3234
70 grs	4831	*175 gr	2924	52,680	3323
71 grs	4831	*175 gr	2975	55,800	3439

*The 175 grain bullet is recommended for use only in 7mm W.M. rifles having 1 in 10″ twist barrels.

WEATHERBY BALLISTICS

.300 WEATHERBY MAGNUM

Primer: Federal #215   Overall cartridge length: 3-9/16"

Charge	Powder	Bullet	Muzzle Velocity in 26" Barrel	Avg. Breech Pressure	Muzzle Energy in Foot-Pounds
86 grs	4350	110 gr	3726	48,950	3390
88 grs	4350	110 gr	3798	51,180	3528
90 grs	4350	110 gr	3863	53,460	3649
81.0 grs	Norma 203	110 gr	3900	53,050	3714
82 grs	4350	130 gr	3488	49,540	3510
84 grs	4350	130 gr	3567	52,570	3663
86 grs	4350	130 gr	3627	54,730	3793
80 grs	4350	150 gr	3343	48,000	3710
82 grs	4350	150 gr	3458	52,380	3981
84 grs	4350	150 gr	3538	56,230	4167
84 grs	4831	150 gr	3305	47,620	3632
86 grs	4831	150 gr	3394	51,990	3831
88 grs	4831	150 gr	3470	54,570	4004
88.0 grs	Norma MRP	150 gr	3545	53,490	4185
77 grs	4350	180 gr	3066	50,830	3755
78 grs	4350	180 gr	3110	53,130	3857
79 grs	4350	180 gr	3145	53,610	3946
80 grs	4831	180 gr	3060	50,240	3742
82 grs	4831	180 gr	3145	54,310	3946
84 grs	4831	180 gr	3223	57,370	4147
81.8 grs	Norma MRP	180 gr	3245	51,800	4208
77.2 grs	Norma MRP	200 gr Nosler	3000	49,000	3996
76 grs	4831	200 gr Nosler	2858	46,480	3632
78 grs	4831	200 gr Nosler	2926	50,620	3800
80 grs	4831	200 gr Nosler	3029	54,690	4078
73 grs	4350	220 gr	2878	54,890	4052
75 grs	4350	220 gr	2926	56,510	4180
74 grs	4831	220 gr	2740	47,920	3667
76 grs	4831	220 gr	2800	51,060	3830
78 grs	4831	220 gr	2881	55,760	4052
77.2 grs	Norma MRP	220 gr	2905	52,850	4122

WEATHERBY BALLISTICS

.340 WEATHERBY MAGNUM

Primer: Federal #215   Overall cartridge length: 3-9/16″

Charge	Powder	Bullet	Muzzle Velocity in 26″ Barrel	Avg. Breech Pressures	Muzzle Energy in Foot-Pounds
80 grs	4350	200 gr	3075	48,290	4200
82 grs	4350	200 gr	3151	53,180	4398
84 grs	4350	200 gr	3210	54,970	4566
84 grs	4831	200 gr	2933	43,240	3824
86 grs	4831	200 gr	3004	45,940	4012
88 grs	4831	200 gr	3066	48,400	4172
90 grs	4831	200 gr	3137	52,730	4356
91.0 grs	Norma MRP	200 gr	3210	50,185	4575
92.0 grs	Norma MRP	210 gr Nosler	3180	51,290	4714
84 grs	4350	210 gr Nosler	3115	51,450	4515
85 grs	4350	210 gr Nosler	3148	53,300	4618
86 grs	4350	210 gr Nosler	3172	54,960	4675
74 grs	4350	250 gr	2741	49,240	4168
76 grs	4350	250 gr	2800	51,370	4353
78 grs	4350	250 gr	2862	55,490	4540
80 grs	4831	250 gr	2686	44,970	4005
82 grs	4831	250 gr	2764	49,180	4243
84 grs	4831	250 gr	2835	53,370	4460
85 grs	4831	250 gr	2860	54,400	4540
86 grs	4831	250 gr	2879	55,500	4605
87 grs	4831	250 gr	2886	56,270	4623
84.9 grs	Norma MRP	250 gr	2850	49,600	4508

.378 WEATHERBY MAGNUM

Primer: Federal #215   Overall cartridge length: 3-11/16″

Caution: Use only the #215 primer in reloading the .378 W. M.

Charge	Powder	Bullet	Muzzle Velocity in 26″ Barrel	Avg. Breech Pressure	Muzzle Energy in Foot-Pounds
106 grs	4350	270 gr	3015	44,800	5446
107 grs	4350	270 gr	3015	49,700	5713
108 grs	4350	270 gr	3112	54,620	5786
116 grs	4831	270 gr	3080	50,190	5689
117 grs	4831	270 gr	3102	50,930	5748
118 grs	4831	270 gr	3128	51,930	5862
101 grs	4350	300 gr	2831	49,500	5334
103 grs	4350	300 gr	2922	54,300	5679
110 grs	4831	300 gr	2897	51,050	5583
111 grs	4831	300 gr	2933	52,270	5736
112 grs	4831	300 gr	2958	53,410	5835

.460 WEATHERBY MAGNUM

Primer: Federal #215   Overall cartridge length: 3¾″

Caution: Use only the #215 primer in reloading the .460 W. M.

Charge	Powder	Bullet	Muzzle Velocity in 26″ Barrel	Avg. Breech Pressure	Muzzle Energy in Foot-Pounds
115 grs	4350	500 gr	2513	44,400	6995
118 grs	4350	500 gr	2577	47,460	7390
120 grs	4350	500 gr	2601	48,330	7505
122 grs	4350	500 gr	2632	50,370	7680
124 grs	4350	500 gr	2678	52,980	7980
126 grs	4350	500 gr	2707	55,130	8155
102 grs	4064	500 gr	2486	49,000	6860
104 grs	4064	500 gr	2521	51,340	7050
106 grs	4064	500 gr	2552	53,280	7220
92 grs	3031	500 gr	2405	49,530	6420
94 grs	3031	500 gr	2426	50,170	6525
96 grs	3031	500 gr	2470	53,560	6775

WINCHESTER AMMUNITION CENTERFIRE PISTOL & REVOLVER BALLISTICS

| 25 Auto | 256 Win | 30 Luger | 32 Auto | 32 S&W | 32 S&W Long | 32 Short Colt | 32 Long Colt | 32-20 Win | 357 Mag | 9mm Luger | 38 S&W | 38 Special |

CENTERFIRE PISTOL AND REVOLVER

Cartridge	Symbol	Wt. Grs.	Bullet Type
25 Automatic (6.35mm)	X25AXP	45	XP
25 Automatic (6.35mm)	X25AP	50	FMC
256 Winchester Magnum Super-X	X2561P	60	HP
30 Luger (7.65mm)	X30LP	93	FMC
32 Automatic	X32AP	71	FMC
32 Automatic	X32ASHP	60	STHP
32 Smith & Wesson (inside lubricated)	X32SWP	85	Lead
32 Smith & Wesson Long (inside lubricated)	X32SWLP	98	Lead
32 Short Colt (greased)	X32SCP	80	Lead
32 Long Colt (inside lubricated)	X32LCP	82	Lead
357 Magnum Jacketed Hollow Point Super-X	X3573P	110	JHP
357 Magnum Jacketed Hollow Point Super-X	X3576P	125	JHP
357 Magnum Silvertip Hollow Point Super-X	X357SHP	145	STHP
357 Magnum Super-X (inside lubricated)	X3571P	158	Lead
357 Magnum Jacketed Hollow Point Super-X	X3574P	158	JHP
357 Magnum Jacketed Soft Point Super-X	X3575P	158	JSP
9mm Luger (Parabellum)	X9MMJSP	95	JSP
9mm Luger (Parabellum)	X9LP	115	FMC
9mm Luger (Parabellum)	X9MMSHP	115	STHP
38 Smith & Wesson (inside lubricated)	X38SWP	145	Lead
38 Special (inside lubricated)	X38S1P	158	Lead
38 Special Semi-Wad Cutter (inside lubricated)	X38WCPSV	158	Lead-SWC
38 Special Metal Point (inside lubricated, lead bearing)	X38S2P	158	Met. Pt.
38 Special Super-Police (inside lubricated)	X38S3P	200	Lead
38 Special Super-X Jacketed Hollow Point + P	X38S6PH	110	JHP
38 Special Super-X Jacketed Hollow Point + P	X38S7PH	125	JHP
38 Special Super-X Silvertip Hollow Point + P	X38SSHP	95	STHP
38 Special Super-X Silvertip Hollow Point + P NEW	X38S8HP	125	STHP
38 Special Super-X (inside lubricated) + P	X38S4P	150	Lead
38 Special Super-X (inside lubricated) + P	X38SPD	158	Lead-HP
38 Special Super-X Semi-Wad Cutter (inside lubricated) + P	X38WCP	158	Lead-SWC
38 Special Super-Match and Match Mid-Range Clean Cutting (inside lubricated)	X38SMRP	148	Lead-WC
38 Special Super Match (inside lubricated)	X38SMP	158	Lead
38 Short Colt (greased)	X38SCP	130	Lead
38 Long Colt (inside lubricated)	X38LCP	150	Lead
38 Super Automatic Silvertip Hollow Point + P	X38ASHP	125	STHP
38 Super Automatic + P	X38A1P	130	FMC
38 Automatic (For all 38 Colt Automatic Pistols)	X38A2P	130	FMC
380 Automatic	X380AP	95	Lead
380 Automatic	X380ASHP	85	STHP
41 Remington Magnum Super-X (inside lubricated)	X41MP	210	Lead
41 Remington Magnum Super-X Jacketed Soft Point	X41MJSP	210	JSP
41 Remington Magnum Super-X Jacketed Hollow Point	X41MHP	210	JHP
44 Smith & Wesson Special	X44STHPS	200	STHP
44 Smith & Wesson Special (inside lubricated)	X44SP	246	Lead
44 Remington Magnum Super-X (Gas Check) (inside lubricated)	X44MP	240	Lead
45 Colt Silvertip Hollow Point	X45CSHP	225	STHP
45 Colt (inside lubricated)	X45CP	255	Lead
45 Automatic	X45ASHP	185	STHP
45 Automatic	X45A1P	230	FMC
45 Automatic Super-Match Clean Cutting	X45AWCP	185	FMC-WC
45 Winchester Magnum Super-X	X45WM	230	FMC

Key

FMC-Full Metal Case
JHP-Jacketed Hollow Point
JSP-Jacketed Soft Point
Met. Pt.-Metal Point
XP-Expanding Point
WC-Wad Cutter
SWC-Semi Wad Cutter
STHP-Silvertip Hollow Point
HP-Hollow Point
L-Lubaloy
**Wax Coated

WINCHESTER AMMUNITION CENTERFIRE PISTOL & REVOLVER BALLISTICS

| 38 Special S.M. | 38 Short Colt | 38 Long Colt | 38 Auto | 380 Auto | 41 Rem Mag. | 44 S&W | 44 Rem Mag. | 44-40 Win | 45 Colt | 45 Auto | 45 Auto S.M. |

| Velocity-FPS | | | Energy Ft-Lbs. | | | Mid Range Trajectory Inches | | Barrel Length Inches |
Muzzle	50 Yds.	100 Yds.	Muzzle	50 Yds.	100 Yds.	50 Yds.	100 Yds.	
815	729	655	66	53	42	1.8	7.7	2
760	707	659	64	56	48	2.0	8.7	2
2350	2030	1760	735	550	415	0.3	1.1	8½
1220	1110	1040	305	255	225	0.9	3.5	4½
905	855	810	129	115	97	1.4	5.8	4
970	895	835	125	107	93	1.3	5.4	4
680	645	610	90	81	73	2.5	10.5	3
705	670	635	115	98	88	2.3	10.5	4
745	665	590	100	79	62	2.2	9.9	4
755	715	675	105	93	83	2.0	8.7	4
1295	1094	975	410	292	232	0.8	3.5	4V
1450	1240	1090	583	427	330	0.6	2.8	4V
1290	1155	1060	535	428	361	0.8	3.5	4V
1235	1104	1015	535	428	361	0.8	3.5	4V
1235	1104	1015	535	428	361	0.8	3.5	4V
1235	1104	1015	535	428	361	0.8	3.5	4V
1355	1140	1008	387	274	214	0.7	3.3	4
1155	1047	971	341	280	241	0.9	3.9	4
1225	1095	1007	383	306	259	0.8	3.6	4
685	650	620	150	135	125	2.4	10.0	4
755	723	693	200	183	168	2.0	8.3	4V
755	721	689	200	182	167	2.0	8.4	4V
755	723	693	200	183	168	2.0	8.3	4V
635	614	594	179	168	157	2.8	11.5	4V
995	926	871	242	210	185	1.2	5.1	4V
945	898	858	248	224	204	1.3	5.4	4V
1100	1002	932	255	212	183	1.0	4.3	4V
945	898	858	248	224	204	1.3	5.4	4V
860	825	794	246	227	210	1.5	6.3	4V
890	855	823	278	257	238	1.4	6.0	4V
890	855	823	278	257	238	1.4	6.0	4V
710	634	566	166	132	105	2.4	10.8	4V
755	723	693	200	183	168	2.0	8.3	4V
730	685	645	150	130	115	2.2	9.4	6
730	700	670	175	165	150	2.1	8.8	6
1240	1130	1050	427	354	306	0.8	3.4	5
1215	1099	1017	426	348	298	0.8	3.6	5
1040	980	925	310	275	245	1.0	4.7	4½
955	865	785	190	160	130	1.4	5.9	3¾
1000	921	860	189	160	140	1.2	5.1	3¾
965	898	842	434	376	331	1.3	5.4	4V
1300	1162	1062	788	630	526	0.7	3.2	4V
1300	1162	1062	788	630	526	0.7	3.2	4V
900	860	822	360	328	300	1.4	5.9	6½
755	725	695	310	285	265	2.0	8.3	6½
1350	1186	1069	971	749	608	0.7	3.1	4V
920	877	839	423	384	352	1.4	5.6	5½
860	820	780	420	380	345	1.5	6.1	5½
1000	938	888	411	362	324	1.2	4.9	5
810	776	745	335	308	284	1.7	7.2	5
770	707	650	244	205	174	2.0	8.7	5
1400	1232	1107	1001	775	636	0.6	2.8	5

+P Ammunition with (+P) on the case head stamp is loaded to higher pressure. Use only in firearms designated for this cartridge and so recommended by the gun manufacturer.

V-Data is based on velocity obtained from 4" vented test barrels for revolver cartridges (38 Special, 357 Magnum, 41 Rem. Mag. and 44 Rem. Mag.) Specifications are nominal. Test barrels are used to determine ballistics figures. Individual firearms may differ from test barrel statistics.

Specifications subject to change without notice.

Handloader's Guide

WINCHESTER-AMMUNITION
CENTERFIRE RIFLE BALLISTICS

218 Bee   22 Hornet   22-250 Rem   222 Rem   223 Rem   225 Win   243 Win   6 MM Rem   25-06 Rem   25-20 Win   25-35 Win   250 Savage

CENTERFIRE RIFLE

Cartridge	Symbol	Game Selector Guide	Bullet Wt. Grs.	Bullet Type	Barrel Length Inches	Muzzle	Velocity In Feet Per Second 100	200	300	400	500
218 Bee Super-X	X218B	S	46	HP	24	2760	2102	1550	1155	961	850
22 Hornet Super-X	X22H1	S	45	SP	24	2690	2042	1502	1128	948	840
22 Hornet Super-X	X22H2	S	46	HP	24	2690	2042	1502	1128	948	841
22-250 Remington Super-X	X222501	S	55	PSP	24	3680	3137	2656	2222	1832	1493
222 Remington Super-X	X222R	S	50	PSP	24	3140	2602	2123	1700	1350	1107
222 Remington Super-X	X222R1	S	55	FMC	24	3020	2675	2355	2057	1783	1537
223 Remington Super-X NEW	X223RH	S	53	HP	24	3330	2882	2477	2106	1770	1475
223 Remington Super-X	X223R	S	55	PSP	24	3240	2747	2304	1905	1554	1270
223 Remington Super-X	X223R1	S	55	FMC	24	3240	2877	2543	2232	1943	1679
225 Winchester Super-X	X2251	S	55	PSP	24	3570	3066	2616	2208	1838	1514
243 Winchester Super-X	X2431	S	80	PSP	24	3350	2955	2593	2259	1951	1670
243 Winchester Super-X	X2432	D,O/P	100	PP(SP)	24	2960	2697	2449	2215	1993	1786
6mm Remington Super-X	X6MMR1	S	80	PSP	24	3470	3064	2694	2352	2036	1747
6mm Remington Super-X	X6MMR2	D,O/P	100	PP(SP)	24	3100	2829	2573	2332	2104	1889
25-06 Remington Super-X	X25061	S	90	PEP	24	3440	3043	2680	2344	2034	1749
25-06 Remington Super-X	X25062	D,O/P	120	PEP	24	2990	2730	2484	2252	2032	1825
25-20 Winchester	X25202	S	86	SP	24	1460	1194	1030	931	858	798
25-35 Winchester Super-X	X2535	D	117	SP	24	2230	1866	1545	1282	1097	984
250 Savage Super-X	X2501	S	87	PSP	24	3030	2673	2342	2036	1755	1504
250 Savage Super-X	X2503	D,O/P	100	ST	24	2820	2467	2140	1839	1569	1339
256 Winchester Mag. Super-X	X2561P	S	60	HP	24	2760	2097	1542	1149	957	846
257 Roberts + P Super-X	X257P2	D,O/P	100	ST	24	3000	2633	2295	1982	1697	1447
257 Roberts + P Super-X	*X257P3	D,O/P	117	PP(SP)	24	2780	2411	2071	1761	1488	1263
264 Winchester Mag. Super-X	X2641	S	100	PSP	24	3320	2926	2565	2231	1923	1644
264 Winchester Mag. Super-X	X2642	D,O/P	140	PP(SP)	24	3030	2782	2548	2326	2114	1914
270 Winchester Super-X	X2701	S	100	PSP	24	3430	3021	2649	2305	1988	1699
270 Winchester Super-X	X2705	D,O/P	130	PP(SP)	24	3060	2802	2559	2329	2110	1904
270 Winchester Super-X	X2703	D,O/P	130	ST	24	3060	2776	2510	2259	2022	1801
270 Winchester Super-X	X2704	D,L	150	PP(SP)	24	2850	2585	2336	2100	1879	1673
284 Winchester Super-X	X2841	D,O/P	125	PP(SP)	24	3140	2829	2538	2265	2010	1772
284 Winchester Super-X	X2842	C,O/P,L	150	PP(SP)	24	2860	2595	2344	2108	1886	1680
7mm Mauser (7x57) Super-X	X7MM	D	175	SP	24	2440	2137	1857	1603	1382	1204
7mm Remington Mag. Super-X	X7MMR3	D,O/P	125	PP(SP)	24	3310	2976	2666	2376	2105	1852
7mm Remington Mag. Super-X	X7MMR1	D,O/P	150	PP(SP)	24	3110	2830	2568	2320	2085	1866
7mm Remington Mag. Super-X	X7MMR2	D,O/P,L	175	PP(SP)	24	2860	2645	2442	2244	2057	1879
30 Carbine	X30M1	S	110	HSP	20	1990	1567	1236	1035	923	842
30 Carbine	X30M2	S	110	FMC	20	1990	1596	1278	1070	952	870
30-30 Winchester Super-X	X30301	D	150°	HP	24	2390	2018	1684	1398	1177	1036
30-30 Winchester Super-X	X30306	D	150	PP(SP)	24	2390	2018	1684	1398	1177	1036
30-30 Winchester Super-X	X30302	D	150	ST	24	2390	2018	1684	1398	1177	1036
30-30 Winchester Super-X	X30303	D	170	PP(SP)	24	2200	1895	1619	1381	1191	1061
30-30 Winchester Super-X	X30304	D	170	ST	24	2200	1895	1619	1381	1191	1061
30-06 Springfield Super-X	X30060	S	110	PSP	24	3330	2799	2325	1901	1532	1239
30-06 Springfield Super-X	X30062	S	125	PSP	24	3140	2780	2447	2138	1853	1595
30-06 Springfield Super-X	X30061	D,O/P	150	PP(SP)	24	2920	2580	2265	1972	1704	1466
30-06 Springfield Super-X	X30063	D,O/P	150	ST	24	2910	2617	2342	2083	1843	1622
30-06 Springfield Super-X NEW	X30065	D,O/P	165	PSP	24	2800	2573	2357	2151	1956	1772
30-06 Springfield Super-X	X30064	D,O/P,L	180	PP(SP)	24	2700	2348	2023	1727	1466	1251
30-06 Springfield Super-X	X30066	D,O/P,L	180	ST	24	2700	2469	2250	2042	1846	1663
30-06 Springfield Super-X	X30068	L	220	PP(SP)	24	2410	2130	1870	1632	1422	1246
30-06 Springfield Super-X	X30069	L	220	ST	24	2410	2192	1985	1791	1611	1448

HSP-Hollow Soft Point PEP-Positive Expanding Point PSP-Pointed Soft Point PP(SP)-Power-Point® Soft Point FMC-Full Metal Case SP-Soft Point HP-Hollow Point ST-Silvertip® JHP-Jacketed Hollow Point GAME SELECTOR CODE S=Small Game L=Large Game O/P=Open or Plains shooting XL=Extra Large Game D=Deer (i.e. Moose, Elk) (i.e. Antelope, Deer) (i.e. Kodiak Bear)

WINCHESTER-AMMUNITION CENTERFIRE RIFLE BALLISTICS

256 Win | 257 Roberts | 264 Win +P | 270 Win | 284 Win | 7 MM Mauser | 7 MM Rem Mag. | 30 Carbine | 30-30 Win | 30-06 Springfield

Energy In Foot Pounds						Short Range — Yards						Long Range — Yards						
Muzzle	100	200	300	400	500	50	100	150	200	250	300	100	150	200	250	300	400	500
778	451	245	136	94	74	0.3	0	−2.3	−7.2	−15.8	−29.4	1.5	0	−4.2	−12.0	−24.8	−71.4	−155.6
723	417	225	127	90	70	0.3	0	−2.4	−7.7	−16.9	−31.3	1.6	0	−4.5	−12.8	−26.4	−75.6	−163.4
739	426	230	130	92	72	0.3	0	−2.4	−7.7	−16.9	−31.3	1.6	0	−4.5	−12.8	−26.4	−75.5	−163.3
1654	1201	861	603	410	272	0.2	0.5	0	−1.6	−4.4	−8.7	2.3	2.6	1.9	0	−3.4	−15.9	−38.9
1094	752	500	321	202	136	0.5	0.9	0	−2.5	−6.9	−13.7	2.2	1.9	0	−3.8	−10.0	−32.3	−73.8
1114	874	677	517	388	288	0.5	0.9	0	−2.2	−6.1	−11.7	2.0	1.7	0	−3.3	−8.3	−24.9	−52.5
1305	978	722	522	369	256	0.3	0.7	0	−1.9	−5.3	−10.3	1.7	1.4	0	−2.9	−7.4	−22.7	−49.1
1282	921	648	443	295	197	0.4	0.8	0	−2.2	−6.0	−11.8	1.9	1.6	0	−3.3	−8.5	−26.7	−59.6
1282	1011	790	608	461	344	0.4	0.7	0	−1.9	−5.1	−9.9	1.7	1.4	0	−2.8	−7.1	−21.2	−44.6
1556	1148	836	595	412	280	0.2	0.6	0	−1.7	−4.6	−9.0	2.4	2.8	2.0	0	−3.5	−16.3	−39.5
1993	1551	1194	906	676	495	0.3	0.7	0	−1.8	−4.9	−9.4	2.6	2.9	2.1	0	−3.6	−16.2	−37.9
1945	1615	1332	1089	882	708	0.5	0.9	0	−2.2	−5.8	−11.0	1.9	1.6	0	−3.1	−7.8	−22.6	−46.3
2139	1667	1289	982	736	542	0.3	0.6	0	−1.6	−4.5	−8.7	2.4	2.7	1.9	0	−3.3	−14.9	−35.0
2133	1777	1470	1207	983	792	0.4	0.8	0	−1.9	−5.2	−9.9	1.7	1.5	0	−2.8	−7.0	−20.4	−41.7
2364	1850	1435	1098	827	611	0.3	0.6	0	−1.7	−4.5	−8.8	2.4	2.7	2.0	0	−3.4	−15.0	−35.2
2382	1985	1644	1351	1100	887	0.5	0.8	0	−2.1	−5.6	−10.7	1.9	1.6	0	−3.0	−7.5	−22.0	−44.8
407	272	203	165	141	122	0	−4.1	−14.4	−31.8	−57.3	−92.0	0	−8.2	−23.5	−47.0	−79.6	−175.9	−319.4
1292	904	620	427	313	252	0.6	0	−3.1	−9.2	−19.0	−33.1	2.1	0	−5.1	−13.8	−27.0	−70.1	−142.0
1773	1380	1059	801	595	437	0.5	0.9	0	−2.3	−6.1	−11.8	2.0	1.7	0	−3.3	−8.4	−25.2	−53.4
1765	1351	1017	751	547	398	0.2	0	−1.6	−4.9	−10.0	−17.4	2.4	2.0	0	−3.9	−10.1	−30.5	−65.2
1015	586	317	176	122	95	0.3	0	−2.3	−7.3	−15.9	−29.6	1.5	0	−4.2	−12.1	−25.0	−72.1	−157.2
1998	1539	1169	872	639	465	0.6	0.9	0	−2.4	−4.9	−12.3	2.9	3.0	1.6	0	−6.4	−23.2	−51.2
2009	1511	1115	806	576	373	0.8	1.1	0	−2.9	−7.8	−15.1	2.6	2.2	0	−4.2	−10.8	−33.0	−70.0
2447	1901	1461	1105	821	600	0.3	0.7	0	−1.8	−5.0	−9.7	2.7	3.0	2.2	0	−3.7	−16.6	−38.9
2854	2406	2018	1682	1389	1139	0.5	0.8	0	−2.0	−5.4	−10.2	1.8	1.5	0	−2.9	−7.2	−20.8	−42.2
2612	2027	1557	1179	877	641	0.3	0.6	0	−1.7	−4.6	−9.0	2.5	2.8	2.0	0	−3.4	−15.5	−36.4
2702	2267	1890	1565	1285	1046	0.4	0.8	0	−2.0	−5.3	−10.1	1.8	1.5	0	−2.8	−7.1	−20.6	−42.0
2702	2225	1818	1472	1180	936	0.5	0.8	0	−2.0	−5.5	−10.4	1.8	1.5	0	−2.9	−7.4	−21.6	−44.3
2705	2226	1817	1468	1175	932	0.6	1.0	0	−2.4	−6.4	−12.2	2.2	1.8	0	−3.4	−8.6	−25.0	−51.4
2736	2221	1788	1424	1121	871	0.4	0.8	0	−2.0	−6.4	−10.1	1.7	1.5	0	−2.8	−7.2	−21.1	−43.7
2724	2243	1830	1480	1185	940	0.6	1.0	0	−2.4	−6.3	−12.1	2.1	1.8	0	−3.4	−8.5	−24.8	−51.0
2313	1774	1340	998	742	563	0.4	0	−2.3	−6.8	−13.8	−23.7	1.5	0	−3.7	−10.0	−19.1	−48.1	−95.4
3040	2458	1972	1567	1230	952	0.3	0.6	0	−1.7	−4.7	−9.1	2.5	2.8	2.0	0	−3.4	−15.0	−34.5
3221	2667	2196	1792	1448	1160	0.4	0.8	0	−1.9	−5.2	−9.9	1.7	1.5	0	−2.8	−7.0	−20.5	−42.1
3178	2718	2313	1956	1644	1372	0.6	0.9	0	−2.3	−6.0	−11.3	2.0	1.7	0	−3.2	−7.9	−22.7	−45.8
967	600	373	262	208	173	0.9	0	−4.5	−13.5	−28.3	−49.9	0	−4.5	−13.5	−28.3	−49.9	−118.6	−228.2
967	622	399	280	221	185	0.9	0	−4.3	−13.0	−26.9	−47.4	2.9	0	−7.2	−19.7	−38.7	−100.4	−200.5
1902	1356	944	651	461	357	0.5	0	−2.6	−7.7	−16.0	−27.9	1.7	0	−4.3	−11.6	−22.7	−59.1	−120.5
1902	1356	944	651	461	357	0.5	0	−2.6	−7.7	−16.0	−27.9	1.7	0	−4.3	−11.6	−22.7	−59.1	−120.5
1902	1356	944	651	461	357	0.5	0	−2.6	−7.7	−16.0	−27.9	1.7	0	−4.3	−11.6	−22.7	−59.1	−120.5
1827	1355	989	720	535	425	0.6	0	−3.0	−8.9	−18.0	−31.1	2.0	0	−4.8	−13.0	−25.1	−63.6	−126.7
1827	1355	989	720	535	425	0.6	0	−3.0	−8.9	−18.0	−31.1	2.0	0	−4.8	−13.0	−25.1	−63.6	−126.7
2708	1913	1321	882	573	375	0.4	0.8	0	−2.1	−5.8	−11.5	1.8	1.6	0	−3.2	−8.3	−26.4	−59.6
2736	2145	1662	1269	953	706	0.4	0.8	0	−2.1	−5.6	−10.7	1.8	1.5	0	−3.0	−7.7	−23.0	−48.5
2839	2217	1708	1295	967	716	0.6	1.0	0	−2.4	−6.6	−12.7	2.2	1.8	0	−3.5	−9.0	−27.0	−57.1
2820	2281	1827	1445	1131	876	0.6	0.9	0	−2.3	−6.3	−12.0	2.1	1.8	0	−3.3	−8.5	−25.0	−51.8
2873	2426	2036	1696	1402	1151	0.7	1.0	0	−2.5	−6.5	−12.2	2.2	1.9	0	−3.6	−8.4	−24.4	−49.6
2913	2203	1635	1192	859	625	0.2	0	−1.8	−5.5	−11.2	−19.5	2.7	2.3	0	−4.4	−11.3	−34.4	−73.7
2913	2436	2023	1666	1362	1105	0.2	0	−1.6	−4.8	−9.7	−16.5	2.4	2.0	0	−3.7	−9.3	−27.0	−54.9
2837	2216	1708	1301	988	758	0.4	0	−2.3	−6.8	−13.8	−23.6	1.5	0	−3.7	−9.9	−19.0	−47.4	−93.1
2837	2347	1924	1567	1268	1024	0.4	0	−2.2	−6.4	−12.7	−21.6	1.5	0	−3.5	−9.1	−17.2	−41.8	−79.9

TRAJECTORY inches above (+) or below (−) line of sight 0 = indicates yardage at which rifle is sighted in.
Specifications are normal. Test barrels are used to determine ballistics figures. Individual firearms may differ from these test barrels statistics. Specifications subject to change without notice.

WINCHESTER-AMMUNITION
CENTERFIRE RIFLE BALLISTICS

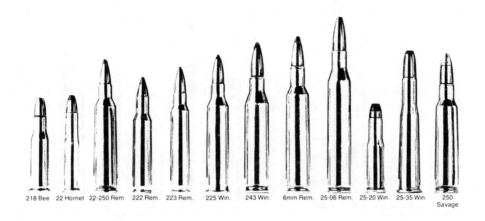

218 Bee   22 Hornet   22-250 Rem.   222 Rem.   223 Rem.   225 Win.   243 Win.   6mm Rem.   25-06 Rem.   25-20 Win.   25-35 Win.   250 Savage

Cartridge	Symbol	Game Selector Guide	Wt. Grs.	Bullet Type	Barrel Length Inches	Muzzle	100	200	300	400	500
30-40 Krag Super-X	X30401	D	180	PP(SP)	24	2430	2099	1795	1525	1298	1128
30-40 Krag Super-X	X30403	D	180	ST	24	2430	2213	2007	1813	1632	1468
300 Winchester Mag. Super-X	X30WM1	D,O/P	150	PP(SP)	24	3290	2951	2636	2342	2068	1813
300 Winchester Mag. Super-X	X30WM2	O/P,L	180	PP(SP)	24	2960	2745	2540	2344	2157	1979
300 Winchester Mag. Super-X	X30WM3	L,XL	220	ST	24	2680	2448	2228	2020	1823	1640
300 H. & H. Magnum Super-X	X300H2	O/P,L	180	ST	24	2880	2640	2412	2196	1991	1798
300 Savage Super-X	X3001	D,O/P	150	PP(SP)	24	2630	2311	2015	1743	1500	1295
300 Savage Super-X	X3003	D,O/P	150	ST	24	2630	2354	2095	1853	1631	1434
300 Savage Super-X	X3004	D	180	PP(SP)	24	2350	2025	1728	1467	1252	1098
300 Savage Super-X	X3005	D	180	ST	24	2350	2137	1935	1745	1570	1413
303 Savage Super-X	X3032	D	190	ST	24	1890	1612	1372	1183	1055	970
303 British Super-X	X303B1	D	180	PP(SP)	24	2460	2233	2018	1816	1629	1459
307 Winchester	X3075	D	150	PP(SP)	24	2760	2321	1924	1575	1289	1091
307 Winchester	X3076	D	180	PP(SP)	24	2510	2179	1874	1599	1362	1177
308 Winchester Super-X	X3081	S	110	PSP	24	3180	2666	2206	1795	1444	1178
308 Winchester Super-X	X3087	S	125	PSP	24	3050	2697	2370	2067	1788	1537
308 Winchester Super-X	X3085	D,O/P	150	PP(SP)	24	2820	2488	2179	1893	1633	1405
308 Winchester Super-X	X3082	D,O/P	150	ST	24	2820	2533	2263	2009	1774	1560
308 Winchester Super-X	X3086	D,O/P,L	180	PP(SP)	24	2620	2274	1955	1666	1414	1212
308 Winchester Super-X	X3083	D,O/P,L	180	ST	24	2620	2393	2178	1974	1782	1604
308 Winchester Super-X	X3084	L	200	ST	24	2450	2208	1980	1767	1572	1397
32 Win. Special Super-X	X32WS2	D	170	PP(SP)	24	2250	1870	1537	1267	1082	971
32 Win. Special Super-X	X32WS3	D	170	ST	24	2250	1870	1537	1267	1082	971
32-20 Winchester	X32202	S	100	SP	24	1210	1021	913	834	769	712
32-20 Winchester	X32201	S	100	Lead	24	1210	1021	913	834	769	712
8mm Mauser (8x57) Super-X	X8MM	D	170	PP(SP)	24	2360	1969	1622	1333	1123	997
338 Winchester Mag. Super-X	X3381	D,O/P	200	PP(SP)	24	2960	2658	2375	2110	1862	1635
338 Winchester Mag. Super-X	X3383	L,XL	225	SP	24	2780	2570	2374	2184	2003	1832
348 Winchester Super-X	X3482	D,L	200	ST	24	2520	2215	1931	1672	1443	1253
35 Remington Super-X	X35R1	D	200	PP(SP)	24	2020	1646	1335	1114	985	901
35 Remington Super-X	X35R3	D	200	ST	24	2020	1646	1335	1114	985	901
351 Winchester S.L.	X351SL2	D	180	SP	20	1850	1556	1310	1128	1012	933
356 Winchester	X3561	D,L	200	PP(SP)	24	2460	2114	1797	1517	1284	1113
356 Winchester	X3563	L	250	PP(SP)	24	2160	1911	1682	1476	1299	1158
358 Winchester Super-X	X3581	D,L	200	ST	24	2490	2171	1876	1610	1379	1194
375 Winchester	X375W	D,L	200	PP(SP)	24	2200	1841	1526	1268	1089	980
375 Winchester	X375W1	D,L	250	PP(SP)	24	1900	1647	1424	1239	1103	1011
375 H. & H. Magnum Super-X	X375H1	L,XL	270	PP(SP)	24	2690	2420	2166	1928	1707	1507
375 H. & H. Magnum Super-X	X375H2	L,XL	300	ST	24	2530	2268	2022	1793	1583	1397
375 H. & H. Magnum Super-X	X375H3	L,XL	300	FMC	24	2530	2171	1843	1551	1307	1126
38-40 Winchester	X3840	D	180	SP	24	1160	999	901	827	764	710
38-55 Winchester	X3855	D	255	SP	24	1320	1190	1091	1018	963	917
44 Remington Magnum Super-X	X44MHSP	D	240	HSP	20	1760	1362	1094	953	861	789
44-40 Winchester	X4440	D	200	SP	24	1190	1006	900	822	756	699
45-70 Government	X4570H	D,L	300	JHP	24	1880	1650	1425	1235	1105	1010
458 Winchester Mag. Super-X	X4580	XL	500	FMC	24	2040	1823	1623	1442	1287	1161
458 Winchester Mag. Super-X	X4581	L,XL	510	SP	24	2040	1770	1527	1319	1157	1046

HSP- Hollow Soft Point PEP-Positive Expanding Point PSP-Pointed Soft Point PP(SP)-Power-Point Soft Point® FMC-Full Metal Case SP-Soft Point HP-Hollow Point ST-Silvertip® JHP-Jacketed Hollow Point GAME SELECTOR CODE S=Small Game L=Large Game O/P=Open or Plains shooting XL=Extra Large Game D=Deer (i.e. Moose, Elk) (i.e. Antelope, Deer) (i.e. Kodiak Bear)

WINCHESTER-AMMUNITION
CENTERFIRE RIFLE BALLISTICS

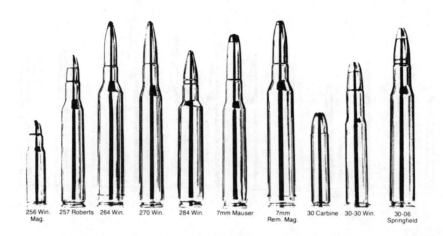

256 Win. Mag.   257 Roberts   264 Win.   270 Win.   284 Win.   7mm Mauser   7mm Rem. Mag.   30 Carbine   30-30 Win.   30-06 Springfield

Muzzle	Energy In Foot Pounds 100	200	300	400	500	Short Range 50	100	150 Yards	200	250	300	Long Range 100	150	200	250 Yards	300	400	500
2360	1761	1288	929	673	508	0.4	0	−2.4	−7.1	−14.5	−25.0	1.6	0	−3.9	−10.5	−20.3	−51.7	−103.9
2360	1957	1610	1314	1064	861	0.4	0	−2.1	−6.2	−12.5	−21.1	1.4	0	−3.4	−8.9	−16.8	−40.9	−78.1
3605	2900	2314	1827	1424	1095	0.3	0.7	0	−1.8	−4.8	−9.3	2.6	2.9	2.1	0	−3.5	−15.4	−35.5
3501	3011	2578	2196	1859	1565	0.5	0.8	0	−2.1	−5.5	−10.4	1.9	1.6	0	−2.9	−7.3	−20.9	−41.9
3508	2927	2424	1993	1623	1314	0.2	0	−1.7	−4.9	−9.9	−16.9	2.5	2.0	0	−3.8	−9.5	−27.5	−56.1
3315	2785	2325	1927	1584	1292	0.6	0.9	0	−2.3	−6.0	−11.5	2.1	1.7	0	−3.2	−8.0	−23.3	−47.4
2303	1779	1352	1012	749	558	0.3	0	−1.9	−5.7	−11.6	−19.9	2.8	2.3	0	−4.5	−11.5	−34.4	−73.0
2303	1845	1462	1143	886	685	0.3	0	−1.8	−5.4	−11.0	−18.8	2.7	2.2	0	−4.2	−10.7	−31.5	−65.5
2207	1639	1193	860	626	482	0.5	0	−2.6	−7.7	−15.6	−27.1	1.7	0	−4.2	−11.3	−21.9	−55.8	−112.0
2207	1825	1496	1217	985	798	0.4	0	−2.3	−6.7	−13.5	−22.8	1.5	0	−3.6	−9.6	−18.2	−44.1	−84.2
1507	1096	794	591	469	397	1.0	0	−4.3	−12.6	−25.5	−43.7	29	0	−6.8	−18.3	−35.1	−88.2	−172.5
2418	1993	1627	1318	1060	851	0.3	0	−2.1	−6.1	−12.2	−20.8	1.4	0	−3.3	−8.8	−16.6	−40.4	−77.4
2538	1795	1233	826	554	397	0.2	0	−1.9	−5.6	−11.8	−20.8	1.2	0	−3.2	−8.7	−17.1	−44.9	−92.2
2519	1898	1404	1022	742	554	0.3	0	−2.2	−6.5	−13.3	−22.9	1.5	0	−3.6	−9.6	−18.6	−47.1	−93.7
2470	1736	1188	787	509	339	0.5	0.9	0	−2.3	−6.5	−12.8	2.0	1.8	0	−3.5	−9.3	−29.5	−66.7
2582	2019	1559	1186	1887	656	0.5	0.8	0	−2.2	−6.0	−11.5	2.0	1.7	0	−3.2	−8.2	−24.6	−51.9
2648	2061	1581	1193	888	657	0.2	0	−1.6	−4.8	−9.8	−16.9	2.4	2.0	0	−3.8	−9.8	−29.3	−62.0
2648	2137	1705	1344	1048	810	0.2	0	−1.5	−4.5	−9.3	−15.9	2.3	1.9	0	−3.6	−9.1	−26.9	−55.7
2743	2066	1527	1109	799	587	0.3	0	−2.0	−5.9	−12.1	−20.9	2.9	2.4	0	−4.7	−12.1	−36.9	−79.1
2743	2288	1896	1557	1269	1028	0.2	0	−1.8	−5.2	−10.4	−17.7	2.6	2.1	0	−4.0	−9.9	−28.9	−58.8
2665	2165	1741	1386	1097	867	0.4	0	−2.1	−6.3	−12.6	−21.4	1.4	0	−3.1	−9.0	−17.2	−42.1	−81.1
1911	1320	892	606	442	356	0.6	0	−3.1	−9.2	−19.0	−33.2	2.0	0	−5.1	−13.8	−27.1	−70.9	−144.3
1911	1320	892	606	442	356	0.6	0	−3.1	−9.2	−19.0	−33.2	2.0	0	−5.1	−13.8	−27.1	−70.9	−144.3
325	231	185	154	131	113	0	−6.3	−20.9	−44.9	−79.3	−125.1	0	−11.5	−32.3	−63.6	−106.3	−230.3	−413.3
325	231	185	154	131	113	0	−6.3	−20.9	−44.9	−79.3	−125.1	0	−11.5	−32.3	−63.6	−106.3	−230.3	−413.3
2102	1463	993	671	476	375	0.5	0	−2.7	−8.2	−17.1	−29.8	1.8	0	−4.5	−12.4	−24.3	−63.8	−130.7
3890	3137	2505	1977	1539	1187	0.5	0.9	0	−2.3	−6.1	−11.6	2.0	1.7	0	−3.2	−8.2	−24.3	−50.4
3862	3306	2816	2384	2005	1677	1.2	1.3	0	−2.7	−7.1	−12.9	2.7	2.1	0	−3.6	−9.4	−25.0	−49.9
2820	2178	1656	1241	925	697	0.3	0	−2.1	−6.2	−12.7	−21.9	1.4	0	−3.4	−9.2	−17.7	−44.4	−87.9
1812	1203	791	551	431	360	0.9	0	−4.1	−12.1	−25.1	−43.9	2.7	0	−6.7	−18.3	−35.8	−92.8	−185.5
1812	1203	791	551	431	360	0.9	0	−4.1	−12.1	−25.1	−43.9	2.7	0	−6.7	−18.3	−35.8	−92.8	−185.5
1368	968	508	409	348		0	−2.1	−7.8	−17.8	−32.9	−53.9	0	−4.7	−13.6	−27.6	−47.5	−108.8	−203.9
2688	1985	1434	1022	732	550	0.4	0	−2.3	−7.0	−14.3	−24.7	1.6	0	−3.8	−10.4	−20.1	−51.2	−102.3
2591	2028	1571	1210	937	745	0.6	0	−3.0	−8.7	−17.4	−30.0	2.0	0	−4.7	−12.4	−23.7	−58.4	−112.9
2753	2093	1563	1151	844	633	0.4	0	−2.2	−6.5	−13.3	−23.0	1.5	0	−3.6	−9.7	−18.6	−47.2	−94.1
2150	1506	1034	714	527	427	0.6	0	−3.2	−9.5	−19.5	−33.8	2.1	0	−5.2	−14.1	−27.4	−70.1	−138.1
2005	1506	1126	852	676	568	0.9	0	−4.1	−12.0	−24.0	−40.9	2.7	0	−6.5	−17.2	−32.7	−80.6	−154.1
4337	3510	2812	2228	1747	1361	0.2	0	−1.7	−5.1	−10.3	−17.6	2.5	2.1	0	−3.9	−10.0	−29.4	−60.7
4263	3426	2723	2141	1669	1300	0.3	0	−2.0	−5.9	−11.9	−20.3	2.9	2.4	0	−4.5	−11.5	−33.8	−70.1
4263	3139	2262	1602	1138	844	0.3	0	−2.2	−6.5	−13.5	−23.4	1.5	0	−3.6	−9.8	−19.1	−49.1	−99.5
538	399	324	273	233	201	0	−6.7	−22.2	−47.3	−83.2	−130.8	0	−12.1	−39.9	−66.4	−110.6	−238.3	−425.6
987	802	674	587	525	476	0	−4.7	−15.4	−32.7	−57.2	−89.3	0	−8.4	−23.4	−45.6	−75.2	−158.8	−277.4
1650	988	638	484	395	232	0	−2.7	−10.2	−23.6	−44.2	−73.3	0	−6.1	−18.1	−37.4	−65.1	−150.3	−282.5
629	449	360	300	254	217	0	−6.5	−21.6	−46.3	−81.8	−129.1	0	−11.8	−33.3	−65.5	−109.5	−237.4	−426.2
2355	1815	1355	1015	810	680	0	−2.4	−8.2	−17.6	−31.4	−51.5	0	−4.6	−12.8	−25.4	−44.3	−95.5	—
4620	3689	2924	2308	1839	1496	0.7	0	−3.3	−9.6	−19.2	−32.5	2.2	0	−5.2	−13.6	−25.8	−63.2	−121.7
4712	3547	2640	1970	1516	1239	0.8	0	−3.5	−10.3	−20.8	−35.6	2.4	0	−5.6	−14.9	−28.5	−71.5	−140.4

TRAJECTORY inches above (+) or below (−) line of sight 0 = indicates yardage at which rifle is sighted in.
Specifications are normal. Test barrels are used to determine ballistics figures. Individual firearms may differ from these test barrels statistics.
Specifications subject to change without notice.

WINCHESTER-AMMUNITION
RIMFIRE CARTRIDGE BALLISTICS

Lead   **Silhouette**

Hollow Point

**Jacketed
Hollow Point**

**Full
Metal Case**

RIMFIRE RIFLE

Cartridge	Symbol	Bullet Wt. Grs.	Type	Velocity (ft./s.) Muzzle	100 yds	Energy (ft. lbs.) Muzzle	100 yds.	Nominal Mid-Range Traj. (in.) 100 yds.
22 Short Super-X	X22S	29	L**	1095	903	77	52	4.5
22 Short H.P. Super-X	X22SH	27	L**	1120	904	75	49	4.4
22 Long Rifle Super-X	X22LR	40	L**	1255	1017	140	92	3.6
22 Long Rifle H.P. Super-X	X22LRH	37	L**	1280	1015	135	85	3.5
22 Long Rifle Shot Super-X (#12 Shot)	X22LRS	—	—	—	—	—	—	—
22 Winchester MAGNUM R.F. Super-X	X22WMR	40	JHP	1910	1326	324	156	1.7
22 Winchester MAGNUM R.F. Super-X	X22MR1	40	FMC	1910	1326	324	156	1.7
22 Short T22	XT22S	29	Lead**	1045	872	70	49	4.8
22 Long Rifle T22	XT22LR	40	Lead**	1150	976	117	85	4.0
22 Long Rifle Silhouette	XS22LR	42	Lead**	1220	1003	139	94	3.6
22 Short C.B.	WW22CBS2	29	Lead**	715	—	33	—	—

RIMFIRE PISTOL AND REVOLVER

Cartridge	Symbol	Bullet Wt. Grs.	Type	Barrel Length	Muzzle Velocity (ft/s)	Muzzle Energy (ft. lbs.)
22 Short Blank	22 BL	—	—	—	—	—
22 Short Super-X	X22S	29	L**	6"	1010	66
22 Short T22	XT22S	29	Lead**	6"	865	48
22 Long Super-X	X22L	29	L**	6"	1095	77
22 Long Rifle Super-X	X22LR	40	L**	6"	1060	100
22 Long Rifle T22	XT22LR	40	Lead**	6"	950	80
22 Long Rifle Silhouette	XS22LR	42	Lead**	6"/10"	1025/1105	98/114
22 Long Rifle Super-Match Mark IV	SM22LR4	40	Lead**	6¾"	1060	100
22 Winchester MAGNUM Rimfire Super-X	X22WMR	40	JHP	6½"	1480	195
22 Winchester MAGNUM Rimfire Super-X	X22MR1	40	FMC	6½"	1480	195

FMC-Full Metal Case
JHP-Jacketed Hollow Point
JSP-Jacketed Soft Point
L-Lubaloy
**Wax Coated

+P Ammunition with (+P) on the case head stamp is loaded to higher pressure. Use only in firearms designated for this cartridge and so recommended by the gun manufacturer.
V-Data is based on velocity obtained from 4" vented test barrels for revolver cartridges (38 Special, 357 Magnum, 41 Rem. Mag. and 44 Rem. Mag.)

Specifications are nominal. Test barrels are used to determine ballistics figures. Individual firearms may differ from test barrel statistics.
Specifications subject to change without notice.

Reference Section

HORNADY RIFLE BULLETS

RIFLE BULLETS
"I" denotes interlock bullets.

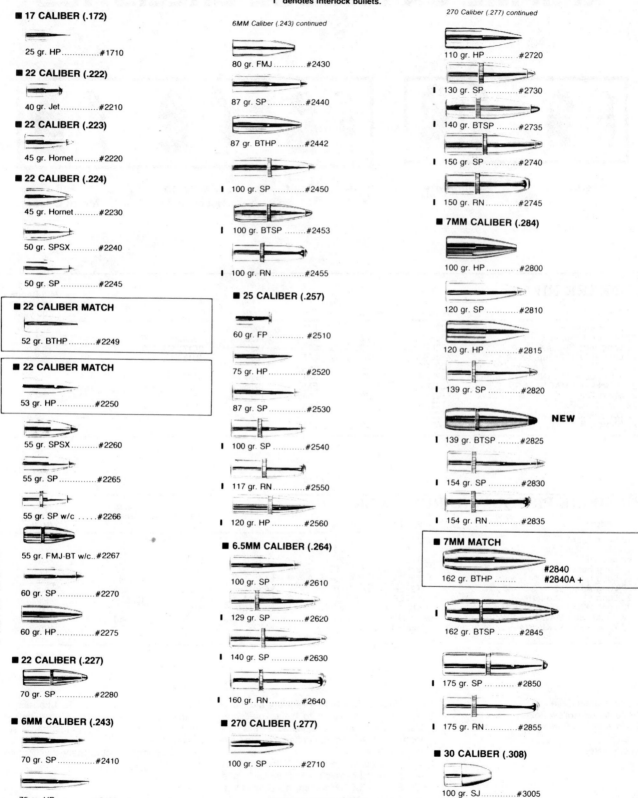

■ 17 CALIBER (.172)

25 gr. HP............#1710

■ 22 CALIBER (.222)

40 gr. Jet............#2210

■ 22 CALIBER (.223)

45 gr. Hornet......#2220

■ 22 CALIBER (.224)

45 gr. Hornet........#2230

50 gr. SPSX..........#2240

50 gr. SP.............#2245

■ 22 CALIBER MATCH

52 gr. BTHP..........#2249

■ 22 CALIBER MATCH

53 gr. HP.............#2250

55 gr. SPSX..........#2260

55 gr. SP.............#2265

55 gr. SP w/c.....#2266

55 gr. FMJ-BT w/c..#2267

60 gr. SP.............#2270

60 gr. HP.............#2275

■ 22 CALIBER (.227)

70 gr. SP.............#2280

■ 6MM CALIBER (.243)

70 gr. SP.............#2410

75 gr. HP.............#2420

6MM Caliber (.243) continued

80 gr. FMJ............#2430

87 gr. SP.............#2440

87 gr. BTHP..........#2442

I 100 gr. SP.........#2450

I 100 gr. BTSP.......#2453

I 100 gr. RN.........#2455

■ 25 CALIBER (.257)

60 gr. FP............#2510

75 gr. HP.............#2520

87 gr. SP.............#2530

I 100 gr. SP.........#2540

I 117 gr. RN.........#2550

I 120 gr. HP.........#2560

■ 6.5MM CALIBER (.264)

100 gr. SP...........#2610

I 129 gr. SP.........#2620

I 140 gr. SP.........#2630

I 160 gr. RN.........#2640

■ 270 CALIBER (.277)

100 gr. SP...........#2710

500 BP = Bulk Packaged

---

270 Caliber (.277) continued

110 gr. HP...........#2720

I 130 gr. SP.........#2730

I 140 gr. BTSP.......#2735

I 150 gr. SP.........#2740

I 150 gr. RN.........#2745

■ 7MM CALIBER (.284)

100 gr. HP...........#2800

120 gr. SP...........#2810

120 gr. HP...........#2815

I 139 gr. SP.........#2820

NEW

I 139 gr. BTSP.......#2825

I 154 gr. SP.........#2830

I 154 gr. RN.........#2835

■ 7MM MATCH

162 gr. BTHP........ #2840
#2840A +

I 162 gr. BTSP.....#2845

I 175 gr. SP.........#2850

I 175 gr. RN.........#2855

■ 30 CALIBER (.308)

100 gr. SJ............#3005

HORNADY RIFLE BULLETS

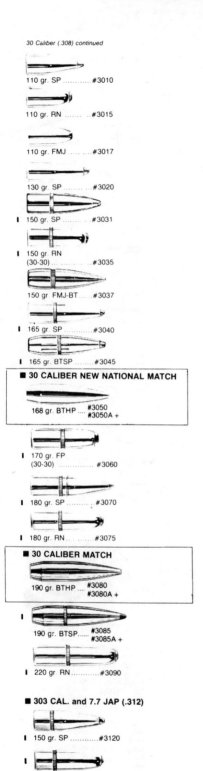

30 Caliber (.308) continued

110 gr. SP .... #3010

110 gr. RN .... #3015

110 gr. FMJ .....#3017

130 gr. SP .... #3020

150 gr. SP ......#3031

150 gr. RN
(30-30) ....#3035

150 gr. FMJ-BT .....#3037

165 gr. SP ......#3040

165 gr. BTSP ....#3045

■ 30 CALIBER NEW NATIONAL MATCH

168 gr. BTHP .... #3050
#3050A +

170 gr. FP
(30-30) .... #3060

180 gr. SP ....#3070

180 gr. RN ....#3075

■ 30 CALIBER MATCH

190 gr. BTHP .... #3080
#3080A +

190 gr. BTSP ...... #3085
#3085A +

220 gr. RN ....#3090

■ 303 CAL. and 7.7 JAP (.312)

150 gr. SP ....#3120

174 gr. RN. ....#3130

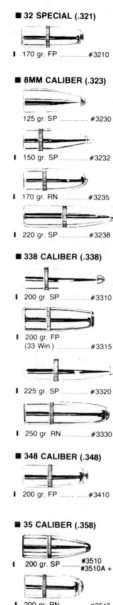

■ 32 SPECIAL (.321)

170 gr. FP ....#3210

■ 8MM CALIBER (.323)

125 gr. SP .... #3230

150 gr. SP ....#3232

170 gr. RN ....#3235

220 gr. SP ....#3238

■ 338 CALIBER (.338)

200 gr. SP ....#3310

200 gr. FP
(33 Win.) ....#3315

225 gr. SP ....#3320

250 gr. RN ....#3330

■ 348 CALIBER (.348)

200 gr. FP .... #3410

■ 35 CALIBER (.358)

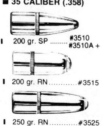

200 gr. SP .... #3510
#3510A +

200 gr. RN ....#3515

250 gr. RN ....#3525

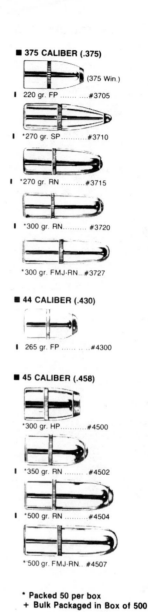

■ 375 CALIBER (.375)

(375 Win.)

220 gr. FP .... #3705

*270 gr. SP...........#3710

*270 gr. RN ....#3715

*300 gr. RN......... #3720

*300 gr. FMJ-RN.. #3727

■ 44 CALIBER (.430)

265 gr. FP ....#4300

■ 45 CALIBER (.458)

*300 gr. HP...........#4500

*350 gr. RN .... #4502

*500 gr. RN ....#4504

*'500 gr. FMJ-RN.. #4507

* Packed 50 per box
\+ Bulk Packaged in Box of 500

LEGEND

BBWC—Bevel Base Wadcutter	RN—Round Nose
BT—Boat Tail	SJ—Short Jacket
DEWC—Double End Wadcutter	SP—Spire Point
FMJ—Full Metal Jacket	SWC—Semi-Wadcutter
FP—Flat Point	SX—Super Explosive
HBWC—Hollow Base Wadcutter	JTC—Jacketed Truncated Cone
HP—Hollow Point	SIL—Silhouette

HORNADY BULLETS

PISTOL BULLETS

■ 25 CALIBER (.251)

50 gr. FMJ-RN.......#3545

■ 32 Caliber (.308)

71 gr. FMJ-RN.... #3200

■ 9MM CALIBER (.355)

90 gr. HP..........#3550

100 gr. FMJ ....#3552

115 gr. HP ....#3554

124 gr. FMJ-FP......#3556

124 gr. FMJ-RN.. #3557

■ 38 CALIBER (.357)

110 gr. HP ....#3570

125 gr. HP ....#3571

---

38 Caliber (.357) continued

125 gr. FP ....#3573

140 gr. JHP..........#3574

158 gr. HP ....#3575

158 gr. FP ....#3578

160 gr. JTC-SIL **NEW** #3572 / #3572A +

180 gr. JTC-SIL **NEW** #3577 / #3577A +

■ 41 CALIBER (.410)

210 gr. HP ....#4100

210 gr. FMJ/FP ....#4103

■ 44 CALIBER (.430)

200 gr. HP .... #4410

■ 44 CALIBER (.430)

240 gr. HP ....#4420

240 gr. JTC-SIL. **NEW** #4425 / #4425A +

■ 45 CALIBER (.451)

185 gr. HP, ACP ...#4510

185 gr. Target SWC, ACP..........#4513

200 gr. FMJ-C/T **(Match)** .# 4515

230 gr. FMJ-RN ....#4517

230 gr. FMJ-FP......#4518

■ 45 CALIBER (.452)

250 gr. Long Colt HP ....#4520

LEAD PISTOL BULLETS

32 cal. (.314)

90 gr. SWC .... #3250 / #1000

38 cal. (.358)

148 gr. BBWC............ #3580 / #1010

38 cal. (.358)

148 gr. HBWC............ #3582 / #1020

38 cal. (.358)

148 gr. DEWC............ Bulk only) / #1030

Bulk lead bullets must be ordered in increments of carton quantities per bullet. 5000 bullets per carton except 44 caliber is 4000 per carton.

38 cal. (.358)

158 gr. RN .... #3586 / #1050

38 cal. (.358)

158 gr. SWC .... #3588 / #1040

44 cal. (.430)

240 gr. SWC .... #4430 / #1110

45 cal. (.452)

200 gr. SWC .... #4526 / #1210

500 Per Box except 44 cal. (400 Per Box)

ROUND LEAD BALLS

Here is an item for Black Powder shooters. Round Lead Balls in 15 sizes, from .310 through .570

.310 .... #6000
.315 .....**NEW**.... #6003
.350 .... #6010
.375 .... #6020
.433 .... #6030
.440 .... #6040
.445 .... #6050
.451 .... #6060
.454 .... #6070
.457 .... #6080
.490 .... #6090
.495 .....**NEW** .... #6093
.530 .... #6100
.535 .... #6110
*.570 .... #6120

* Packed 50 Per Box
   All Others Packed 100 Per Box

NOSLER BULLETS

Nosler Trophy Grade Bullets

Whether your trophy is a bull elk of Boone and Crockett proportions or an engraved cup awarded in competitive shooting, the performance of every bullet you shoot has to measure up to the job at hand. Nosler designs and manufactures every bullet it makes, both Partition and Solid Base, to perform every time as if your target were a trophy. Because Nosler believes *every* shot you take is important, *every* Nosler bullet has trophy performance built in...in accuracy, in flight characteristics, in striking power. That is why Nosler bullets can truly be called "Trophy Grade" bullets.

NEW—Solid Base 6mm, 75 Gr: Spitzer; 7mm, 162 Gr. Spitzer

Caliber	Diameter	Partition	Bullet Weight and Style
6mm	.243″		95 Gr. Spitzer
	.243″		100 Gr. Semi Spitzer
.25	.257″		100 Gr. Spitzer
	.257″		120 Gr. Spitzer
6.5mm	.264″		125 Gr. Spitzer
	.264″		140 Gr. Spitzer
.270	.277″		130 Gr. Spitzer
	.277″		150 Gr. Spitzer
	.277″		160 Gr. Semi Spitzer
7mm	.284″		140 Gr. Spitzer
	.284″		150 Gr. Spitzer
	.284″		160 Gr. Spitzer
	.284″		175 Gr. Semi Spitzer
.30	.308″		150 Gr. Spitzer
	.308″		165 Gr. Spitzer
	.308″		180 Gr. Spitzer
	.308″		180 Gr. Protected Point
	.308″		200 Gr. Round Nose
.338	.338″		210 Gr. Spitzer
	.338″		250 Gr. Round Nose

Caliber	Diameter	Solid Base	Bullet Weight and Style
.22	.224″		50 Gr. Spitzer
	.224″		50 Gr. Hollow Point
	.224″		50 Gr. Expander
	.224″		52 Gr. Hollow Point
	.224″		52 Gr. Hollow Pt. Match
	.224″		55 Gr. Spitzer
	.224″		60 Gr. Spitzer
6mm	.243″		70 Gr. Hollow Point
	.243″		70 Gr. Hollow Pt. Match
	.243″		85 Gr. Spitzer
	.243″		100 Gr. Spitzer
.25	.257″		100 Gr. Spitzer
	.257″		120 Gr. Spitzer
6.5mm	.264″		120 Gr. Spitzer
.270	.277″		100 Gr. Spitzer
	.277″		130 Gr. Spitzer
	.277″		150 Gr. Spitzer
7mm	.284″		120 Gr. Spitzer
	.284″		140 Gr. Spitzer
	.284″		150 Gr. Spitzer
.30	.308″		150 Gr. Flat Point
	.308″		150 Gr. Spitzer
	.308″		150 Gr. Hollow Point
	.308″		150 Gr. Hollow Pt. Match
	.308″		165 Gr. Spitzer
	.308″		168 Gr. Hollow Point
	.308″		168 Gr. Hollow Pt. Match
	.308″		170 Gr. Flat Point
	.308″		180 Gr. Spitzer

REMINGTON BULLETS

"Core-Lokt® Bullets

The "Number One Mushroom"—a name given by hunters everywhere to the Remington center fire cartridges with "Core-Lokt" bullets.

Superior mushrooming and one-shot stopping power are the results of the advanced design of "Core-Lokt" bullets: metal jacket and lead core are locked together by the jacket's heavy mid-section. "Core-Lokt" bullets are available in a wide variety of types and weights.

Bronze Point Expanding Bullet

A top performing all-around bullet of a unique design for extra long range accuracy and controlled expansion. Travels in a flat trajectory and has great wind bucking qualities.

"Power-Lokt"® Bullets

Remington "Power-Lokt" bullets are uniquely designed with the core and jacket electrolytically bonded into a one-piece unit. This exclusive process produces a better balance and more concentric bullet of uniformly high performance, rapid expansion and amazing accuracy.

ABBREVIATIONS

BrPt—Bronze Point	PL—Power-Lokt
CL—Core-Lokt	PSP—Pointed Soft Point
GC—Gas Check	SJ—Semi-Jacketed
HP—Hollow Point	SP—Soft Point
J—Jacketed	WC—Wadcutter
LD—Lead	SWC—Semi-Wadcutter
MC—Metal Case	

NEW ORDER NO.	OLD ORDER NO.		DESCRIPTION	WT. (LBS.) PER 100
		17 cal. (.172)		
B1705	B22936		25 gr. PLHP	0.3
		22 cal. (.224)		
B2210	B22704		45 gr. SP	0.7
B2220	B27710		50 gr. PSP	0.7
B2230	B22708		50 gr. MC	0.7
B2240	B22950		50 gr. PLHP	0.7
B2250	B22956		50 gr. PL Match	0.7
B2260	B22948		52 gr. HPBR	0.8
B2270	B22924		55 gr. PSP	0.8
B2280	B22952		55 gr. PLHP	0.8
B2290	B22958		55 gr. PL Match	0.8
B2265	B23558		55 gr. MC WO/C	0.8
		6mm (.243)		
B2420	B22966		80 gr. PSP	1.2
B2430	B22954		80 gr. PLHP	1.2
B2440	B22960		80 gr. PL Match	1.2
B2460	B22920		100 gr .PSPCL	1.5
		25 cal. (.257)		
B2510	B22752		87 gr. PLHP	1.4
B2520	B22730		100 gr. PSPCL (25-06)	1.5
B2540	B22736		120 gr. PSPCL (25-06)	1.8
		6.5mm (.264)		
B2610	B22926		120 gr. PSPCL	1.8
		270 cal. (.277)		
B2710	B23744		100 gr. PSP	1.5
B2720	B22746		130 gr. PSPCL	1.9
B2730	B22748		130 gr. BrPt	1.9
B2740	B22750		150 gr. SPCL	2.2
		7mm (.284)		
B2830	B22756		150 gr. PSPCL	2.2
B2850	B22918		175 gr. PSPCL 7mm Rem.	2.6
		30 cal. (.308)		
B3010	B22796		110 gr. SP Carbine	1.6
B3020	B22770		150 gr. BrPt (30-06)	2.2
B3025	B22774		150 gr. SPCL (30-30)	2.2
B3030	B22776		150 gr. PSPCL	2.2
B3040	B23594		165 gr. PSPCL	2.4
B3050	B22782		170 gr. SPCL	2.5
B3060	B22784		180 gr. BrPt	2.6
B3070	B22786		180 gr. SPCL	2.6

* .360 dia. for best accuracy. † Also available in bulk pack.

NEW ORDER NO.	OLD ORDER NO.		DESCRIPTION	WT. (LBS.) PER 100
		30 Cal. (.308) Cont'd		
B3080	B22788		180 gr. PSPCL	2.6
B3090	B22792		220 gr. SPCL	3.2
		32 cal. (.320)		
B3250	B22828		170 gr. SPCL	2.5
		8mm (.323)		
B3270	B22984		185 gr. PSPCL	2.8
B3280	B22986		220 gr. PSPCL	3.3
		35 cal. (.358)		
B3510	B22868		200 gr. SPCL	2.9
		9mm (.354)		
B3550	B22942		115 gr. JHP	1.8
B3552	B22842		124 gr. MC	1.9
		38 cal.		
B3810	B22944		95 gr. SJHP	1.4
		357/38 cal. (.357)		
B3570	B23586		110 gr. SJHP	1.6
B3572	B22866		125 gr. SJHP	1.9
B3574	B22846		158 gr. SP	2.3
B3576	B22938		158 gr. SJHP	2.3
		357 cal. (.358)		
B3578	B22856		158 gr. LEAD SWC†	2.3
		38 cal. (.360)*		
B3830	B22850		148 gr. LD WC†	2.2
		38 cal. (.358)		
B3840	B22854		158 gr. LEAD†	2.3
B3850	B23568		158 gr. LEAD HP	2.3
		41 mag. (.310)		
B4110	B22888		210 gr. SP	3.1
		41 mag. (.411)		
B4120	B22922		210 gr. LEAD	3.1
		44 cal. (.430)		
B4405	B23588		180 gr. SJHP	2.8
B4410	B22906		240 gr. SP	3.5
B4420	B22940		240 gr. SJHP	3.5
		44 cal. (.432)		
B4430	B22884		240 gr. LEAD GC	3.5
B4440	B22768		240 gr. LEAD	3.5
		45 cal. (.451)		
B4530	B22892		230 gr. MC†	3.4
B4510	B22890		185 gr. MCWC†	2.7
B4520	B22586		185 gr. JHP	2.7

SIERRA BULLETS

Stock No.	Description	
.22 Caliber (.224 Diameter)		
1100	40 gr. Hornet	(.223 Dia.)
1110	45 gr. Hornet	(.223 Dia.)
1200	40 gr. Hornet	
1210	45 gr. Hornet	
1300	45 gr. SMP	
1310	45 gr. SPT	
1320	50 gr. SMP	
1330	50 gr. SPT	
1340	50 gr. Blitz	
1410	52 gr. HPBT	
1400	53 gr. HP	
1345	55 gr. Blitz	
1350	55 gr. SMP	
1355	55 gr. FMJBT	
1360	55 gr. SPT	
1365	55 gr. SBT	
1370	63 gr. SMP	
6MM .243 Caliber (.243 Diameter)		
1500	60 gr. HP	
1505	70 gr. HPBT	
1510	75 gr. HP	
1520	85 gr. SPT	
1530	85 gr. HPBT	
1535	90 gr. FMJBT	
1540	100 gr. SPT	
1550	100 gr. SMP	
1560	100 gr. SBT	
.25 Caliber 6.3MM (.257 Diameter)		
1600	75 gr. HP	
1610	87 gr. SPT	
1615	90 gr. HPBT	
1620	100 gr. SPT	

Stock No.	Description	
1630	117 gr. SBT	
1640	117 gr. SPT	
1650	120 gr. HPBT	
6.5MM .264 Caliber (.264 Diameter)		
1700	85 gr. HP	
1710	100 gr. HP	
1720	120 gr. SPT	
1730	140 gr. SBT	
1740	140 gr. HPBT	
.270 Caliber 6.8MM (.277 Diameter)		
1800	90 gr. HP	
1810	110 gr. SPT	
1820	130 gr. SBT	
1830	130 gr. SPT	
1835	140 gr. HPBT	
1840	150 gr. SBT	
1850	150 gr. RN	
7MM .284 Caliber (.284 Diameter)		
1900	120 gr. SPT	
1905	140 gr. SBT	
1910	140 gr. SPT	
1915	150 gr. HPBT	
1920	160 gr. SBT	
1930	168 gr. HPBT	
1950	170 gr. RN	
1940	175 gr. SBT	
.30 Caliber (.308 Diameter)		
2020	125 gr. HP	(30-30)
2000	150 gr. FN	(30-30)
2010	170 gr. FN	(30-30)
2100	110 gr. RN	
2105	110 gr. FMJ	
2110	110 gr. HP	

SIERRA BULLETS

Stock No.	Description
2120	125 gr. SPT
2130	150 gr. SPT
2125	150 gr. SBT
2190	150 gr. HPBT
2135	150 gr. RN
2145	165 gr. SBT
2140	165 gr. HPBT
2200	168 gr. HPBT
2150	180 gr. SPT
2160	180 gr. SBT
2220	180 gr. HPBT
2170	180 gr. RN
2210	190 gr. HPBT
2165	200 gr. SBT
2230	200 gr. HPBT
2240	220 gr. HPBT
2180	220 gr. RN

.303 Caliber 7.7MM (.311 Diameter)

Stock No.	Description
2320	125 gr. FMJ
2300	150 gr. SPT
2310	180 gr. SPT

8MM .323 Caliber (.323 Diameter)

Stock No.	Description
2400	150 gr. SPT
2410	175 gr. SPT
2420	220 gr. SBT

.338 Caliber 8.38MM (.338 Diameter)

Stock No.	Description
2600	250 gr. SBT

.35 Caliber 8.9MM (.358 Diameter)

Stock No.	Description
2800	200 gr. RN

.375 Caliber 9.3MM (.375 Diameter)

Stock No.	Description
3000	300 gr. SBT

.45 Caliber (45-70) 11.4MM (.458 Diameter)

Stock No.	Description
8900	300 gr. HP

.32 Caliber 7.65MM (.308 Diameter)

Stock No.	Description
8010	71 gr. FMJ

9MM .355 Caliber (.355 Diameter)

Stock No.	Description
8100	90 gr. JHP
8105	95 gr. FMJ
8110	115 gr. JHP

Stock No.	Description
8115	**115 gr. FMJ**
8120	125 gr. FMJ
8345	130 gr. FMJ

.38 Caliber (.357 Diameter)

Stock No.	Description
8300	110 gr. JHC Blitz
8310	125 gr. JSP
8320	125 gr. JHC
8325	140 gr. JHC
8360	158 gr. JHC
8340	158 gr. JSP
8365	170 gr. JHC
8350	170 gr. FMJ Match
8370	**180 gr. FPJ**

.41 Caliber 10.2MM (.410 Diameter)

Stock No.	Description
8500	170 gr. JHC
8520	210 gr. JHC
8530	220 gr. FPJ Match

.44 Magnum 10.7MM (.4295 Diameter)

Stock No.	Description
8600	180 gr. JHC
8620	210 gr. JHC
8605	220 gr. FPJ Match
8610	240 gr. JHC

.45 Caliber 11.4MM (.4515 Diameter)

Stock No.	Description
8800	185 gr. JHP
8810	185 gr. FPJ Match
8815	230 gr. FMJ Match
8820	240 gr. JHP
8825	**200gr. FPJ**

*50 bullets per box

SPEER BULLETS

22 CALIBER (.223)

1005   40 Gr. Spire Point

1011   45 Gr. Spitzer

22 CALIBER (.224)

1017   40 Gr. Spire

1023   45 Gr. Spitzer

1029   50 Gr. Spitzer

1035   52 Gr. Hollow Point

1045   55 Gr. F M J

1047   55 Gr. Spitzer

1049   55 Gr. Spitzer

1053   70 Gr. Semi-Spitzer

6mm CALIBER (.243)

1205   75 Gr. Hollow Point

1211   80 Gr. Spitzer

1213   85 Gr. Boat Tail

1215   90 Gr. F M J

1217   90 Gr. Spitzer

1223   105 Gr. Round Nose

1229   105 Gr. Spitzer

25 CALIBER (.257)

1241   87 Gr. Spitzer

1405   100 Gr. spitzer

1407   100 Gr. Hollow Point

1410   120 Gr. Boat Tail

1411   120 Gr. Spitzer

6.5mm CALIBER (.263)

1435   120 Gr. Spitzer

1441   140 Gr. Spitzer

270 CALIBER (.277)

1447   100 Gr. Hollow Point

1453   100 Gr. Spitzer

1458   130 Gr. Boat Tail

1459   130 Gr. Spitzer

1465   130 Gr. Grand Slam

1604   150 Gr. Boat Tail

1605   150 Gr. Spitzer

1608   150 Gr. Grand Slam

7mm CALIBER (.284)

1617   115 Gr. Hollow Point

1623   130 Gr. Spitzer

1628   145 Gr. Boat Tail

1629   145 Gr. Spitzer

1631   145 Gr. Match Boat Tail

1634   160 Gr. Boat Tail

1635   160 Gr. Spitzer

1637   160 Gr. Mag-Tip

1638   160 Gr. Grand Slam

1641   175 Gr. Mag-Tip

1643   175 Gr. Grand Slam

30 CALIBER (.308)

1805   100 Gr. Plinker ®

1835   110 Gr. Hollow Point

1845   110 Gr. Round Nose

1855   110 Gr. Spire Point

2005   130 Gr. Hollow Point

2007   130 Gr. Flat Point

2011   150 Gr. Flat Point

2017   150 Gr. Round Nose

2022   150 Gr. Boat Tail

2023   150 Gr. Spitzer

2025   150 Gr. Mag-Tip

2029   165 Gr. Round Nose

2034   165 Gr. Boat Tail

2035   165 Gr. Spitzer

2038   165 Gr. Grand Slam

2040   168 Gr. Match Boat Tail

2041   170 Gr. Flat Point

2047   180 Gr. Round Nose

2052   180 Gr. Boat Tail

2053   180 Gr. Spitzer

2059   180 Gr. Mag-Tip

2063   180 Gr. Grand Slam

2080   190 Gr. Match Boat Tail

2211   200 Gr. Spitzer

SPEER BULLETS

303 CALIBER (.311)

2217
150 Grain
Spitzer

2223
180 Grain
Round Nose

32 CALIBER (.321)

2259
170 Grain
Flat Nose

8mm CALIBER (.323)

2277
150 Grain
Spitzer

2283
170
Semi-Spitzer

2285
200 Grain
Spitzer

338 CALIBER (.338)

2405
200 Grain
Spitzer

2408
250 Grain
Grand Slam

2411
275 Grain
Semi-Spitzer

35 CALIBER (.358)

2435
180 Grain
Flat Nose

2453
250 Grain
Spitzer

375 CALIBER (.375)

2471
235 Grain
Semi-Spitzer

2473
285 Grain
Grand Slam

45 CALIBER (.458)

2479
400 Grain
Flat Nose

9mm CALIBER (.355)

4000
88 Grain
Hollow Point

3983
100 Grain
Hollow Point

4005
125 Grain
Soft Point

38 CALIBER (.357)

4007
110 Grain
Hollow Point

4011
125 Grain
Soft Point

4013
125 Grain
Hollow Point

4203
140 Grain
Hollow Point

4205
146 Grain
Hollow Point

4211
158 Grain
J H P

4217
158 Grain
Soft Point

4223
160 Grain
Soft Point

41 CALIBER (.410)

4405
200 Grain
Soft Point

4417
220 Grain
Soft Point

44 CALIBER (.429)

4425
200 Grain
Mag Hollow Point

4435
225 Grain
Hollow Point

4447
240 Grain
Soft Point

4453
240 Grain
Mag
Hollow Point

4457
240 Grain
Mag Soft Point

45 CALIBER (.451)

4477
200 Grain
Hollow Point

4479
225 Grain
Mag Hollow Point

4481
260 Gr.
Hollow Point

(Lead)

9mm CALIBER (.356)

4601
125 Grain
Round Nose

38 CALIBER (.358)

4605
148 Grain
BBWC

4617
148 Grain
HBWC

4623
158 Grain
SWC

4647
158 Grain
Round Nose

44 CALIBER (.430)

4660
240 Grain
SWC

45 CALIBER (.452)

4677
200 Grain
SWC

4690
230 Grain
Round Nose

4683
250 Grain
SWC

ROUND BALL

#5113 .375	#5135 .454"
#5127 .433"	#5137 .457"
#5129 .440"	#5139 .490"
#5131 .445"	#5142 .530"
#5133 .451"	#5180 .570"

FEDERAL PRIMERS

PRIMERS Non-Corrosive/Non-Mercuric

ITEM NUMBER	DESCRIPTION	NOMINAL DIAMETER IN INCHES	COLOR CODING	PACKAGED	WEIGHT PER CASE
100	Small Pistol	.175	Green		4.8 lbs.
150	Large Pistol	.210	Green		6.1
155	Large Magnum Pistol	.210	Blue		6.7
200	Small Rifle & Mag. Pistol	.175	Red	100 per Box	4.9
205	Small Rifle	.175	Purple	10 Boxes per ctn.,	4.9
210	Large Rifle	.210	Red	5 ctn. per Case,	6.5
215	Large Magnum Rifle	.210	Purple	of 5000	6.5
205M	Small Rifle Match	.175	Purple		4.9
210M	Large Rifle Match	.210	Red		6.5
209	Shotshell (12, 16 & 20 Ga.)	.243	—		16.7
410	Shotshell (.410 & 28 Ga.)	.243	—		16.7

FEDERAL UNPRIMED CASES

UNPRIMED BRASS PISTOL CASES

ITEM NUMBER	DESCRIPTION	RECOMMENDED FEDERAL PRIMER NUMBER FOR HAND LOADS	PACKAGED	APPR. WEIGHT PER CASE
380UP	380 Auto	100		8.4 lbs.
9UP	9mm Luger Auto	200		10.0
38UP	38 Special	100	50 per Box,	10.6
357UP	357 Magnum	200	20 Boxes	12.4
357MXUP	357 Maximum	200	per Case of	18.0
44UP	44 Rem. Magnum	150 or 155	1000 Rounds	18.6
45UP	45 Auto	150		14.1
45LCAUP	45 Colt	150		19.6

UNPRIMED BRASS RIFLE CASES

ITEM NUMBER	DESCRIPTION	RECOMMENDED FEDERAL PRIMER	PACKAGED	APPR. WEIGHT PER CASE
222UP	222 Remington	200 or 205		18.2 lbs.
22250UP	22-250 Remington	210		29.4
223UP	223 Remington	200 or 205		18.3
243UP	243 Winchester	210		30.4
2506UP	25-06 Remington	210		34.0
270UP	270 Winchester	210	20 per Box,	34.2
7RUP	7mm Rem. Magnum	215	50 Boxes	40.5
30CUP	30 Carbine	200	per Case of	13.1
3030UP	30-30 Winchester	210	1000 Rounds	26.0
3006UP	30-06 Springfield	210		34.4
300WUP	300 Win. Magnum	215		42.0
308UP	308 Winchester	210		31.0
4570UP	4570 Government	210		16.1

UNPRIMED NICKEL PLATED MATCH RIFLE CASES

ITEM NUMBER	DESCRIPTION	RECOMMENDED FEDERAL PRIMER	PACKAGED	APPR. WEIGHT PER CASE
222MUP	222 Remington Match	205M	20 per Box, 50 Boxes	18.5 lbs.
308MUP	308 Winchester Match	210M	per Case of 1000 Rounds	30.6

UNPRIMED CASES

SYMBOL	CALIBER
U218	218 Bee
U22H	22 Hornet
U2250	22-250 Rem
U220S	220 Swift
U222R	222 Rem
U223R	223 Rem
U225	225 Win
U243	243 Win
U6mmR	6mmR
U2520	25/20 Win
U256	256 Win Mag
U250	250 Savage
U2506	25-06 Rem
U257	257 Roberts
U257F	257 Roberts +P
U264	204 Win Mag
U270	270 Win
U284	284 Win
U7mm	7mm Mauser
U7 Mag	7mm Rem Mag
U30C	30 Carbine
U3030	30-30 Win
U3006	30-06 Springfield
U3040	30-40 Krag
U300WM	300 Win Mag
U300H	300 H & H Mag
U300	300 Savage
U307	307 Win
U308	308 Win
U303	303 British
U32W	32 Win Special
U3220	32-20 Win

SYMBOL	CALIBER
U8mm	8mm Mauser
U338	338 Win Mag
U348	348 Win
U35R	35 Rem
U356	356 Win
U358	358 Win
U375H	375 H & H Mag
U375W	375 Win
U3840	38-40 Win
U3855	38-55 Win
U440	44-40 Win
U44M	44 Rem Mag
U4570	45-70 Govt
U458	458 Win Mag
U25A	25 Auto
U256	256 Win Mag
U32A	32 Auto
U32SW	32 S & W
U32SWL	32 S & W Long
U357	357 Mag (Nickel)
U9mm	9mm Luger
U38SW	38 S & W
U38SP	38 Special
U38A	38 Auto
U380A	380 Auto
U41	41 Rem Mag
U44S	44 S & W Special
U44M	44 Rem Mag
U45C	45 Colt
U45A	45 Auto

PRIMERS

Symbol		
W209	#W209	Shot Shell
WLR	#8½-120	Large Rifle
WSR	#6½-116	Small Rifle
WSP	#1½-108	Small (Regular) Pistol
WLP	#7-111	Large (Regular) Pistol
WSPM	#1½M-108	Small (Mag) Pistol

PLASTIC WADS

WAA 12
WAA 12R
WAA 12F 114
WAA 12F 1
WAA 20
WAA 20F 1
WAA 28
WAA 41

NORMA EMPTY UNPRIMED RIFLE CASES

Caliber
220 Swift
222 Remington
22 SAV High Power
243 Winchester
6.5 Jap
6.5 Norma (6.5x55)
6.5 Carcano
270 Winchester
7mm Mauser
7x57 R (Rimmed)
7mm Rem. Mag.
7x64
7.5x55 (7.5 Swiss)

Caliber
30 U.S. Carbine
7.62 Russian
30-06 Springfield
22-250 Rem.
30-30 WIN
308 Winchester
308 Norma Magnum
7.65 Argentine Mauser
303 British
7.7mm Jap
8x57J (.318 dia.)
8mm Mauser (.323 dia.)

Caliber
358 Norma Belted Magnum
9.3x57 Dual Core
9.3x62 Dual Core

NORMA EMPTY UNPRIMED PISTOL CASES

32 S & W Long
9mm Luger
38 Special
357 Magnum
44 Magnum
44 Auto Mag

REMINGTON CASES & PRIMERS

Remington brass cases with 5% more brass for extra strength in head section—annealed neck section for longer reloading life—primer pocket dimension controlled to .0005 inch to assure precise primer fit—heavier bridge and sidewalls—formed and machined to exacting tolerances for consistent powder capacity—choice of seventy-one center fire rifle, pistol and revolver cases—

Rifle Cases (Unprimed)

	QTY. PER BOX	"KLEANBORE" PRIMER NO.
17 REMINGTON • U17REM ★	20	7½
22 HORNET • U22HRN	50	6½
222 REMINGTON • U222R	20	7½ .
222 REMINGTON MAGNUM • U222MG	20	7½
22-250 REMINGTON • U22250	20	9½
223 REMINGTON • U223	20	7½
6mm REMINGTON • U6MM	20	9½
243 WINCHESTER • U243	20	9½
25-06 REMINGTON • U2506	20	9½
270 WINCHESTER • U270	20	9½
7mm-08 REMINGTON • U7MM08	20	9½
7mm EXPRESS REMINGTON • U7MM06 ‡	20	9½
7mm REMINGTON MAGNUM • U7MMAG	20	9½M
30 CARBINE • U30CAR	50	6½
30-06 SPRINGFIELD • U3006	20	9½
30-30 WINCHESTER • U3030	20	9½
300 WINCHESTER MAGNUM • U300W	20	9½M
8mm REMINGTON MAGNUM • U8MMAG	20	9½M
308 WINCHESTER • U308	20	9½
45-70 GOVERNMENT • U4570	20	9½

Pistol and Revolver Cases

	QTY. PER BOX	"KLEANBORE" PRIMER NO.
357 MAGNUM (BRASS) • U357B	50	5½
9mm LUGER AUTO PISTOL • U9MLUR	50	1½
38 SPECIAL (BRASS) • U38SPR	50	1½
41 REMINGTON MAGNUM • U41MAG	50	2½
44 REMINGTON MAGNUM • U44MAG	50	2½
45 COLT • U45CLT	50	2½
45 AUTO • U45AP	50	2½

★ Designed for Remington No. 7½ primer only. Substitutions not recommended. U number is unprimed.

‡ Interchangeable with 280 Rem.

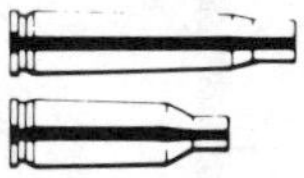

Bench Rest Cases

	QTY. PER BOX	"KLEANBORE" PRIMER NO.
	20	7½

Order No. URBR Remington .308 BR case ready for sizing, shortened and necked down to .224, 6mm, or 7mm.

Remington "Kleanbore" CENTER FIRE PRIMERS

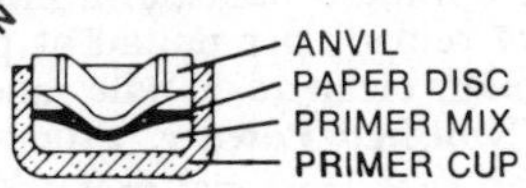

ANVIL
PAPER DISC
PRIMER MIX
PRIMER CUP

PRIMER NO.	ORDER NO.	DESCRIPTION
Small Pistol 1½	X 22600	Brass. Nickel-plated. For small revolver and pistol cartridges.
Large Pistol 2½	X 22604	Brass. Nickel-plated. For large revolver and pistol cartridges.
Small Pistol 5½	X 22626	Brass. Nickel-plated. Specially designed for 32 S & W and 357 Magnum cartridges.
Small Rifle 6½	X 22606	Brass. Nickel-plated. For small rifle cartridges other than those noted under Primer No. 7½.
Small Rifle Bench Rest 7½	X 22628	Brass. Copper-plated. Specially designed for 17 Rem., 221 Rem., "Fire Ball," 222 Rem., 222 Rem. Mag., 22 Rem. BR and 223 Rem. cartridges.
Large Rifle 9½	X 22608	Brass. For large rifle cartridges.
Magnum Rifle 9½M	X 22622	Brass. For use in belted magnum cartridges, 264 Win., 6.5mm Rem. Magnum., 7mm Rem. Magnum, 300 Win. Magnum, 300 H&H Magnum, 8mm Rem. Magnum, 350 Rem. Magnum, 375 H&H Magnum, 458 Win. Magnum cartridges.

PERCUSSION CAPS

SIZE	INSIDE DIA.	ORDER NO.	DESCRIPTION
10	.162"	X 22616	A hotter primer mix to assure more reliable ignition of both black powder and substitutes. Uniform, dependable performance. F.C. trimmed edge, foil-lined, center fire. Identical in length, priming mixture, weight of charge.
11	.167"	X 22618	

All Remington Center Fire Primers and Percussion Caps packed 100 per box (PC caps—tin), 1,000 per carton, 5,000 per case.

DU PONT SMOKELESS POWDERS

SHOTSHELL POWDER

Hi-Skor 700-X Double-Base Shotshell Powder. Specifically designed for today's 12-gauge components. Developed to give optimum ballistics at minimum charge weight (means more reloads per pound of powder). 700-X is dense, easy to load, clean to handle and loads uniformly.

PB Shotshell Powder. Produces exceptional 20- and 28-gauge skeet reloads; preferred by many in 12-gauge target loads, it gives 3-dram equivalent velocity at relatively low chamber pressures.

Hi-Skor 800-X Shotshell Powder. An excellent powder for 12-gauge field loads and 20- and 28-gauge loads.

SR-4756 Powder. Great all-around powder for target and field loads.

SR-7625 Powder. A fast growing "favorite" for reloading target as well as light and heavy field loads in 4 gauges. Excellent velocity-chamber pressure.

IMR-4227 Powder. Can be used effectively for reloading .410-gauge shotshell ammunition.

RIFLE POWDER

IMR-3031 Rifle Powder. Specifically recommended for medium-capacity cartridges.

IMR-4064 Rifle Powder. Has exceptionally uniform burning qualities when used in medium- and large-capacity cartridges.

IMR-4198. Made the Remington 222 cartridge famous. Developed for small- and medium-capacity cartridges.

IMR-4227 Rifle Powder. Fastest burning of the IMR Series. Specifically designed for the 22 Hornet class of cartridges.

SR-4759. Brought back by shooter demand. Available for Cast bullet loads.

IMR-4320. Recommended for high-velocity cartridges.

IMR-4350 Rifle Powder. Gives unusually uniform results when loaded in magnum cartridges. Slowest burning powder of the IMR series.

IMR-4831. Produced as a canister-grade handloading powder. Packaged in 1 lb. canister, 8 lb. caddy and 20 lb. kegs.

IMR-4895 Rifle Powder. The time-tested standard for caliber 30 military ammunition is now being manufactured again. Slightly faster than IMR-4320. Loads uniformly in all powder measures. One of the country's favorite powders.

PISTOL POWDER

PB Powder. Another powder for reloading a wide variety of center-fire handgun ammunition.

IMR-4227 Powder. Can be used effectively for reloading "magnum" handgun ammunition.

"Hi-Skor" 700-X Powder. The same qualities that make it a superior shotshell powder contribute to its excellent performance in all the popular handguns.

SR-7625 Powder. For reloading a wide variety of center-fire handgun ammunition.

SR-4756, IMR-3031 and IMR-4198. Three more powders in a good selection—all clean burning and with uniform performance.

HERCULES SMOKELESS POWDERS

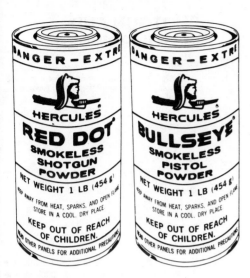

Eight types of Hercules smokeless sporting powders are available to the handloader. These have been selected from the wide range of powders produced for factory loading to provide at least one type that can be used efficiently and economically for each type of ammunition. These include:

Powder	Packaging				
	1-lb Canisters	4-lb Canisters	5-lb Canisters	8-lb Keg	15-lb Keg
Bullseye	X	X		X	X
Red Dot	X	X		X	X
Green Dot	X	X		X	X
Unique	X	X		X	X
Herco	X	X		X	X
Blue Dot	X		X		
Hercules 2400	X	X		X	X
Reloder 7	X				

BULLSEYE®

A high-energy, quick-burning powder especially designed for pistol and revolver. The most popular powder for .38 special target loads. Can also be used for 12 gauge-1 oz. shotshell target loads.

RED DOT®

The preferred powder for light-to-medium shotshells; specifically designed for 12-gauge target loads. Can also be used for handgun loads.

GREEN DOT®

Designed for 12-gauge medium shotshell loads. Outstanding in 20-gauge skeet loads.

UNIQUE®

Has an unusually broad application from light to heavy shotshell loads. As a handgun powder, it is our most versatile, giving excellent performance in many light to medium-heavy loads.

HERCO®

A long-established powder for high velocity shotshell loads. Designed for heavy and magnum 10-, 12-, 16-, and 20-gauge loads. Can also be used in high-performance handgun loads.

BLUE DOT®

Designed for use in magnum shotshell loads, 10-, 12-, 16-, 20- and 28-gauge. Also provides top performance with clean burning in many magnum handgun loads.

HERCULES 2400®

For use in small-capacity rifle cartridges and .410-Bore shotshell loads. Can also be used for large-caliber magnum handgun cartridges.

RELODER®7

Designed for use in center-fire rifle cartridges. Has outstanding accuracy in small-capacity rifle cartridges used in bench rest shooting.

HODGDON SMOKELESS POWDER

RIFLE POWDER

H4227 and H4198
H4227 is the fastest burning of the IMR series. Well adapted to Hornet, light bullets in 222 and all bullets in 357 and 44 magnum pistols. Cuts leading with lead bullets. H4198 was developed especially for small and medium capacity cartridges.

H322
A new extruded bench-rest powder which has proved to be capable of producing fine accuracy in the .22 and .308 Bench-rest guns. This powder fills the gap between H4198 and BL-C(2). Performs best in small to medium capacity cases.

SPHERICAL BL-C®, Lot No. 2
A highly popular favorite of the Bench-rest shooters. Best performance is in the 222, and in other cases smaller than 30/06.

SPHERICAL H335®.
Similar to BL-C(2), H335 is popular for its performance in medium capacity cases, especially in 222 and 308 Winchester.

4895®
4895 may well be considered the most versatile of all propellants. It gives desirable performance in almost all cases from 222 Rem. to 458 Win. Reduced loads, to as low as $^3/_5$ of maximum, still give target accuracy.

SPHERICAL H380®
This number fills a gap between 4320 and 4350. It is excellent in 22/250, 220 Swift, the 6mm's, 257 and 30/06.

SPHERICAL H414®
A new development in spherical powder. In many popular medium to medium-large calibers, pressure velocity relationship is better.

SPHERICAL H870®
Very slow burning rate adaptable to over-bore capacity magnum cases such as 257, 264, 270 and 300 mags with heavy bullets.

SPHERICAL H4350
Introduced in April, 1982, this powder is fast becoming a favorite of many handloaders. It gives superb accuracy at optimum velocity for many large capacity metallic rifle cartridges.

H4831®
Here is a new batch of the original 4831. The most popular of all powders. Use same loading data as our original surplus powder. Outstanding performance with medium and heavy bullets in the 6mm's, 25/06, 270 and magnum calibers.

SHOTGUN AND PISTOL POWDER

HP38
A fast pistol powder for most pistol loading. Especially recommended for mid-range 38 special.

TRAP 100
Trap 100 is a spherical trap and light field load powder, also excellent for target loads in centerfire pistol. Mild recoil.

HS-6 and HS-7
HS-6 and HS-7 for magnum field loads are unsurpassed since they do not pack in the measure. They deliver uniform charges and are dense so allow sufficient wad column for best patterns.

H110
A spherical powder made especially for the 30 M1 carbine. H110 also does very well in 357, 44 Spec., 44 Mag. or 410 ga. Shotshell. Magnum primers are recommended for consistent ignition.

NORMA SMOKELESS POWDER
RIFLE POWDERS

NORMA 200
A fast-burning powder, for small capacity cartridge cases as the 222, but also for use with light bullets and/or light loads in larger calibers.

NORMA 201
Slower than the 200, used with lighter bullets in medium-size cases, or with big-caliber cartridges where a large bore volume is to be filled up quickly by expanding gases. case capacity.

NORMA 202
A rifle powder of medium-burning rate that makes it the right choice for cartridges in the 6. 5mm-7mm—30-06 caliber range of regular

NORMA MAGNUM RIFLE POWDER
Exceptionally slow-burning, high-energy powder for highest velocity with large capacity cases. A must for Magnums.

HANDGUN POWDERS

NORMA POWDER R-1
Is a fast-burning, easily ignited powder especially adapted for revolver cartridges with lead bullets, such as 38 Special target loads. It is clean burning, and the granules are of such size and shape that they flow easily in the powder measure and without binding the cylinder. It also handles very easily in the spoon or powder trickler for shooters who prefer weighing their loads.

NORMA POWDER R-123
Is a slow-burning handgun powder for heavier loads in cartridges such as 357 and 44 Magnum, especially when using jacketed bullets. This powder gives a lower breech pressure and the charge weight can therefore be increased for higher bullet velocities.

NORMA RELOADING POWDERS

Rifle Powders/Pulver für Büchsenpatronen

Caliber	Bullet index no	Bullet weight (grains)	Max Cartridge length (inch)	(mm)	Norma primer	Norma powder	Load (grains)	(grams)	Muzzle vel Feet per sec	Meter per sec	Pressure[1] (psi)	(bar)
220 Swift	65701	50	2.62	66.5	LR	202	39.3	2.55	3980	1213	53700	3700
222 Rem	65701 +65702	50	2.11	53.5	SR	200	21.0	1.36	3200	975	46400	3200
						200	20.2	1.31	3000	914	46400	3200
						200	17.7	1.15	2790	850	46400	3200
	65704	53	2.16	55.0	SR	200	20.8	1.35	3115	950	46400	3200
22-250	65704	53	2.38	60.5	LR	202	36.6	2.37	3710	1130	53700	3700
5.6x52 R	65604	71	2.50	63.5	LR	202	27.0	1.75	2835	864	42100	2900
	65605	71	2.50	63.5	LR	202	27.0	1.75	2835	864	42100	2900
243 Win	66002 +66003	100	2.62	66.5	LR	204	45.1	2.92	3070	936	52200	3600
						204	43.8	2.84	2870	875	52200	3600
						204	42.0	2.72	2670	814	52200	3600
6.5 Jap.	66531	139	2.82	71.5	LR	202	30.9	2.00	2270	692	32200	2220
						201	28.2	1.83	2230	680	32200	2220
						200	24.0	1.55	2030	618	32200	2220
	66532	156	2.89	73.5	LR	202	28.2	1.83	2035	620	32200	2220
						201	24.7	1.60	1865	568	32200	2220
						200	20.5	1.33	1665	508	32200	2220
6.5x55	66551	77	2.62	66.5	LR	200	33.2	2.15	2725	830	45000	3100
						200	37.8	2.45	3115	950	45000	3100
						200	34.1	2.21	2915	889	45000	3100
	66512	139	2.99	76.0	LR	204	46.6	3.02	2790	850	45000	3100
						MRP	49.4	3.20	2815	858	45000	3100
						MRP	47.8	3.10	2740	835	45000	3100
	66532	156	3.07	78.0	LR	204	44.2	2.86	2495	760	45000	3100
						204	42.5	2.75	2295	700	45000	3100
						204	39.8	2.58	2095	639	45000	3100
6.5 Carc.	66532	156	2.97	75.5	LR	202	35.5	2.30	2340	713	37700	2600
						200	25.2	1.63	1800	549	37700	2600
270 Win.	66902	130	3.15	80.0	LR	204	57.0	3.69	3140	957	52200	3600
						204	55.0	3.56	2940	896	52200	3600
						204	52.0	3.37	2740	835	52200	3600
	66903	150	3.23	82.0	LR	204	52.4	3.39	2800	853	52200	3600
						204	50.5	3.27	2600	792	52200	3600
						204	46.7	3.02	2400	731	52200	3600
7x57	67002	150	3.05	77.5	LR	202	44.0	2.85	2690	820	49300	3400
						201	40.0	2.59	2555	779	49300	3400
						201	36.5	2.36	2355	718	49300	3400
7x57 R	67002 +67003	150	3.02	76.7	LR	202	42.9	2.78	2620	799	43500	3000
						201	36.3	2.35	2290	698	43500	3000
Super 7x61	67002	150	3.19	81.0	LR	MRP	67.4	4.37	3165	965	55100	3800
						204	58.5	3.79	2950	899	55100	3800
						204	55.3	3.58	2750	838	55100	3800
7 mm Rem. M	67002	150	3.25	82.5	LR	MRP	71.4	4.63	3250	990	55100	3800
						204	66.6	4.31	3060	933	55100	3800
						204	62.4	4.04	2860	872	55100	3800
7x64	67002	150	2.13	84.0	LR	204	57.1	3.70	2890	880	52200	3600
						204	52.9	3.43	2690	819	52200	3600
						204	49.5	3.21	2490	758	52200	3600
	67036	175	2.13	84.0	LR	MRP	56.6	3.67	2725	830	52200	3600
						MRP	51.7	3.35	2475	754	52200	3600
						MRP	48.3	3.13	2275	693	52200	3600
280 Rem	67002	150	3.29	83.5	LR	MRP	59.4	3.85	2980	910	50800	3500
7.5x55 Swiss	67625	180	2.91	74.0	LR	204	52.2	3.38	2650	808	45000	3100
						204	54.0	3.50	2690	820	45000	3100
7.62 Russ	67623	130	2.66	67.5	LR	201	51.4	3.33	3100	945	47900	3300
	67624	150	2.75	70.0	LR	201	47.8	3.10	2800	853	47900	3300
	67625	180	2.82	71.5	LR	202	47.1	3.05	2595	791	47900	3300
						201	37.2	2.41	2225	678	47900	3300
30 US Carb.	67621	110	1.67	42.5	SR	–	–	–	1970	600	46400	3200
30-06	67621	110	2.87	73.0	LR	201	54.5	3.53	3280	1000	50800	3500
	67623	130	3.11	79.0	LR	202	56.3	3.65	3205	977	50800	3500
	67624	150	3.13	79.5	LR	202	52.5	3.40	2955	901	50800	3500
						MRP	62.4	4.04	2820	860	50800	3500
	67628	180	3.17	80.5	LR	204	56.3	3.65	2700	823	50800	3500
						202	48.5	3.14	2645	806	50800	3500
						201	41.6	2.69	2300	701	50800	3500
	67648	180	3.15	80.0	LR	204	56.3	3.65	2700	823	50800	3500
						202	48.5	3.14	2645	806	50800	3500
						201	41.6	2.69	2300	701	50800	3500
30-30 Win	67630	150	2.50	63.5	LR	201	35.5	2.30	2410	735	43500	3000
						201	32.5	2.10	2210	674	43500	3000
						200	26.1	1.69	2010	613	43500	3000
	67631	170	2.50	63.5	LR	201	32.4	2.10	2220	677	43500	3000
						200	26.3	1.70	2020	616	43500	3000
						200	23.3	1.51	1820	555	43500	3000
308 Win	67621	110	2.38	60.5	LR	200	40.1	2.60	2740	835	52200	3600
	67623	130	2.62	66.5	LR	200	40.6	2.63	2900	884	52200	3600
						200	38.2	2.47	2780	823	52200	3600
						200	35.1	2.27	2500	762	52200	3600
	67624	150	2.65	67.5	LR	201	45.5	2.95	2860	872	52200	3600
						201	43.3	2.80	2660	811	52200	3600
						201	40.6	2.63	2460	750	52200	3600
	67628	180	2.70	68.5	LR	202	42.1	2.73	2525	770	52200	3600
308 Norma M.	67623	130	3.17	80.5	LR	204	78.4	5.08	3545	1080	55100	3800
	67624	150	3.21	81.5	LR	204	76.7	4.97	3330	1015	55100	3800
	67628	180	3.25	82.5	LR	MRP	74.3	4.81	3020	920	55100	3800
						204	71.8	4.65	2900	884	55100	3800
						204	70.0	4.53	2700	823	55100	3800
7.65 Arg.	67701	150	2.85	72.5	LR	201	47.8	3.10	2920	890	49300	3400
						201	44.0	2.85	2720	829	49300	3400
						201	42.5	2.75	2520	768	49300	3400
303 British	67701	150	2.95	75.0	LR	201	44.6	2.89	2720	829	46400	3200
						201	41.4	2.68	2520	768	46400	3200
						200	33.9	2.19	2320	707	46400	3200
	67713	180	2.97	75.5	LR	202	43.0	2.79	2540	774	46400	3200
						202	43.5	2.82	2600	792	46400	3200
						201	36.2	2.34	2140	652	46400	3200
7.7 Jap.	67711	130	2.84	72.0	LR	202	51.7	3.35	3005	916	39200	2700
	67713	180	3.03	77.0	LR	202	46.0	2.98	2515	767	39200	2700
8x57 J	67901	196	2.97	75.5	LR	202	48.0	3.11	2485	757	48500	3300
						201	39.8	2.58	2125	648	48500	3300
8x57 JS	68003	196	2.95	75.0	LR	202	48.3	3.13	2485	757	49300	3400
						200	36.4	2.36	2125	648	49300	3400
	68007	196	2.97	75.5	LR	202	48.3	3.13	2485	757	49300	3400
						200	36.4	2.36	2125	648	49300	3400
358 Norma M.	69001	250	3.23	82.0	LR	202	66.3	4.30	2710	826	53400	3700
						201	57.0	3.69	2400	731	53400	3700
9.3x57	69303	286	3.01	76.5	LR	201	44.6	2.89	2065	630	36300	2500
						201	40.6	2.63	1865	569	36300	2500
						200	34.2	2.22	1665	508	36300	2500
9.3x62	69303	286	3.23	82.0	LR	201	54.7	3.54	2360	720	49300	3400
						201	51.2	3.32	2160	659	49300	3400
						200	44.0	2.85	1960	598	49300	3400

NORMA RELOADING POWDERS

MRP/Magnum Rifle Powder

An exceptionally slow burning, high-energy powder for highest velocity with large capacity cases. Replaces the famous Norma 205 powder. A must for magnums.

Caliber	Bullet index no.	Bullet weight (grains)	Max Cartridge length (inch)	(mm)	Norma primer	Norma powder	Load (grains)	(grams)	Muzzle vel. Feet per sec.	Meter per sec.	Pressure [1] (psi)	(bar)
243 Win.	–	80	2.54	64.5	LR	MRP	50.6	3.28	3347	1020	52200	3600
243 Win.	66003	100	2.62	66.5	LR	MRP	49.2	3.19	3199	975	52200	3600
6 mm Rem.	66003	100	2.82	71.6	LR	MRP	46.4	3.01	3117	950	54400	3750
6 mm Rem.	66003	100	2.82	71.6	LR	MRP	48.2	3.12	3248	990	54400	3750
6.5 Carc.	66551	77	2.52	64.0	LR	MRP	46.5	3.01	2965	904	37700	2600
6.5 Carc.	66522	80	2.50	63.5	LR	MRP	46.6	3.02	2950	899	37700	2600
6.5 Carc.	66512	139	2.85	72.5	LR	MRP	43.2	2.80	2570	783	37700	2600
6.5 Carc.	66510	144	2.95	75.0	LR	MRP	43.2	280	2550	777	37700	2600
6.5 Carc.	66532	156	2.95	75.0	LR	MPR	42.4	2.75	2435	744	37700	2600
6.5 Jap.	66512	139	2.81	71.5	LR	MRP	37.7	2.44	2335	712	37700	2600
6.5 Jap.	66532	156	2.89	73.3	LR	MRP	38.1	2.47	2310	704	37700	2600
6.5x55	66531	139	2.99	76.0	LR	MRP	47.8	3.10	2740	835	45000	3100
6.5x55	66512	139	2.99	76.0	LR	MRP	49.4	3.20	2815	858	49300	3400 [2]
6.5x55	66510	144	3.05	77.5	LR	MRP	48.6	3.15	2780	847	49300	3400 [2]
6.5x55	66532	156	3.07	78.0	LR	MRP	48.0	3.11	2645	806	49300	3400 [2]
270 Win.	–	110	3.15	80.0	LR	MRP	61.5	3.98	3166	965	52200	3600
270 Win.	66902	130	3.15	80.0	LR	MRP	60.9	3.95	3133	955	52200	3600
270 Win.	66903	150	3.23	82.0	LR	MRP	58.4	3.78	2969	905	52200	3600
7x57	67002	150	3.03	77.0	LR	MRP	50.9	3.30	2615	797	49300	3400
7x57 R	67002	150	3.02	76.7	LR	MRP	51.3	3.32	2690	820	43500	3000
7x57 R	–	160	3.06	77.7	LR	MRP	50.4	3.27	2608	795	43500	3000
7x61 Super	–	160	3.19	81.0	LR	MRP	66.5	4.31	3100	945	55100	3800
7x61 Super	–	175	3.19	.81.0	LR	MRP	64.8	4.20	2904	885	55100	3800
7x64	67002	150	3.27	83.0	LR	MRP	59.6	3.86	2960	902	52200	3600
7 mm Rem.	–	160	3.19	81.0	LR	MRP	70.2	4.55	3166	965	55100	3800
7 mm Rem.	–	175	3.21	81.5	LR	MRP	68.0	4.41	2986	910	55100	3800
7.5x55	67621	110	2.56	65.0	LR	MRP	60.9	3.95	3085	940	45000	3100
7.5x55	67623	130	2.80	71.0	LR	MRP	60.2	3.90	3060	933	45000	3100
7.5x55	67602	146	2.81	71.5	LR	MRP	57.1	3.70	2920	890	45000	3100
7.5x55	67624	150	2.80	71.0	LR	MRP	57.1	3.70	2890	881	45000	3100
7.5x55	67625	180	2.80	71.0	LR	MRP	55.6	3.60	2730	832	45000	3100
30–06	67624	150	3.13	79.5	LR	MRP	62.4	4.04	2822	860	50800	3500
30–06	67628	180	3.17	80.5	LR	MRP	60.1	3.89	2658	810	50800	3500
30–06	–	200	3.23	82.0	LR	MRP	59.4	3.85	2608	795	50800	3500
30–06	67628	180	3.17	80.5	–	MRP	61.7	4.00	2790	850	50800	3500

Loading data for Weatherby Magnums/Ladedata für Weatherby Magnum Patronen

Caliber	Bullet index no.	Bullet weight (grains)	Max Cartridge length (inch)	(mm)	Norma primer	Norma powder	Load (grains)	(grams)	Muzzle vel. Feet per sec.	Meter per sec.	Pressure [1] (psi)	(bar)
240 WM	–	70	3.15	80.0	–	MRP	59.4	3.85	3838	1170	55100	3800
240 WM	–	85	3.15	80.0	–	MRP	54.9	3.56	3497	1066	55100	3800
240 WM	–	87	3.15	80.0	–	MRP	54.5	3.53	3497	1066	55100	3800
240 WM	–	100	3.15	80.0	–	MRP	54.0	3.50	3395	1035	55100	3800
257 WM	–	87	3.42	87.0	–	MRP	74.1	4.80	3757	1145	55100	3800
257 WM	–	100	3.42	87.0	–	MRP	71.3	4.62	3555	1084	55100	3800
257 WM	–	117	3.42	87.0	–	MRP	67.1	4.35	3300	1006	55100	3800
270 WM	–	100	3.42	87.0	–	MRP	77.2	5.00	3760	1146	55100	3800
270 WM	–	130	3.42	87.0	–	MRP	73.3	4.75	3375	1029	55100	3800
270 WM	–	150	3.42	87.0	–	MRP	71.7	4.65	3245	990	55100	3800
7 mm WM	–	139	3.42	87.0	–	MRP	74.1	4.80	3300	1006	55100	3800
7 mm WM	–	154	3.42	87.0	–	MRP	72.8	4.72	3160	963	55100	3800
7 mm WM	–	160	3.42	87.0	–	MRP	72.5	4.70	3150	960	55100	3800
7 mm WM	–	175	3.42	87.0	–	MRP	71.0	4.60	3070	935	55100	3800
300 WM	–	110	3.58	91.0	–	MRP	81.0	5.25	3900	1189	55100	3800
300 WM	–	150	3.58	91.0	–	MRP	88.0	5.70	3545	1081	55100	3800
300 WM	–	180	3.58	91.0	–	MRP	83.3	5.40	3245	990	55100	3800
300 WM	–	200	3.58	91.0	–	MRP	78.7	5.10	3000	914	55100	3800
300 WM	–	220	3.58	91.0	–	MRP	79.2	5.13	2905	885	55100	3800
340 WM	–	200	3.70	94.0	–	MRP	91.0	5.90	3210	978	55100	3800
340 WM	–	210	3.70	94.0	–	MRP	91.0	5.90	3180	969	55100	3800
340 WM	–	250	3.70	94.0	–	MRP	85.2	5.52	2850	869	55100	3800
378 WM	–	270	3.70	94.0	–	MRP	115.5	7.48	3180	969	58785	4055
378 WM	–	300	3.70	94.0	–	MRP	111.8	7.20	2925	892	58785	4055

Handgun Powders

Caliber	Bullet index no.	Bullet weight (grains)	Max Cartridge length (inch)	(mm)	Norma primer	Norma powder	Load (grains)	(grams)	Muzzle velocity Feet per sec.	Meter per sec.	Pressure [1] (psi)	(bar)
9 mm Luger	69010	116	1.16	29.5	SP	R-1	3.8	0.246	1115	340	36300	2500
38 Special	69110	148	1.16	29.5	SP	R-1	2.5	0.162	800	244	17000	1170
	69112	158	1.50	38.0	SP	R-1	3.5	0.227	870	265	20000	1380
	69107	158	1.48	37.5	SP	R-1	4.2	0.272	900	274	20000	1380
	69101	158	1.46	37.0	SP	R-1	4.2	0.272	900	274	20000	1380
357 Mag.	69101	158	1.59	40.5	SP	R-123	13.9	0.900	1450	442	40600	2800
	69107	158	1.59	40.5	SP	R-123	13.9	0.900	1450	442	40600	2800
38 S & W	–	146	1.16	29.5	SP	R-1	2.0	0.130	730	222	13800	950
44 Mag.	61103	240	1.61	41.0	LP	R-123	19.1	1.240	1675	511	40600	2800

INDEX

Alox/beeswax—144
antelope—42, 170, 188, 191
aoudad—183
Apple IIe—197

ballistic coefficient—41, 91, 101, 172
ballistic putty—130
ballistics, external, 127–28
   internal, 127–28
   terminal, 127–29, 172
bear—40, 42, 163, 173, 186
Bell, W.D.M.—165
bench press—9, 21–24, 150, 152, 154, 195
Berdan primer—123
black powder—75, 115, 149
bullet rotation—13, 128, 131

cannelure—170
caribou—163, 170
cases, belted magnum, 33, 37, 76
   rebated rimless, 33–34, 145
   rimmed, 33
   semi-rimmed, 33
   straight-walled, 25

case volume—37, 43, 76, 105, 111, 124, 135, 147, 159–60, 189
Cast Bullet Association—144
copper units of pressure (c.u.p.)—34, 107, 133, 138
Corbett, Major Jim—165
Crawford, Dick—190
crimp, roll—40, 106, 126
   taper—40, 106, 111, 123, 26, 192
custom moulds—144

Data Tech Ballistics Program—197
deer—16, 40, 42, 128, 170, 173, 187–89, 196, 197
Dietz, Dick—168
double rifle—158
drilling—158
dross—141
duplex loads—77

ear protection—92, 138
elephants—165
elk—42, 163, 189, 191
expander dies—26, 59, 135, 193

fallow deer—183
fireformed brass—35, 112
flame cutting—134
full length resizing—26

gemsbok—165
German Mausers—165

headspace—33–35, 37, 40, 60, 106, 110, 123, 145, 160
Herrett, Steve—112

Keith, Elmer—118–19, 186

leade—163

machine rest—94, 98, 122
magnumizing—111, 194
maintenance—195
moose—42, 158

neck sizing—146, 151
neck tension—59, 105, 170
nitrocellulose—75
nitroglycerine—75
Noise Reduction Rating—92
NRA formula—144

O'Conner, Jack—165
ogive—126, 147
ordnance gelatin—130

plastic bullets—196
plinking—12, 41
potassium sulfate—76
prairie dogs—187

pressure, signs of abnormal, 60, 108, 132
progressive powder—75

Ruger, Bill—104
Russian boar—183

sable (antelope)—165
Sharpe, Philip B.—118
shooting glasses—91–92, 138
shooting muffs—92, 112
.22 shorts—196
SHOT show—24
silhouette shooting—109, 113, 129, 135–36, 138–39, 194
slugging bullets—144
Spanish American War—165
spotting scopes—93, 151
sprue—140–42
straight-line bullet seater—147
swaging—141, 144

trapdoor Springfield—139
tungsten carbide dies—22, 25–26, 32, 106, 123, 135, 195
turkey—186

Union Metallic Cartridge Company—11

varmint hunting—13, 39, 41, 130, 149, 168, 186–88, 197–98

wadcutter bullets—38, 106, 116–19, 184, 192
wax bullets—196
Wesson, Douglas B.—118
woodchucks—102, 185, 187, 197

zebra—165